The International Handbook on Non-Market Environmental Valuation

T0319451

Edited by

Jeff Bennett

Professor of Environmental Management, Crawford School of Economics and Government, The Australian National University, Canberra, Australia

Edward Elgar
Cheltenham, UK • Northampton, MA, USA

© Jeff Bennett 2011

All rights reserved. No part of this publication may be reproduced, stored in a retrieval system or transmitted in any form or by any means, electronic, mechanical or photocopying, recording, or otherwise without the prior permission of the publisher.

Published by
Edward Elgar Publishing Limited
The Lypiatts
15 Lansdown Road
Cheltenham
Glos GL50 2JA
UK

Edward Elgar Publishing, Inc.
William Pratt House
9 Dewey Court
Northampton
Massachusetts 01060
USA

A catalogue record for this book
is available from the British Library

Library of Congress Control Number: 2010939196

MIX
Paper from
responsible sources
FSC® C018575

ISBN 978 1 84844 425 6 (cased)

Typeset by Servis Filmsetting Ltd, Stockport, Cheshire
Printed and bound by MPG Books Group, UK

Contents

Contributors

Stuart Bain is a Post-doctoral Research Fellow at the Institute of Transport and Logistics Studies (ITLS), University of Sydney. Stuart completed his doctoral studies in 2007 in the field of computer science, developing new methods for the automatic development of algorithms to solve different classes of optimization problems. Stuart joined ITLS in 2006, primarily developing new optimization methods for the Vehicle Routing Problem. His research activities at ITLS have since broadened, and now include fields as diverse as algorithm design for stated choice experiment construction to transport modelling. His primary teaching responsibilities at ITLS are to teach computational logistics at the institute.

Ian J. Bateman is Professor of Environmental Economics and Director of the Centre for Social and Economic Research on the Global Environment (CSERGE) at the University of East Anglia and also holds professorships in Australia and New Zealand. His main research interests include: integrated and spatially sensitive modelling of physical, biological and economic systems and their associated ecosystem services; the formation and valuation of preferences for non-market goods and services (environment, health, and so on); preference anomalies and behavioural economics; working with policy-makers to address real-world environmental resource management issues. He heads the economics team for the UK National Ecosystem Assessment (NEA) and is adviser to a number of national and international bodies.

Jeff Bennett is Professor in the Crawford School of Economics and Government at the Australian National University. Professor Bennett has over 30 years' experience researching, consulting and teaching in the fields of environmental economics, natural resource economics, agricultural economics and applied micro-economics. He is currently leading research projects investigating the use of non-market techniques to estimate the value of the environment, the use of auctions to encourage land-use change in western China and private sector conservation initiatives. Jeff is a Distinguished Fellow of the Australian Agricultural and Resource Economics Society, was President of that Society in 2004 and is a member of the Mont Pelerin Society. He is co-editor of the *Australian Journal of Agricultural and Resource Economics* and Director of the Environmental Economics Research Hub.

Elena Y. Besedin is a Senior Economist with Abt Associates in Cambridge, MA. She received a PhD in environmental and natural resource economics from the University of Rhode Island and an MS in economics from the Moscow Telecommunication Institute. Dr Besedin has published expertise in areas that include non-market valuation methods, benefits analysis, cost–benefit analysis, environmental risk assessment, benefit transfer, and integrated ecological and economic assessment. She specializes in economic analysis of environmental policy and regulatory programs, including analysis of economic benefits from reducing risks to the environment and human health. She has extensive experience in policy analysis for the US Environmental Protection Agency (EPA) and other government agencies, and in the management of large-scale multidisciplinary projects for benefit–cost analysis.

Michiel C.J. Bliemer is Associate Professor of Transportation Modelling at Delft University of Technology at the Department of Transport and Planning and also works as consultant at Goudappel Coffeng in the Netherlands. Since 2003 he has also been affiliated with the University of Sydney as a yearly visiting academic at the Institute of Transport and Logistics Studies. His research interests include dynamic network modelling, travel behaviour, design of stated choice experiments and road pricing.

Roy Brouwer is Professor in the Department of Environmental Economics at the Institute for Environmental Studies, VU University Amsterdam. He holds a PhD in environmental economics from the University of East Anglia in the UK. His research interests include economic valuation of the environment, in particular payments for ecosystem services.

Richard T. Carson is Professor in the Department of Economics at the University of California (UC), San Diego, and is a past President and Fellow of the Association of Environmental and Resource Economists. Previously he served as Research Director for International Environmental Policy at the UC Institute on Global Conflict and Cooperation. He has worked on a range of environmental economics and econometric issues with a particular emphasis on the valuation of non-marketed and new goods. He has served as principal investigator on several major projects including the benefit assessment for the US Clean Water Act and the damage assessment for the *Exxon Valdez* oil spill. Carson has also served as a consultant to a number of local, state, federal agencies, foreign governments and international organizations as well as to several Fortune 500 companies. He has been a member of US National Academy of Sciences committees reviewing oil spill prevention policies and water resource planning procedures.

Joseph Champ is an Associate Professor in the Department of Journalism and Technical Communication at Colorado State University (CSU) in Fort Collins, Colorado. Champ was a television journalist for ten years before returning to graduate school. He is interested in issues related to environmental communication, while keeping up his television/video skills, primarily as an instructor for CSU's intermediate television production course. His work has been published in *Leisure Sciences*, *Society & Natural Resources*, *Human Dimensions of Wildlife*, *Popular Communication: International Journal of Media and Culture* and *Journal of Media and Religion*.

Jeremy Cheesman is a senior resource and environmental economist with Marsden Jacob Associates. He advises public and private organizations on matters spanning infrastructure investment decisions, production efficiency analysis, market demand analysis, the non-market valuation of environmental and natural resources, social cost–benefit analysis, public sector reform and policy development, and the macroeconomic (CGE) effects of public and private infrastructure investments. Prior to joining Marsden Jacob Associates, Jeremy worked for five years as a senior water economist on a sustainable water resource management project in the Central Highlands region of Vietnam. This project was funded by the Australian Centre for International Agricultural Research (ACIAR). Jeremy has published widely in the areas of applied water, environmental and agricultural economics. His publications include professional peer-reviewed journal papers, book chapters, technical reports and conference papers.

Sergio Colombo is a senior researcher at IFAPA in Granada, Spain. He obtained his PhD from the University of Granada. He has worked extensively in the area of choice experiments, especially on issues of benefit transfer.

John Downing is a Professor of Ecology, Evolution, and Organismal Biology at the Department of Agricultural and Biosystems Engineering, Iowa State University (ISU). His research interests include limnology, aquatic ecology, terrestrial ecology, microbial ecology, biogeochemistry, population conservation, and whole ecosystem restoration and management. John is a member of the Board of Directors of the American Society of Limnology and Oceanography, an invited member of the North American Nitrogen Center, and has advised many policy-makers and citizens groups concerning water quality management. He received his BS from Hamline University (St. Paul, MN), his MS from NDSU (Fargo, ND) and his PhD from McGill University (Montreal, Canada). He was formerly a Professor at McGill University and the University of Montreal where he was Director of the Laurentian Biological Station. He has been at ISU since 1995 and is the Director of the Iowa State University Limnology Laboratory and has surveyed water quality in Iowa's lakes since 2000. Dr Downing has published his research in a wide variety of journals, including *Limnology and Oceanography*, *Ecosystems*, the *Canadian Journal of Fisheries and Aquatic Science*, the *Journal of Soil and Water Conservation* and the *Ecology of Fresh Water Fish*.

Jeffrey Englin received his PhD in Economics from the University of Washington in 1986. His research is focused on applied econometrics with an emphasis on the valuation of natural resources. He is currently a Professor in the Department of Resource Economics at the University of Nevada, Reno.

Sonia Garcia is an environmental consultant in Kaneohe, Hawaii.

Marek Giergiczny is Assistant Professor in Applied Economics at the University of Warsaw, Poland. He also works as a senior researcher in the Warsaw Ecological Economic Center. His research interests focus mainly on valuation of non-market resources and ecosystem services.

Armando González-Cabán is Research Economist with the Forest Service, Pacific Southwest Research Station, Forest Fire Laboratory in Riverside, California. He has worked for over thirty years in the field of fire economics, with emphasis on the economic effects of wildland fires on natural resources, non-market resource valuation, fire management decision-making in large fires, and the attitudes and values of individuals towards Forest Service fire management policies. His work has been published, among others, in journals such as *Land Economics*, *International Journal of Wildland Fire*, *Ecological Economics* and *Journal of Environmental Management*.

Theodore Groves received his BA from Harvard and his PhD in Economics from the University of California, Berkeley in 1970. Prior to coming to the University of California, San Diego (UCSD) as a Professor of Economics in 1979, he was a faculty member at the University of Wisconsin, Madison, Northwestern University's Kellogg School of Management and Stanford University. He was a founder of mechanism design theory and the discoverer of the 'Groves Mechanism', for eliciting truthful information in an incentive-compatible manner. He and co-author John Ledyard also developed the first general equilibrium solution to the 'free rider problem' of public goods. Professor Groves has also studied the Chinese economy's transition to a market economy, optimal policies for minimizing the occurrence of oil spills, the incentive compatibility of stated-preference surveys and improved methods for video multiplexing. He is the Director of the Center for Environmental Economics in the Department of Economics at UCSD and is involved in ongoing research on water pricing, consumer responses to smart-metre technology for electrical energy consumption, and numerous projects for managing marine resources and the protection of endangered species. He is an elected Fellow of the Econometric Society and the American Academy of Arts and Sciences.

Nick Hanley is Professor of Environmental Economics at the University of Stirling. He has been undertaking stated preference studies since 1985, and implemented the first UK choice experiment study of environmental management issues in 1997. He is the author of several textbooks, including *Pricing Nature* (with Edward Barbier), *Environmental Economics in Theory and Practice* and *Introduction to Environmental Economics* (both with Jason Shogren and Ben White).

Joseph A. Herriges is a Professor of Economics at Iowa State University, where he has been on the faculty since 1988. Prior to that, he was a Senior Economist at Laurits R. Christensen Associates in Madison, Wisconsin, where he specialized in incentive design and evaluation in the electric power industry. He holds a PhD in Economics from the University of Wisconsin-Madison (1983). Much of his recent research has focused on non-market valuation techniques, including both stated and revealed preference methods. Dr Herriges was the managing editor of the *Journal of Environmental Economics and Management* from 2001 to 2006, and has served on the editorial boards of the *Journal of Choice Modeling*, *Environmental and Resource Economics* and *Australian Economic Papers.* He has published his research results in a wide variety of journals, including the *Review of Economic and Statistics*, the *Journal of Business and Economic Statistics*, *Environmental and Resource Economics*, the *Journal of Environmental Economics and Management*, the *Journal of Econometrics* and the *American Journal of Agricultural Economics.*

Sebastiaan Hess works as an independent environmental economist. Between 2003 and 2008 he was employed as a researcher at the VU University in Amsterdam. His research experience is mostly linked to developing countries, having worked on topics such as payments for environmental services, valuation of watershed functions, environmental taxation, rangeland management and the sustainable development contribution of clean development mechanism (CDM) projects. Outside the developing country context, his experience is related to the valuation of coral reef services, ground and surface water quality, among others.

Thomas Holmes received his PhD in Agricultural and Resource Economics from the University of Connecticut in 1986. He has worked extensively in the areas of non-market valuation, environmental policy and timber markets and harvesting. He is currently a Research Forest Economist with the US Forest Service located in the Southern Research Station in Research Triangle Park, North Carolina.

Yongsik Jeon is currently a Research Fellow at the Strategic Management and Research Center of Woori Finance Holdings in Seoul, South Korea. He received his PhD in Economics from Iowa State University in 2005, where his dissertation research focused on valuing water quality in lake ecosystems. A portion of this research is published in *Environmental and Resource Economics*.

Robert J. Johnston is Director of the George Perkins Marsh Institute and Professor of Economics at Clark University. He received his BA from Williams College and PhD from the University of Rhode Island. He is currently President of the Northeastern Agricultural and Resource Economics Association and Vice President of the Marine Resource Economics Foundation, and is on the Program Committee for the Charles Darwin Foundation, the Science Advisory Board for the Communication Partnership for Science and the Sea, and the Gulf of Maine Regional Ocean Science Council. Professor Johnston is an environmental and resource economist with extensive publications on the valuation of non-market commodities and ecosystem services, benefit transfer and meta-analysis, and the management of aquatic, coastal and ecological resources. His work on valuation, benefit transfer, coastal and ocean management, and environmental economics has contributed to national, state and local policy in the US, Canada and elsewhere.

H. Allen Klaiber is an Assistant Professor of Agricultural and Environmental Economics in the Department of Agricultural Economics and Rural Sociology at the Pennsylvania State University. He holds a PhD in Economics from North Carolina State University. His research areas broadly include topics in environmental economics and applied econometrics. An area of emphasis in his research is valuation of amenities using revealed preference data on housing markets in a general equilibrium setting.

Catherine L. Kling is Professor of Economics at Iowa State University and the Center for Agricultural and Rural Development. She received her PhD from the University of Maryland and began her professional career at the University of California, Davis. Her research interests include non-market valuation methods, the design of agricultural conservation policy, and incentives for the provision of ecosystem services. Cathy is a Fellow of the Agriculture and Applied Economics Association (AAEA), a member EPA's Science Advisory Board, president-elect of the Association of Environmental and Resource Economists and past board member of the AAEA. She has held editorial positions with the *American Journal of Agricultural Economics*, *Journal of Environmental Economics and Management* and *Land Economics*. She has been the recipient of over $7 million in grants and has published in the *Economic Journal*, the *Review of Economics and Statistics*, the *American Journal of Agricultural Economics*, *the Journal of Environmental Economics and Management*, *Economic Inquiry*, the *Journal of Public Economics*, *Land Economics* and elsewhere.

Yi Liu received his B Eng. degree from Jilin University, Changchun, China in 2003, and his MSc degrees from the VU University Amsterdam, the Netherlands in 2005 and 2007, majoring in Environment and Resource Management, and Hydrology respectively. After working in Commonwealth Scientific and Research Organization (CSIRO) Land and Water, Canberra, Australia for one year as a research officer, he is currently pursuing his PhD degree at the University of New South Wales, Sydney, Australia, applying remote sensing observations to the hydrological cycle.

John Loomis is a Professor in the Department of Agricultural and Resource Economics at Colorado State University. He is the author of three books (*Integrated Public Lands Management*, *Environmental Policy Analysis for Decision Making*, and *Recreation Economic Decisions, 2nd edn*) as well as over one hundred journal articles dealing with economic valuation of non-marketed natural resources using the contingent valuation, travel cost and hedonic property methods. He is a Distinguished Scholar of the Western Agricultural Economics Association.

Pierre-Alexandre Mahieu obtained his PhD on valuation in December 2009 at the University of Rouen (France) after having spent some time at the Autonomous University of Barcelona (Spain). He is currently a guest researcher at the Centre for Environmental and Resource Economics (Sweden). His main interests within stated preferences are uncertainty, hypothetical bias and monetary illusion.

Kenneth E. McConnell is Professor in the Department of Agricultural and Resource Economics at the University of Maryland where he has been on the faculty since 1979. His research has been in the area of environmental and natural resource economics, with emphasis on non-market valuation. His papers have been published in leading economics journals and in the principal field journals for environmental and resource economics.

Ståle Navrud is a Professor of Environmental and Resource Economics at the Department of Economics, Norwegian University of Life Sciences. His main research topic is environmental valuation, with applications to ecosystem services and biodiversity, externalities of renewable energy, recreation, climate induced extreme events, oil pollution and marine ecosystems, cultural heritage, environmentally related health impacts and transportation noise. He has conducted about fifty original contingent valuation, choice experiments, hedonic price, and travel cost studies in Europe, Latin America, Asia, Africa and the Middle East, and has worked extensively on benefit transfer. He has published about 50 journal articles and edited the books *Pricing the European Environment* (Oxford University Press, 1992), *Valuing Cultural Heritage* (Edward Elgar, 2002) and *Environmental Value Transfer: Issues and Methods* (Springer, 2007).

Arwin Pang received her PhD in Public Finance from National Chengchi University, Taiwan in 2008. Her dissertation comprises three essays about environmental economics including examining Environmental Kuznets Curve in Mainland China, the health effect of green tax reform and the optimal second-best environmental tax rate in the presence of pre-existing distortions by taxing emissions. She is a Research Associate who works with Professor Jeffrey Englin at the Department of Resource Economics, University of Nevada, Reno. Her research interests are public finance, applied econometrics and non-market valuation.

Gregory L. Poe is a Professor of Environmental and Resource Economics in the Department of Applied Economics and Management at Cornell University. His present appointment involves research and teaching in environmental economics and policy, and his corresponding research program focuses on applied welfare economics, non-market valuation, experimental economics and water pollution policy. While much of his work involves policy relevant field research, in recent years he has also worked extensively on developing and evaluating public goods provision mechanisms in experimental economics laboratory settings. He has published over forty journal articles in economics, public economics, environmental economics and agricultural economics journals, and is the co-editor of the book, *The Economic Value of Water Quality* (Edward Elgar, 2001).

Pere Riera is Professor in Applied Economics at the Autonomous University of Barcelona, Spain. His research is in the area of environmental economics and policy, and non-market valuation.

John Rolfe is a resource economist who has specialized in the use of choice modelling and other non-market valuation techniques. He is Professor in the Faculty of Arts, Business, Informatics and Education and the Director of the Centre for Environmental Management at the CQ University in Australia. John has a number of research interests, including regional development, environmental, resource and agricultural economic issues, resource tradeoffs and economic impact assessment in regional areas. His location in Rockhampton, Queensland, means that he is closely involved with many issues relevant to northern Australia and the tropics.

John M. Rose is Associate Professor in Transport and Logistics Management at the Institute of Transport and Logistics Studies, The University of Sydney. John's research expertise lies in the areas of discrete choice modelling, advanced econometric modelling and efficient stated choice experiments. John has published in the fields of marketing, transportation and health economics as well as environmental economics.

Eric T. Schultz is an Associate Professor in the Department of Ecology and Evolutionary Biology at the University of Connecticut. He earned his PhD in 1990, in Aquatic and Population Biology within the Department of Biological Sciences at the University of California, Santa Barbara, and was awarded a two-year Coastal Marine Scholar Post-doctoral Fellowship at the Marine Sciences Research Center, State University of New York at Stony Brook. Professor Schultz teaches undergraduate courses in introductory biology, physiological ecology of animals and biology of fishes. His research encompasses the population biology, evolutionary ecology and physiological ecology of fishes. His particular areas of expertise include: life history strategies, particularly evolutionary responses to seasonal environments; advection of marine fish larvae and recruitment patterns in oceanic and estuarine systems; evolution of intromittent organs in live-bearers; evolution of osmoregulatory systems. He has received research funding from the National Science Foundation, the Environmental Protection Agency, Sea Grant, private foundations and the State of Connecticut.

Kathleen Segerson is Philip E. Austin Professor of Economics at the University of Connecticut. She holds a BA in mathematics from Dartmouth College and a PhD in agricultural and resource economics from Cornell University. She is a fellow of the Association of Environmental and Resource Economists (AERE) and of the American Agricultural Economics Association, and is immediate past-president of AERE. She is also a member of the Chartered Board of the US Environmental Protection Agency's Science Advisory Board (SAB) and the Board on Agriculture and Natural Resources for the National Academy of Sciences. Dr Segerson's research focuses on the incentive effects of alternative environmental policy instruments, with emphasis on the application of legal rules and principles to environmental problems. Specific research areas include: the impact of legal liability for environmental damages in a variety of contexts, including groundwater contamination, hazardous waste management and workplace accidents; land use regulation and the takings clause; voluntary approaches to environmental protection; the impacts of climate change on US agriculture; and incentives for nonpoint pollution control.

V. Kerry Smith is a Professor of Economics at the W.P. Carey School of Business, School of Sustainability and School of Geographical Sciences and Urban Policy, Arizona State University. He is a University Fellow at Resources for the Future and a Research Associate at the National Bureau of Economic Research. Smith is a member of the National Academy of Sciences. His current research has two components: (a) the development of methods to estimate consistently the role of environmental resources in household choice using the properties of market equilibrium; and (b) then using these results to incorporate environmental services into static and dynamic general equilibrium models.

Jon Strand is Senior Economist in the Development Research Group, Environment and Energy Team, at the World Bank in Washington, DC. His work area is environmental and energy economics, focusing on climate-related issues. He also holds (and is currently on leave from) a chair as Professor of Economics at the University of Oslo. Within the fields of environmental, resource and energy economics, his main topics for research have been environmental valuation using both non-market and market methods, including the valuation of statistical life; natural resource issues focusing on developing countries; and environmental policy design issues including environmental taxation and climate policy. He has published widely, with about sixty published articles in international economics journals. He has served as consultant for the Organisation for Economic Co-operation and Development (OECD), the World Bank, the Inter-American Development Bank and various Norwegian government agencies, on environmental policy matters. During 2005–08, he worked in the Fiscal Affairs Department of the International Monetary Fund (IMF), as its environmental economist.

Paul J. Thomassin is an Associate Professor of Agricultural and Environmental Economics in the Agricultural Economics Program in the Department of Natural Resource Sciences at McGill University. He is also an Associate Member of McGill's School of Environment, is a Research Fellow at the Center for Interuniversity Research and Analysis of Organizations (CIRANO) with the Experimental Economics Group and was a Visiting Professor at the William S. Richardson School of Law at the University of Hawaii, Visiting Fellow at the National Centre for Development Studies at the Australian National University and Honorary Professor in the Division of Science and Technology at the University of Auckland. Professor Thomassin's research includes: the non-market valuation of the environment and benefit transfer, macroeconomic and environmental impacts of economic development; consumer perceptions of food, agriculture, health and the environment; the integration of economic and biological models of agricultural systems; and the convergence of agriculture and health policies to address problems with chronic disease. He is currently a member of the editorial board of the *Canadian Journal of Agricultural Economics*.

Dugald Tinch is a post-doctoral researcher within the Environmental Economics Research Group at the University of Stirling, where he also studied for his PhD. His main research interests are in the valuation of ecosystem services. He has also worked on the economics of climate change and on water quality issues.

Pieter van Beukering is Associate Professor in Environmental Economics at the Institute for Environmental Studies, VU University Amsterdam. His main research interests are economic valuation, natural resource management, solid waste management, poverty and environment. Most of his work is conducted in developing countries. His current research efforts focus predominantly on the economics of ecosystem services and the role of renewable energy in developing countries.

Christian A. Vossler is an Associate Professor in the Department of Economics at the University of Tennessee-Knoxville. His main research interests are in environmental and resource economics, public economics, experimental economics and applied econometrics. Within environmental economics, much of his research focuses on non-market valuation methods, with special attention on mechanism design and validity issues related to survey-based valuation methods; and environmental regulation, with emphasis on regulatory compliance and the development of policy instruments for controlling non-point source pollution. He has published in leading environmental economics and general interest journals, including *Journal of Public Economics*, *Journal of Environmental Economics and Management*, *Journal of Economic Behavior and Organization* and *American Journal of Agricultural Economics*. Recent funding for his research has come from the US EPA and the Internal Revenue Service (IRS).

Xuehong Wang was Post-doctoral Fellow with the Crawford School of Economics and Government of the Australian National University at the time the chapter contained in this book was drafted. Her research interests extend across environmental and natural resource management, valuation of environmental goods and services, climate change mitigation and adaptation, and land use policy. Currently she is based in Bonn working at the Secretariat of the United Nations Framework Convention on Climate Change.

Acknowledgements

In any endeavour, one stands on the shoulders of those who have gone before and are supported by those around. This applies in the case of the preparation of this volume. My appreciation therefore goes to those in the economics profession who pioneered the discipline's application to issues of environmental and natural resource management and to the scholars who have supported the compilation of this volume through their contributed chapters. It also applies personally. The efforts of my parents in helping me to establish my career, and my wife and sons' willingness to foster it, are gratefully acknowledged.

1 The rise and rise of non-market environmental valuation
Jeff Bennett

The aim of this handbook is to advance the development and application of non-market environmental valuation (NMEV) as a tool for policy-making. To achieve this goal, a range of state-of-the-art applications across the spectrum of revealed preference and stated preference NMEV techniques is presented. These applications are instructive illustrations of what can be achieved using NMEV. The contexts of the case studies are deliberately diverse to show the flexibility of these techniques. Applications are drawn from Europe, North America, Asia and Australia with valuation targets ranging across both use and non-use values of the environment. Despite this variety of contexts there is a common denominator: all the applications are practically based in their provision of information relevant to real resource allocation decisions. This demonstrates the policy 'power' of the techniques.

The focus of this handbook on developing NMEV techniques is achieved through a sequence of chapters that address key, cutting-edge research issues. These chapters provide insights into the directions being taken by leading researchers in the NMEV field.

The intended audience for this handbook is therefore wide-ranging. For example, policy-makers and their advisers will find it useful to their gaining a better appreciation of what NMEV can do. Practitioners will be able to use the chapters to update their skills or to find out more about techniques they have yet to use. Researchers will benefit from the widening and deepening of their knowledge base that these chapters provide. Students will find the chapters an invaluable source of information to further their understanding of established and emerging tools.

The importance of the contributions made through the chapters of this handbook cannot be overstated. They appear at a time when NMEV is undergoing a period of increased growth in both application and development because of a growing recognition of the role of economics in the consideration of environmental policy issues. This increased recognition is the result of numerous factors, including greater political pressure to account for the environment in policy decision-making and a surge in professional capacity to carry out NMEV studies. It is timely to consider in more detail each of these dimensions of growth.

In the advanced western democracies, political pressure to accommodate the environment in policy formulation has come about for a number of reasons. First, community awareness of the environment and problems associated with human impacts on the environment has expanded as incomes, wealth and associated levels of public education have grown. People are simply more aware of the environment now. This awareness has also come about as environmental resources (clean air, natural places, species and ecosystem diversity) have become scarcer. So as resource exploitation has fuelled economic growth and increased wealth, the environmental degradation that has often, but not universally, occurred simultaneously has become more of an issue for the general public. Growing sophistication in the business of lobbying and rent-seeking has spilt over to environmental pressure groups, and politicians in advanced democracies today are only too well aware of the electoral influence that the environmental movement can deliver.

The increased environmental awareness and political pressure does not, by itself, explain why there has been a rise in NMEV activity. To take the argument further, it must also be recognized that economics as a discipline has achieved a prominence in western democracies not enjoyed by any of the physical or social sciences. In part that has occurred because of the rapid growth of market-based economies, seen on the whole to be a function of the macro and micro policy prescriptions developed by economists. In another part, economics has also been seen to be capable of 'defusing' conflicts where rent-seekers from opposing camps (developers versus conservationists) put politicians in invidious positions where there appears to be no easy answer from a political perspective.

With economics in the ascendancy, even environmentally motivated policy proposals have been subjected to economic analysis. Central to the carriage of that analysis is the capacity to consider the trade-offs that are either implicit or explicit in decisions that have environmental impacts. Such considerations require the use of a common numeraire: money. Because, so often, environmental impacts – either positive or negative, that is, either benefits or costs – are not bought or sold directly in markets, they do not have market-based estimates of value. Hence there is a requirement for NMEV.

In some jurisdictions, the use of NMEV is mandated by law. In others, there is simply a recognition that an economic analysis of policies with environmental dimensions is necessary to see the policy pass through the processes of government vetting. Environmental agencies seeking policy reform may, for instance, be required to have their proposals approved by economists employed in finance or treasury agencies. In some settings, private developers may be required to submit environmental assessments inclusive of cost–benefit analyses that incorporate NMEVs. In others, development interests may volunteer to such analytical rigour as a pre-emptive move.

In association with the increased demand for NMEV has come an increased capacity within the profession to meet the demand. This association has had 'chicken and egg' features in that it is unclear whether it was the increased capacity that saw the emergence of the demand for application or whether the demand induced the growth in professional capacity. Doubtless there are elements of both in the progression that has occurred.

Early applications of all the NMEV techniques suffered from significant pitfalls. All have had considerable research investments made to address those issues. The degree of sophistication in application has increased to the point in some techniques that improvements at the margin are now significantly diminished. For others, advances are still being made at lower points on the learning curve. Some research challenges remain stubbornly unresolved. For others, increased computing power has allowed what were once impractical-to-solve algorithms to be crunched by a laptop computer in a few minutes. Lessons have been learnt from associated disciplines such as psychology and econometrics as well as parallel sub-disciplines such as marketing, transport and health economics. More practitioners have developed more experience in adding art to the science embedded in NMEV.

All this has meant that NMEV has been a fast-evolving area of research. Coupled with this has been a pattern of rapid adoption in policy circles, at least in major western democracies. A feature of this coupling has been the funding of NMEV research initiatives by government agencies seeking solutions to specific policy issues. This has assured policy relevance for the research work as well as timely adoption of research innovation by policy-makers.

The focus of this volume is on two types of NMEV. The first relies on the revealed preferences of people in markets that are specifically related to the environmental good or service of interest. These are the revealed preference (RP) techniques. Second are the group of techniques that involve asking people to state their preferences for environmental goods or services using hypothetical choice contexts. These are referred to as stated preference (SP) techniques.

Omitted from consideration are techniques that, while often applied to estimate NMEV because of their ease of application, have conceptual weaknesses that render them dubious as appropriate providers of policy-relevant information. In particular, they are the cost-based measures such as replacement cost and costs of aversion. They involve the collection of information relating to the monetary costs associated with actions taken either to replace supplies of environmental goods and services with substitutes in the event of loss or to avoid such losses. For instance, the value of a loss in air quality might be estimated by the extent of expenditure on purifying air conditioners, or water quality benefits arising from catchment protection may be estimated by reference to the costs of a water treatment plant. Such estimates are conceptually weak for a number of reasons but, most critically, they are based on cost rather than economic surplus as the appropriate measure of 'value'. Furthermore, those costs are associated with what are at best imperfect substitutes: how well does a water treatment plant substitute for water from a protected catchment, and is purified air from an air conditioner the same as being able to breath clean air from an open window?

The RP techniques included in the handbook are the hedonic pricing method and the travel cost method. Both take advantage of specific relationships existing between marketed goods and services and non-marketed goods and services. Both enjoy the status of being based on people's behaviour and so have been regarded as accurate indicators of people's true preferences. Both are well established in the literature and in application. Even with this established 'pedigree', the RP techniques are evolving. Hence, the four RP-focused application chapters in this volume – two each for the hedonic pricing and travel cost methods – are aimed at providing insights into some of the latest developments that have taken place in this evolution as well as providing indications of future research directions.

The hedonic pricing method recognizes that the environmental characteristics of a marketed good or service can have a role in determining its price. By examining the relationship between the extent of the environmental characteristic and the good or service's market price, some inferences may be made about the value of the environmental characteristic. Most hedonic pricing studies have used real estate prices to infer values for characteristics such as exposure to negative environmental characteristics such as noise or air pollution and to positive environmental features such as pleasant views or proximity to a recreation area. Others have used labour markets to estimate values associated with environmental risk factors in the work place.

A particular challenge facing applications of the hedonic pricing method involves the development of value estimates from the relationship between market price and environmental characteristic. While the relationship allows us to gauge the effect on market price of a unit increment in the environmental characteristic, that is not a conceptually sound measure of value. A second step is required to achieve that, but it is data intensive, requiring information on the characteristics of the buyers of the good or service to establish the heterogeneity of the demand side of the market.

Chapter 2, by Ståle Navrud and Jon Strand, demonstrates the application of the first stage of the hedonic pricing method using a case study of the estimation of implicit prices of road externalities (as indicated by noise exposure) in Norway. It does not make the assumption that these are welfare estimates but rather advances them as information on the marginal costs faced by home owners when their properties are impacted by new roads. They are therefore measures of marginal costs rather than consumer surplus as is required for inclusion in cost–benefit analyses. The study does not attempt the problematic second stage of the method whereby marginal values, and hence demand functions, are estimated. Even addressing this restricted goal faces challenges associated with market segmentation and the prospect of market mobility. Yet the results produced are of policy use as refinements to the information provided by 'experts' on the levels of compensation that may be paid to affected residents.

The second hedonic price method application, Chapter 3 by Roy Brouwer, Sebastiaan Hess, Yi Liu, Pieter van Beukering and Sonia Garcia investigates the impact of proximity to coral reefs on house prices in Hawaii. A particular feature of this work is its integration of spatial impacts into the economic analysis through the use of geographical information systems (GIS). This streamlines the process of data collection when distance is a key variable. A second feature of the work is its use of two approaches to the modelling of the data: a generalized least squares (GLS) regression and a maximum likelihood random effects panel data model. The first approach is used to verify the use of the random effects model to account for the spatial hierarchy present in the data. The study demonstrates the capacity to interact spatially explicit data, specifically environmental attributes that may be the focus of public policy, to generate a better understanding of price relationships. In this case, the question addressed is: what would be the impact on house prices of a policy to protect/remediate coral reefs?

The travel cost method has undergone a remarkable transformation since its inception and has been perhaps the most widely applied NMEV method. The concept that underpins the method is straightforward: the further people have to travel to visit a site of environmental significance and hence the greater are their costs of visiting, the less likely they are to make the visit. The original formulation of the method involved the estimation of this relationship between travel costs and visitation so that a demand curve for the site could be simulated. This required the assumption that visitors would respond to an access fee in the same way as they react to higher travel costs. For sites where people made frequent visits, the individual was used as the basis for estimating the relationship between visit rate and travel cost. Where individuals visit a site only rarely, then the 'zonal' approach was used. This involved establishing geographical zones of visitors' places of origin and visit rate was calculated on the basis of number of visits per head of population in each zone.

In Chapter 4, Pere Riera, Ted McConnell, Marek Giergiczny and Pierre-Alexandre Mahieu provide a brief summary of this evolution going back to Harold Hotellings's original specification of the travel cost model dated in the late 1940s. They describe how the zonal and individual variants, estimated using multiple regression techniques have given way to the random utility model based discrete choice analysis of visitation decisions. This has occurred as the associated econometrics and computing power have developed. Under this approach, survey respondents' choices to visit a recreational site are recorded, given that site's characteristics along with the range of substitute sites' characteristics. The cost of travelling to a site is one characteristic. This allows the use of the random utility model to develop econometric estimates of the respondent's utility function for a site and, hence, estimates of values associated with changes in site characteristics or access. Riera et al.'s application is in the context of beach recreation in Minorca, a Mediterranean island well known as a summer beach recreation centre. Their straightforward application demonstrates how powerful the method can be in developing policy useful information. By simulating an oil spill that forces the closure of selected beaches around the island, estimates of the losses so caused are made. Such estimates would be useful *ex post* to an oil spill in developing a compensation case, or *ex ante* to the assessment of policies aimed at reducing the probability of such a spill.

The second travel cost study – Chapter 5 by Yongsik Jeon, Joe Herriges, Catherine Kling and John Downing – also estimates the relationship between the travel costs expended in accessing a site and the frequency of visitation using the random utility model. Trip decisions to Iowa lakes are explained with reference to travel costs (as a proxy for price), socio-economic characteristics and water quality date. A key feature of the chapter is the development and testing of objectively determined water quality data and respondents' subjective assessments of the condition of the lakes as parameters that explain lake destination choice. Using the random utility model as a conceptual base for this approach to using the travel cost method does not avoid some of the prevailing challenges facing the technique. Hence Jeon et al. take steps such as eliminating data provided by respondents who undertook multiple day visits. However, an important advantage of the approach is its explicit recognition of substitute sites. This is something that the older approaches to the travel cost method were unable to do explicitly. As a result, these earlier applications may have delivered overestimates of visitation value.

Both of the RP techniques, the travel cost and the hedonic pricing methods, have their specific limitations. However, as a class of methods, both provide *ex post* estimates of environmental values in that they involve the analysis of actions that have already taken place and thus in contexts that may no longer exist or that are irrelevant to contexts that are being proposed by policy. Hence, their application is limited to situations where the context remains relevant. In addition, the range of environmental values they are able to estimate is limited to so-called 'use values' which involve people having direct contact with the environment in question.

So despite their foundations in people's actual behaviour, the RP techniques are not applicable in all circumstances where environmental value estimates are required to inform policy formulation. In particular, where non-use values are involved or when the context of a proposed policy has not been experienced before, RP techniques will not be suitable as NMEV tools. To fill this gap, SP techniques have been developed and now have a history of application that extends at least 30 years. The first SP method developed was contingent valuation. Early applications involved simply asking survey respondents what they would be willing to pay to enjoy an environmental benefit or to have an environmental cost diminished. With improved understanding of the various biases that seemed to be a feature of these 'open-ended' contingent valuation responses along with expanded econometric and computing power came a range of method variants. The dominant approach remains the single binary choice in which survey respondents are asked if they would pay a pre-assigned cost level for the policy change advanced in the questionnaire.

Not withstanding the 30 years of development and application, contingent valuation has remained controversial largely because of concerns regarding the accuracy of the NMEV estimates produced. Perhaps the pinnacle of that controversy occurred when the method was used to substantiate claims for environmental damages experienced after the *Exxon Valdez* oil spill. With such substantial amounts of money riding on the method's results, substantial effort was applied by both sides of the legal argument into validating/discrediting contingent valuation.

The method continues to evolve in response to pressures relating to criticism. The scrutiny to which contingent valuation studies are put, especially those in the policy arena, continues to pressure the technique to experimentation and improvement. Changes include developments in the technicalities of its application as well as theoretical advances.

That evolutionary process is demonstrated by Chapter 6 in which John

Loomis, Armando González-Cabán and Joseph Champ contribute two developments. The first relates to the technology of questionnaire delivery and the second is a refinement of the approach used to treat 'protest votes'. Loomis et al show how the use of video/DVD recordings could lower the costs of large-scale surveys relative to the cost of distributing a conventional information booklet. They also suggest an improved method for dealing with protest votes that involves asking 'No' respondents in the dichotomous choice version of the technique if they would be willing to pay $1. Their application is in the context of estimating willingness to pay for a reduction in catastrophic wild land forest fires via prescribed burning.

The second contingent valuation focused chapter is Chapter 7, authored by Greg Poe and Christian Vossler. They explore the key issue of hypothetical bias in contingent valuation studies. A range of past studies is presented in which the impact of 'consequentiality' in the design of questionnaires is considered. Consequentiality is the understanding that respondents have as to the significance of the survey process in the determination of policy outcomes. They argue that many previous tests of the validity of contingent valuation results have not taken into account differences in consequentiality and that this has delivered incorrect assessments. The analysis presented follows the arguments advanced by Richard Carson and Ted Groves in Chapter 15 of this volume. Poe and Vossler are advocates of contingent valuation in its 'consequentialist' format, given adherence to other incentive compatibility constructs such as the use of referendum/dichotomous choice questioning and a majority voting provision rule. However they also recognize that a consequential format is not always feasible or that some respondents will react to surveys as though they are not consequential. Here they suggest that the established tool for dealing with hypothetical bias – such as cheap talk script – is likely to be necessary.

One dimension of the evolution of contingent valuation was its extension to the format now known as choice modelling or choice experiments. The contingent valuation method, in its dichotomous choice format, involves asking survey respondents to choose once between a 'status quo' option involving no cost and an alternative characterized by an improved environmental outcome and a financial cost. In contrast, choice experiment questionnaires include multiple choice questions where the selection is often between more than two options. Options are defined by attributes that describe environmental and cost implications of choice. Options are differentiated by the attributes taking different levels. The combinations of choices presented to respondents are developed with reference to experimental designs.

The different stated preference format offered by choice experiments allows more detailed preference data to be collected and offers some advantage over contingent valuation in that the focus of the trade-offs involved in each question is not solely on money. Having been developed in applications across marketing, transport and health economics, choice experiments have added a new dimension to NMEV even though both contingent valuation and choice experiments are based on the same random utility model.

That is not to imply that choice modelling has been the 'holy grail' of NMEV. Rather its application has confronted many of the same challenges in application as met by contingent valuation. In addition, it has faced other specific research issues. Debate as to the relative merits of these two stated preference techniques continues, with a growing recognition that both have strengths and weaknesses in differing contexts.

Dugald Tinch, Sergio Colombo and Nick Hanley's use of the choice experiment method, detailed in Chapter 8, is focused on an exploration of any distinction between utility as measured prior to a visit to the Peak District National Park, during a visit and subsequently. These are described as decision- and experience-based utilities. The research is motivated by a debate in the literature that extends back to Bentham and Marshall as to the validity of the direct estimation of utility versus a backward induction approach using observed behaviour. The chapter is also instructive in that the data collection approach involves relatively small numbers of respondents who answer relatively large numbers of choice questions in the setting of a 'workshop'. This is a significant departure from the conventional approach of sampling large numbers of respondents and the use of telephone, mail or web-based questionnaire delivery.

A particular challenge facing economists using stated preference methods is the development of linkages between the biophysical science that documents the relationship between policy options and environmental outcomes and the estimation of the values held by the community for those outcomes. It has frequently been the case that economic value analysis has been poorly grounded in the biophysical science. Rob Johnston, Eric Schultz, Kathleen Segerson and Elena Besedin in Chapter 9 seek to redress this situation by establishing a formal process of attribute selection and definition in choice experiment applications. Their goal is to ensure that value estimates are relevant inputs to cost–benefit assessments of policy proposals as well as being soundly based in the bio-physical science. They demonstrate the application of their attribute protocol in the context of an ecological restoration project in Rhode Island. As well as showing that respondents have the capacity to deal with ecological complexity, they also conclude that values are held at multiple levels. These relate to specific aspects of restoration works as well as the overall ecological integrity of the restored area.

A further evolution of the stated preference approach has been the development of the contingent behaviour method. In seeking to anchor survey respondents' stated intentions in actual behaviour, researchers supplemented observations of people's resource use choices with information collected using 'what if' type contingent choice questions. Hence, stated preference data are collected alongside revealed preference data. The goal is to ensure the answers to contingent questions had some basis in actual choices. Applications of the contingent behaviour method have been primarily in the estimation of recreational values associated with environmental assets. Hence they have effectively been extensions of the travel cost method.

The study by Jeff Englin, Arwin Pang and Thomas Holmes reported in Chapter 10 is an example. They use the travel cost method logic as a base and observe recreational behaviour. The context is off-highway vehicle recreation in North Carolina. The stated preference, contingent behaviour data were collected using a choice experiment framework. Englin et al. observe how recreation activity could change given variations in a number of choice parameters. The other key feature of their work is the consideration of respondent heterogeneity in modelling the count data that emerges from the revealed and stated preference questioning. They demonstrate the importance of modelling heterogeneity in ensuring unbiased estimates of the surplus arising from recreational activities.

In a study that departs from recreation value estimation, Jeremy Cheesman and Jeff Bennett in Chapter 11 use the contingent behaviour method to estimate demand for domestic water in a regional city in Vietnam. Survey respondents were asked about their current water consumption and then were led through a sequence of 'what if' questions regarding their behavioural responses to hypothetical changes in water prices. So unlike the Englin et al. approach displayed in the previous chapter, which uses a choice experiment style of question, Cheesman and Bennett use a single alternative question to elicit the contingent behaviour response. An added strength of the approach used was the process used to verify respondents' perceptions of their current water use patterns: statements of current use levels were checked against records of use provided by water bills. Through this merging of revealed and stated preference data, confidence regarding the validity of the estimates produced is improved. The study also demonstrates the capacity of contingent behaviour to work in less developed country contexts, especially given the complexities of water use involving multiple sources of supply.

The sequence of ten chapters – from 2 to 11 – demonstrates the application of five different NMEV methods. Each is shown to have strengths and weaknesses, with all methods displaying prospects for further research to aid in their ongoing evolution. With such prospects in mind, the final sequence of chapters – from 12 to 17 – explores six fields of research that are high priorities in overcoming some of the barriers that remain to the ongoing advancement of NMEV methods.

Allen Klaiber and Kerry Smith in Chapter 12 set out three approaches for tackling the complexity of recognizing preference heterogeneity into the hedonic primary technique. This is key to the pursuit of the second stage of the method that was not undertaken in either of the applications presented in this volume (Navrud and Strand in Chapter 2 and Brouwer et al. in Chapter 3). In doing so, they address the prospect of people adjusting their locations, in the housing market context, in response to the set of characteristics offered by alternatives. In addition to the well-established multiple regression based hedonic price model in which supply is exogenous, two varieties of sorting models – horizontal and vertical – are detailed. It is these models' capacity to integrate taste heterogeneity and choice flexibility that allow them to move from the estimation of partial equilibrium to general equilibrium estimates of welfare changes associated with changes in public good provision specific to locations. Klaiber and Smith also detail a range of applications drawn from the literature to illustrate the challenges facing analysts using this form of revealed preference technique.

Chapter 13, by John Rolfe and Xuehong Wang, explores issues related to the design of the questionnaires used in stated preference valuation methods. These issues include the establishment of the overall context or frame of the study as well as setting up the contingent market within the survey. The chapter provides a key contribution as it clarifies a long-standing confusion in the literature relating to the definitions of the 'scope' and 'scale' effects in both contingent valuation and choice experiment applications. By defining these effects and then relating them to the primary features of a stated preference questionnaire, Rolfe and Wang give guidance for future applications. They especially point out the importance of this clarification to the process of benefit transfer, a process of using value estimates that is further analysed in Chapter 17 by Paul Thomassin and Rob Johnston. The scales and scopes implicit in value estimates are critical to the accuracy of benefit transfer exercises.

The move within the stated preference valuation literature from contingent valuation to choice experiments brought with it several additional degrees of complexity in application. One of those related to the construction of choice-sets using experimental design. The development of experimental designs remains at the forefront of the research effort in choice experiments. John Rose, Stuart Bain and Michiel Bliemer, in Chapter 14, present an overview of the process of experimental design and how it has developed to date. Their particular focus is on the efficiency of experimental designs, and they show how more advanced designs are able to reduce the sampling effort required to estimate statistically robust models. They also point out ongoing research in the direction of reconciling differences between efficient and orthogonal design approaches and the integration of statistical efficiency with behavioural aspects of designs.

One of the most influential papers in the development of stated preference methods over the past decade was Carson and Groves (2007). The chapter in this volume authored by the same Richard Carson and Ted Groves (Chapter 15) is a commentary on the findings presented in their original paper and some extensions of the logic employed. In particular, the focus is on perhaps the most widely debated feature of stated preference methods – hypothetical bias. Carson and Groves examine the incentive compatibility or otherwise of alternative stated preference questioning styles. In particular, they consider the difference between contingent valuation questions – especially the incentive compatible, single bid choice type – and the choice modelling point that frequently involves multiple alternatives as well as multiple choices. As a research frontier for stated preference techniques, the establishment of approaches that provide satisfaction to the wider community of economists in terms of incentive compatibility is a priority that this chapter addresses.

Ian Bateman's concern in Chapter 16 regarding the validity of stated preference studies' results, focuses on the understanding that respondents hold for the goods and services being investigated and their familiarity with the institutional framework in which they are being asked to express their preferences. His argument is that biased value estimates, unfit for policy deliberation, will result from stated preference method applications where respondents are not sufficiently familiar with the goods and services involved, or experienced in the operation of contingent markets. The findings from a number of studies are used to support this argument. They show, for instance, breaches of straightforward economic principles when unfamiliar goods are involved and demonstrate how estimates are malleable to changes in contexts in such cases. However, the studies also indicate how information strategies and experience can be used to overcome these issues. The overriding conclusion is that those using stated preference techniques must take care to ensure respondents know what they are being asked to value and how the valuation process works.

The estimation of environmental values is an expensive and time-consuming process. Such are the magnitudes of the investments involved or the resources available for the valuation task that it is unlikely that the process will be initiated in every policy decision case. But with increasing emphasis being given to cost–benefit analysis as a decision tool, non-market values are still sought by policy-makers with responsibilities for modest investments and/or with access to modest research resources. Hence the growing interest in the benefit transfer process under which values estimated in one context are used as inputs into the policy determination process for another (related) context. Along with that growth in interest has come growth in concern that benefit transfer is unable to deliver results that are sufficiently accurate representation of values for policy deliberation purposes. It is this research frontier that is explored by Paul Thomassin and Rob Johnston in the final chapter of the book. Specifically, they use the Environmental Valuation Reference Inventory (EVRI) database as a source of water quality value estimates and seek ways to capitalize on the rich array of studies undertaken in the USA to estimate values in Canada where comparatively few studies have been carried out. They demonstrate the importance of the few Canadian studies in the benefit transfer process: the meta regression model formed from combining data from the US and Canadian studies significantly outperforms the model based on US value data alone in predicting values in specific contexts.

In summary, the chapters of this volume present a rich array of methods, contexts and applications focused on the estimation of NMEV. Its role is as a handbook for those engaged in the use of these techniques, either as researchers or consultants, as well as those seeking to do so in the future. It has also sought to point out challenges that remain to be overcome, as well as reporting on some efforts under way to advance these techniques. The field will, no doubt, continue to evolve given the growth in demand for NMEV coupled with the rigorous scrutiny to which this research effort is put. A long-term goal of this handbook is the continued development of the capacity to supply those future applications and advances.

REFERENCE

Carson, R.T. and T. Groves (2007), 'Incentive and information properties of preference questions', *Environmental and Resource Economics*, **37**, 181–210.

2 Using hedonic pricing for estimating compensation payments for noise and other externalities from new roads
Ståle Navrud and Jon Strand

1 INTRODUCTION

Hedonic pricing (HP) uses multiple regression techniques to isolate implicit prices: that is, differences in property prices attributable to marginal differences in property characteristics. One of the most frequent applications has been to transportation noise, mainly from road traffic, aircraft and, to a lesser extent, railways. Bateman et al. (2001) provides a good review of HP studies of transportation noise, while Schipper et al. (2001) and Nelson (2004) are examples of meta-analyses of HP studies of aircraft noise.[1] Hedonic Pricing models have been used to value peace and quiet for more than 35 years; ever since the seminal paper of Rosen (1974). Even though there were early comparative studies of HP and contingent valuation (CV) (Brookshire et al. 1982),[2] the use of stated preference (SP) methods like CV and choice experiments (CE) to value noise are much more recent (see Navrud, 2002, for a review). Stated preference methods for valuing noise gained popularity since they can more easily isolate the effect of noise from other externalities caused by road traffic; including vibration, barrier effects, air pollution, safety concerns).[3] Since most HP models do not contain variables for these other externalities, the estimated implicit price of noise reflects house buyers' marginal willingness-to-pay (WTP) to avoid all the externalities from roads rather than just noise. Using these estimates in cost–benefit analyses (CBAs) of measures and policies that reduce noise only (and not these other externalities from road traffic) will then overestimate the benefits of noise reducing measures.[4] Stated preference methods can also directly calculate individuals' WTP and thus the welfare change from changes in noise levels, whereas the implicit prices from HP models (like all market prices) will be market specific and reflect the particular conditions of supply and demand that exist in that property market.

According to Day et al. (2007) an implicit price for noise estimated in a 'first stage' HP study in one urban area offers little indication of the benefits of changes in noise experienced elsewhere. Far better would be to use the information provided by observations of households' choices of noise exposure when faced by different implicit prices to identify the demand relationship for peace and quiet. Areas under such a demand curve provide valid approximations to the welfare benefits of non-marginal changes in noise exposure (Bartik, 1988) and, because they are based on underlying preferences (and not market prices), indicate values that might be used in benefits transfer exercises. As Day et al. (2007) point out, estimating demand relationships from hedonic pricing data is a theoretically and analytically very challenging task. Different approaches have been used to obtain the 'correct' individual WTP in the few studies that have gone on to this 'second stage' HP analysis, but these methods have generally been abandoned due to identification problems and other methodological issues (Haab and McConnell, 2002). Thus, Day et al. (2007) represent only a handful of HP studies that have attempted to estimate demand relationships using the HP method in a theoretically consistent manner, and is the only one of these few that conducts this 'second stage' HP analysis for transportation noise.

The study reported here, like most HP analyses, is a 'first stage' HP method. However, our aim is neither to isolate the effect of noise (from other traffic externalities) on property prices nor to provide welfare estimates. Thus, the most common critique of most HP studies of road traffic noise does not apply to our study. Our HP analysis aims to provide the Norwegian Directorate for Public Roads (DPR) with a market-based framework for estimating the compensation to be paid to house owners in order to offset the depreciation in market price of their homes due to *all* externalities from new roads. Thus, average estimated noise level dbA[5] is used as an indicator of *all* externalities from road traffic. Also, we do not claim to estimate welfare losses but only the loss in market value of the residential property, which is the legal basis for compensation payments to property owners in Norway when new roads are constructed (or existing roads are widened, extended or changed in other ways).

2   THE HEDONIC PRICE TECHNIQUE AND APPLICATIONS TO ROAD NOISE

In his seminal paper, Rosen (1974) showed that under the assumption of utility maximizing individuals, the marginal WTP for attributes of composite goods will equal their implicit prices. In our study, the composite good is a residential property, let A and $\mathbf{C} = [c_1, \ldots, c_n]$ denote road noise and a vector of other utility-bearing attributes (or characteristics), respectively. The hedonic price function (P) may then be written as

$$P = P(A, \mathbf{C}). \qquad (2.1)$$

In Rosen's model, the relationship between hedonic attributes such as noise or other environmental aspects, on the one hand, and residential property prices, on the other, is determined from interactions of demand and supply in the housing market, assuming that all markets are perfectly competitive and that commodities are perfectly divisible.[6]

Rosen (1974) showed that the consumer's WTP for the good will equal its market price. Since, in optimum, the consumer's marginal WTP equals his marginal rate of substitution between the price of the good and any of the attributes, the slope of the price function may be used to determine the consumer's marginal WTP. Focusing on noise, the marginal WTP ($MWTP$) can then be estimated as:

$$MWTP = \partial P(A, \mathbf{C})/\partial A \qquad (2.2)$$

The information about individuals' preferences from equation 2.2 only reveals the marginal WTP at the market equilibrium. It does not reveal the underlying preference structure. To derive the price function and to estimate the marginal WTP using the HP technique is often referred to as the 'first stage' HP of the technique. In the 'second stage' HP, where the preference parameters are estimated, the results from the 'first stage' together with information on house owners, are used. The 'second stage' enables the analyst to calculate 'theoretically consistent' values for non-marginal changes, which was done in Day et al. (2007). In this study only the 'first stage' is executed.

A theoretically consistent measure of welfare estimates for non-marginal changes of the noise levels requires the estimation of the second stage of HP technique (Freeman, 1974; Rosen, 1974). Freeman (2003, p.379) shows that if the price function does not shift as a result of changes in the noise level (for example if the number of properties with a change is small relative to the total market), the first stage HP function may be used to calculate the welfare measure. Brookshire et al. (1982) show theoretically that this will be an upper bound of the true welfare measure.

However, we do not attempt to derive a monetized welfare measure in terms of 'true' social externality impacts of roads and road construction. Rather, we limit ourselves to studying the effects that such road projects have on housing market characteristics, in particular, on average or predicted residential prices. We argue that this is a relevant measure, albeit mainly in the legal context of possible compensation for losses sustained by home owners, in the view of road projects.

A large number of HP studies of road noise have been conducted over

the years. Table 2.1 provides an overview of these studies, and their estimate of the 'first stage' implicit prices for noise in terms of the NSDI (Noise
Sensitivity Depreciation Index). The NSDI shows the percentage decrease
in house price per dbA increase in noise level, and range from 0.08 to 2.22.
These studies span data from four decades and three continents, and naturally vary according to methodological differences (especially the omission
of important attributes in some studies), and how housing markets and
home buyers' preferences for noise and other attributes vary in time and
space. In the following, we will review some of the methodological differences and results of some of these studies.

The study of road noise in Birmingham, UK (Bateman et al. 2004;
Day et al. 2007) is one of very few HP studies addressing the problem of
multiple noise sources by including noise data for road traffic, aircrafts
and railways. They show, as expected, that failing to include several independent sources of noise will typically lead to a too high estimate of the
effect of road noise on house prices. The main reason for this is that the
different noise levels tend to be positively correlated: if they had been negatively correlated omissions of several sources, the estimate of the effect of
road noise on home prices would instead have been biased downwards.
Andersson et al. (2010) also address this issue for road and railway noise,
and find (as opposed to Day et al. 2007) that noise from railroads has
less impact on property prices then road noise. This result is more in line
with the noise annoyance research which finds that railway noise has to
be about 5 dBA higher than noise from roads, in order to create the same
percentage of the affected population highly annoyed by noise (Miedema
and Oudshoorn, 2001).

Most studies rely on information for single-family houses, but Grue et
al. (1997) and Rich and Nielsen (2002) produce separate hedonic pricing
estimates for single-family homes and apartments and both find lower
NSDI for apartments. As Bue-Bjørner et al. (2003) point out, one reason
for this might be that single-family house owners are also disturbed by
noise when they are in their garden, while the outdoor life of owners of
apartments is not as closely linked to the location of the dwelling (or they
have a lower preference for outdoor activities).[7]

Bateman et al. (2001) illustrate the impact of omitted attributes (environmental and other) on the estimated NSDI. If they only (in addition
to noise) include characteristics of the house, they obtain an NSDI of
0.84 per cent. When they add neighbourhood characteristics and then a
number of accessibility variables the NSDI is reduced to 0.57 and 0.42 per
cent, respectively. Finally, when they also include variables indicating the
visual (dis)amenities of the land use surrounding the property the implicit
price of road noise drops to 0.2 per cent.

Table 2.1   *A review of hedonic price (HP) studies of road noise; the*
NSDI (Noise Sensitivity Depreciation Index) shows the
percentage decrease in house price per dbA increase in noise
level

Study	Study area	Study year	NSDI
Allen (1980)	Northern Virginia, USA	1978	0.15
Allen (1980)	Tidewater, USA	1977–79	0.14
Anderson and Wise (1977)	North Springfield, USA	1969–71	0.14
Anderson and Wise (1977)	Towson, USA	1970	0.43
Bailey (1977)	North Springfield, USA	1968–76	0.30
Gamble et al. (1974)	Bogota, USA	1971	2.22
Gamble et al. (1974)	Towson, USA	1969–71	0.43
Gamble et al. (1974)	Rosedale, USA	1969–71	0.24
Gamble et al. (1974)	North Springfield, USA	1969–71	0.21
Hall et al. (1978)	Ontario, USA	1975–77	1.05
Langey (1976, 1980)	North Springfield, USA	1962–72	0.32
Nelson (1978)	Washington, USA	1970	0.87
Palmquist (1980)	North King County, USA	1958–76	0.30
Palmquist (1980)	Kingsgate, USA	1962–76	0.48
Palmquist (1980)	Spokane, USA	1950–78	0.08
Vaughan and Huckins (1975)	Chicago, USA	1971–72	0.65
Grue et al. (1997)	Oslo, Norway; apartments in cooperatives	1995	0.24
Grue et al. (1997)	Oslo, Norway; regular apartments	1995	0.48
Grue et al. (1997)	Oslo, Norway; small single-family houses	1995	0.54
Pommerehne (1988)	Basel, Switzerland	1986	1.29
Soguel (1991)	Neuchatel, Switzerland	1990–92	0.91
Vainio (1995)	Helsinki, Finland	1991	0.36
Baranzini and Ramirez (2005)	Geneva, Switzerland	2001	0.70
Bateman et al. (2001)	Glasgow, UK	1986	0.20
Bateman et al. (2004)	Birmingham, UK	1997	0.55
Bateman et al. (2004)	Birmingham, UK	1997	0.67
Wilhelmsson (2000)	Stockholm, Sweden	1986–95	0.6
Rich and Nielsen (2002)	Copenhagen, Denmark; houses	2000	0.54
Rich and Nielsen (2002)	Copenhagen, Denmark; apartments	2000	0.47
Bue-Bjørner et al. (2003)	Copenhagen, Denmark	2002	0.49
Damgaard (2003)	Copenhagen, Denmark; large roads	1982–2001	1.20
Damgaard (2003)	Copenhagen, Denmark; highways	1982–2001	1.60

Table 2.1   (continued)

Study	Study area	Study year	NSDI
Salvi (2008)	Zürich, Switzerland	1995–2007	0.82
Pommerehne (1988)	Switzerland, Basel	1986	1.29
Baranzini and Ramirez (2005)	Switzerland, Geneva	2001	1.10
Bateman et al. (2001)	UK, Glasgow	1986	0.25
Gautrin (1975)	UK, London Heathrow	1968–69	0.62
Abelson (1979)	Australia, Marrickville (Sydney)	1972–73	0.40
Abelson (1979)	Australia, Rockdale (Sydney)	1972–73	0.50
Andersson et al. (2010)	Sweden, Lerum (Gothenburg) > 50 dbA	1996–2006	1.17
Andersson et al. (2010)	Sweden, Lerum (Gothenburg) > 55 dbA	1996–2006	1.68

Source: Updated and expanded from Bateman et al. (2001). Full reference to publications from 2002 onwards can be found in the References list. Full reference details of studies prior to 2002 can be found in Bateman et al. (2001).

Most studies assume that the impact of noise on the price of the dwelling can be ignored below a certain threshold noise level. Cut-off points typically used are either 50 dB or 55 dB. However, which of these cut-off points is used turns out to matter. Rich and Nielsen (2002) found in their sample of 238 houses and 472 apartments from the greater Copenhagen area exposed to noise levels above 50 dB, a NSDI of 0.54 for single-family homes and 0.47 for apartments. The NSDI increased to 1.08 for houses and 0.63 for apartments when they only included dwellings exposed to noise levels above 55 dbA. The same effect is observed by Andersson et al. (2010) and Damgaard (2003) in Sweden and Denmark, respectively.

Damgaard (2003), Rich and Nielsen (2002) and Bue-Bjørner et al. (2003) are all HP studies of road noise in Copenhagen, Denmark. However, as Table 2.1 shows, the NSDI from Damgaard is much higher than that from the other two. One explanation for this could be the omission of accessibility or neighbourhood attributes in Damgaard (2003), but this study of 760 single-family houses from eight areas in the greater Copenhagen used dummies for each area to compensate for this. Another possible explanation (launched by Bue-Bjørner et al. 2003) is that in Damgaard (2003) the variation in noise levels was obtained by including houses in the first row, second row and so on up to a 500-metre range from the road, whereas Rich and Nielsen (2002) and Bue-Bjørner et al. (2003) obtained variations in noise levels by including first-row houses from roads with different levels of traffic and noise. A single-family house located in the second, third or fourth row away from a large road or highway in a single-family housing area, will in addition to not being close to the noisy road also have the advantage of a higher level of 'safety from traffic' (for example, 'a local road where the children can play'). Differences in levels of 'safety' when comparing dwellings in streets with different traffic volumes (which generally represent more than just local traffic) are likely to generally imply lower levels of safety with greater traffic volumes, thereby implying a negative correlation between safety and noise level. This suggests that when safety cannot be directly observed and corrected for, it is likely that the noise variable to some degree also picks up a 'safety' variable. We, however, do not normally expect such a correlation to be as high as that found in Damgaard's sample. Potentially, this may clearly have led to an upward bias in the Damgaard's (2003) NSDI. A similar general argument can also be made with respect to barrier effects: that such effects are reduced with distance to large roads and highways.

This discussion illustrates the general difficulty of isolating the impact of noise on house prices, and separating it from that of other externalities associated with roads, in the context of HP models where not all externalities are directly observable, and are correlated. Thus, our study uses noise as an indicator for *all* externalities of roads, instead of trying to isolate the effect of noise.

3   DATA AND MODEL

The data-set applied in this analysis has been created by combining data-sets from two major Norwegian databases. One of these is Statistics Norway's database on residential house sales, which provides a complete set of sold residential housing units in Norway for the period from the first quarter of 1999 to the first quarter of 2002. The other data-set is provided by the Norwegian Directorate of Public Roads (DPR), from their VSTØY database, which contains data on road traffic noise levels and other environmental variables at the level of the individual property for residential units with close proximity to large roads and highways. Only single-family homes, which comprise detached houses and row houses (and thus not apartments), are included in our data-set. This was motivated by the overriding purpose of the study, which was to design a model for calculating compensation for the damage experienced due to the construction of new roads, where claims are typically raised only by single-family house owners. The combined data-set consists of a total of about 11 000 observations of residential housing units sold all over Norway. Among these are about 4500 detached houses, and about 6500 row houses. Within these two groups of properties, about 1300 and 5000, respectively are from the Greater Oslo Area (that is, the counties of Oslo and Akershus, which account for about a quarter of the aggregate Norwegian population).

It should be stressed that the environmental variables (including the noise level) are generally not observed at the level of the individual property, but rather imputed on the basis of a parameterized and estimated model held by the DPR. This may be a source of error at the individual property level; but, we argue, not generally on the average. Still the resulting observational errors may cause some bias in the estimated coefficients, which are discussed below.

Various characteristics of the residential units are provided in the combined data-set. First, from the data-set for sold housing units, several variables describe attributes of the housing unit itself, such as the number of rooms and bathrooms, floor space, whether the unit has a garage or not, its year of construction and its geographical location (including its post code).

Secondly, from the data provided from VSTØY by the DPR, information about road noise related to the individual dwelling in terms of:

1. Distance to road, in metres
2. Average outdoor noise level (in dbA)[8] calculated at the exterior wall of the house
3. Average indoor noise (in dbA)
4. Variable expressing view towards nearest road, which takes the value 1 if there is a 90-degree view or more, and 0 otherwise.
5. Variable expressing shielding of noise from the nearest road. This variable takes three values: the value 0 with no shielding; 1 with partial shielding; and 2 when fully shielded from the road. There is no information on whether the shield is natural (for example, a hill) or artificial (for example, a constructed noise barrier).
6. Calculated reduction of average outside noise level (in dbA) due to specific noise-reducing measures
7. Calculated reduction of average indoor noise level (in dbA) due to specific noise-reducing measures
8. Other measures to reduce noise including façade shielding, noise barriers, insulated/triple glazed window, and so on.

Whereas information from variables (1) to (5) were included in our HP model, variables (6), (7) and (8) were not, for various reasons. First, there are very few observations for these categories. Secondly, these variables were deemed likely to create endogeneity problems, as any noise-reducing

Table 2.2   Distribution of dwellings in the data-set, by county and level of urbanity

County	Rural	Semi-urban	Urban	Total
Østfold	217	303	314	834
Akershus	566	2979	2041	5586
Oslo	0	268	536	804
Hedemark	254	108	1022	1384
Oppland	71	68	55	194
Buskerud	2	0	0	2
Vestfold	16	11	17	44
Vest-Agder	0	0	312	312
Aust-Ager	2	64	33	99
Hordaland	46	0	715	761
Sør-Trøndelag	531	128	232	891
Nordland	0	2	0	2
Troms	24	39	208	271
Total	1729	3970	5485	11184

measures are likely to be determined simultaneously with the (initial and final) noise situation. We did, however, run some models with these variables on the aggregate data-set (as the split in subsamples we otherwise use would yield too few observations). These calculations showed that these variables had very little or no systematic effects on housing prices. In addition, VSTØY also had data on how urbanized the area was where the dwelling was located.[9] Table 2.2 describes some summary statistics of our final data-set. We lack observations from some of Norway's 20 counties, because few people live there and/or there are few major roads and highways and/or there were no houses sold there during this specific time period. Most of our observations are from semi-urban (in most cases, suburban) and urban areas. It is noticeable that most of the observations are from the central parts of South-east Norway (which includes the greater Oslo area). Apart from this region, a substantial number of observations are from only four city regions:[10] Kristiansand (Vest-Agder), Bergen (Hordaland), Trondheim (Sør-Trøndelag) and Tromsø (Troms).

Since the houses in our data-set have been selected based on their proximity to roads, and few households in Norway are affected by multiple transportation noise sources, the bias introduced by not having data for other noise sources like aircraft and railways, should be small in our data-set.

Our first stage HP model, following Rosen (1974), assumes that the sales price of residential housing units is systematically affected by the observable variables in our data set, including the proximity of homes to roads and the road noise level:

$$\log(P) = \alpha_1 A + \alpha_2 \log(H) + \alpha_3 V + \alpha_4 S + \sum_i \beta_i \log(Y_i)$$

$$+ \sum_j \gamma_j \log(Z_j) + \sum_k \mu_k D_k + \delta t + \varepsilon \qquad (2.3)$$

where P is the sales price of the residential property, A is average outdoor noise level (measured in decibels; dbA), H is the distance of the home from the nearest road (in meters), V is a dummy variable indicating view to the road (taking the value 1 when there is a view of the road; and zero otherwise), while S indicates the degree of shielding of the home from road traffic noise. Y is a vector of variables characterizing the property itself (floor area, number of bedrooms, number of bathrooms, and so on) and Z is a vector of variables characterizing the neighbourhood. Apart from V and S, all these variables are either continuous or take several different values. D is a vector of additional binary explanatory variables. t represents time, so that δ represents a systematic national development in home prices over time.[11] All Greek letters (apart from ε) represent coefficients, associated with the respective variables, these are generally taken as constants in the respective model specifications to be estimated, and determined by the analysis. ε is a stochastic, residual term, assumed in the model to be normally distributed with mean value zero and constant variance, σ^2.

Generally speaking, equation (2.3) implies the assumption that the value of a particular residential property is affected systematically by three groups of variables: 'environmental' variables (related to road traffic noise, proximity to roads); variables identifying aspects and qualities of the residential unit itself (such as the type of residential property (detached house, row house), floor area, number of bedrooms, and so on); and neighbourhood variables (including geographical location and the general view from the home). The purpose of our study is to identify partial effects of the noise variable (including the distance and shielding variables) on sales prices.

A key assumption behind this analysis is that error terms ε are exogenous and randomly distributed. The basic underlying assumption behind this is that the explanatory variables (on the right-hand side of equation 2.3) are uncorrelated with ε, which means that there is no 'feedback' effect on the explanatory variables from sales prices, nor any 'feedback' effects of some explanatory variables on other such variables. This may seem a reasonable starting hypothesis for most of the (non-environmental) explanatory variables, which are, in most cases, not likely to be much influenced by home prices or by the environmental variables. In some cases this assumption may be more problematic. Some of the explanatory variables (including 'shielding against noise', which may represent deliberate efforts to shield the particular residence) may themselves be affected by the noise level, in which case the respective variable will not be autonomous as assumed. This is, however, not necessarily a serious basic concern that will significantly upset our estimates; but it is one we need to be aware of when interpreting the coefficients.

A particular problem in this regard is that road traffic noise, also noted above, is not directly observed at each property, but is instead model generated or imputed.[12] Since model-generated data can never fully represent the actual noise level at each property site, it implies that noise (used as an explanatory variable) generally is recorded with an error. From basic statistical theory, this implies that, generally, the regression coefficient related to noise will be biased, and generally in the downward direction.[13] The degree of bias will depend on the variance of the model error, and in addition on any bias in the noise model itself.

There exist ways in which model specification, in particular independence of right-hand side variables from the error term, can be tested. One set of such tests relies on using instrumental variables, which (by construction) are uncorrelated with the error term, as right-hand side variables. We have carried out a number of such prospective tests, however, without conclusive results. A problem here is that few suitable instrumental variables are available for such a procedure.[14]

4   RESULTS AND DISCUSSION

Results are presented in Tables 2.3–2.9. As noted we use data only for detached homes and row houses (not apartments in multi-unit buildings), and for outside noise levels in the range 55–70 dbA only.[15] Several ways of categorizing our data have been attempted, by geographical region, type of residence, and so on. More explanatory variables have been included in our analysis than those shown in the tables (generally, the number of variables used equals the difference between the number observation and the degrees of freedom for each model). Some of these variables are related to characteristics of the property itself (number of rooms, baths, and so on). Most importantly, we correct for geographical location by including dummies for individual postcodes.[16] Overall, the total explanatory power of the relationship is high, in most cases with an adjusted R-squared in the range 0.8 or even higher.[17]

Table 2.3   Regression models with residential house prices for the full data-set; the dependent variable is the log of house sales prices

Explanatory Variable	Model 1	Model 2	Model 3	Model 4	Model 5
Log gross floor area	0.156***	0.156***	0.156***	0.153***	0.155***
Log net floor area	0.394***	0.393***	0.393***	0.394***	0.394***
Detached unit	0.038***	0.039***	0.040***	0.038***	0.041
Have garage	0.031***	0.032***	0.031***	0.031***	0.031***
Log age of house	−0.081***	−0.080***	−0.079***	−0.077***	0.081***
Distance to road				0.0207***	
Decibel noise	−0.0043***	−0.0041***	−0.0038***	−0.0029***	−0.0043***
Noise specific for row houses					0.00005
View of road		−0.0248***	−0.0239***	−0.0167	
Partially shielded			0.016*	0.015*	
Fully shielded			0.014	0.011	
Adjusted R^2	0.7963	0.7965	0.7965	0.7968	0.7963
No of observations	8128	8128	8128	8128	8128
d.f.	7415	7414	7412	7411	7414

Note: * Significant at the 10 per cent level, ** = 5 per cent level, ***= 1 per cent level. d.f. = degrees of freedom.

Table 2.3 provides model results for the full set of housing data applied. The five regression models differ in the number of explanatory variables included. The key result is the effect of noise on house price. In all five models, the impact on the property price is highly significant. Since the independent variable is log of house sales prices and the average noise level in dbA is measured on a logarithmic scale, the coefficient can be interpreted as an elasticity. Thus, model 1 shows that the house price is reduced by 0.43 per cent per decibel increase in average road traffic noise level. Thus, the Noise Depreciation Sensitivity Index is 0.43. Considering the entire noise range covered by our models (55–70 dbA), the value of the house would, on average, be reduced by nearly seven per cent (that is, 0.46 per cent per dbA × 15 dbA) if the average road traffic noise level were to increase from 55 to 70 dbA *ceteris paribus*. The noise coefficient changes little when including other environmental variables (but gets smaller when distance to road is included separately, as these two variables are highly

Table 2.4   Regression models with log of residential house prices, separate for three main geographical regions of Norway

Explanatory variable	Oslo region	Rest of South/East	Rest of country
Log gross floor area	0.172***	0.201***	0.093***
Log net floor area	0.388***	0.402***	0.305***
Detached unit	0.149***	−0.005	0.011*
Have garage	−0.01	0.124***	0.043***
Log age of house	−0.051***	−0.111***	−0.098***
Decibel noise	−0.0046***	−0.0027*	0.0005
View of road	−0.065***	0.010	0.0136*
Partially shielded	−0.026**	0.084**	0.0336
Fully shielded	−0.050***	0.103***	−0.0299*
Adjusted R^2	0.7967	0.7065	0.7660
Number of observations	4821	1852	1361
d.f.	4544	1590	1124

Note: * Significant at the 10 per cent level, ** = 5 per cent level, ***= 1 per cent level.
d.f. = degrees of freedom.

correlated). We note that all other variables have reasonable coefficients. Note also that 'view to road' appears to have a negative and highly significant effect on house prices in models 2 and 3. There is no measurable difference in the impact on noise on sales prices for detached houses and row houses (as evident from model 5).

Table 2.4 shows regression models separate for three different regions, which can be viewed as separate housing markets: the Greater Oslo area, the rest of South and East Norway, and the rest of the country. Note here there are far more data for the Oslo area, both in terms of number of observations, and in terms of representing different parts of the region. The impact of noise level on property prices is also highest for the Oslo area, nearly half in the rest of the South and East Norway, and there is no significant impact of noise for the region covering the rest of the country. Note also that the variable 'view to road' has a significant negative effect on residential property prices for the Greater Oslo area, but not for other areas. This may reflect a general problem, to be discussed below in connection with Table 2.8, that the 'view of the road' variable may have different implications depending on the distance of the house from the road and which region we look at.

In the Oslo area, the main effect of 'view of the road' is likely to be negatively correlated with having a view in general (something that, in isolation, is valued positively). In the rest of the country, 'view to the road'

Table 2.5 *Regression models of residential house prices, for exclusive houses only; defined here as sales prices exceeding NOK2 million for the Greater Oslo area and exceeding NOK1.5 million for the rest of Norway*

Explanatory variable	Model 1	Model 2	Model 3
Log gross floor	0.102***	0.095***	0.095**
Log net floor	0.130***	0.126***	0.131***
Detached unit	0.061***	0.058***	0.047**
Have garage	0.086***	0.088***	0.086***
Log age of house	−0.030***	−0.029***	−0.033***
Distance to road		0.0207***	
Decibel noise	−0.0087***	−0.0077***	−0.0078
View of road	−0.027***	−0.0157	
Partially shielded	0.001	−0.0054	
Fully shielded	0.116***	0.1084***	
Adjusted R^2	0.7260	0.7273	0.7244
No. of observations	1564	1564	1564
d.f.	1268	1267	1271

Note: * Significant at the 10 per cent level, ** = 5 per cent level, ***= 1 per cent level.
d.f. = degrees of freedom.
NOK 1 = US$ 0.16 (March 2010).

is more likely to be positively correlated with general view. A further issue is the 'shielding' variable which has a negative effect for the Oslo area but is positive elsewhere. One possible explanation here could be that in urban areas (Oslo being the main such area), shielding is largely artificial, in terms of the construction of wooden or concrete noise barriers which reduce noise but are in themselves not aesthetically attractive. In mostly rural areas (which are 'The Rest of South/East Norway' and 'The rest of the country' regions, shielding is likely to be largely natural, with aesthetically more attractive features.

Table 2.5 provides results for what we have defined (from sales price) as 'exclusive' residences only.[18] Here we find greater relative effects of noise on house prices; about twice the average effect for the full sample presented in Table 2.3. The overall NDSI (from model 1 where the distance variable is excluded) here is 0.87. Internationally speaking this is relatively high; it is near the high end of international estimates given in Table 2.1. Considering model 2 in Table 2.5 (where the distance variable is included; and which contains the highest number of explanatory variables when we consider exclusive houses in all of Norway), we find that an increase in the outdoor noise level from 55 to 70 dbA leads to a reduction in sales price

Table 2.6   Regression models of residential house prices, for ordinary (non-exclusive) houses only; defined here as sales prices below NOK2 million for the Greater Oslo area and below NOK1.5 million for the rest of Norway

Explanatory variable	All	Detached Houses only	Row houses only
Log gross floor	0.104***	0.017***	0.100***
Log net floor	0.357***	0.372***	0.373***
Detached unit	−0.059***		
Have garage	0.025***	0.080***	0.001
Log age of house	−0.062***	−0.121***	−0.012**
Distance to road	−0.002	−0.001	0.0004
Decibel noise	−0.0024**	−0.0010	−0.0044***
Partially shielded	0.051***	0.114***	0.0023
Fully shielded	−0.007	−0.003	0.0156
Adjusted R^2	0.776	0.714	8285
No. of observations	6551	2421	4130
d.f.	5936	1963	3824

Note: * Significant at the 10 per cent level, ** = 5 per cent level, ***= 1 per cent level.
d.f. = degrees of freedom.
NOK 1 = US$ 0.16 (March 2010).

by about 11.6 per cent. Because these are high-value homes, the absolute price change is even greater. These results are not very surprising. They may simply reflect a tendency for environmental factors to have income elasticities in excess of unity (thus being 'luxury goods'). Also note that the partial effect of noise changes little by inclusion of distance to road as a separate variable (model 2 compared with model 1).

Table 2.6 shows the results for the 'non-exclusive' houses, defined as the full set of houses except that the 'exclusive' ones presented in Table 2.5 are now excluded. Here, not surprisingly, the effect of noise on house prices is substantially lower; the coefficient representing noise in model 1 is now only one quarter of that found for 'exclusive' homes (in Table 2.5), and about one half of the effect for the full sample (in Table 2.3). In contrast to the 'exclusive' houses, there is no effect of distance to road and being fully shielded from the road on sales prices of these 'non-exclusive' houses.

Table 2.7 shows regression models separately for rural and semi-urban/urban areas. We find that noise has the greatest impact on house prices in rural areas, and the smallest effect in urban areas. This is not surprising. First, road traffic noise is likely to be more conspicuous in rural areas, so that house price values are likely to be more affected. Secondly, some may

Table 2.7   Regression models of residential house prices; separate for rural and urban/semi-urban areas

Explanatory variable	Rural, excluding distance to road	Rural, including distance to road	Urban/ semi-urban; excluding distance to road	Urban/ semi-urban, including distance to road
Log gross floor	0.172***	0.165***	0.167***	0.163***
Log net floor	0.339***	0.340***	0.382***	0.384***
Detached unit	0.036*	0.042*	0.060***	0.057***
Have garage	−0.030	−0.026	0.035***	0.034***
Log age	−0.132***	−0.133***	−0.063***	−0.060***
Distance to road		0.046*		0.021**
Decibel noise	−0.0087***	−0.0077***	−0.0034***	−0.0024**
View of road	−0.0157	0.0110	−0.026**	−0.020*
Partially shielded	0.0615	0.0562	0.12	0.013
Fully shielded	0.0606	0.0559	0.014**	0.040**
Adjusted R^2	0.8063	0.8073	0.8120	0.8123
No. of observations	1162	1162	6966	6953
d.f.	910	909	6363	6352

Note: * Significant at the 10 per cent level, ** = 5 per cent level, *** = 1 per cent level. d.f. = degrees of freedom.

settle in rural areas to avoid certain environmental disturbances including road traffic noise. Thus, there is some self-selection with house buyers in rural areas putting greater emphasis on avoiding noise. Thirdly, house prices are lower in rural areas; with a log-linear model this yields a greater relative price change in rural areas for a given absolute value attached to the noise nuisance. We note that other environmental variables lose much of their significance when splitting up the data-set in this way.[19]

Tables 2.8 and 2.9 look more closely at some special issues that arise in estimating hedonic price models of the type considered here. In Table 2.8, we attempt to look closer at the issue of shielding, in particular, whether the two shielding variables ('partly' and 'fully' shielded, as opposed to the house not being shielded from the house) are correlated with the 'view of road' variable. A problematic issue is that while general view from a home may tend to increase home value, the view of a road with traffic may tend to reduce it. The correlation between these two variables is therefore important.

To exemplify, consider first a perfect positive correlation between the two, so that all houses with a view towards the road also have a general

Table 2.8   *Regression models of residential house prices, including dummy variables for houses with a view towards the road at increasing distance from the road (view 1–7); for the full data-set (all houses) and separate for rural, semi-urban and urban houses*

Explanatory variable	All houses	Exclusive houses	Rural houses	Semi-urban house	Urban houses
Log gross floor area	0.150**	0.107**	0.173**	0.025	0.224**
Log net floor area	0.392**	0.113**	0.338**	0.463**	0.334**
Detached house	0.038**	0.055**	0.038	0.163**	0.039**
Have garage	0.030**	0.093**	−0.027	0.013	0.041**
Log age of house	−0.078**	−0.031**	−0.130**	−0.065**	−0.074**
Distance to road	0.060**	0.075**	−0.020	−0.014	0.091**
Decibel noise	−0.0040**	−0.0097**	−0.0097**	−0.0072**	−0.0044**
View 1	0.041**	0.042*	−0.059	−0.000	0.064**
View 2	0.0069	0.053**	−0.095**	−0.013	0.022
View 3	0.0086	−0.057**	0.037	0.020	−0.033**
View 4	−0.029**	−0.014	−0.043	−0.010	−0.029
View 5	−0.083**	−0.033	0.087	−0.038**	−0.079**
View 6	−0.072**	−0.210**	0.019	−0.287**	−0.036
View 7	0.039	−0.248**			−0.050
Partially shielded	0.0107	−0.016	0.060	0.034	−0.016
Fully shielded	0.0063	0.106**	0.056	0.022	0.026
Adjusted R^2	0.8162	0.7394	0.8528	0.8533	0.8456
No. of observations	8115	1564	1162	3248	3705
d.f.	7395	1261	904	2998	3277

Note: * Significant at the 10 per cent level, ** = 5 per cent level, ***= 1 per cent level.
d.f. = degrees of freedom.
The dummy variables 'view' 1 through to 7 are defined as the house having a view towards the road, and the distances to the road being, respectively: < 15 metres; 15–25 metres; 25–35 metres; 35–50 metres; 50–80 metres; 80–150 metres; and > 150 metres.

(and attractive) view. It is then reasonable to assume that the view (including view towards the road) on average tends to increase house prices. We would then expect the coefficient representing the 'view of road' variable to be positive.

Consider instead the case where most houses with a general view do not have view of the road, and vice versa. In that case, the 'view of road' variable might be more likely to have a negative impact on house prices, implying that the coefficient will be negative.

One working hypothesis is that such correlations vary systematically

Table 2.9 *Regression models of residential house prices, for houses below and above the cut-off levels used in the previous models; that is, below 55 dbA and above 70 dbA, respectively*

Explanatory variable	Below 55 dbA	Above 70 dbA
Log gross floor area	0.145***	0.196*
Log net floor area	0.540***	0.499***
Detached	−0.089**	0.190**
Have garage	−0.032**	0.007
Log age of house	−0.061***	−0.016
Distance to road	0.043***	0.0771
Decibel noise	−0.00127	0.0052
View of road	−0.023	0.167*
Partially shielded	0.064**	0.025
Fully shielded	0.088***	−0.031
Adjusted R^2	0.8814	0.9338
No. of observations	1621	335
d.f.	1324	209

Note: * Significant at the 10 per cent level, ** = 5 per cent level, ***= 1 per cent level.
d.f. = degrees of freedom.

with distance to the road, so that, with generally short distances to the road, road view tends to be positively correlated with general view, while with greater distances to the road, this correlation is negative (since, in this case, most tend to have a view, but not all have a view of the road).

To test for such effects, we have, in the regression models reported in Table 2.8, included specific dummy variables for view at different distances to the road. The variables view 1–view 7 take the value 1, if and only if, the house has a view towards the road, and distances to the road are, respectively: <15 metres; 15–25 metres; 25–35 metres; 35–50 metres; 50–80 metres; 80–150 metres; and >150 metres.

From the reasoning above, we might expect the coefficients of these dummy variables to take positive values for small distances to road, and negative values for greater distances. For the full sample, these patterns are not entirely clear. It is, however, interesting to note that, for 'exclusive' residences, there is a strong such effect. This is an interesting result, in particular as environmental variables are likely to have their greatest effects on house sales prices for exactly this class of residences. We also find that the impact of noise on house prices increases when these dummy variables are included. Given an assumption that the model is better specified in this way, this tends to support the relatively strong effect of noise on house prices in 'exclusive' price ranges.

Table 2.9 studies the effect of having limited the exterior road traffic noise level range to 55–70 dbA, by presenting HP models for houses experiencing noise below 55 dbA and above 70 dbA, respectively. An initial hypothesis is that noise levels below 55 dbA are too small to have a noticeable effect on house values. Noise levels above 70 dbA, by contrast, are so high that a further increase might be relatively unnoticeable. The number of homes in this category is very small; owners of such homes also likely to take strong protective measures against noise; and there could be a strong selection effect among the population into such homes, implying that only households highly resistant to noise buy such dwellings.

We find no significant effect of noise on house prices, neither for dwellings experiencing road noise below 55 dbA, nor above 70 dbA. On this basis, we conclude that there is little to lose by excluding these data from our analysis. These results also seem to support the current practice in Norway, of not paying compensation to house owners experiencing an average road noise level below 55 dbA.

5   CONCLUSIONS

Many hedonic price studies claim, rather heroically, to be able to estimate the welfare loss from the externality that is the subject of the respective analysis. We argue that nearly all these studies fail to calculate the 'true' welfare loss as they estimate only the 'first stage' HP model, and report the implicit price of noise from this model.[20] In the case of noise, the implicit price is expressed in terms of the Noise Sensitivity Depreciation Index, which describes the percentage decrease in house price per decibel (dbA) increase in noise level. In most HP studies of road noise, the observed NSDI represents *all* external effects of road traffic; not only noise but also barrier effects, vibrations, safety concerns about living near roads, and dust and air pollution causing annoyance and health effects. This is because house-specific data for such other environmental variables for inclusion in the HP function is generally lacking. As a consequence, we argue, the estimated welfare effects of road noise, and of changes in such noise, tend to be biased in most studies to date.

In the current study, our main objective is *not* to provide welfare estimates to be used in cost–benefit analyses of noise-reducing measures, but rather deciding the correct level of tort compensations for *all* externalities that may result from new road construction. With this perspective, we present an example of how a 'first stage' HP analysis of road noise can provide very useful information about the appropriate level of compensation.

The main aim of our HP study was to develop a market-based model for the Norwegian Directorate for Public Roads, to be used in calculating the appropriate monetary compensation for single-family home owners in Norway when a new road is constructed near their house. We argue that our model can serve favourably as a substitute for, or supplement to, the expert-based model currently in use by the DPR. Using noise as an indicator of *all* externalities caused by the road, we show how the NSDI, estimated from the HP function, varies between different market segments, in terms of the type of single-family house (semi-detached and row house), exclusivity of the house (defined as high market price), population density/pressure (urban versus. semi-urban and rural) and geographical location (that is, different parts of Norway). Our results indicate that no compensation for externalities from new roads should be paid for noise levels below 55 dbA, but that compensation should be paid above this threshold level and up to 70 dBA. *Payments per dbA* should be higher for detached single-family houses than for row houses; higher in rural and semi-urban areas than in urban areas; higher for exclusive than for non-exclusive homes; and higher than average for homes located in the Greater Oslo area; and lower than average for homes located in Middle and North Norway (with the rest of East and South Norway as a reference group).

ACKNOWLEDGEMENTS AND DISCLAIMERS

Funding for this hedonic pricing study from the Norwegian Directorate of Public Roads is gratefully acknowledged. Ståle Navrud would also like to thank the Department of Economics, University of New Mexico, for their hospitality and for providing an inspiring working environment for writing up this chapter. Special thanks go to Bob Berrens, David Brookshire, Kristine Grimsrud and Jenn Thacher. The views expressed in this chapter are solely those of the authors, and do not necessarily represent those of the World Bank or its members.

NOTES

1. See Smith and Huang (1993, 1995) for the first meta-analyses of HP studies, which concerned air quality.
2. The first combined HP and CV study of road traffic noise seems to be Vainio (1995).
3. This is especially true for SP studies based on the damage function approach of linking noise levels to an annoyance scale (an ISO-standard with currently five levels from 'not annoyed' to 'extremely annoyed'; see Miedema and Oudshoorn (2001) for

such exposure-response functions between noise and level of annoyance) and asking people for their willingness-to-pay (WTP) to eliminate their annoyance from noise (but keeping the other externalities from road traffic constant); see Navrud (2002) for a review of these studies, and Navrud (2000), Bue-Bjørner et al. (2003) and Navrud et al. (2006) for CV surveys using this approach. Arsenio et al (2006) and Wardman and Bristow (2004, 2008) apply the CE approach to transportation noise.

4. In the event that people are affected by multiple noise sources, it is also of vital importance to include data and variables for each of the noise sources in the HP function.
5. dbA' = noise level in decibels averaged over 24 hours of the day and over the year. We use the equivalent level for a full 24-hour period, LAEq, 24h, which is the most commonly used noise indicator. Another indicator, used in the European Noise Directive, that better reflects both general annoyance and sleep disturbance is the Lden (level day evening night).
6. Perfect divisibility in this context simply means that each house unit is 'small' relative to the entire house market, and that there is, in principle, a continuum of possible attributes. These are relatively innocuous assumptions that are likely to be fulfilled, at least in relatively large (or 'thick') housing markets. For a further discussion and illustration of the principles underlying the hedonic price model, see for example, Palmquist (1984, 1991), Bateman et al. (2001, ch. 2) and Kolstad (2000, ch. 16).
7. Our HP study looks only at detached houses and row houses, which are both single-family units with gardens.
8. dbA' = average noise level, in decibels.
9. VSTØY contain data on two such variables. The first of these splits each of the 20 Norwegian counties into three types of regions: 'rural', 'densily built up' and 'largest city'. The second variable splits each of these regions into areas that are 'scattered', 'medium dense' and 'dense' population. Here, we use only the first of these, and rename the categories 'rural', 'semi-urban' and 'urban', respectively.
10. The name of the county in parenthesis.
11. Over the entire period for which we have data, there has been a relatively stable trend of growth in house prices. Thus, we found no particular reason to introduce a more complex price growth function.
12. Based on the VSTØY model of the Norwegian Directorate of Public Roads.
13. See Greene (2000, ch. 9). This problem occurs even when the model as such provides consistent estimates of noise at each property site.
14. See again Greene (2000, p. 275), who discusses difficulties in finding suitable instruments. A common problem is that any available instruments will often have a low degree of correlation with the underlying variables that they replace. See also Hansen (1982) and White (1984) for further discussion, also for considerations of optimal instrument choice.
15. Outside this range we find little effect on residential house prices, and there is little to gain in terms of efficiency or explanatory power by including a larger range. Table 2.9 reports results from noise levels outside of the 55–70 dbA range. The insulated walls in Norwegian detached and row houses (mostly wooden houses) reduce the indoor noise level by about 25–30 dbA. Thus, outdoor noise levels of 55 dbA correspond to 25–30 dbA indoors.
16. This is crucial it turns out, as there are large and systematic differences in house prices between postcodes.
17. This is considerably higher than in most other comparable analyses; see, for example, Bateman et al. (2001), who in a similar study in the UK find R-squared in the range of 0.7, which they consider to be unusually high.
18. We define 'exclusivity' by sales price only. All housing units sold at prices above NOK2 million in Oslo and Akershus, and above NOK1.5 million elsewhere, are considered to be 'exclusive'. This is of course a rough approximation. In particular, in some regions of Oslo and suburban community of Bærum it is difficult to find single-family homes at prices below NOK2 million. Thus many of these houses will in reality not be 'exclusive'.

In other parts of the country it is by contrast difficult to find houses (many of which are 'exclusive') valued above NOK1.5 million.
19. We also note that there is little to gain, in terms of explanatory power or precision, by splitting the material further into semi-urban and urban residential property sites.
20. Day et al. (2007) appears to be the only exception, among studies we are aware of that apply HP models to road noise.

REFERENCES

Andersson, H., L. Jonsson and M. Ögren (2010), 'Property prices and exposure to multiple noise sources: hedonic regression with road and railway noise', *Environmental and Resource Economics*, **45**, 73–89.

Arsenio, E., A.L. Bristow and M. Wardman (2006), 'Stated choice valuations of traffic related noise', *Transportation Research Part D*, **11** (1), 15–31.

Baranzini A., and J.V. Ramirez (2005), 'Paying for quietness: the impact of noise on Geneva rents', *Urban Studies*, **42** (4), 633–46.

Bartik, T.J. (1988), 'Measuring the benefits of amenity improvements', *Land Economics*, **64** (2), 172–83.

Bateman, I.J., B.H. Day, A.A. Lake and I. Lovett (2001), *The Effect of Road Traffic on Residential Property Value: A Literature Review and Hedonic Pricing Study*, Edinburgh: Scottish Executive and The Stationery Office.

Bateman I.J., B.H., Day, and I. Lake (2004), 'The valuation of transport-related noise in Birmingham', non-technical report to the Department for Transport, Centre for Social and Economic Research on the Global Environment (CSERGE), University of East Anglia.

Brookshire, D.S., M.A. Thayer, W.D. Schulze and R.C. D'Arge (1982), 'Valuing public goods: a comparison of survey and hedonic approaches', *American Economic Review*, **72** (1), 165–77.

Bue-Bjørner, T., T. Lundhede and J. Kronbak (2003), *Valuation of Noise Reduction – Comparing Results from Hedonic Pricing and Contingent Valuation*, Copenhagen: AKF Forlaget.

Damgaard, C. (2003), *What is the Cost of Noise? Valuation of Road Noise using the Hedonic Price Method* (in Danish), Copenhagen: Danish Environmental Protection Agency.

Day, B., I.J. Bateman and I. Lake (2007), 'Beyond implicit prices: recovering theoretically consistent and transferable values for noise voidance from a hedonic property price model', *Environmental and Resource Economics*, **37** (1), 211–32.

Freeman, A.M. (1974), 'Air pollution and property values: a further comment', *Review of Economics and Statistics*, **56**, 554–6.

Freeman, A.M. (2003), *The Measurement of Environmental and Resource Values*, 2nd edition, Washington, DC: Resources for the Future.

Greene, W.H. (2000), *Econometric Analysis*, Upper Saddle River, NJ: Prentice-Hall.

Grue, B., J.L. Langeland and O.I. Larsen (1997), *Housing Prices – Impacts of Exposure to Road Traffic and Location*, report 351/1997, Oslo: Institute of Transport Economics.

Haab, T.C. and K.E. McConnell (2002), *Valuing Environmental and Natural Resources: The Econometrics of Nonmarket Valuation*, Northampton, MA: Edward Elgar.

Hansen, L.P. (1982), 'Large sample properties of generalized method of moments estimators', *Econometrica*, **50**, 1029–54.

Kolstad, C.D. (2000), *Environmental Economics*, New York: Oxford University Press.

Miedema, H.M.E. and C.G.M. Oudshoorn (2001), 'Annoyance from transportation noise: relationships with exposure metrics DNL and DENL and their confidence intervals', *Environmental Health Perspectives*, **109** (4), 409–16.

Navrud, S. (2000), 'Economic benefits of a program to reduce transportation and community noise – a contingent valuation survey', *Proceedings of Internoise 2000*, Nice, France.

Navrud, S. (2002), *The State-of-the-art on Economic Valuation of Noise. Report to the European Commission DG Environment, Brussels*, final report, 14 April 2002, available at: http://ec.europa.eu/environment/noise/pdf/020414noisereport.pdf. (accessed 15 November 2010) An updated version was published as Navrud, S. (2004), 'What is silence worth? Economic valuation of road traffic noise', in M. Scasny and J. Melichar (eds), *Lectures in Non-market Valuation Methods in the Environment Area. Development of the Czech Society in the European Union V*, Prague: Matfyz Press, Charles University, pp. 145–77.

Navrud S., Y. Trædal, A. Hunt, A. Longo, A. Gressmann, C. Leon, R. Espino, R. Markovits-Somogyi and F. Meszaros (2006), *Economic Values for Key Impacts Valued in the Stated Preference Surveys*, Deliverable 4, HEATCO – Developing Harmonized European Approaches for Transport Costing and Project Assessment, report to European Commission DG Research, Brussels.

Nelson, J.P. (2004), 'Meta-analysis of airport noise and hedonic property values. Problems and prospects', *Journal of Transport Economics and Policy*, **38** (1), 1–28.

Palmquist, R.B. (1984), 'Estimating the demand for characteristics of housing', *Review of Economics and Statistics*, **66**, 394–404.

Palmquist, R.B. (1991), 'Hedonic methods', in J.B. Braden and C.D. Kolstad (eds), *Measuring the Demand for Environmental Quality*, North-Holland: Elsevier Science, pp. 77–120.

Rich, J.H. and O.A. Nielsen (2002), *Hedonic Evaluation of Traffic Noise – an empirical Study*, Centre of Traffic and Transport, Technical University of Denmark.

Rosen, S. (1974), 'Hedonic prices and implicit markets: product differentiation in perfect competition', *Journal of Political Economy*, **82**, 34–55.

Salvi, M. (2008), 'Little house in the city: estimation of the willingness-to-pay for housing attributes, location and amenities', mimeo. Zurich Kantonal Bank, Switzerland.

Schipper, Y., P. Nijkamp and P. Rietveld (2001), 'Aircraft noise valuation studies and meta analysis', *International Journal of Environmental Technology and Management*, **1** (3), 317–20.

Smith, V.K. and J.C. Huang (1993), 'Hedonic models and air pollution. Twenty-five years and counting', *Environmental and Resource Economics*, **3**, 381–94.

Smith, V.K. and J.C. Huang (1995), 'Can markets value air quality? A meta-analysis of hedonic property value models', *The Journal of Political Economy*, **103** (1), 209–27.

Vainio, M. (1995), Traffic noise and air pollution: valuation of externalities with the hedonic price and contingent valuation methods, PhD thesis, School of Economics and Business Administration, Helsinki.

Wardman, M. and A.L. Bristow (2004), 'Noise and air quality valuations: evidence from stated preference residential choice models', *Transportation Research Part D*, **9** (1), 1–27.

Wardman, M.R. and A.L. Bristow (2008), 'Valuation of aircraft noise: experiments in stated preference', *Environmental and Resource Economics*, **39**, 459–80.

White, H. (1984), *Asymptotic Theory for Econometricians*, New York: Cambridge University Press.

3   A hedonic price model of coral reef quality in Hawaii

*Roy Brouwer, Sebastiaan Hess, Yi Liu,
Pieter van Beukering and Sonia Garcia*

1   INTRODUCTION

Coral reefs have significant economic value (for example, Brander et al., 2007). They are, however, under imminent threat worldwide, from processes such as coral bleaching, especially as a result of climate change. Twenty per cent of the world's coral reefs have been effectively already destroyed and another 50 per cent are under serious threat (Wilkinson, 2004). Most economic valuation studies of coral reefs focus on their recreational benefits derived from activities such as snorkelling and diving, and the income generation from associated tourism. Coral reefs also provide important nursery habitats and hence are a source of income for the commercial fishing industry (for example, McConnell and Strand, 2000). This study examines whether a value relationship can also be detected between coral reefs and house prices using a hedonic price model. Such a relationship has not yet been established in the coral reef valuation literature. Hedonic price models are more widely used to assess the impact of living near the waterfront and the impact of beach quality on coastal residential property (for example, Pompe and Rinehart, 1995).

The main objective of this chapter is to estimate a hedonic price model for residential property in Hawaii and test the impact of coral reef quality and proximity on property values. The Hawaiian Islands are surrounded by 1180 square kilometres of coral reefs of different sizes, structure, density and quality. Based on a statistical analysis of available property sales data over the period 2000–05, and additional census, land use and coral reef monitoring data, we test the hypothesis that property values are not only determined by conventional house and neighbourhood characteristics, but also affected by the presence and quality of coral reefs. Given the hierarchical spatial nature of the available data, special attention is paid to spatial interdependencies, and their effect on the statistical efficiency of the estimated models. Our interest here is to correct for possible bias introduced by this correlation due to the use of spatial data (Anselin,

2001). To this end, we account for spatial heterogeneity in property values in a hierarchical mixed modelling framework.

2   ECONOMETRIC MODEL

In a hedonic price study, preferences for and economic values of non-priced environmental goods and services are revealed through the price house owners paid for their residential property as a composite bundle of attributes (Rosen, 1974). This bundle of attributes includes house characteristics and characteristics related to the property's location and environment (for example, Boyle and Kiel, 2001; Freeman, 2003). Each of these characteristics adds to the observed transaction price. By regressing individual (i) property transaction prices (P) on structural house (S), location (L) and environmental (E) characteristics, their implicit shadow prices can be estimated based on the hedonic price function's partial derivatives:

$$P_i = f(X_i) = f(S_i, L_i, E_i) \tag{3.1}$$

$$P_i = \Sigma \beta X_i + \varepsilon_i = \beta_S'S_i + \beta_L'L_i + \beta_E'E_i + \varepsilon_i \tag{3.2}$$

$$\varepsilon_i \sim N(0, \sigma^2) \tag{3.3}$$

Depending on the nature of the attribute and change involved (positive or negative), the implicit shadow price is, in most cases, also expected to be either positive or negative. In the case of environmental characteristics, the general assumption is that the implicit price of a property increases the nearer it is located to an environmental 'good' such as a natural park ($\delta P/\delta D < 0$ where D is the distance to the environmental good), and decreases the nearer it is located to an environmental 'bad', such as a landfill ($\delta P/\delta D > 0$ where D is the distance to the environmental bad). The derivative of the hedonic price function to a specific attribute represents marginal willingness-to-pay (WTP) for this attribute based on the aggregate uncompensated demand curve. In order to estimate the theoretically correct Hicksian welfare measure, a second step is needed where estimated marginal WTP is regressed on income and other individual house-owner characteristics. However, this second step is usually skipped due to lack of information (Bockstael and McConnell, 2007).

In this case study, an attempt is made to derive the implicit price of coral reefs encapsulated in the price of coastal and non-coastal properties in Hawaii. Accounting for property characteristics (for example house type, age, lot size, number of bedrooms), socio-economic characteristics of the neighbourhood in which these properties are located (for example degree of urbanization, presence of schools, ethnic composition, income), and the environment (for example, presence of parks, beaches, surf hot spots), house prices are regressed on the distance houses are located from the coast, the presence of shoreline coral reef and the quality of this coral reef. Autonomous trends in house prices over time are filtered out with the help of monthly dummy variables. A more detailed description of the variables used in the regression analysis is provided in the next section.

Given the nature of house price data in general and the Hawaiian archipelago context in particular in this study, house values are likely to be part of spatial clusters, causing spatial heterogeneity. It is generally acknowledged that property markets are not homogenous entities (Day et al., 2007). Demand and supply on the house market are expected to differ in this case study between the four islands, for instance in view of important population differences, and (as we show in the next section) also the supply of coral reefs. Not accounting for these spatial differences may lead to estimation errors in both the significance and magnitude of the estimates.[1] The available house market data described in more detail in the next section refer to four distinct islands of the Hawaiian archipelago: Oahu, Maui, Hawaii, and Kauai. Each of these islands consists of five to nine residential zones.

In order to test the significance of the hierarchical nature of the available data, two approaches are used. In the first approach, a flexible mixed generalized least squares (GLS) model is specified for the hedonic price function (for example, Greene, 2003):

$$P_i = \Sigma \beta X_i + \varepsilon_i = \Sigma \beta_{fe} X_i + \Sigma \beta_{re} Z_i + \varepsilon_i \qquad (3.4)$$

$$\varepsilon_i \sim N(0, \sigma^2) \qquad (3.5)$$

$$\beta_{re} \sim N(0, \sigma^2 \theta) \qquad (3.6)$$

where the subscript '*fe*' refers to the fixed effects variables X_i and '*re*' to the random effects variables Z_i. The random effects variables are set equal to the residential zones across the four islands, and the marginal effects of house and environmental characteristics on residential property prices are assumed to be common (fixed) across the islands and residential zones. The error term ε_i is assumed to be independently and identically distributed (i.i.d.) and the random parameters addressing heteroskedasticity are assumed to be drawn from a multivariate normal (Gaussian) distribution with mean zero and variance-covariance matrix θ. The theta equals the variance of the random parameter relative to the scalar variance σ^2 of the error ε associated with the individual observations. The GLS model is solved using the generalized method of moments (GMM) estimation procedure (for example Kelejian and Prucha, 1999).

Groupwise heteroskedasticity or cross-sectional dependence is tested in this first step using the Breusch and Pagan (1980) Lagrange multiplier test (λ):

$$\lambda = T \sum_{i=1}^{N} \sum_{j=1}^{i-1} r_{ij}^2 \tag{3.7}$$

where N is the number of cross-sectional units, in this case the zones, and r_{ij}^2 the ij^{th} residual correlation coefficient. Under the null hypothesis, the test statistic has a chi-square distribution with degrees of freedom equal to the number of cross-sectional units. An alternative approach is the Hausman (1978) specification test to examine whether the regressors are uncorrelated with the error term:

$$Q = (\hat{\beta}_1 - \hat{\beta}_0)'(\hat{V}_1 - \hat{V}_0)^{-1}(\hat{\beta}_1 - \hat{\beta}_0) \tag{3.8}$$

where $\hat{\beta}_1$ is a consistent estimator for β under the null and alternative hypothesis, but inefficient under the null hypothesis and $\hat{\beta}_0$ is an efficient and consistent estimator for β under the null hypothesis, but inconsistent under the alternative hypothesis (making $\hat{\beta}_1$ more robust to inconsistency). $\hat{V}$ refers to the variance-covariance matrix of the estimators. The Hausman test statistic is also chi-square distributed with degrees of freedom set equal to the number of estimators.

A positive outcome of these tests means that the null hypothesis of zero cross-sectional variance is rejected based on the Breusch and Pagan LM test and the difference between parameter estimates from the fixed and random effects model specification is not systematic based on the Hausman test. The hierarchical structure of the model initially specified in equation 3.4 and further detailed below is then estimated in a second approach that uses a maximum likelihood (ML) random effects panel data model.

$$P_{ij} = \beta_{0j} + \beta_S' S_{ij} + \beta_E' E_{ij} + \beta_L' L_{ij} + \varepsilon_{ij} \tag{3.9}$$

$$\beta_{0j} = \beta_0 + \upsilon_j \tag{3.10}$$

$$\varepsilon_{ij} \sim N(0, \sigma^2) \tag{3.11}$$

$$\upsilon_j \sim N(0, \sigma_\upsilon^2) \tag{3.12}$$

The random term υ_j captures the variance (heterogeneity) across the residential zones j, while the error term ε_{ij} is (as before) specific to a particular observation. The ML random effects estimator is an efficient estimation procedure that fully maximizes the likelihood of the random effects model under the assumption of normality (for example, Henning Olsson et al., 2000). The ML model explicitly accounts for the evidenced spatial heterogeneity in the first approach in the random component of the price equation in the second approach.

3   DATA DESCRIPTION

House market data for four of the Hawaiian islands were obtained from the Hawaii Information Service (HIS) for the period 2000–05. With a surface area of 4028 square miles Hawaii is the largest island with 173 000 inhabitants. Oahu is smaller (597 square miles), but has the largest population (876 000), most of whom live in Honolulu. Maui is bigger than Oahu with 727 square miles, but has fewer inhabitants (141 000). Finally, Kauai is the smallest island considered, both in terms of size (552 square miles) and population (63 000). Residential property sales data for the four islands were linked to a unique nine-digit tax map key (TMK) number. The first digit refers to the island, the second to the residential zones mentioned in the previous section, and the remaining digits to individual parcels in sections within these zones. The geographical location of the different zones across the four islands, including the number of observations per zone, is presented in Figure 3.1.

The relative sample size for each island equals the actual population distribution across the four islands (68 per cent of the total observations relate to Oahu, 13 per cent to Hawaii and Maui, and 6 per cent to Kauai). The distribution across years is also fairly equal (the number of transactions is slightly higher in the last three years). However, the spatial distribution of observations across the residential zones is far from equal. Most observations in Oahu are, as expected, found in the island's south-western urban zones of Honolulu (38 per cent) and Ewa (45 per cent), and in Maui in the urban centre of Wailuku (55 per cent) located in the island's northern bottleneck. The distribution of the available observations across the residential zones is more concentrated in the eastern part of Kauai and the eastern and western coastal strips of Hawaii and Kauai.

House sales prices differ significantly between the four islands (Figure 3.2).[2] The average house price is highest in Maui (except in 2000), followed by Oahu and Kauai. Average house prices are lowest in Hawaii. Sales prices increased significantly across all four islands from 2000 until

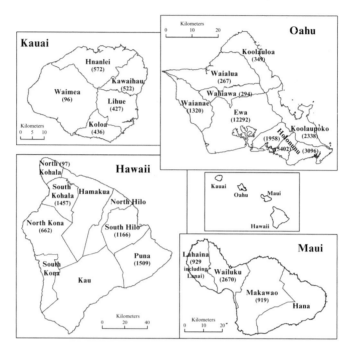

Figure 3.1   Number of observations across residential zones on the four islands

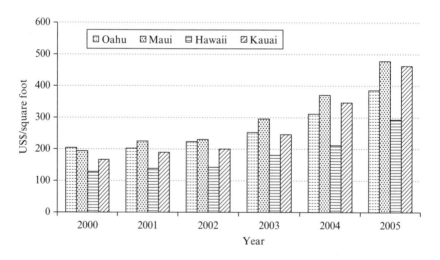

Figure 3.2   Average nominal sales price per island across the period 2000–05

2005. In these six years, the average house price per square foot in the database doubled in nominal terms, from US$190 per square foot in 2000 to US$390 per square foot in 2005 for the four islands taken together. The price increase was highest in Kauai, followed by Maui and Hawaii.

Besides the sales price of each transaction and the exact date of the sale (day, month, year), data were available about house and plot size, whether the house was a condominium or not (the definition of a condominium is that the property's plot of land is shared), building year, number of bedrooms, number of bathrooms, number of floors (the majority of properties only have one floor, that is, the ground floor), whether the house has a swimming pool, whether the parcel of land of the property is directly located on the oceanfront, building quality based on the type of materials used (ranging from 1 = very poor to 7 = excellent), flooring (the majority of houses have carpet) and whether the house is occupied by the owner or rented out. The summary statistics of these house characteristics across the four islands are presented in Appendix 3.1 to this chapter.

Additional geographical information system (GIS) computations were carried out in ArcGIS and ArcView 3.3 and related to the unique TMK codes to characterize each parcel's neighbourhood using available census data on the official website of the State of Hawaii. The geographical boundaries of a 'neighbourhood' coincide with the 2000 census blocks. The number of census blocks ranged from 46 in Kauai to 398 in Oahu and represent a separate layer below the residential zones presented in Figure 3.1. On average, a census block contains about 1700 people (ranging from 1250 in Kauai to 2065 in Oahu) or 495 households (ranging from 340 in Kauai to 670 in Oahu). Transactions and their TMK code were allocated to a census block and the census block was characterized in terms of population size, average household size, poverty (percentage), and presence of various race groups, including white, black, Asian, Native Hawaiian, other Pacific Islander and Hispanic. Each census block was also categorized as urban or rural. Urban areas are defined by the Office of Planning in the State of Hawaii based on the archipelago's land use map as areas including residential land, industrial and commercial complexes, transportation infrastructure, utilities, mixed urban and other built-up land. Based on the available information distances were calculated from each TMK code to the nearest beach, park, public school, reserve and body-surfing site.

Coral-related GIS data were obtained from the National Oceanic and Atmospheric Administration's (NOAA's) National Centers for Coastal Ocean Science. Distances were calculated from each TMK to the coast. The coastal shore was characterized in terms of the proportion (percentage) of coral reef structures and live coral cover found within concentric zones of 1000 metres around the nearest coastal point from each TMK

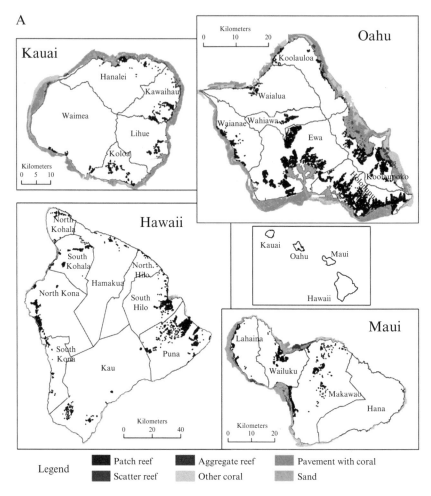

A

Figure 3.3   Coral structures (A) and biological cover (B) around the four islands (black dots represent the transaction locations)

(see Appendix 3.2 to this chapter). In the case of coral cover, four classes were originally distinguished (NOAA, 2007). The lowest class (0–10 per cent live coral) was used as the baseline level in the analysis. Since the highest category (91–100 per cent live coral) is only found around Hawaii at a small number of locations, this category was merged with the class 51–90 per cent live coral. Hence, the analysis was conducted for three coral cover categories: 0–10 per cent, 11–50 per cent and 51–100 per cent. The quality classes 10–50 per cent and 51–100 per cent live coral are presented in Figure 3.3.

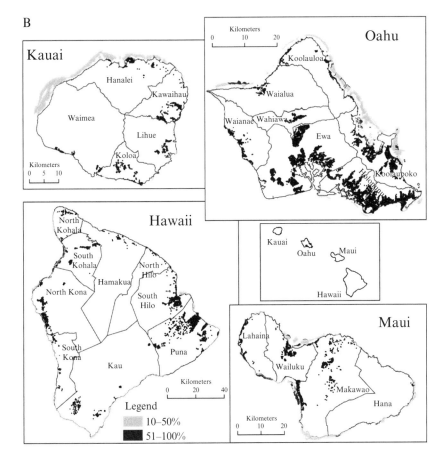

Figure 3.3   (continued)

The average share of live coral found within the concentric zones of 1000 metres for the property sales data in our database is relatively low. This becomes clear from Figure 3.4. Coral reefs are under threat in the main Hawaiian islands.[3] The 51–100 per cent live coral coverage category is only found around the islands Oahu, Maui and Hawaii.

Reef structures were classified into seven categories (NOAA, 2007): aggregate reef, scatter reef, patch reef, pavement with coral, other coral, sand, and other non-coral structures.[4] The latter two categories were merged in Figure 3.3 for convenience. Although variation exists between the islands, the general observation is that, on average, around 45 per cent of the ocean bed surrounding the islands consists of coral structures, primarily pavement with coral and other coral, while the remainder is sand (20

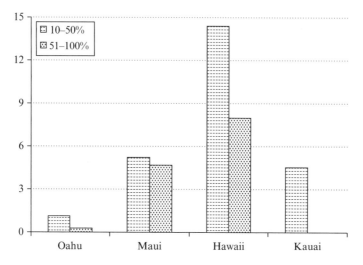

Figure 3.4   Average share (percentage) of live coral cover found within the 1000 metres concentric zones along the coast of the four islands

per cent) and other non-coral structures (30 per cent). These ratios more or less apply irrespective of the distance from the coast (for example, 500 or 1000 metres).[5] Aggregate reef structures increase as one moves deeper into the ocean, but are still less than 10 per cent between 500 and 1000 metres offshore. Less than 1 per cent of the ocean bed around the islands consists, on average, of scatter and patch reef. The question whether there exists a relationship between coral reef proximity and prices paid for residential properties on the four islands will be addressed in the next section.

4   GLS ESTIMATION HEDONIC PRICE MODEL

In view of the large database and the limited data-storing capacity of statistical and econometric software, three biannual models were estimated (in Stata10): one for the period 2000–01, one for 2002–03, and one for the period 2004–05. The model results appeared to be robust across these three time periods. We present the findings for the last time period 2004–05, for which 38 906 observations were available, 70 per cent of which relate to transactions in Oahu, 12 per cent to Maui, 13 per cent to Big island and 5 per cent to Kauai. The number of residential zones on the four islands was reduced from 25 to 22 because of the small number of biannual observations for some zones.[6]

The statistically best fit GLS model results are presented in Table 3.1. The dependent price variable is transformed in its natural logarithmic form as this produced a better statistical fit. A monthly trend variable (1–24) was included to account for possible autonomous trends during the two year time period. The monthly dummy variables T2–T24 are presented on the left-hand side of the table and are all significantly different from the baseline category T1 (January 2004) at the 1 per cent level except the first one (T2). The whole model is statistically significant given the outcome of the Wald test statistic, and the variables included explain 62 per cent of the observed variation. The outcome of the Breusch and Pagan Lagrange multiplier test shows that there exists significant clustering of house prices across the 22 different residential zones. The null hypothesis of zero residual variance (uncorrelated error terms) is convincingly rejected at the one per cent confidence level (chi-square $= 110\,000$; $p < 0.001$). A similar result is found for the Hausman test (chi-square $= 3160$; $p < 0.001$), indicating that the random effects model is the appropriate specification. The estimated GLS model explains 53 per cent of the variation within the residential zones and 85 per cent between the zones.

The variables presented on the right-hand side of Table 3.1 are all statistically significant at the 1 per cent confidence level. The three island dummy variables show significant price variation over and above the residual variance picked up by the residential zones, suggesting that while accounting for a host of control factors, the house markets nevertheless differ significantly across the four islands. The most densely populated island, Oahu, is included in the model as the baseline level. Hence, prices are *ceteris paribus* significantly higher in Maui and Kauai than in Oahu and significantly lower in Hawaii. Also the differences between the coefficient estimates for Maui and Kauai are significant (Wald chi-square $= 5.64$; $p < 0.018$), and between Hawaii and Maui (Wald chi-square $= 1925.62$; $p < 0.001$) and Hawaii and Kauai (Wald chi-square $= 1484.83$; $p < 0.018$).

The next ten variables relate to house characteristics. The variables all show the expected signs. House characteristics that significantly explain the observed variation in house transaction prices include whether or not the property is a condominium (condominiums are *ceteris paribus* around 3 per cent lower priced than other houses in 2004–05), plot size (the double log functional structure implies that a 1 per cent increase of land around the house results *ceteris paribus* in a 5 per cent increase of the house price), number of bedrooms (an additional bedroom means *ceteris paribus* a price increase of almost 14 per cent), whether or not the property was restructured (if it was, then this leads *ceteris paribus* to a mark-up of 8 per cent), the quality of the building (the higher the quality, the higher the price),

Table 3.1 GLS regression results

Variable	Value range	Beta	St error	Variable	Value range	Beta	St error
Constant		11.175	0.023	Maui	0–1	0.103	0.008
T2	0–1	0.004†	0.017	Hawaii	0–1	−0.400	0.011
T3	0–1	0.045	0.015	Kauai	0–1	0.118	0.011
T4	0–1	0.103	0.015	Condominium	0–1	−0.029	0.009
T5	0–1	0.109	0.015	Plot size (natural log)	0.0–14.7	0.054	0.001
T6	0–1	0.129	0.015	Bedrooms	0–14	0.136	0.002
T7	0–1	0.144	0.015	Restructured	0–1	0.082	0.008
T8	0–1	0.161	0.015	Building quality	1–7	0.277	0.003
T9	0–1	0.181	0.015	Floor – tiles	0–1	0.167	0.017
T10	0–1	0.203	0.016	Floor – hardwood	0–1	0.068	0.012
T11	0–1	0.216	0.016	Floor – pinewood	0–1	0.137	0.011
T12	0–1	0.220	0.015	Pool	0–1	0.331	0.013
T13	0–1	0.238	0.017	Oceanfront	0–1	0.422	0.013
T14	0–1	0.270	0.017	Urban	0–1	−0.016	0.005
T15	0–1	0.293	0.015	Multicultural pct	0.00–0.56	−0.977	0.030

Poverty pct	0.00–0.52	−0.527	0.031
Distance to coast DTC	3–24 188	$-0.261*10^{-4}$	$0.204*10^{-5}$
DTC^2 (squared)		$0.799*10^{-9}$	$0.158*10^{-9}$
Distance to reef DTR	0–14 572	$-0.998*10^{-4}$	$0.369*10^{-5}$
DTR^2 (squared)		$0.111*10^{-7}$	$0.467*10^{-9}$
Coral quality 10–50% C1	0.00–70.30	0.0134	0.0004
Coral quality 51–100% C2	0.00–39.02	0.0180	0.0007
DTR * C1		$-0.108*10^{-5}$	$0.773*10^{-7}$
DTR * C2		$-0.692*10^{-6}$	$0.144*10^{-6}$

T16	0–1	0.321	0.016
T17	0–1	0.373	0.016
T18	0–1	0.401	0.015
T19	0–1	0.400	0.016
T20	0–1	0.437	0.015
T21	0–1	0.387	0.015
T22	0–1	0.419	0.016
T23	0–1	0.462	0.016
T24	0–1	0.463	0.016
R^2 within		0.532	
R^2 between		0.851	
R^2 overall		0.622	
Wald χ^2		60 339.18	$p < 0.001$
N		37 628	

Note: [†] Not statistically significant at 10 per cent.

floor type (compared to carpet as the most common floor type), whether or not the property has a private pool (if so, then the price was 33 per cent higher), and whether the house was directly located at the oceanfront (if so, then this too yields a price mark-up of 42 per cent).[7] No significant difference exists between floors made of ceramic tiles and pinewood (Wald chi-square = 2.31; $p < 0.129$). However, both floor types result in significantly higher property prices than hardwood.[8]

Adding the neighbourhood characteristics to the set of house characteristics results in a 5 per cent increase of the model's explanatory power. The neighbourhood characteristics all have a negative impact on the price of a house. Compared to rural areas, houses located in urban areas were sold, on average and *ceteris paribus*, at a 1.6 per cent lower price in the period 2004–05. Houses in neighbourhoods with a higher share of different cultures, that is, higher share in the census block of two or more races, and a higher poverty rate are also lower priced.[9] The latter relationship between individual house prices and a neighbourhood's poverty rate is as expected. The impact of these two neighbourhood characteristics on house prices is substantial. An increase in the share of different cultures by 1 percentage point results *ceteris paribus* in a decrease of house price of 98 per cent. This decrease is 53 per cent in the case of a 1 percentage point increase in the poverty rate. No expected effect could be detected for any of the other available neighbourhood variables, such as the distance from house to schools or parks located in the neighbourhood. A significant linear decay effect was, as expected, found for distance to the nearest beach, but including this variable resulted in non-significance of the variable whether the neighbourhood was urban or rural. Including distance to the nearest coastal point instead (irrespective whether this is a beach or not) results in a significant non-linear distance-decay effect. This variable also matches best with the coral reef variables discussed below. With every metre further away from the coast, the house price decreases, on average and *ceteris paribus*, by \$26.[10] However, this decay factor is not linear nor constant and wears off after 8.1 km.

Finally, including the coral reef variables in addition to the house and neighbourhood characteristics yields an improvement of the overall model fit of 7 per cent. A significant distance-decay effect is found for living near coral reefs over and above the effect of living near the coast and having an ocean view. On average and *ceteris paribus*, property prices decrease by \$51 with every metre they are located further away from the nearest coral reef structure.[11] This decay effect is significantly different from the one found for living near the coast (Wald chi-square = 64.59; $p < 0.001$). Again, this decay factor is not linear and wears off after 5.5 km. A significant positive effect is found for the share of live coral in the concentric zones of 1000 metres drawn around the nearest point from each house to the coast. The effect is sensitive to scale: a 1 per cent point increase in the share of 10–50 per cent live coral results *ceteris paribus* in a price increase of 1.3 per cent, while the same increase in the share of 51–100 per cent live coral gives an increase of 1.8 per cent. The difference between the two coefficient estimates is statistically significant as evidenced from the outcome of the Wald test (chi-square $= 30.48$; $p < 0.001$). The interaction terms between the coral reef distance variable and the two coral quality indicators yields an additional negative impact on property prices, implying that the further away a house is located from coral reefs of a certain quality, the lower the impact of coral reef quality improvement on house prices. The distance effect is significantly higher if the coral reef falls into a higher quality category (Wald test chi-square $= 3.96$; $p < 0.05$).

5 ML ESTIMATION HEDONIC PRICE MODEL

In the second approach, the same statistically best fit model presented in the previous section is estimated as a ML random effects model, explicitly accounting this time for the evidenced spatial heterogeneity in the first step in the random component of the price equation. The dependent variable is again the natural log-transformed house price, and three main groups of independent variables are distinguished: house characteristics, neighbourhood characteristics and coral reef characteristics. Although the contribution of each group to the model's explanatory power in the previous section was relatively small, the outcome of the Likelihood Ratio tests carried out based on the estimated ML-model confirms that their contribution is statistically significant.[12]

The results are presented in Table 3.2, including this time the standard deviation of the random variable residential zone (σ_υ) and the standard deviation of the regression (σ_ε). The standard deviation of the random variable is, as expected, statistically significant at the 1 per cent confidence level. The null hypothesis that the standard deviation of the random variable is not significantly different from zero is tested using the Likelihood Ratio test based on a chi-square distribution (chi-square $= 5543.41$; $p < 0.001$). The rho in Table 3.2 shows which fraction of the model variance is explained by the standard deviation of the random term.

Compared with the GLS results presented in Table 3.1, the main differences are the insignificant impact of the dummy variable for Kauai and the insignificant quadratic term for distance to the closest coral reef.[13] Hence, when allowing the error terms to vary with the independent variables due to spatial clustering of observations across the residential zones, no

Table 3.2 Random effects ML regression results

Variable	Value range	Beta	St error	Variable	Value range	Beta	St error
Constant		11.198	0.087	Maui	0–1	0.297	0.168
T2	0–1	0.005†	0.015	Hawaii	0–1	−0.252	0.141
T3	0–1	0.037	0.014	Kauai	0–1	0.135†	0.141
T4	0–1	0.096	0.014	Condominium	0–1	−0.049	0.009
T5	0–1	0.102	0.014	Plot size (natural log)	0.0–14.7	0.052	0.001
T6	0–1	0.124	0.014	Bedrooms	0–14	0.135	0.002
T7	0–1	0.140	0.014	Restructured	0–1	0.074	0.007
T8	0–1	0.153	0.014	Building quality	1–7	0.233	0.003
T9	0–1	0.176	0.014	Floor – ceramic tiles	0–1	0.176	0.016
T10	0–1	0.194	0.015	Floor – hardwood	0–1	0.052	0.011
T11	0–1	0.209	0.015	Floor – pinewood	0–1	0.075	0.010
T12	0–1	0.210	0.014	Pool	0–1	0.259	0.012
T13	0–1	0.229	0.015	Oceanfront	0–1	0.332	0.012
T14	0–1	0.259	0.016	Urban	0–1	−0.092	0.005
T15	0–1	0.297	0.014	Multicultural pct	0.00–0.56	−0.352	0.035

Variable	Range	Coefficient	Std error
T16	0–1	0.315	0.014
T17	0–1	0.369	0.015
T18	0–1	0.398	0.014
T19	0–1	0.403	0.014
T20	0–1	0.426	0.014
T21	0–1	0.386	0.014
T22	0–1	0.416	0.015
T23	0–1	0.453	0.015
T24	0–1	0.445	0.015
Distance to coast DTC	3–24 188	$-0.302*10^{-4}$	$0.206*10^{-5}$
DTC^2 (squared)		$0.204*10^{-8}$	$0.158*10^{-9}$
Distance to reef DTR	0–14 572	$-0.398*10^{-4}$	$0.392*10^{-5}$
DTR^2 (squared)		$0.612*10^{-9}$ [†]	$0.534*10^{-9}$
Coral quality 10–50% C1	0.00–70.30	0.0078	0.0004
Coral quality 51–100% C2	0.00–39.02	0.0140	0.0007
DTR * C1		$-0.792*10^{-6}$	$0.805*10^{-7}$
DTR * C2		$-0.265*10^{-5}$	$0.147*10^{-6}$
σ_ε		0.390	0.001
σ_υ		0.252	0.038
ρ		0.294	0.063
Log likelihood		−18007.805	
LR χ^2		30 456.24	$p < 0.001$
N		37 628	

Note: [†] Not statistically significant at 10 per cent.

additional significant difference can be detected anymore at the island level between Oahu and Kauai. The differences between Oahu and Hawaii, Oahu and Maui, and Hawaii and Maui remain statistically significant (the latter difference is tested using the Wald test: chi-square = 8.89; $p <$ 0.003).

Small differences are found between the coefficient estimates for house characteristics in Tables 3.1 and 3.2. The influence of a private swimming pool and living on the oceanfront is slightly less than in the estimated GLS model. More substantial differences are found for the neighbour-hood variables. The impact of living in an urban area has increased (houses located in an urban neighbourhood are sold for a price which is now 9 per cent instead of 2 per cent lower than in rural areas), whereas the influence of a neighbourhood's cultural mix has diminished by a factor of almost 3.

The non-linear decay effect for distance to the nearest coral reef is no longer significant. The impact of distance to the nearest coastal point is slightly higher, but the effect reduces quicker to zero (at 7.6 km instead of 8.1 km). The linear effect of distance to the nearest coral reef in Table 3.2 is much lower than in Table 3.1 ($36 per metre further away from the coral reef structure). The same applies to the relationship between property prices and the two live coral variables. The previously observed sensitiv-ity to scale between the two coral quality variables has grown in strength (Wald chi-square = 48.61; $p < 0.001$). Correspondingly, the impact of the interaction term between distance to the nearest coral reef and the first coral quality category is less, while the influence of the interaction term between distance to coral reef and the second coral quality category has increased (also the difference between the two interaction terms remains significant as before; chi-square = 85.14; $p < 0.001$).

6   SUMMARY AND CONCLUSIONS

The main objective of this study was to estimate a hedonic price model for residential property in the Hawaiian archipelago and test whether a significant impact could be detected of coral reefs on property values located at different distances from the shoreline. To this end, house market data were collected for the four main islands of Oahu, Hawaii, Maui and Kauai over the period 2000–05. The available residential property sales data had a unique nine-digit TMK number, which allowed us to identify the geographical location and surrounding of each single property. Based on these TMK numbers, properties were linked to residential zones and GIS data about neighbourhood, land use and coral reef characteristics.

Owing to the large amount of data, it was impossible to pool all data and fit the data into one aggregate, spatially hierarchical (multi-level) model for all four islands together. Therefore, the data were split into three biannual samples. The results for the model fitted on the data covering the time period 2004–05 are reported here. However, the results were robust irrespective of the biannual split sample. Monthly dummy variables were included to account for autonomous time trends in the data.

To account for the spatial hierarchy present in the data owing to the clustering of observations across islands and residential zones on each individual island, two types of estimation procedures are used. First, tests were carried out to assess the significance of data clustering across the zones (using the Breusch and Pagan Lagrange Multiplier test), and the appropriateness of fitting the data in a random effects model (using the Hausman specification test). Following the outcome of these tests, a second approach using a statistically efficient maximum likelihood random effects model was applied, explicitly to account for cross-section variance. Besides fixed control variables for standard house and neighbourhood characteristics, dummy variables were included to capture global house market differences between the four islands. Island-specific spatial heterogeneity (responsible for around 30 per cent of the model variance) was modelled in the random component of the estimated ML-model. Not accounting for the spatial hierarchy present in the data would result in biased coefficient estimates for the variables of interest in this study, that is, the coral reef characteristics.

Adding the distance of a property to the nearest coral reef structure and its quality (measured in terms of share of live coral) into the hedonic price function besides the house and neighbourhood characteristics led to a small, but statistically significant improvement of the model's explanatory power. This suggests that the presence of coral reef has a significant impact on house prices while controlling for other conventional house and neighbourhood characteristics, including the distance a property is located from the coast and whether it has an ocean view. Based on the average house price in the database over the period 2004–05 (around $450000), the implicit value for each 100 metres a property is located closer to a coral reef structure on one of the main Hawaiian islands is $1790. A value of $3510 is encapsulated in property prices for every 1 per cent increase in the share of 10–50 per cent live coral located roughly within 1 kilometre off the coastline, and $5400 in the case of 51–100 per cent live coral. A further $35 can be added to the price of a property for every 100 metres it is located closer to 10–50 per cent live coral and $112 for 51–100 per cent live coral.

ACKNOWLEDGEMENTS

We are grateful for the help and assistance provided by the employees of the Hawaii Information Service, especially Colleen Yasuhara, Novena Saludares, Jocelyn Yanos and Bob Schoenthal, for collecting and interpreting the sales data and house characteristics from their database. We would also like to thank Will Smith from the University of Hawaii for helping with the interpretation of the coral reef data. The usual disclaimer applies.

NOTES

1. In general, two approaches exist to account for spatial interdependency in regression models: spatial lags and spatial error models (Kim et al., 2003). The former model assumes that there exists an indirect spatially weighted effect of the average price of a neighbouring house on the price of an individual house in addition to the direct effect of house, neighbourhood and environmental characteristics. A spatial error model assumes that there is one or more spatially determined omitted variable causing spatial autocorrelation. The hierarchical nature of the available data in this study requires another type of model.
2. Differences in mean and median prices were tested for their statistical significance with the help of the non-parametric Kruskal-Wallis and Median test.
3. Note that Figure 3.4 reflects the average over the concentric circles drawn around the closest coastal points for the houses in the database. This may not necessarily represent the average of the whole Hawaiian archipelago. In general, there may be fewer coral reefs around residential areas.
4. Other coral mainly includes rock and boulder, rubble, spur and groove. Other non-coral structures include mud and artificial structures.
5. Concentric circles of different sizes were drawn and tested. No significant differences were detected between concentric circles of 500 m and 1000 m. In this chapter we present the results found for 1 km.
6. Zones for which less than 100 observations were available were removed from the database: Hana on Maui, North Hilo on Hawaii and Hamakua on Hawaii.
7. All available variables were tested for their impact on house prices. Some appeared to be correlated, such as age of the house and building quality or whether or not the property was restructured, and interior area and number of bedrooms and bathrooms. In those cases, only one of the variables was included in the estimated model.
8. The Wald chi-square equals 23.50 ($p < 0.001$) in the case of ceramic tiles and hardwood and 21.95 ($p < 0.001$) for the difference between pinewood and hardwood.
9. Tests conducted to see whether the variables were correlated are negative. The highest correlation is found between the indicators for urban and poverty (26 per cent). No correlation can be detected between the poverty rate and multicultural mix.
10. Based on the original property price instead of the natural log transformed price regressed on distance to the coast.
11. Based on the original property price regressed on distance to the nearest coral reef.
12. The LR chi-square equals 805.93 ($p < 0.001$) for adding the neighbourhood characteristics (including distance to the coast) and 1623.18 ($p < 0.001$) for the coral reef characteristics.
13. The variable 'poverty rate' was excluded from the ML-model, because this variable unexpectedly changed sign (that is, became positive instead of negative). This was only the case for the models estimated for 2004–05, not the other time periods.

REFERENCES

Anselin, L. (2001), 'Spatial econometrics', in B. Baltagi (ed.), *A Companion to Theoretical Econometrics*, Oxford: Basil Blackwell, pp. 310–30.

Bockstael, N.E. and K. McConnell (2007), *Environmental and Resource Valuation with Revealed Preferences: A Theoretical Guide to Empirical Models*, Dordrecht: Springer.

Boyle, M.A. and K.A. Kiel (2001), 'A survey of house price hedonic studies of the impact of environmental externalities', *Journal of Real Estate Literature*, **9** (2), 117–44.

Brander, L.M., P. Van Beukering and H.S.J. Cesar (2007), 'The recreational value of coral reefs: a meta-analysis', *Ecological Economics*, **63**, 209–18.

Breusch, T. and A. Pagan (1980), 'The LM test and its application to model specification in econometrics', *Review of Economic Studies*, **47**, 239–54.

Day, B., I.J. Bateman and I. Lake (2007), 'Beyond implicit prices: recovering theoretically consistent and transferable values for noise avoidance from a hedonic property price model', *Environmental and Resource Economics*, **37**, 211–32.

Freeman, A.M. (2003), *The Measurement of Environmental and Resource Values: Theory and Methods*, Washington, DC: Resources for the Future.

Greene, W.H. (2003), *Econometric Analysis*, 5th edn, Englewood Cliffs, NJ: Prentice Hall.

Hausman, J.A. (1978), 'Specification tests in econometrics', *Econometrica*, **46** (6), 1251–71.

Henning Olsson, U., T. Foss, S.V. Troye and R.D. Howell (2000), 'The performance of ML, GLS, and WLS estimation in structural equation modeling under conditions of misspecification and nonnormality', *Structural Equation Modeling: A Multidisciplinary Journal*, **7** (4), 557–95.

Kelejian, H. and I. Prucha (1999), 'A generalized moments estimator for the autoregressive parameter in a spatial model', *International Economic Review*, **40**, 509–33.

Kim, C.W., T.T. Phipps and L. Anselin (2003), 'Measuring the benefits of air quality improvement: a spatial hedonic approach', *Journal of Environmental Economics and Management*, **45**, 24–39.

McConnell, K.E. and I.E. Strand (2000), 'Hedonic prices for fish: tuna prices in Hawaii', *American Journal of Agricultural Economics*, **82** (1), 133–44.

National Oceanic and Atmospheric Administration (NOAA) (2007), 'Shallow-water benthic habitats of the main Hawaiian Islands – 2007', NOAA's National Centers for Coastal Ocean Science, available at: http://ccma.nos.noaa.gov/products/biogeography/hawaii_cd_07/welcome.html.

Pompe, J.J. and J.R. Rinehart (1995), 'Beach quality and the enhancement of recreational property values', *Journal of Leisure Research*, **27** (2), 143–54.

Rosen, S. (1974), 'Hedonic prices and implicit markets: production differentiation in pure competition', *Journal of Political Economy*, **82**, 34–55.

Wilkinson, C. (2004), *Status of Coral Reefs of the World: 2004*, vols 1 and 2. Global Coral Reef Monitoring Network and Australian Institute of Marine Science Townsvalle, Australia.

APPENDIX 3.1

Table 3A.1   House and neighbourhood characteristics

Characteristic	Oahu	Maui	Hawaii	Kauai
House				
Age (years)	27.0	20.2	21.2	22.3
	(17.0)	(14.1)	(18.0)	(14.3)
Share restructured (%)	11.0	4.2	5.6	27.2
Building quality (1–7)	3.9	3.7	3.5	4.0
	(0.8)	(1.1)	(1.0)	(0.8)
Share condominium (%)	56.6	47.3	22.2	46.9
Plot size (sq feet)	3649	8262	26088	11787
	(8223)	(25640)	(75757)	(30356)
Interior area (sq feet)	1306	1427	1510	1452
	(759)	(862)	(756)	(677)
Bedrooms (#)	2.7	2.7	2.8	2.7
	(1.3)	(1.1)	(0.9)	(0.9)
Floor (%)				
– Carpet	66.1	76.9	65.2	59.1
– Ceramic	1.3	2.8	3.2	3.3
– Hardwood	4.3	2.2	5.2	7.4
– Pinewood	5.7	4.3	5.2	3.8
Share oceanfront (%)	3.0	4.1	1.3	6.9
Share pool (%)	4.0	6.4	4.2	2.4
Neighbourhood				
Share urban (%)	62.3	39.9	43.1	59.9
Share multicultural (%)	0.19	0.18	0.29	0.20
	(0.08)	(0.07)	(0.05)	(0.08)
Poverty percentage (%)	0.09	0.10	0.15	0.09
	(0.08)	(0.04)	(0.09)	(0.06)
Distance to nearest coast (m)	2504	1908	5273	1603
	(2792)	(3261)	(4280)	(1457)
Distance to nearest beach (m)	3178	2835	7895	2450
	(3027)	(3386)	(4768)	(1518)
Coral reef				
Distance to nearest reef (m)	946	222	1749	791
	(985)	(213)	(2810)	(757)
Share live coral 10–50%	1.163	5.234	14.373	4.566
	(4.272)	(6.965)	(14.319)	(12.603)
Share live coral 51–100%	0.064	4.659	8.043	0
	(0.358)	(8.066)	(12.784)	

APPENDIX 3.2

Concentric circles were used to calculate the share of coral structures and biological cover within for example 500 and 1000 metres from the nearest distance from each residential property to the coast.

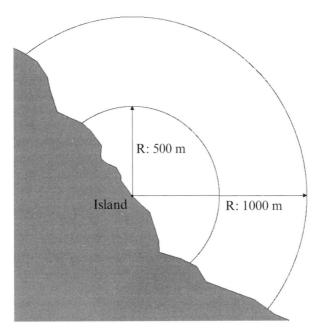

Figure 3A.1   Calculating coral and biological cover shares

4 Applying the travel cost method to Minorca beaches: some policy results
Pere Riera, Kenneth E. McConnell,
Marek Giergiczny and Pierre-Alexandre Mahieu

INTRODUCTION

Valuation methods can be applied for several purposes. Land management based on social recreational values, and natural resource damage assessment are only two examples where both revealed and stated preference valuation methods can be used. Among the revealed preference techniques, the travel cost method (TCM) is particularly suitable for valuing coastal recreational uses in the formulation of management strategies.

The TCM can take different forms. The first variant of TCM applied was the so-called zonal travel cost method. The original idea was outlined by Harold Hotelling (1949) in a letter dated June 1947 to the US National Park Service, answering a request for ideas on how to measure the value of parks. Hotelling made the connection between average frequency of visitation from a given geographic zone of the population and the average cost of the visit depending on how close or how far the zone was from the park, and briefly described how the consumer surplus from visits could be derived. This idea was later applied by Clawson (1959) and Clawson and Knetsch (1966), with much influence on future studies.

With the development of econometrics, TCM was able to capture variations in cost and visit frequency at an individual level instead of relying on zonal averages, giving way to the individual travel cost method (Brown and Nawas, 1973). This required that the researcher address the problems of selection and truncation of the number of trips per user, which is the typical dependent variable in the individual travel cost approach (Bockstael et al., 1987a). This was feasible with truncated normal distributions, or more conveniently with count data models (Smith, 1988). Thus, the number of visits per period of the individuals is regressed against the cost of the visit and other explanatory co-variables. Then the average individual consumer surplus can be estimated (Creel and Loomis, 1990). This is probably the most applied TCM variant.

With the introduction of the random utility model (RUM) and its econometric treatment (McFadden, 1974), another TCM variant appeared. It was based on the observation of choices made by individuals (Bockstael et al., 1987b). For instance, an individual wanting to spend a recreational day on a beach may have several to choose from. Each beach might have some different characteristics and the cost associated with travelling to each beach might also differ. Observing choices made and characteristics of each beach in the choice set allows the researcher to apply a discrete choice model consistent with the RUM (Haab and McConnell, 2002). The sound theoretical properties and practical applicability of the RUM make it widely used.

This chapter illustrates the use of a discrete choice TCM to estimate the recreational value of visitors to the beaches of Minorca Island, in Spain. It also illustrates its policy use in the context of natural resource damage assessment. The next section develops the theoretical and econometric modelling. It is followed by an explanation of the case study and the results estimated. It ends with some conclusions.

THE MODEL

The analysis is based on a RUM model, where participants choose among a set of alternatives, which in this application are the beaches of Minorca. Each beach has different levels of attributes. For the empirical analysis, the choice corresponds to the beach the recreationist went to on the day of the interview. Choices are conditional in the sense that the participants choose which beach to visit, given that they do visit a beach. A 'do-nothing' alternative, such as staying at home, is not included in the choice set, since participants are surveyed on site, that is, at the beach.

The conditional logit model (McFadden, 1974) is commonly used in recreational valuation. It begins by specifying individual random utility for each of the alternatives as a function of the characteristics of the alternatives, $u_{ij}, j = 1, \ldots, J$ for individual i, and breaks these utilities into a deterministic and random component: $u_{ij} = v_{ij} + \varepsilon_{ij}$ where v_{ij} are the deterministic components of utility and ε_{ij} are random components, distributed type I extreme value independently across alternatives and individuals. The deterministic components depend on the attributes of the alternatives that affect the utility. These are derived by considering the income given up to reach the alternative and the attributes of alternatives that people enjoy. We denote the attributes for alternative j, individual i as $X_{ij}\beta$ so that we can write $u_{ij} = X_{ij}\beta$. This model gives the probability that individual i chooses alternative j as a function of attributes that vary by alternative and unknown parameters (Haab and McConnell, 2002).

A feature of the conditional logit model is the possibility of including variables that differ among alternatives and respondents. This is the case for the cost attribute in our empirical application. The cost attribute varies among alternatives; the cost may differ for individuals for given alternatives. It is feasible to allow individuals from different locations to select their best alternative from different choice sets. However, in our application individuals may choose from all of the island's beaches, regardless of their initial location. Random utility models applied to recreational choices typically assume that the impact of a change in cost is constant both with respect to increasing costs and among different alternatives. This is a consequence of assuming a constant marginal utility of income in the RUM.

Let X_{ij} denote the vector of attributes of site j. The probability that individual i chooses alternative j is

$$\Pr_i(j) = \frac{e^{X_{ij}\beta}}{\sum_{k=1}^{J} e^{X_{ik}\beta}},$$

where β is a vector of unknown parameters to be estimated and J the number of alternatives.

Unlike in the multinomial logit model, individual characteristics, such as age or gender, cannot be directly included in the model, as they do not vary among alternatives. It is, however, possible to interact those with beach characteristics, or the alternatives, to check, for instance, whether men attach a different importance to the orientation of the beach than women. To do so we would interact the personal characteristics with attributes that vary across alternatives.

We are interested in estimating the welfare impact of a variety of beach closures on Minorca. To estimate the loss of welfare implied by the closure of several sites, we calculate a representative WTP. Stated purely in behavioural terms, the value of lost access to a beach j for the individual i would be

$$WTP_{ij} = -\ln\,(1\,-\,\Pr_i(j))/\beta_y,$$

where WTP_{ij} corresponds to the willingness to pay of individual i for beach j, $\Pr_i(j)$ the probability for the individual to choose beach j and β_y the marginal utility of income. When several sites are involved, the WTP for each beach cannot be added up to obtain the total WTP, since substitution among sites needs to be considered. The following formula may however be used (Haab and McConnell, 2002):

$$WTP_{iJ^*} = -\ln\left(1 - \sum_{h=1}^{J^*}\mathrm{Pr}_i(h)\right)\Big/\beta_y, \qquad (4.1)$$

where J^*, is a subset of the J beaches. For example, to assess the loss of access to a group of five beaches (say some west-facing group), the welfare loss for individual i would correspond to

$$WTP_{i5} = -\ln\left(1 - \mathrm{Pr}_i(1) - \mathrm{Pr}_i(2) - \mathrm{Pr}_i(3) - \mathrm{Pr}_i(4) - \mathrm{Pr}_i(5)\right)/\beta_y.$$

This represents the willingness to pay to avoid loss of access for a given individual. The individual probabilities naturally vary, and when some respondents live close to the sites being lost they will suffer greater losses. This expression in willingness to pay reveals the higher losses as the probabilities get bigger.

CASE STUDY

In summer 2008 we surveyed users of Minorca beaches. Minorca is a Balearic island in the western part of the Mediterranean Sea, belonging to Spain. Its surface is of *circa* 700 square kilometres, with a length of 53 kilometres and a perimeter of 216 kilometres. The combination of nature, beaches and sunny weather makes it a popular tourist attraction in the summer months. With slightly more than 80 000 permanent residents, its population went up to 150 000 in July 2008 and reached an average of 175 000 people present in the island during the month of August. Tourism is the main economic activity of the island, accounting for nearly two-thirds of its gross domestic product (GDP). According to the Consell Insular de Menorca census, an average of *circa* 25 000 people enjoyed the beaches of Minorca during a peak season day, in August of 2008.

Figure 4.1 shows a map of Minorca with the municipalities and the location of the beaches. A common classification used in the island to group beaches goes from type A, with an urbanized environment to type C, or unspoiled beaches only reachable by foot, with type B being non-developed beaches with car access to its vicinity.

The sample followed a distribution based on the frequency of past visitation. For beaches of type A and B, which are the most frequented, the sample was representative of the number of visitors at beach level. Some contiguous beaches that are often considered separately from an ecological perspective were pooled together because they were perceived as a single beach for the purposes of sampling in the study. Thus, 20 type A and 22 type B beaches were taken into account. For C beaches, the least

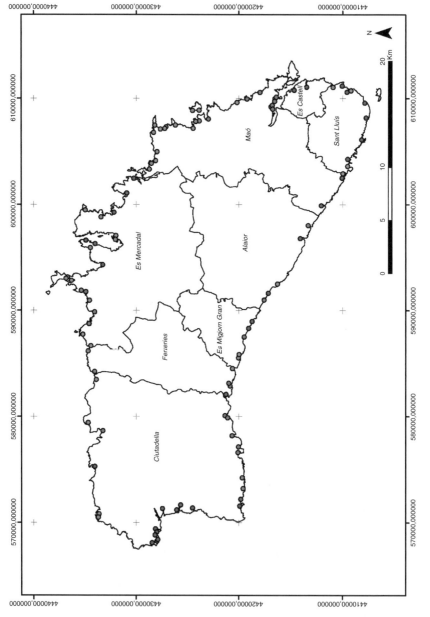

Figure 4.1   Municipal map of Minorca island with the points indicating the location of beaches

Table 4.1   Variables of interest

VARIABLES[a]	Description	Mean	Standard deviation
COST	Travel cost, including time of travelling at 5 Euros per hour (in 2008 euros)	13.467	5.778
EAST	East facing beach	0.176	0.381
SOUTH	South facing beach	0.510	0.500
WEST	West facing beach	0.098	0.297
BLUE_FLAG[b]	Beach awarded blue flag quality	0.196	0.397
NUDISTS	Presence of nudists	0.373	0.483
URBAN	Beach at an urban environment (type A)	0.235	0.424
CLEANING	Beach cleaned periodically	0.490	0.500
TOILET	Toilets available nearby the beach	0.294	0.456
DRINK	Drinks sold nearby the beach	0.412	0.492
TEMPERATURE	Average water temperature (degrees Celsius)	25.235	1.214
CROWDED	Beach crowded	0.627	0.483
ALGAE	Presence of algae	0.118	0.322
CALM	Sea usually calm	0.725	0.446
LIFE_GUARD	Presence of lifeguard	0.627	0.483
THIN_SAND	Presence of thin sand (thick sand – reference level)	0.843	0.364

Notes:
[a]   All variables but travel cost and temperature are indicators variables, taking the value 1 when the statement about the beach is true.
[b]   Blue flags are awarded following criteria dealing with water quality, environmental education and information, environmental management, and safety and other services. The Blue Flag Programme is run by the Foundation for Environmental Education.

frequented were pooled together in one representative beach, because there was much less than one person per beach to be interviewed according to sample proportionality. A total of nine type C beaches were sampled. Altogether, 573 individuals were surveyed at 51 beaches. Interviews were performed face to face, on site, with an average duration of 15 minutes each.

The questionnaire was designed for a travel cost method exercise. It asked questions about the origin of the trip, the means of transportation, party composition, socio-economic characteristics, and attitudinal questions on different beach attributes and leisure activities. Interviewers also had to complete a questionnaire on beach characteristics. Table 4.1 sets out some of the variables collected that were found most significant in the econometric analysis.

The cost of the trip was estimated by means of transportation software. Origin and destination were entered in the trip planning software of the Via Michelin website (http://www.viamichelin.com). The software accounts for speed limits in the different types of roads. The output provided the estimated road distance, time and cost of the trip. The walking distance, for example, from the parking lot to the beach, was estimated using Google maps (http://maps.google.com).

Travel cost is composed of fuel cost, tolls and the value of travel time. Travel time was calculated accounting for the different speed limits of the road involved. Walking time was calculated at an average speed of 4 kilometres per hour. We would expect that individuals' opportunity costs of their travel time to depend on household characteristics. However, the characteristics likely to influence these costs were not available from this survey. Consequently, the value of time was set to 5 euros per hour for all respondents. The cost variable accounts for the round trip.

The data were organized as a panel. It was assumed that the individual choosing the particular beach could have gone to any other beach of the island. Travelling to any beach of the island is doable within a recreational day. We have structured the choice problem such that each interview with an individual forms a choice, with the beach where the individual is interviewed being the beach chosen and all of the other beaches comprising the rest of the choice set. Each interview creates a choice occasion, with the data represented by 51 alternatives with alternative-specific data. The survey completed 573 interviews. 17 interviews were dropped, due to non-recorded or misreported origin of the trip. The 556 remaining interviews create the equivalent of 28 356 observations (51 × 556).

RESULTS

The conditional logit model was estimated with NLOGIT 4.0 statistical software. Three models are reported, starting with a more general one. Results are shown in Table 4.2. The likelihood function is the standard RUM likelihood. Because we have sampled in proportion to the population of users, it is not necessary to weight individual probabilities by the on-site weights.

The most general model included all the variables from Table 4.1. The signs of the significant variables are in accordance with a priori expectations. The COST variable has the expected negative sign – equivalent to the negative value of the marginal utility of income. As is usual in random

Table 4.2   Results of the conditional logit model estimation

Variables	Model I Coefficients (standard errors)		Model II Coefficients (standard errors)		Model III Coefficients (standard errors)	
COST	−0.190***	0.012	−0.190***	0.011	−0.190***	0.011
EAST	−1.224***	0.205	−1.268***	0.202	−1.384***	0.196
SOUTH	−0.357**	0.167	−0.468***	0.134	−0.428***	0.131
WEST	−1.973***	0.258	−2.017***	0.259	−1.957***	0.255
BLUE_FLAG	0.456***	0.136	0.400***	0.129	0.456***	0.126
NUDISTS	0.433***	0.112	0.416***	0.110	0.407***	0.108
URBAN	−.692***	0.184	−0.658***	0.180	−0.695***	0.160
CLEANING	0.358***	0.110	0.326***	0.108	0.390***	0.098
TOILET	0.305**	0.129	0.261**	0.116	0.243**	0.112
DRINK	0.710***	0.147	0.721***	0.138	0.691***	0.131
TEMPERATURE	0.188***	0.050	0.202***	0.049	0.209***	0.047
CROWDED	−0.284*	0.145	−0.259*	0.140	−0.299**	0.137
ALGAE	−0.266*	0.160	−0.242	0.155		
THIN_SAND	0.286*	0.169	0.247	0.171		
CALM	−0.216	0.172				
LIFE_GUARD	0.073	0.119				
Log-likelihood	−1789.833		−1790.621		−1792.571	
Pseudo R2	0.181		0.181		0.180	
N	28 356		28 356		28 356	

Note: * 10 per cent significance level; ** 5 per cent significance level; *** 1 per cent significance level two-tailed tests.

utility models, the travel cost coefficient is highly significant. We classified beaches based on their orientation – facing north, east, south or west. The three included orientations, facing east, south and west, are all negative and significant. This implies the north-facing beach, the excluded alternative, has a positive effect. The impact of facing north probably embeds some landscape characteristics. Other covariates are also significant. A good environmental and educational quality denoted by a blue flag, with lifeguards, the sand being thin, nudism present on the beach, periodical cleaning, and toilets and drink-selling facilities all contribute positively to the utility of the alternative. Also, warmer waters are preferred. On the other hand, urban beaches, crowded beaches and presence of algae contribute negatively to the utility. Finally, people seem to prefer beaches with surf to calm waters, although variable CALM is not significant at 10 per cent level of significance.

The second model excludes the two variables that were not significant at the 10 per cent level in the first model (calm waters and the presence of lifeguards). There was no change in the signs of the remaining variables, although two of them were no longer significant, the presence of algae and the beach having thin sand. The change in the log-likelihood value from the first to the second model was not statistically significant, with a likelihood ratio test statistic of 1.58 whereas the critical value for 0.05 level and two degrees of freedom is 5.99.

A third model was estimated excluding the two non-significant variables from the previous one. This rendered with all variables significant at the 1 per cent level, except for crowded beaches, which was significant at the 5 per cent level. There was no change in the signs of the coefficients and only small changes in their magnitude. The likelihood ratio test of the third model with respect to the second model and to the first model indicates no significant change in the model fit. Furthermore, moving from the first general model to the most restricted one has almost no impact on the estimates of the significant variables. In particular, the COST coefficients vary at the fourth decimal only. Thus, being the most parsimonious, we use the third model for welfare estimates.

One of the clear advantages of the RUM is its flexibility in modelling welfare changes. Researchers can investigate the welfare effects of changes in the attributes at a single site or a group of sites. The welfare implications of closing various sites can also be computed in a straightforward way with the RUM. The manner in which the RUM handles substitution among alternatives makes it an attractive approach to computing welfare. The recreationist is assumed to be fully informed about all sites, and can switch from one to another by paying only the difference in travel costs to the different sites. In practice, individuals are driven to an extent by habits. They find a beach they like and visit it repeatedly. As a consequence, the welfare estimates tend to be quite low, reflecting easy substitution. In the absence of formal models of inertia or habit formation, this might represent the longer run welfare loss, when the individuals have had time to learn about alternatives. In the Minorca case, where the recreationists are tourists, there may be less inertia, and so the direct estimates might give a more accurate measure of welfare gains and losses.

To illustrate the welfare estimation process with the discrete choice travel cost method, assume an environmental damage, for example, caused by an oil spill, results in the closure of the beaches of the west coast, around the city of Ciutadella (see Figure 4.2, scenario 1). The probability of visiting these beaches is 0.043 and the WTP to avoid the recreational loss is of 0.24 euros, in 2008 values, per daily beach visit on the island, which are at 25 000 during the peak period. At the aggregate level, this implies a total daily welfare loss of 6000 euros (Table 4.3). This represents

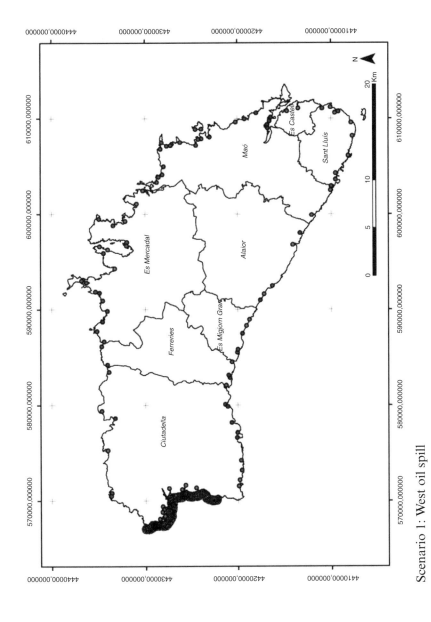

Scenario 1: West oil spill

Figure 4.2   Municipal map of Minorca island with the points indicating the location of beaches and the dark coastal ribbon indicating the extent of the effect of an oil spill in three simulated scenarios

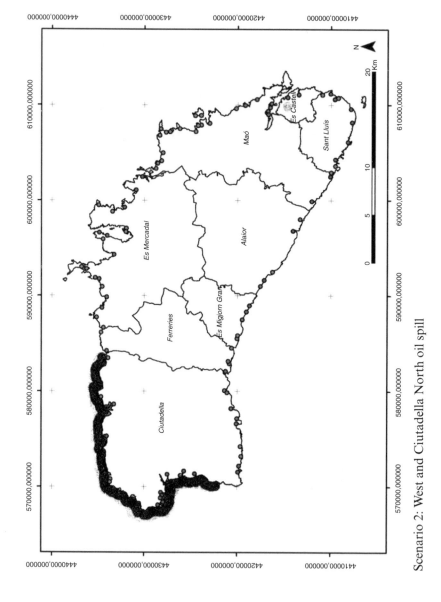

Scenario 2: West and Ciutadella North oil spill

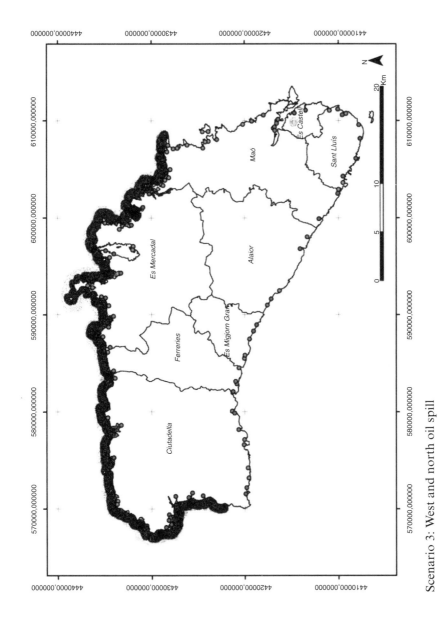

Scenario 3: West and north oil spill

Figure 4.2 (continued)

Table 4.3   Welfare loss associated with closing different beaches from an oil spill in three simulated scenarios

Scenario	Beaches	Probability of visiting	WTP/visit to avoid loss of the sites (euros, 2008)	Total welfare loss per day during peak season (euros, 2008)
1	West	0.045	0.24	6 000
2	West and Ciutadella North	0.084	0.46	11 500
3	West and north	0.280	1.73	43 250

the daily welfare loss to users of the beaches. It does not include losses to vendors of beach services – bars umbrella rentals, and so on.

Assume next that the oil spill spreads northwards to affect the northern beaches of the municipality of Ciutadella (Figure 4.2, scenario 2). The probability of visiting the beaches would then be 0.08, and the welfare loss would be of 0.46 euros per beach recreationist. If the accident happened during peak season, it would decrease the aggregate welfare by 11 500 euros per day.

Finally, suppose the oil spreads further, to the rest of the north on beaches (Figure 4.2, scenario 3). The probability of visiting the west and north beaches would go up to 0.28, and the average individual welfare loss would be 1.73 euros per day, or a total of 43 250 euros per day during peak season.

CONCLUSIONS

The discrete choice travel cost method is becoming more popular, being rooted in the RUM model and requiring relatively little information. A case study of this TCM variant has been presented involving the beaches of the Minorca island, in the Mediterranean Sea. A large data-set (more than 28 000 lines of observations) delivered stable conditional logit model results. The results can be used to estimate the welfare loss from natural resource damages. To illustrate this use, a simulation of closing some of the beaches as a result of an oil spill has been presented. If only the west beaches were affected, the daily welfare loss would be 6000 euros; if the oil spill extends to the northern beaches of Ciutadella, the loss would go up to 11 500 euros; and if western and northern Minorca beaches had to close, the estimated daily recreational loss would be 43 250 euros.

ACKNOWLEDGEMENTS

The authors acknowledge the field work of this study conducted by the Observatori Socioambiental de Menorca (OBSAM).

REFERENCES

Bockstael, Nancy E., Michael W. Hanemann and Catherine L. Kling (1987a), 'Estimating the value of water quality improvements in a recreational demand framework', *Water Resources Research*, **23** (5), 951–60.

Bockstael, Nancy E., Ivar E. Strand and Michael W. Hanemann (1987b), 'Time and the recreational demand model', *American Journal of Agricultural Economics*, **69** (2), 293–302.

Brown, William G. and Farid Nawas (1973), 'Impact of aggregation on the estimation on the demand for outdoor recreation demand functions', *American Journal of Agricultural Economics*, **55** (2), 246–9.

Clawson, Marion (1959), *Methods of Measuring the Demand for and Value of Outdoor Recreation*, Washington, DC: Resources for the Future.

Clawson, Marion and Jack L. Knetsch (1966), *Economics of Outdoor Recreation*, Washington, DC: Resources for the Future.

Creel, Michael D. and John B. Loomis (1990), 'Theoretical and empirical advantages of truncated count data estimators for analysis of deer hunting in California', *American Journal of Agricultural Economics*, **72** (2), 434–41.

Haab, Timothy C. and Kenneth E. McConnell (2002), *Valuing Environmental and Natural Resources: The Econometrics of Non-Market Valuation*, Cheltenham, UK and Northampton, MA, USA: Edward Elgar.

Hotelling, Harold (1949), 'Letter to the Director of the National Park Service', in Roy A. Prewitt (ed.), *The Economics of Public Recreation. The Prewitt Report*, Washington, DC: Department of the Interior.

McFadden, Daniel (1974), 'Conditional logit analysis of qualitative choice behavior', in Paul Zarembka (ed.), *Frontiers in Econometrics: Economic Theory and Mathematical Economics*, New York: Academic Press, pp. 105–42.

Smith, V. Kerry (1988), 'Selection and recreation demand', *American Journal of Agricultural Economics*, **70** (1), 29–36.

5 The role of water quality perceptions in modelling lake recreation demand

Yongsik Jeon, Joseph A. Herriges,
Catherine L. Kling and John Downing

I INTRODUCTION

According to the US Environmental Protection Agency's (USEPA) *2000 National Water Quality Inventory* (2002), 46 per cent of the country's lake acres are categorized as 'impaired' based on physical measures of their water quality. In the state of Iowa, the problem is no better. Indeed, over half of the 132 lakes included in the Iowa Lake Valuation Project are on the USEPA's impaired list (USEPA, water quality inventory for the state of Iowa, 2003).[1] Despite their apparently deteriorated conditions, these same lakes are used extensively by Iowans for recreational boating, fishing, swimming, and so on. Approximately 62 per cent of all Iowa households visited at least one of the 132 lakes in 2002, with an average of eight day-trips per year (Azevedo et al., 2003). At the same time, the study's survey respondents indicated that water quality was the most important factor they consider when choosing a lake for recreation. This raises the question as to whether there is a disconnect between the physical characteristics of the individual lakes as measured by scientists and how those characteristics are perceived by the typical household.

As Ditton and Goodale (1973) suggest, physical water quality variables may not necessarily measure the qualities that attract or deter recreation users. The question is what form of quality attributes drives an individual's site choice decision: physical measures or quality perceptions (or both)? A related issue of interest is whether individual water quality perceptions are correlated with the available physical measures; that is, to what extent do individuals have accurate perceptions of quality. Biases in quality perceptions are of interest to policy-makers from the standpoint of welfare analysis. If perceptions do influence recreation trip behaviour, but these perceptions differ from the corresponding physical measures (or the USEPA's categorization of them), the changes to the physical water quality of a lake may have unintended impacts on lake usage and the corresponding welfare calculations will be in error.

This chapter utilizes detailed data on trip behaviour and water quality perceptions collected from the 2003 Iowa Lake Survey and physical quality measures collected by the Iowa State University Limnology Laboratory to investigate the linkage between physical water quality measures and household perceptions of them, as well as how both subsequently impact recreational demand. The remainder of this chapter is divided into five sections. Section II provides a review of the existing literature on water quality perceptions. Section III describes the trip behaviour and quality assessments data collected in the Iowa Lake Survey 2003 and physical measures of Iowa lakes collected by the Limnology Laboratory at Iowa State University (ISU). The repeated mixed logit model (RXL) to be used in the analysis is described in Section IV. Welfare estimation is discussed in Section V. Section VI provides conclusions and outlines directions for future research.

II   LITERATURE REVIEW

Recent studies of recreation demand show that physical water quality measures significantly impact the site choice decision. Phaneuf et al. (2000), for example, estimate a Kuhn-Tucker model analysing angler behaviour in the Great Lakes. They include catch rates for particular fish species of interest as well as a toxin measure derived from the average toxin levels given in a study by De Vault et al. (1989). The authors find that the toxin level, a measure of the presence of environmental contaminants, significantly influences the recreation decision.

Egan et al. (2009) estimate the demand for day trips to the primary lakes in Iowa using data from the first year of the Iowa Lakes Valuation Project. Included in the analysis are eight physical quality measures (Secchi transparency, chlorophyll, nitrogen, total phosphorus, and so on) and a series of other lake specific characteristics (the presence of boat ramps, wake restrictions, handicap facilities, and so on). The results show that individuals do respond to physical quality characteristics in choosing where to recreate. The Egan et al. (2009) analysis, however, does not explore the crucial link between the physical water quality measures and individual perceptions of them.

Researchers often argue that choices are made on the basis of perceptions. Yet, there has been relatively little use of perceptions of quality attributes in recreation demand modelling in the past due to the cost of collecting individual perception information. One of the few exceptions is Adamowicz et al. (1997), which examines perceived and objective quality attribute measures in discrete choice models of moose-hunting site choice behaviour. They employed data collected from recreational moose-hunters in Alberta, Canada, including actual and perceived hunting site attributes (access, moose population and congestion) of hunters. Their analysis shows that the model with perceived attributes of a hunting place outperforms that of objective quality attribute, though only modestly. Two scenarios are considered for welfare estimation: one involving closure of a site and the other involving a change in perceptions to the agency's objective measure for those individuals who have perceptions that are lower than the target level. The authors find that welfare estimates obtained using their 'perception' model are less than that from 'objective quality' model for both scenarios.

III   DATA AND SURVEY RESULTS

Two sources of data are used in this chapter: results from the 2003 Iowa Lakes Survey and physical water quality measures collected by the ISU Limnology Laboratory. These data sources are described in turn in the following two subsections.

The 2003 Iowa Lakes Survey

The 2003 Iowa Lakes Survey is the second-year survey in a four-year study, jointly funded by the Iowa Department of Natural Resources and the USEPA, aimed at understanding recreational lake usage in Iowa and the value placed on water quality in the state. The 2003 survey was sent by direct mail in January 2004 to 8000 Iowans, collecting information on their recreation behaviour as well as their assessment of the Iowan's principal lakes.[2] Standard follow-up procedures were used to encourage a high response rate to the survey (see, for example, Dillman, 1978, 2000), including a postcard reminder mailed two weeks after the initial mailing and a second copy of the survey mailed one month later. In addition, survey respondents were provided with a $10 incentive for completing the survey.

   The survey asked respondents to report both how frequently they visited each of primary lakes in the state during 2003 and to rate those lakes they are familiar with in terms of water quality. The ten-point water quality ladder (Figure 5.1) employed by EPA was used in this water quality assessment. The water quality ladder has been used in the past both to categorize lakes in terms of quality and in communicating potential water quality improvements (for example, from 'boatable' to 'fishable' or 'drinkable'). Socio-demographic information, including age, gender and education, was also collected.

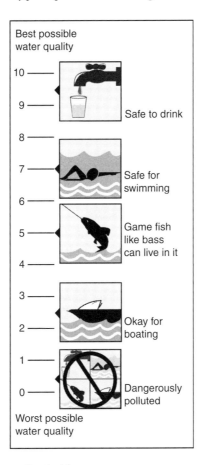

Figure 5.1   Water quality ladder

A total of 5281 surveys were returned. Allowing for the non-deliverables, this corresponds to a 68 per cent response rate. From the 5281 completed surveys, the final sample of 5052 individuals was obtained as follows. Non-Iowans were excluded (47 observations) based on zip code. Anyone reporting more than 52 total single day-trips to the 131 lakes were excluded as well (182 observations).[3] The analysis focuses on single day-trips only in order to avoid the complexity of modelling multiple day visits. Defining the number of choice occasions as 52 trips per year allows one trip to one of the 131 Iowa lakes per week. While the choice of 52 is arbitrary, we chose this cut-off as a conservative approach to ensure our data sample is visitors to the lakes and not residents who may claim many recreational trips simply due to living on the shore of a lake. Indeed, those households

Table 5.1   Socio-demographics summary statistics[a]

	Mean	Std. dev.	Minimum	Maximum
Total day trips	6.97	10.19	0	52
Income	$55 697	$36 444	$7500	$200 000
Male	0.67	0.46	0	1
Age	54.21	15.89	15	82
School	0.67	0.46	0	1
Household size	2.52	1.34	0	21

Note: [a] Sample size = 5052 individuals.

reporting more than 52 trips per year, by and large, live in close proximity to one of the lakes (that is, within a 5-mile radius).

Table 5.1 lists the summary statistics for trips and the socio-demographic data. The average number of total single day trips to all 131 lakes is 6.97, ranging from zero to 52 trips per year. The survey respondents are more likely to be older, male, have a higher income, and be more educated than the general Iowa population. Schooling is entered as a dummy variable equalling 1 if the individual has attended or completed some level of post-high school education.

As indicated above, water quality assessment data were collected by directly asking the respondents to assign a number between 0 and 10 based on the water quality ladder (Figure 5.1) for the lakes they visited in 2003 or considered visiting recently. The water quality ladder, proposed by Carson and Mitchell (1986), was pictured page by page on the survey along with the following verbal description of its meaning:

> One way of thinking about water quality is to use a ladder like the one shown to the right of the list of lakes. The top of the water quality ladder stands for the best possible quality of water, while the bottom of the ladder stands for the worst. On the ladder you can see the different levels of water quality.
>
>   For example: The lowest level is so polluted that it has oil, raw sewage, and/or other things in it like trash; it has almost no plant or animal life, smells bad, and contact with it is dangerous to human health. Water quality that is 'boatable' would not harm an individual if they happened to fall into it for a short time while boating or sailing. Water quality that is 'fishable' is a higher level of quality than 'boatable'. Although some kinds of fish can live in boatable water, it is only when water is 'fishable' that game fish like bass can live in it. Finally, 'swimmable' water is of a high enough quality that it is safe to swim in and ingest in small amounts.

The summary statistics for day trips (per capita) and median, mean and standard deviation of the water quality perception for each lake are

Table 5.2   Summary statistics of water quality (WQ) perception[a]

	Mean	Std. dev.	Minimum	Maximum
Median WQ perception	5.81	0.66	4.00	7.00
Mean WQ perception	5.75	0.51	4.11	6.81
Standard deviation of WQ perception	1.66	0.28	1.06	2.42
Day trips per household	0.36	0.50	0.02	4.26

Note: [a] Sample size = 131 lakes.

listed in Table 5.2. The sample size is 131 lakes. Total day trips per lake is divided by the total number of surveys sent out to the local zone where a lake is located in order to standardize population size effect on trips. On average, Iowans took 0.36 trips per capita to each lake in 2003.

Although there were individuals who perceived some lakes to be dangerously polluted, most respondents rated the 131 lakes as being safe for swimming and boating. The mean water quality assessment ranges across lakes from 4.11 to 6.81. Standard deviation of the water quality assessment of a lake measured across individuals who rated the lake in question ranges from 1.06 to 2.42. This suggests that for some lakes, individuals share very similar perceptions regarding the lake's quality For other lakes, the water quality perceptions are wide-ranging.

An initial question regarding the lake perceptions data is whether or not it influenced which lakes Iowans visited in 2003. To investigate this, Table 5.3 lists number of day trips per household to the 20 best and 20 worst lakes sorted by their mean water quality assessments. Although some lakes had few respondents assessing their water quality, the mean number of day trips to the 'best' lakes (with a mean assessment of 6.46) is roughly two and a half times the mean number of trips to the 'worst' lakes (which had a mean assessment of 4.89). The best lakes, of course, do not have uniformly higher visitation rates. Several of the 'worst' lakes had higher visitation rates than lakes included in the 'best' lakes category. More detailed analysis will be required to tease out other factors influencing recreational site choices, such as proximity to population centres. However, these aggregate data do suggest that water quality perception influence the site choice decision.

It should also be noted that high quality assessments do not necessarily imply that the lake is less contaminated (based on actual physical water quality measures). Some lakes are listed as impaired, even though they have high mean quality assessments. Others among the worst assessment lakes, are not on the list. This implies that individual's perceptions may

Table 5.3   Water quality perception (WQP) and total day trip per capita

	County	Impaired	Day trip[a]	WQP[b]	N[c]
Best 20 water quality perception lakes and day trips					
West Okoboji Lake	Dickinson	0	1.46	6.81	571
Dale Maffitt Reservoir	Madison	0	0.11	6.68	93
Fogle Lake	Ringgold	0	0.09	6.67	12
Three Mile Lake	Union	0	1.37	6.67	156
Pleasant Creek Lake	Linn	0	0.39	6.61	204
Poll Miller Park Lake	Lee	0	0.18	6.59	27
Rathbun Reservoir	Appanoose	0	4.26	6.54	387
Lake Wapello	Davis	0	0.48	6.46	106
Big Spirit Lake	Dickinson	0	0.92	6.44	369
Lake Meyer	Winneshiek	1	0.71	6.43	473
Mill Creek Lake	O'Brien	0	0.12	6.42	31
Twelve Mile Creek Lake	Union	0	0.83	6.37	110
Lake Keomah	Mahaska	1	0.11	6.37	90
Little River Watershed Lake	Decatur	0	0.49	6.36	45
Lake Iowa	Iowa	0	0.17	6.34	86
Lake Smith	Kossuth	1	0.30	6.33	88
Kent Park Lake	Johnson	0	0.20	6.32	165
Lake Icaria	Adams	1	1.12	6.31	101
Lake Ahquabi	Warren	0	0.24	6.31	200
Greenfield Lake	Adair	0	0.16	6.26	34
Average		0.2	0.69	6.46	167
Worst 20 water quality perception lakes and day trips					
George Wyth Lake	Black Hawk	0	0.69	5.25	224
Mariposa Lake	Jasper	1	0.04	5.24	42
Williamson Pond	Lucas	1	0.05	5.22	9
Briggs Woods Lake	Hamilton	0	0.31	5.18	88
Tuttle Lake	Emmet	1	0.08	5.14	22
Ingham Lake	Emmet	1	0.10	5.07	45
Lake Macbride	Johnson	1	1.20	5.06	160
Mitchell Lake	Black Hawk	0	0.05	5.04	26
Meyers Lake	Black Hawk	0	0.12	5.00	49
Lower Gar Lake	Dickinson	1	0.20	4.97	99
Swan Lake	Carroll	1	0.54	4.96	108
Lake Darling	Washington	1	0.43	4.95	148
Little Wall Lake	Hamilton	1	0.25	4.89	111
Silver Lake (Palo Alto)	Palo Alto	1	0.05	4.83	18
Arbor Lake	Poweshiek	1	0.08	4.70	44
Silver Lake (Delaware)	Delaware	1	0.07	4.69	39
Trumbull Lake	Clay	1	0.05	4.59	22

Table 5.3 (continued)

	County	Impaired	Day trip[a]	WQP[b]	N[c]
Carter Lake	Pottawattamie	1	0.39	4.53	98
Manteno Park Pond	Shelby	1	0.04	4.30	10
Ottumwa Central Park Ponds	Wapello	1	0.59	4.11	89
Average		0.8	0.27	4.89	73

Notes:
[a] Day trip per household.
[b] Mean water quality perception.
[c] Number of respondents assessing the lake.

Table 5.4 Water quality variables and 2003 summary statistics

	Mean	Std. dev	Min.	Max.
Secchi transparency (m)	1.44	1.12	0.17	8.10
Chlorophyll (ug/l)	20.12	7.71	2.09	37.62
Nitrogen (ug/l)	294.64	168.69	52.04	1278.84
Nitrates (mg/l)	1.54	3.13	0.02	14.79
Total nitrogen (mg/l)	2.72	3.19	0.49	15.66
Total phosphorus (ug/l)	93.93	65.62	16.87	383.77
Silicon (mg/l)	4.01	2.49	0.88	11.22
pH	8.48	0.27	7.95	9.49
Alkalinity (mg/l)	107.90	33.64	56.33	201.00
Inorganic SS (mg/l)	8.08	7.27	0.60	49.54
Volatile SS (mg/l)	8.40	6.38	0.85	38.55
Total phytoplankton (mg/l)	293.63	827.09	0.01	7178.13
Cyanobacteria (mg/l)	302.60	829.14	3.99	7178.60

not agree with either EPA or physical and chemical water quality assessments.[4] Correlation coefficients of mean water quality assessment with the number of day trips and physical water quality measures are calculated in the following subsection.

Physical Quality Measures

Table 5.4 lists the summary statistics of physical water quality measures. Secchi transparency is a measure of water clarity indicating how far down into the water an object remains visible. Chlorophyll is an indicator of plant biomass or algae and leads to greenness in the water.

Total phosphorus is usually the principal limiting nutrient in Iowa lakes, meaning it most likely determines algae growth. Three nitrogen species are provided, including $NH_3 + NH_4$ (measuring ammonia, which can be toxic), $NO_3 + NO_2$ (measuring nitrates), and total nitrogen (the sum of dissolved and particulate N). Silicon is important to diatoms which extract it from the water to use as a component of their cell walls. Diatoms, in turn, are a key food source for marine organisms. The acidity of the water is measured by 'pH' with levels below 6 or above 8 indicating unhealthy lakes. Alkalinity is the concentration of calcium or calcium carbonate in the water, which indicates the pH-buffering capacity of the water. Inorganic suspended solids (ISS) are basically mineral soil and silt in the water due to erosion. Volatile or organic suspended solids (VSS) indicate the organic soil, silt and living organisms in the water. Total phytoplankton estimates represent the total amount of microscopic plant matter suspended in the water, whereas cyanobacteria represents the part of phytoplankton that is potentially toxic.

It is evident that considerable variation in water quality characteristics is present across the lakes in Iowa. For example, Secchi transparency varies from a low of 0.17 metres to a high of 8.10 metres and total phosphorus varies from 17 to 384 μg/L, some of the highest concentrations in the world. All of the physical measures are the average values for the 2003 season. Samples were taken from each lake three times throughout the year, in spring/early summer, midsummer and late summer/fall, to include seasonal variation. Measurements indicate the upper mixed zone of each lake.

According to the EPA's *Nutrient Criteria Technical Guidance Manual* (USEPA, 2000), the four paramount variables for nutrient criteria are total phosphorus, total nitrogen, chlorophyll and Secchi transparency. Scientists consider inorganic suspended solids and organic suspended solids to be crucial indicators as well. The question is how close are the perceptions of individuals and physical measures of the EPA's and/or scientists? Further, does the EPA's water quality index and/or scientist water quality index explain water quality perception?

The EPA's water quality index used in the water quality ladder is a weighted average of up to nine quality indices based on physical quality measures including total phosphates (PO4), total nitrates (NO3), total suspended solids, dissolved oxygen and pH. A water quality index using the latter five variables is constructed using data from the ISU Limnology Laboratory.[5] In addition, Carlson's (1977) Trophic State Indices (CSTI) for lakes based on Secchi transparency (CTSI_SEC), chlorophyll (CTSI_Chla), total phosphorus (CTSI_TP) are provided from the ISU Limnology Laboratory.[6] A trophic state index is an objective standard of the trophic state of any body of water whereas the water quality ladder index represents a subjective judgement.

Table 5.5 contains the correlation coefficients of the water quality ladder assessment with several physical measures, the EPA's water quality index and Trophic State Indices. The correlations are provided for the sample as a whole and for two subsamples: those reporting that they engaged in water contact activities (for example, swimming and jet skiing) and those who did not (for example, nature appreciation and picnicking). One might expect those engaged in water contact activities might be more aware of and/or affected by the physical water quality conditions.

For the sample as a whole, day trips were found to be positively correlated with the corresponding water quality perception measure. This suggests, as indicated by Table 5.3, that overall quality perceptions do influence trip behaviour. The overall water quality assessments also are generally consistent with the actual physical water quality measures. Specifically, all of the physical measures are negatively correlated with mean water quality assessment except for Secchi transparency; clarity of the water has a positive relationship with the water quality ladder assessment (0.317). However, the degree of correlation varies by the physical water quality measure. For example, there is relatively little correlation between the water quality assessment and nitrates, chlorophyll and pH. Water quality perceptions also appear to be correlated with a number of existing water quality indices, based on physical water quality measures. The EPA's water quality index is positively correlated with water quality perceptions.

The various CTSI, as expected, consistently have negative correlations with water quality perceptions, since lower CTSI's correspond to higher levels of water quality. This indicates that the EPA's and scientists' physical measurements are at least somewhat consistent with individuals' water quality assessments. At the same time, it is important to note that these correlations are by no means perfect. The correlation between the water quality perceptions and the water quality index (both of which use the water quality ladder) is just over 0.21. A number of single water quality measures have higher correlations with the water quality perceptions, including Secchi transparency, ISS, and VSS. The CTSI_SEC index fares somewhat better, but still has a simple correlation coefficient of only −0.327.

The relationship between the physical measures and the overall water quality perceptions also appears to vary by the type of activity engaged in at the lakes. About one-third of the households in the sample did not participate in water body contact recreation. As Ditton and Goodale (1973) suggested, water quality perceptions might not be the same over all respondents. Most recreation users participate in boating (43 per cent),

Table 5.5 Correlation coefficients of quality assessment with several physical measures

	Full sample (n = 5052)			Water contact group (n = 3619)			Non-water contact group (n = 1433)		
	Correlation	Statistics	p-value	Correlation	Statistics	p-value	Correlation	Statistics	p-value
Day trip per capita	0.231	2.693	0.008	0.245	2.874	0.005	0.044	0.486	0.628
Secchi transparency	0.317	3.800	0.000	0.352	4.278	0.000	0.091	1.010	0.314
Chlorophyil	-0.072	-0.823	0.412	-0.093	-1.058	0.292	0.009	0.101	0.920
Total phosphorus	-0.275	-3.243	0.002	-0.299	-3.560	0.001	-0.172	-1.932	0.056
Total nitrogen	-0.185	-2.140	0.034	-0.208	-2.418	0.017	-0.148	-1.662	0.099
NH3 + NH4	-0.327	-3.930	0.000	-0.352	-4.268	0.000	-0.236	-2.696	0.008
NO3 + NO2	-0.052	-0.593	0.554	-0.049	-0.557	0.578	-0.096	-1.064	0.289
pH	-0.001	-0.006	0.995	0.008	0.093	0.926	0.010	0.116	0.908
Alkalinity	-0.181	-2.092	0.038	-0.161	-1.855	0.066	-0.172	-1.940	0.055
Silica	-0.296	-3.516	0.001	-0.315	-3.772	0.000	-0.164	-1.839	0.068
ISS	-0.322	-3.866	0.000	-0.319	-3.823	0.000	-0.172	-1.939	0.055
VSS	-0.290	-3.444	0.001	-0.329	-3.952	0.000	-0.057	-0.629	0.530
TSS	-0.308	-3.676	0.000	-0.339	-4.091	0.000	-0.104	-1.156	0.250
CTSL_SEC	-0.327	-3.930	0.000	-0.360	-4.387	0.000	-0.104	-1.162	0.248
CTSL_Chla	-0.060	-0.685	0.495	-0.087	-0.994	0.322	0.020	0.221	0.825
CTSL_TP	-0.274	-3.238	0.002	-0.299	-3.563	0.001	-0.162	-1.824	0.071
WQI	0.214	2.484	0.014	0.241	2.824	0.005	0.146	1.634	0.105

fishing (52 per cent) and swimming (40 per cent). Non-participants in water contact recreation enjoy camping (30 per cent), picnicking (43 per cent), and nature appreciation and viewing wildlife (42 per cent). Overall, 3619 visitors participated in water contact recreation, whereas 1433 did not.

The mean assessment of the water contact group is more highly correlated with day trips (0.245) than for the non-contact group (0.044). Because they are more likely to participate in boating, swimming and fishing activity on the lake, higher quality assessments correlated with more trips to lake. This group appears aware of the levels of total nitrogen, phosphorus and suspended solids or at least their visible impact. All of the correlation coefficients are statistically different from zero for the contact group at a 10 per cent level except for the nitrates, chlorophyll, and pH. On the other hand, for individuals who want to take a walk along the beach at a lake, ride a bike or simply appreciate the lake's natural surroundings, the water quality itself may not impact them as much or they may have less direct contact with the water in constructing an overall water quality perception. For these households, the correlation coefficient of day trip and most of physical quality measures (except for total phosphorus, nitrogen, silica and inorganic suspended solids) are not statistically different from zero.[7]

These simple summary statistics concerning water quality assessments and physical quality measures data again suggest that there is a linkage, though imperfect, between individual water quality perceptions and the actual physical measures. However, the linkage also appears to depend upon the recreationists' activities. Recreationists' activities influence on their site choice decision and their types of activities might in turn impact their water quality perceptions. For example, if individuals prefer jet skiing or boating to walking around the lake, they may choose a lake where motorized vessels are allowed or one with a boat ramp, regardless of the water's visibility. This leads to the question of whether these facility characteristics in turn end up impacting the individual's water quality assessment.

To investigate this question, the lake site characteristics were obtained from the Iowa Department of Natural Resource. Table 5.6 provides a summary of these site characteristics. As Table 5.6 indicates, the size of the lakes varies considerably, from 10 acres to 19 000 acres. Four dummy variables are included to capture different amenities at each lake. The first is a 'ramp' dummy variable which equals one if the lake has a cement boat ramp, as opposed to a gravel ramp or no boat ramp at all. The second is a 'wake' dummy variable that equals one if motorized vessels are allowed to travel at speeds great enough to create wakes and zero otherwise. About 67 per cent of the lakes allow wakes, whereas 33 per cent are 'no wake' lakes. The 'state park' dummy variable equals one if the lake is located

Table 5.6   Summary statistics for lake site characteristics

	Mean	Std. dev	Min.	Max.
Acres	662.41	2105.41	10	19 000
Ramp	0.86	0.35	0	1
Wake	0.67	0.47	0	1
State Park	0.39	0.49	0	1
Handicap Facility	0.38	0.49	0	1

adjacent to a state park, which is the case for 39 per cent of the lakes in our study. The last dummy variable is the 'handicap facilities' dummy variable, which equals 1 if handicap amenities are provided, such as handicap restrooms or paved ramps.[8]

The correlation coefficient of the boat ramp dummy variable with mean water quality perceptions is positive and significant for the water contact group whereas it is insignificant for the non-water contact group. The disability facilities and state park dummy variables both have positive correlation coefficients with water quality perceptions. However, these correlations are insignificant at the 5 per cent critical level with *p*-values ranging from 7 to 10 per cent. Acreage use of lake has a positive correlation, although it is not statistically significant. These results suggests that individual's water quality perceptions are somewhat correlated with the lake site characteristics, with the boat ramp characteristic having the clearest effect.[9]

To investigate the linkage between water quality perception and physical water quality measures and/or site characteristics, we ran a simple linear regression of mean perceptions on physical measures and site characteristics. Some physical measures are logarithmically transformed because they concern plant growth which is geometric (for example, Chlorophyll, total phosphorus, total nitrogen, total and cyano-bacteria), whereas others (Secchi transparency, the nitrogen, silica and alkalinity) are entered linearly following Egan et al. (2009). Dissolved oxygen, total nitrates, pH, suspended solids and turbidity are transformed to quality indices according to McClelland (1974) on which EPA's water quality index is based. Finally, five lake-characteristic variables (log transformed acres, ramp, wake, state park and wake dummy variables) are entered. All variables are standardized with respect to their standard errors in order to compare the size of the impact. Estimated coefficients are listed in Table 5.7. Overall, these physical measures and lake characteristic variables explain about 39 per cent of water quality perception's variation (adjusted R^2) and the model appears to be significantly explaining the perceptions

Table 5.7   Regression of mean perceptions on physical measures and lake characteristics

	Estimate	Std. err	*p*-value
Constant	−0.093	0.132	0.479
Secchi transparency	0.296	0.154	0.056
Log (chlorophyll)	0.346	0.123	0.006
Nitrogen ($NH_3 + NH_4$)	−0.021	0.119	0.859
Log (total phosphorus)	−0.322	0.139	0.022
Log (total nitrogen)	−0.244	0.302	0.422
Silika	−0.107	0.103	0.303
Alkalinity	−0.191	0.089	0.035
Log (total phytoplankton)	−0.117	0.190	0.541
Log (cyanobacteria)	0.018	0.193	0.925
Quality index of dissolved oxygen	0.513	0.163	0.002
Square of quality index of dissolved oxygen	0.168	0.081	0.042
Quality index of total nitrates	−0.353	0.287	0.222
Quality index of pH	−0.112	0.135	0.408
Square of quality index of pH	0.068	0.063	0.281
Quality index of total suspended solids	−0.113	0.214	0.598
Square of quality index of suspended solids	−0.142	0.072	0.052
Quality index of turbidity	−0.224	0.128	0.083
Boat ramp dummy	0.162	0.083	0.054
Wake dummy	0.208	0.083	0.013
Handicap facilities dummy	−0.004	0.081	0.965
Log (acreage use)	0.156	0.096	0.106
State park dummy	0.038	0.089	0.673

(*F*-value of null hypothesis of all coefficients are zero is 3.93 and *p*-value is less than 0.01). Secchi transparency, log transformed chlorophyll and total phosphorus, alkalinity and square and linear term of dissolved oxygen quality index and square term of total suspended solids quality index are significant at the 10 per cent level. The signs of these terms are generally as one would expect except for the turbidity quality index. Also, boat ramp and wake dummy variables appear to be significant and have positive effects on water quality perception. The results support the evidence of a relationship between water quality perception and the physical measures and site characteristics.

IV   RECREATION DEMAND MODEL

There are two competing hypotheses regarding the role of perceptions and physical water quality measures in recreation demand. The first assumes that physical measures are the primary influence in determining site choices (either directly or indirectly by influencing an individual's overall perception of each lake). The second suggests that the physical attributes influence behaviour in a complex fashion that cannot be readily captured by a single index or water quality ladder so that only measures of perceptions can accurately predict site choice. Of course, there is also the possibility that neither have a significant impact on lake usage, which may be driven instead by other site characteristics such as facilities and proximity to population centres. To investigate these alternatives, we consider a model of the utility derived from visiting site j on choice occasion t that nests both of these alternatives. Specifically, suppose that the utility of individual i associated with site j on choice occasion t denoted:

$$
\begin{aligned}
U_{ijt} &= V(P_{ij}, Z_j, Q_j, X_j, s_i) + \varepsilon_{ijt} \\
&= \begin{cases} \kappa' s_i + \varepsilon_{i0t} \\ \alpha_i - \lambda P_{ij} + \beta' Z_j + \delta' Q_j + \gamma'_i X_j + \varepsilon_{ijt}, \end{cases} \\
&\quad i = 1, \cdots, I, \quad j = 1, \cdots, J, \quad t = 1, \cdots, T
\end{aligned}
\tag{5.1}
$$

where V is the deterministic component of utility and ε_{ijt} is an error component which is an *iid* extreme value random variable. The vector s_i consists of socio-demographic characteristics, while P_{ij} is the travel cost each of the 131 lakes, as calculated using PCMiler.[10] Z_j represents observable water quality attributes for lake j. Q_j denotes the overall water quality perception regarding lake j and X_j denotes other site characteristics (including lake facilities and state park designation). Notice that the parameters on the lake attributes and α_i are allowed to vary across individuals, allowing for heterogeneity of preferences. Specifically, these parameters are assumed to be distributed randomly across individuals in the population. The random parameter α_i was introduced by including a dummy variable, D_j, which equals one for all of the recreation alternatives ($j = 1, \cdots, J$) and equals zero for the stay at home option ($j = 0$), following Herriges and Phaneuf (2002). For simplicity, the subscript t will be suppressed throughout the remainder of this chapter.

The random coefficient vectors for each individual, γ_i and α_i can be expressed as the sum of population means $\bar{\gamma}$ and $\bar{\alpha}$, and individual deviations from the means, τ_i and ϕ_i, which represents the individual's tastes relative to the average tastes in the population (Train, 1998).[11] Therefore, we can redefine

$$\gamma_i = \bar{\gamma} + \tau_i, \text{ and}$$
$$\alpha_i = \bar{\alpha} + \phi_i. \tag{5.2}$$

The partitioned utility function in (5.1) is then

$$U_{ijt} = \begin{cases} \kappa' z_i + \eta_{i0t} \\ \bar{\alpha} - \lambda' P_{ij} + \beta' Z_j + \delta' Q_j + \bar{\gamma} X_j + \eta_{ijt}, \ j = 1, \cdots, J, \end{cases} \tag{5.3}$$

where

$$\eta_{ijt} = \begin{cases} \varepsilon_{i0t}, \ i = 1, \cdots, N \\ \tau'_i X_j + \phi_i + \varepsilon_{ijt}, \ j = 1, \cdots, J; \ i = 1, \cdots, N \end{cases} \tag{5.4}$$

is the unobserved portion of utility. This unobserved portion is correlated over sites and trips because of the common influence of the terms τ_i and ϕ_i, which vary over individuals. For example, an individual with a large negative deviation from the mean of α_i will be more likely to choose the stay-at-home option on each choice occasion, the ϕ_i capturing in this case some unobserved attribute of the individual causing them to prefer staying at home (for example, they cannot swim or do not like fishing). On the other hand, someone with a large positive deviation ϕ_i will tend to take many trips. The variation in the γ_is allows the marginal effects of site characteristics to vary across individuals. The random parameters γ_i and α_i do not vary over sites or choice occasions. Thus, the same preferences are used by the individual to evaluate each site across time periods. Since the unobserved portion of utility is correlated over sites and choice occasions, the familiar IIA assumption does not apply.

Given that the ε_{ijt}s are assumed to be *iid* extreme value, the resulting model corresponds to McFadden and Train's (2000) mixed logit framework. A mixed logit model is defined as the integration of the logit formula over the distribution of unobserved random parameters (Revelt and Train, 1998). Let the vector of random parameters in the model defined above denoted by $\omega_i = (\alpha_i, \gamma_i)$ and let $\xi = (\beta, \delta, \gamma, \lambda, \kappa)$ denote the fixed parameters. If the random parameters, ω_i, were known then the probability of observing individual i choosing alternative j on choice occasion t would follow the standard logit form:

$$L_{ijt}(\omega_i, \xi) = \frac{\exp[V_{ijt}(\omega_i, \xi)]}{\sum_{k=0}^{J} \exp[V_{ikt}(\omega_i, \xi)]}. \tag{5.5}$$

Since the ω_i are unknown, the corresponding unconditional probability, $P_{ijt}(\theta, \xi)$ is obtained by integrating over an assumed probability density function for the ω_is. The unconditional probability is now a function of θ, where θ represents the estimated moments of the random parameters.[12] This repeated mixed logit model assumes the random parameters are *iid* distributed over the individuals with:

$$P_{ijt}(\theta, \xi) = \int L_{ijt}(\omega_i, \xi) f(\omega_i | \theta) \, d\omega. \qquad (5.6)$$

No closed form solution exists for this unconditional probability and therefore simulation is required for the maximum likelihood estimates of θ.[13]

Two hypotheses are of interest. The first hypothesis of interest is $H_0^1: \beta = 0$, that is, whether or not physical quality measures directly predict site choice. The second hypothesis of interest is $H_0^2: \delta = 0$; that is, whether or not the perceptions regarding water quality at the lake, based on the USEPA's water quality ladder predict site choice behaviour. Egan et al. (2009) estimates a model with only the physical measures, implicitly assuming that the physical water quality measures directly influence household behaviour but water quality perceptions do not. Adamowicz et al. (1997) compared two restricted models and estimated WTPs: one is the model under the hypothesis 1 (using perception data only) and the other one is under hypothesis 2 (using physical quality data only). The advantage of the current work is that we have an extensive list of physical water quality measures and perceptions data for a larger set of site alternatives.

One issue in using the water quality perceptions data in modelling site choice is that we do not have data on the water quality perception for each individual and lake combination since if an individual has not visited a lake, he cannot form a perception concerning its quality. This is similar to the problem associated with catch rate data in standard recreation demand models; that is, because a household only visits a limited number of lakes, individual catch rate information is typically only available for these visited lakes. Moreover, the catch rates information itself is endogenous. Following the standard procedure used in case of catch rate, the mean water quality assessment of a lake is used as a proxy variable for water quality perception in this model because some lakes have few visitors and respondents providing water quality assessments.

Estimation Result

Specification

Although the model for testing the null hypothesis and welfare estimation is set in equation (5.1), the functional forms to be useful for the physical water quality measures, lake characteristics and socio-demographic variables are unknown. Economic theory provides little or no guidance in terms of these choices. Egan et al. (2009), however, provide an extensive investigation into the choice of functional form for water quality measures, lake characteristics and socio-economic variables. Specifically, using data from the first year of the Iowa Lakes survey, they split the available sample into three subsamples, using the first for a specification search, the second for estimation and the third for investigating out-of-sample predictions. They focus on modelling the role of water quality characteristics in determining recreation demand patterns, holding constant the manner in which both socio-demographics and other site characteristics impact preferences. The specification search process involved comparing numerous combinations of linear and logarithmic forms for the water quality measures. In the analysis below, we follow Egan et al.'s (2009) final specification for the physical measures, lake characteristics and socio-demographic variables.

Socio-demographic characteristics are assumed to enter through the 'stay-at-home' option. They include age and household size, as well as dummy variables indicating gender and college education. A quadratic age term is included in the model to allow for non-linearities in the impact of age. Site characteristics are included with random coefficients. This is to allow for heterogeneity in individual preferences regarding site characteristics, such as wake restrictions and site facilities. For example, some households may prefer to visit less developed lakes with wake restrictions in place, while others are attracted to sites allowing the use of motorboats, jet skis, and so on. It is assumed that the random parameters γ_i are each normally distributed with the mean ($\bar{\gamma}_k$) and dispersion ($\sigma_{\gamma k}$) for each parameter. Physical water measures (Z_j) are categorized into five groups: (1) Secchi transparency, (2) chlorophyll, (3) Nutrients (total nitrogen and total phosphorus), (4) suspended solids (inorganic and organic) and (5) phytoplankton (cyanobacteria and total). The first four characteristic groups directly impact the visible features of the water quality, making it more likely that households respond to them. Phytoplankton is included because surveyed households report it to be the single most important water quality concern (Azevedo et al., 2003). Egan et al.'s (2009) specification search results suggested phytoplankton, chlorophyll, and nutrients enter logarithmically and the remaining variables enter linearly. This model is referred to as model A. A more complex model, including pH, alkalinity, silicon, nitrates, and ammonium nitrogen is referred to as model B. These additional variables are entered in a linear form, except for pH for which a quadratic term is also included.

A total of seven models are considered. The first four represent variations on models A and B in Egan et al. (2009):

Model A_1: model A as estimated in Egan et al. (2009).
Model A_2: A_1 plus the water quality perceptions variable.
Model B_1: model B as estimated in Egan et al. (2009).
Model B_2: B_1 plus the water quality perceptions variable.

In terms of equation (5.3), the difference between models A_1 and A_2 (B_1 and B_2) is that A_1 (B_1) constrains $\delta = 0$, hypothesis H_0^2. We also include three models to illustrate the consequences of relying on a single measure of water quality, in this case one that is widely used by the US Environmental Protection Agency:

Model C_1: model A, but replacing all physical water quality measures with the single water quality ladder index.
Model C_2: model A_2, but replacing all physical water quality measures with a single water quality ladder index.
Model C_3: model A_1 with the physical water quality attributes constrained to have no impact (that is, $\beta = 0$ in equation 5.3).

Note that it is the comparison of models A1 and C3 that provides the basis for testing hypothesis H_0^1.

Estimation result

The resulting parameter estimates are presented in Tables 5.8a and 5.8b. Table 5.8a lists parameter estimates for socio-demographic variables and mean and dispersion parameters for random coefficients for lake amenities data. All the coefficients are significant at the 5 per cent level except for inorganic suspended solids for models B_1 and B_2 and some of the socio-demographic data including age, age square and school dummy variables. While age variables for models A_1, B_1, B_2 and C_1 are not significant, age-squared is not significant for model A_2. School variable is not significant only for model A_1. Note that the socio-demographic data are included in the conditional indirect utility for the stay-at-home option. Therefore, larger households are all more likely to take a trip to a lake. Age has a convex relationship with the stay-at-home option and therefore has a concave relationship with trips. For model C_2 and C_3, the peak occurs at

Table 5.8a   Repeated mixed logit model parameter estimates[a]

	Model A		Model B		Model C		
Male	−9.11	−7.55	−11.92	−11.91	−5.83	−14.89	−14.85
	(0.429)	(0.428)	(0.475)	(0.473)	(0.432)	(0.487)	(0.484)
Age	−0.12	0.20	0.07	0.09	0.002	−1.26	−1.27
	(0.074)	(0.078)	(0.081)	(0.081)	(0.078)	(0.095)	(0.095)
Age^2	0.005	0.001	0.002	0.002	0.003	0.013	0.014
	(0.001)	(0.001)	(0.001)	(0.001)	(0.001)	(0.001)	(0.001)
School	−0.26	3.67	1.37	1.25	4.88	0.95	0.90
	(0.387)	(0.422)	(0.524)	(0.527)	(0.433)	(0.542)	(0.540)
Household	−0.49	−0.98	−1.10	−1.06	−1.25	−1.65	−1.66
	(0.167)	(0.163)	(0.185)	(0.185)	(0.168)	(0.191)	(0.189)
Price	−0.331	−0.332	−0.334	−0.334	−0.330	−0.334	−0.335
	(0.001)	(0.001)	(0.001)	(0.001)	(0.001)	(0.001)	(0.001)
Mean estimate for random coefficient							
Log(acres)	3.45	3.38	3.71	3.56	3.11	3.20	3.21
	(0.063)	(0.066)	(0.069)	(0.069)	(0.065)	(0.066)	(0.066)
Ramp	14.46	14.49	13.69	13.11	14.39	10.79	10.74
	(0.828)	(0.833)	(0.843)	(0.851)	(0.826)	(0.719)	(0.719)
Facilities	1.42	1.29	0.96	1.13	0.90	1.00	0.96
	(0.235)	(0.247)	(0.241)	(0.242)	(0.234)	(0.241)	(0.242)
State park	2.99	3.59	3.43	3.59	4.23	3.82	3.86
	(0.260)	(0.267)	(0.307)	(0.305)	(0.252)	(0.254)	(0.254)
Wake	4.10	3.54	2.13	1.58	3.43	4.27	4.33
	(0.258)	(0.260)	(0.320)	(0.323)	(0.255)	(0.297)	(0.297)
α	−8.91	−10.09	−10.29	−10.28	−10.42	−10.28	−10.37
	(0.214)	(0.229)	(0.040)	(0.040)	(0.039)	(0.040)	(0.040)
Dispersion estimate for random coefficients							
Log(acres)	0.35	0.35	0.33	0.33	0.34	0.32	0.32
	(0.01)	(0.01)	(0.01)	(0.01)	(0.01)	(0.05)	(0.01)
Ramp	19.92	21.05	18.01	18.09	21.99	18.69	18.72
	(0.62)	(0.71)	(0.63)	(0.63)	(0.58)	(0.58)	(0.57)
Facilities	13.13	13.38	12.68	12.54	13.24	13.20	13.25
	(0.26)	(0.27)	(0.24)	(0.24)	(0.26)	(0.26)	(0.27)
State park	11.75	12.26	14.29	14.27	12.54	12.77	12.75
	(0.26)	(0.27)	(0.28)	(0.28)	(0.26)	(0.27)	(0.27)
Wake	13.38	13.28	15.79	15.70	13.63	16.30	16.34
	(0.25)	(0.27)	(0.32)	(0.32)	(0.27)	(0.33)	(0.33)
α	2.38	2.50	2.46	2.46	2.51	2.47	2.47
	(0.03)	(0.03)	(0.03)	(0.03)	(0.03)	(0.03)	(0.03)

Notes:
Parentheses are standard errors.
[a]   All of the parameters are scaled by 10, except α (which is unscaled).

Table 5.8b   Repeated mixed logit model parameter estimates[a]

Variable	Model A		Model B		Model C		
Secchi	2.51	2.28	2.59	2.36			
	(0.096)	(0.098)	(0.100)	(0.100)			
Log (chlorophyll)	2.50	2.21	3.01	2.63			
	(0.223)	(0.224)	(0.234)	(0.234)			
$NH_3 + NH_4$			−0.01	−0.01			
			(0.001)	(0.001)			
$NO_3 + NO_2$			−1.59	−1.71			
			(0.071)	(0.072)			
Log (total nitrogen)	0.32	0.41	4.87	5.48			
	(0.068)	(0.068)	(0.283)	(0.284)			
Log (total phosphorus)	−1.38	−1.12	−4.03	−3.90			
	(0.135)	(0.141)	(0.160)	(0.164)			
Silicon			1.10	1.08			
			(0.035)	(0.035)			
pH			−69.89	−64.04			
			(10.836)	(11.099)			
pH2			4.25	3.88			
			(0.627)	(0.643)			
Alkalinity			0.04	0.05			
			(0.003)	(0.003)			
Inorganic SS	−0.083	−0.079	−0.008	−0.009			
	(0.009)	(0.009)	(0.010)	(0.010)			
Volatile SS	0.24	0.26	0.03	0.08			
	(0.014)	(0.014)	(0.019)	(0.019)			
Log (cyanobacteria)	−1.64	−1.71	−1.36	−1.41			
	(0.079)	(0.085)	(0.091)	(0.091)			
Log (total phytoplankton)	1.82	1.97	0.87	1.01			
	(0.099)	(0.109)	(0.116)	(0.120)			
Mean perception		1.47		2.22		3.50	3.40
		(0.127)		(0.141)		(0.100)	(0.096)
Water quality index					0.40	−0.02	
					(0.057)	(0.006)	
Log-likelihood	−59 319	−59 278	−59 096	−59 071	−59 614	−59 502	−59 503

Notes:
Parentheses are standard errors.
[a]   All of the parameters are scaled by 10, except for α (which is unscaled).

about age 48, which is consistent with the estimate of larger households taking more trips, as at this age the household is more likely to include children. Higher-educated individuals appear to be likely to stay at home, with positive coefficients. The price (travel cost) coefficient is negative as expected and virtually identical in all seven models.

Turning to the site amenities, all of the parameters are of the expected sign. As the size of a lake increases, has a cement boat ramp, gains handicap facilities or is adjacent to a state park, the average number of visits to the site increases. Notice, however, the large dispersion estimates. For example, in model A_1 the dispersion on the size of the lake indicates almost all people prefer bigger lakes. The large dispersion on the 'wake' dummy variable seems particularly appropriate given the potentially conflicting interests of anglers and recreational boaters. Anglers would possibly prefer 'no wake' lakes, while recreational boaters prefer lakes that allow wakes. It seems the population is roughly split, with 62 per cent preferring a lake that allows wakes and 38 per cent preferring a 'no wake' lake. Lastly, the mean of α_i, the trip dummy variable, is negative, indicating that on average the respondents receive higher utility from the stay-at-home option, which is expected considering the average number of trips is seven out of a possible 52 choice occasions.

The physical water qualities and mean perception coefficients are reported in Table 5.8b. Entering mean perception in the model A and/or model B does not notably change the coefficients. For four models, the effect of Secchi transparency is positive, while inorganic (volatile) suspended solids have a negative impact, indicating that respondents strongly value water clarity. However, the coefficients on chlorophyll and volatile suspended solids are positive, suggesting that on average respondents prefer 'greenish' to brown water. The negative coefficient on total phosphorus, the most likely principal limiting nutrient, indicating higher algae growth, leads to fewer recreational trips. Total nitrogen, having a positive coefficient, is consistent with expectation given the negative sign on total phosphorus because lakes with high ratios of nitrogen to phosphorous have lower risk of noxious plankton blooms. Two other forms of nitrogen, $NO_3 + NO_2$ and $NH_3 + NH_4$, have negative effects, likely due to the toxic nature of these substances. Continuing with the additional measures in model B, alkalinity has a positive coefficient, consistent with alkalinity's ability to both act as a buffer on how much acidification the water can withstand before deteriorating and as a source of carbon, keeping harmful phytoplankton from dominating under low CO_2 stress. The positive coefficient on silicon is also consistent since silicon is important for the growth of diatoms, which in turn are a preferred food source for many aquatic organisms. The pH is entered quadratically, reflecting the fact that low or high pH levels are signs of poor water quality. However, as mentioned, in our sample of lakes, all of the pH values are neutral or high. The coefficients for pH show a convex relationship (the minimum is reached at a pH of 8.3) to trips, indicating that as the pH level rises above 8.3, trips are predicted to increase. This is the opposite of what we expected.

The water quality perception has a positive and statistically significant impact in model A_2 and model B_2. Entering mean perception in model A and B does not change the signs or general size of the physical water quality measures. The coefficients on water quality perceptions indicate that lakes which have higher mean perception are more likely to be places where individuals want to visit, as we expected. Clearly we reject the hypothesis H_0^2 that the physical water quality measures above capture the full impact of water quality on the household's trip patterns. Water quality perceptions, as captured by Q_j, also significantly affect where people choose to recreate. However, it is also clear that the perceptions index is an incomplete measure of how water quality affects household behaviour. We clearly reject the restriction $\beta = 0$ (H_0^1) using either models A or B.[14]

V   WELFARE ESTIMATION

Based on the test results in section IV and the random parameter vector estimates, $\theta_i = (\gamma_i, \alpha_i)'$, the conditional compensating variation associated with a change in water quality from Q to Q' for individual i on choice occasion t is:

$$CV_{it}(\theta_i) = -\frac{1}{\beta^P}\left\{ \ln\left[\sum_{j=0}^{J}\exp(V_{ijt}[Q';\theta_i]) \right] - \ln\left[\sum_{j=0}^{J}\exp(V_{ijt}[Q;\theta_i]) \right] \right\},$$
(5.7)

which is the compensating variation for the standard logit model. The unconditional compensating variation does not have a closed form, but it can be simulated by

$$CV_{it}(\theta_i)$$
$$= \frac{1}{R}\sum_{r=1}^{R} -\frac{1}{\beta^P}\left\{ \ln\left[\sum_{j=0}^{J}\exp(V_{ijt}[Q';\theta_i^r]) \right] - \ln\left[\sum_{j=0}^{J}\exp(V_{ijt}[Q;\theta_i^r]) \right] \right\},$$
(5.8)

where R is the number of draws and r represents a particular draw from its distribution. The simulation process involves drawing values of $\theta_i = (\gamma_i, \alpha_i)'$ and then calculating the resulting compensating variation for each vector of draws, and finally averaging over the results for many draws. Following Von Haefen (2003), 2500 draws were used in the simulation.

Three water quality improvement scenarios are considered with the results from models C1 and C3 used. The first scenario improves all 130 lakes to the water quality of West Okoboji Lake, the clearest, least impacted lake in the state. Table 5.9 compares the water quality

Table 5.9   West Okoboji Lake versus the other 130 lakes

	West Okoboji Lake	Average of the other 130 lakes	Average of the 9 zone lakes
Mean perception	6.81	5.74	5.67
Water quality index	90.8	77.91	79.03

Table 5.10   The 65 non-impaired lakes versus the 66 impaired lakes

	Median of the 65 non-impaired lakes	Averages of the 66 impaired lakes
Mean perception	5.94	5.60
Water quality index	81.67	74.48

Table 5.11   Annual compensating variation estimates

Average CV	All 130 lakes improved to W.Okb.	9 zone lakes improved to W.Okb.	65 impaired lakes improved to median
Using model C1: water quality index only			
Per choice occasion	$0.24	$0.02	$0.05
Per Iowa household	$12.39	$0.90	$3.06
Predicted trips (6.45 with current water quality index)	6.68	6.47	6.53
Using model C3: mean water quality perception			
Per choice occasion	$1.40	$0.16	$0.14
Per Iowa household	$73.03	$8.26	$7.28
Predicted trips (7.35 with current mean perception)	8.64	7.50	7.49

perception and water quality index of West Okoboji Lake with the average of the other 130 lakes. Two of West Okoboji Lake's measures are considerably better than the other 130. The water quality index and water quality perception are second highest (90.8 and 6.81 respectively) among 130 lakes. For these large changes, 'boatable' to 'swimmable' and 'swimmable' to 'drinkable', the annual compensating variation estimates are $12.39 and $73.03 using model C1 and C3 respectively (Table 5.11) for every Iowa household. Table 5.10 also reports the average predicted trips before and after the water quality improvement. Improving all 130 lakes to the water quality perception of West Okoboji Lakes leads to an 18 per cent increase in average trips while improving to the water quality index of West Okoboji Lakes leads to 16 per cent increase in average trips.

The next scenario is a less ambitious, more realistic scenario of improving nine lakes to the water quality of West Okoboji Lake (see Table 5.9 for comparison). The state is divided into nine zones with one lake in each zone, allowing every Iowan to be within a couple of hours of a lake with superior water quality. The nine lakes are chosen based on recommendations by the Iowa Department of Natural Resources for possible candidates of a clean-up project. The annual compensating variation estimate is $0.90 when water quality improvement is measured by the water quality index and $8.26 when the quality improvement is measured by the water quality perception. As expected, this estimate is 7 per cent and 11 per cent of the value if all lakes were improved. This suggests location of the improved lakes is important and, to maximize Iowan's benefit from improving a few lakes, policy-makers should consider dispersing them throughout the state.

The last scenario is also a policy-oriented improvement. Currently, of the 131 lakes, 65 are officially listed on the EPA's impaired water list. Total maximum daily leads (TMDLs) are being developed for these lakes and by 2009 the plans must be in place to improve the water quality at these lakes enough to remove them from the list. Therefore, in this scenario, the 65 impaired lakes would be improved to the median mean water quality perception and/or water quality index level of the 66 non-impaired lakes. Table 5.10 compares the median values for the non-impaired lakes with the averages of the impaired lakes. This scenario is valued considerably lower than the first water quality improvement scenario. The estimated compensating variation per Iowa household is $3.06 when the water quality index is used and $7.28 when water quality perceptions are used. Consistent with this, the predicted trips only increase 1.24 per cent for water quality index increase and 1.90 per cent for water quality perception increase.

As discussed above, there is a big margin between compensating variation calculated using water quality perception versus the water quality index. In terms of predicted trip change, the impact of water quality perceptions is bigger than that of the water quality index (14.19, 1.73 per cent point for the first two scenarios and 0.7 per cent point for the last scenario). Further, the fact that compensating variation calculated using water quality perception is bigger than that calculated using water quality index suggests that agent's cost–benefit analysis of improving water quality, ignoring lake visitor's perception, could be underestimated.

VI CONCLUSION

Household-level day trip data collected from the Iowa Lake Survey in 2003 shows that subjective quality assessment influences individual's site choice decision. In addition, the perceptions of water quality are correlated with objective quality measures that limnologists typically collect; however, correlation coefficients suggest that there is a disparity in this regard between two recreation groups: those who participate in water body contact and those who do not.

Repeated mixed logit model estimation suggests that individuals' site choice decisions that are modelled to depend on physical water quality measures, a water quality index and water quality perceptions provides the best fit of the data. As Adamowicz et al. (1997) found, the models with water quality perception entered outperform the models without water quality perception.

These results suggest that there is a considerable amount of information about consumer preferences for recreation sites that can be gleaned from physical, chemical and biological measures of water quality, but that perceptions information provides valuable additional information.

NOTES

1. The Iowa Lakes Valuation Project is a four-year study of recreational lake usage in the state of Iowa, funded by both the Iowa Department of Natural Resources and the USEPA. The project gathered information on household level visitations to the 132 primary lakes in the state from a randomly selected sample of state residents.
2. The sample itself consisted of two subsamples. The first subsample corresponded to the approximately 4500 households that completed the 2002 Iowa Lakes Survey, originally mailed to 8000 randomly selected Iowa households. The second subsample consisted of 3500 randomly selected Iowa households.
3. While there are 132 lakes included in the Iowa Lakes Valuation Project, only 131 lakes were included in the 2003 survey because one of the lakes had been drained for that year as part of a restoration project.
4. Of course, factors other than physical water quality conditions may play a role in listing a lake on the impaired water quality list.
5. Jeon (2005) provides details regarding the construction of these water quality indices.
6. For details of Carson's Trophic State Index, see Jeon (2005).
7. Of course, the sample size is also smaller for this group, which will impact the precision with which the correlation coefficients are estimated.
8. A concern may be that handicap facilities would be strongly correlated with the state park dummy variable. However, while 50 of the lakes in the study are located in state parks and 50 have accessible facilities, only 26 of these overlap.
9. It should be noted that the causation may run in the other direction in the case of lake attributes. For example, boat ramps and lake facilities may be constructed at a lake site because they are generally of high quality and the demand for such facilities is there.
10. *PCMiler* is a software package commonly used in the recreation demand literature to calculate travel times and travel distances, from which travel costs are computed.

11. Specifically, we assume that $\gamma_i \sim N(\bar{\gamma}, \Sigma)$ where Σ is a $(k \times k)$ diagonal variance co-variance matrix, with diagonal element $\sigma^2_{\gamma k}$ for the kth site characteristic. Similarly, $\alpha_i \sim N(\bar{\alpha}, \sigma^2_\alpha)$.
12. In the current model, $\theta = (\bar{\gamma}, \bar{\alpha}, \sigma_{r1}, \cdots, \sigma_{rk}, \sigma_\alpha)$
13. Train (2003) describes simulation methods for use with mixed logit models, in particular maximum simulated likelihood which we employ. Software written in GAUSS to estimate mixed logit models is available from Train's home page at: http://elsa.berkeley.edu/~train.
14. The corresponding likelihood ratio test statistics or $\chi^2 = 82$ (p-value < 0.001) for model A whereas χ^2 (p-value < 0.001) for model B.

REFERENCES

Adamowicz, Wiktor, Joffre Swait, Peter Boxall, Jordan Louvier and Michale Williams (1997), 'Perceptions versus objective measures of environmental quality in combined revealed and stated preference models of environmental valuation', *Journal of Environmental Economics and Management*, **32**, 65–84.

Azevedo, C.D., K.J. Egan, J.A. Herriges and C.L. Kling (2003), 'The Iowa Lakes Valuation Project: summary and findings from year one', CARD report.

Carlson, Robert E. (1977), 'A trophic state index for lakes', *Limnology and Oceanography*, **22** (2), 361–9.

Carson, R.T. and R.C. Mitchell (1986), 'The value of clear water: the public's willingness to pay for boatable, fishable, and swimmable quality of water', Discussion Paper QE85-08, rev., Resources for the Future, Washington, DC.

De Vault, D.S., D. Dunn, P. Bergqvist, K. Wiberg and C. Rappe (1989), 'Polychlorinated dibenzofurans and polychlorinated dibenzo-p-dioxins in Great Lakes fish: a baseline and interlake comparison', *Environmental Toxicology and Chemistry*, **8**, 1013–22.

Dillman, D.A. (1978), *Mail and Telecom Surveys: The Total Design Method*, New York: Wiley.

Dillman, D.A. (2000), *Mail and Telecom Surveys: The Tailored Design Method*, New York: John Wiley and Sons.

Ditton, Robert and Thomas L. Goodale (1973), 'Water quality perception and the recreational uses of Green Bay, Lake Michigan', *Water Resources Research*, **9** (3), 569–79.

Egan, Kevin J., Joseph A. Herriges, Catherine L. Kling and John A. Downing (2009), 'Recreation demand using physical measures of water quality', *American Journal of Agricultural Economics*, **91** (1), 106–23.

Herriges, J. and D. Phaneuf (2002), 'Introducing patterns of correlation and substitution in repeated logit models of recreation demand', *American Journal of Agricultural Economics*, **84**, 1076–90.

Jeon, Y. (2005), 'Essays on improving nonmarket valuation techniques', doctoral dissertation, Iowa State University.

McClelland, Nina I. (1974), 'Water quality index application in the Kansas River Basin', Environmental Protection Agency report EPA-907/9-74-001, February.

McFadden, D. and K. Train (2000), 'Mixed MNL models for discrete response', *Journal of Applied Econometrics*, **15** (5), 447–70.

Phaneuf, D.J., C.L. Kling and J.A. Herriges (2000), 'Estimation and welfare calculations in a generalized corner solution model with an application to recreation demand', *The Review of Economics and Statistics*, **82** (1), 83–92.

Revelt, D. and K. Train (1998), 'Mixed logit with repeated choices: households' choices of appliance efficiency level', *The Review of Economics and Statistics*, **80**, 647–57.

Train, K. (1998), 'Recreation demand models with taste differences over people', *Land Economics*, **74** (2), 230–9.

Train, K. (2003), *Discrete Choice Methods with Simulation*, Cambridge: Cambridge University Press.

US Environmental Protection Agency (USEPA) (2000), *Nutrient Criteria Technical Guidance Manual: Lakes and Reservoir*, USEPA, Office of Water, EPA-822-B00-001, Washington, DC.

US Environmental Protection Agency (USEPA) (2002), *2000 National Water Quality Inventory*, USEPA, Office of Water, Washington, DC.

US Environmental Protection Agency (USEPA) (2003), 'Assessment data for the state of Iowa Year 2002', available at: http://iaspub.epa.gov/waters10/w305b_report_v2.state?p_state=IA (accessed 3 March 2005).

Von Haefen, Roger H. (2003), 'Incorporating observed choice into the construction of welfare measures from random utility models', *Journal of Environmental Economics & Management*, **45** (2), 145–65.

6 Testing the robustness of contingent valuation estimates of WTP to survey mode and treatment of protest responses

John Loomis, Armando González-Cabán and Joseph Champ[1]

INTRODUCTION

Over the past four decades the contingent valuation method (CVM) has become a technique frequently used by economists to estimate willingness-to-pay (WTP) for improvements in environmental quality and protection of natural resources. The CVM was originally applied to estimate recreation use values (Davis, 1963; Hammack and Brown, 1974) and air quality (Brookshire et al., 1982; Randall et al., 1974). In the second decade the CVM was extended to valuing the general public's option and existence values of environmental improvements (Walsh et al., 1984). As part of this evolution, the overall design of CVM studies now attempts to construct a market for the public good (Carson, 1991). As such, a typical CVM survey describes the public good to be valued, how the good will be paid for (that is, payment vehicle), the WTP question format (that is, open ended or closed ended) and a rule for deciding whether the good will be supplied (for example, majority rule in a referendum or total benefits exceed total cost). Each of these design elements has received substantial testing to determine whether the CVM WTP estimates are sensitive to the payment vehicle or WTP question format (Boyle, 2003). The key concern of CVM regarding the validity of the WTP estimates has also received extensive testing from the early days of CVM (Bishop and Heberlein, 1979) to the more recent (Murphy et al., 2005).

Survey Mode

The CVM relies more heavily on survey research than many other economic valuation techniques such as the hedonic property method. Thus, it is important to understand the sensitivity of CVM WTP estimates to various aspects of survey design such as mode (for example, phone, mail, in person). One of the conditions needed for mainstream economists and policy-makers to take the CVM estimates of WTP seriously is that they should be robust for different survey modes. The most commonly used survey mode is mail, owing to it being relatively inexpensive and allowing presentation of graphics and photos. Phone surveys are used when visual aids are not critical. In-person interviews are considered by some as the 'gold' standard (Arrow et al., 1993; Mitchell and Carson, 1989). Their expense has resulted in such interviews primarily being used in large natural resource damage cases (Carson et al., 2003) or other high-profile public policy studies. Internet surveys have slowly been gaining ground as an approach for conducting CVM surveys. With commercial companies providing consumer panels with representative demographics and hosting the surveys, CVM surveys using the Internet, especially for large nationwide surveys, have become more common (Banzhaf et al., 2006; Berrens et al., 2004). Basic research is now being conducted to compare WTP responses of Internet surveys with more traditional surveys such as mail (Banzhaf et al., 2006).

Because no one survey mode is ideal for CVM, mixed mode surveys emerged in the late 1980's as a means of utilizing the strengths of each method (Loomis and King, 1994). Hanemann et al. (1991) conducted one of the first mixed mode CVM surveys. They used random digit dialling to initiate contact with a random sample of respondents. Then a survey booklet with visual aids and questions were sent to respondents prior to the phone interviews. Finally, the phone interviews were conducted by leading the respondent through the booklet and obtaining their answers. This was argued to combine the best features of the phone survey such as its use of a random digit dialling sample frame, a live interviewer to motivate respondents to complete each question and answer questions for the respondent, along with the advantages of mail, that is, providing the respondent a booklet with visual aids. While more expensive than mail surveys alone, the approach was shown to yield lower item non-response than mail surveys (Loomis and King, 1994). In this chapter this approach will be referred to as a phone–mail booklet–phone interview approach.

This chapter reports on a comparison of this phone–mail booklet–phone interview approach with a new video survey mode. Both of these approaches attempt to mimic the preferred but expensive survey administration format, in-person interviews (Arrow et al., 1993; Mitchell and Carson, 1989). An alternative to the phone–mail booklet–phone approach and to Internet surveys is to send the respondent a videotape or DVD that utilizes an on-camera interviewer who explains the elements of the constructed market and asks the survey questions. The respondent records their answers on a sheet that is mailed back. This videotape method mimics an in-person interview, may appeal to a 'video' generation and can be inexpensively applied to large samples. In contrast, large samples in the phone–mail booklet–phone can quickly become expensive due to repeated phone contacts and in-depth (10–15 minute) phone interviews.

Protest Responses

In a constructed market, economists rely on visitors' or households' intended behaviour as manifested in their statements of value towards the natural resource of interest. In order for a survey to have face validity, these respondents must be valuing the same public good as intended by the researcher. Thus, the design elements of the constructed market (for example, description of the good, payment vehicle) should be credible or realistic enough to facilitate rather than interfere with eliciting a household's true WTP. However, some respondents object to the particular method of paying for the public good (for example, rejecting the fairness of the payment vehicle – Morrison et al., 2000), the method of provision (for example, a particular government agency) or doubt whether the proposed public programme will solve the environmental problem described in the survey. In these cases, their WTP responses reflect a rejection of one or more premise of the constructed market, rather than their value of the public good. These responses have been labelled protest responses (Boyle, 2003; Mitchell and Carson, 1989).

If the WTP question format is open ended (what is the maximum you would pay?) or payment card, then some respondent's statements of zero WTP may reflect protest responses rather than lack of value for the public good or inability to pay for the public good. In the closed-ended dichotomous choice or voter referendum format, where respondents are asked whether they would pay a specific monetary amount for the public good, detecting protest responses is more difficult (Boyle, 2003). If a respondent is asked whether they would pay a particularly high monetary amount (US$450), they may respond 'No', but still have a positive value for the good that is less than $450. However, the respondent's 'No' response may also be a protest response, in which case they are rejecting some element of the constructed market rather than indicating no value for the public good. Much of the past research has evaluated how to detect or deal with zero WTP responses, but not identification or handling of protest responses in dichotomous choice CVM (Collins and Rosenberger 2007).

In this chapter we compare two different protocols for detecting and handling protest responses in voter referendum CVM WTP responses. The first method relies on written statements of respondents as to why they would not pay. The second approach utilizes these written statements in combination with a follow-up WTP question asking whether the respondent would pay $1 for the programme. This allows us to better identify those who completely reject the CVM constructed market and those who have some positive value for public program, but just less than the bid amount they are asked to pay. We then test whether the WTP amounts from these two different approaches to excluding protest responses are statistically different from one another, and different from the WTP estimate from including all responses, whether protest or not. These tests allow us to investigate whether the WTP estimates are robust for the treatment of protest responses.

The empirical application is to the use of prescribed burning to reduce wildland forest fires. This problem is a policy relevant issue throughout the world, as wildfires are becoming increasing large and destructive in countries such as the USA, Australia, Spain and Greece, to name a few.

DESCRIPTION OF PHONE–MAIL BOOKLET–PHONE INTERVIEW AND VIDEO SURVEY MODES

There are many features of a CVM survey that can potentially influence the validity of respondents' WTP (Barro et al., 1996). An important area that has seen less investigation is that of the convergent validity of traditional and new survey administration modes (Loomis and King, 1994). While in-person surveys are preferred, the most frequently used survey administration form is mail surveys. However, mail surveys require significant reading ability on the part of the respondent. Arrow et al. (1993) suggests that phone interviews may be able to mimic some of the strong features of in-person interviews. However, pure phone surveys are limited due to their inability to provide the respondent with visual aids. A combination of phone recruitment-mailed survey booklet–phone interview with the aid of the survey booklet (hereafter called phone–mail booklet–phone) has proved an effective combination in a number of CVM surveys (Hanemann et al., 1991; Loomis et al., 2002). The respondent has the questions and visual aids in front of them while the phone interviewer asks the questions. However, these phone–mail booklet–phone interviews can also be quite expensive, ranging from $50 to $100 per completed interview owing to the multiple contacts required and the cost of the in-depth interviews. Internet surveys may be the way of the future, but inconsistent web browsers and incomplete coverage of low-income households make them less than ideal at present, despite the efforts of Internet panel companies.

However, according to the US Census Bureau, in 1999 approximately 85 per cent of American households with televisions also had video cassette recorders (VCRs). We suspect with the introduction of low-cost digital versatile disk (DVD) players that nearly every household in America with a television has either a VCR or DVD player, or both. The technology of DVDs and VCRs is easy to use, and the medium offers many of the advantages of the Internet, but few of the drawbacks. In addition, using a videotape with an on-camera narrator and visual aids has the potential to mimic an in-person interview, at a fraction of the cost. Once produced, videotape and especially DVD distribution is relatively inexpensive. To our knowledge, no one has yet taken advantage of even the basic features that videotapes offer for conducting a contingent valuation method survey. We hypothesize that the videotape/DVD medium is as effective as the phone–mail booklet–phone interview method at obtaining an adequate response rate, reducing protest refusals to pay and estimating willingness-to-pay (WTP). Thus, the objective of this study is to evaluate the convergent validity of a new video approach with the more traditional phone–mail booklet–phone survey method with respect to response rates, protest refusals to pay versus non-protest refusals to pay responses, and WTP estimates. We emphasize this is a test of convergent, not criterion validity with respect to survey mode, since phone surveys are not perfect in sample coverage and have their own biases.

SCREENING FOR PROTESTS IN THE DICHOTOMOUS CHOICE WTP QUESTION FORMAT

To investigate whether zero bids or 'No' votes reflect a true expression of respondent values or rejection of some feature of the constructed market, follow-up questions to the WTP question are often asked, particularly of those stating zero WTP or voting against the program. These follow-up questions can be open-ended like 'Why did you answer zero?' or 'Why did you vote against?' These responses are then postcoded into two categories, protests and non-protests following criteria described below. Alternatively, some surveys (Loomis, 1987; Walsh et al., 1984) use a checklist approach which prompts the user to select the main reason or all the reasons why they would not pay. These reasons include what are typically considered non-protest such as 'I do not receive any benefits from the public program' or 'I cannot afford to pay for the public program'. It is in fact heartening to obtain these responses, as it indicates respondents took the obligation for payment seriously even though they were not required to actually pay.

Typically protest responses include one of several factors. As summarized by Jorgensen and Syme (2000), these include (a) it is unfair to be asked to pay additional money for this public good; (b) existing taxes or funding should be used; (c) government wastes money; (d) this public good is a right that I should not have to pay for; (e) money collected may not actually be used to provide the good; (f) taxes already too high; (g) only users of the good should pay. In our traditional postcoding of respondent's open-ended reasons for not paying (described in more detail below), we were guided by these categories in determining what was a protest response.

HYPOTHESES REGARDING SURVEY MODE RESPONSE RATES AND PROTEST RESPONSES

Test of Response Rate Differences by Survey Mode

There are two contacts in both the phone–mail booklet–phone approach and the videotape/DVD approach. In the phone–mail booklet–phone approach there is an initial random digit dialling phone call with a short initial interview. The address to mail a survey booklet is verified, and a time is scheduled for an in-depth (20-minute) interview. The videotape/DVD survey proceeds in a similar fashion with an initial contact, except a videotape is mailed and the respondent mails back the answer booklet. Thus, the first test of convergent validity is whether households respond equally to the initial phone call, and then whether they follow through on answering the in-depth CVM questionnaire with the two survey administration modes.

$$\text{Ho: RESPONSE}_{video} = \text{RESPONSE}_{phone\text{-}booklet} \tag{6.1}$$

This will be tested using separate contingency tables and χ^2 tests for both the first and second interviews.

Test of Differences in WTP by Survey Mode

Comparisons of mean WTP estimates across survey administration mode will be tested by equality of the mean WTP estimates from each survey mode. The null hypothesis is:

$$\text{Ho: WTP}_{video} = \text{WTP}_{phone\text{-}booklet} \tag{6.2}$$

The results are determined by whether the confidence intervals overlap or not.

Test of Different Protest Rates by Survey Mode

The response to the WTP questions elicited during the in-depth interview is the main focus of our analysis. First, the phone–mail booklet–phone and video survey responses are compared in terms of the reasons given for refusing to pay anything for the public program. As noted above, some refusals are valid expressions of zero WTP since they reflect lack of value for the good or low income (that is, inability to pay), while others may be considered protest responses.

Our second survey mode related hypothesis is that different survey administration modes may result in different protest rates. Comparing the overall protest reasons given, we will test the null hypothesis of no difference between the two survey administration modes in terms of proportions of protests and non-protest refusals to pay. The null hypothesis is that the distribution of refusals to pay and protest responses to the CVM survey is independent of survey administration mode:

$$\text{Ho: PROTEST}_{\text{video}} = \text{PROTEST}_{\text{phone–booklet}} \qquad (6.3)$$

This will be tested using a contingency table and the test performed using a χ^2 statistic.

Comparison of Traditional Protest Classification and 'Increased Information' Protests

Within the video survey we compare the traditional approach to screening for protest responses that uses only what the respondent stated to the open-ended question of why they would not pay their monetary bid amount. The reasons were content-analysed by the authors to classify answers by similar reasons given by the respondent, according to the classifications of Jorgensen and Syme (2000).

However, unlike an open-ended WTP question or payment card where the respondent can express a zero WTP, the standard binary dichotomous choice or voter referendum approach does not directly allow for a zero WTP response. Rather, individuals indicate whether they would pay the random bid amount assigned to them. This range of bid amounts respondents are asked to pay is usually quite wide, that is, the monetary amounts some respondents are asked to pay can be quite high. Thus, it is possible that some respondents who rejected paying a very high bid amount might still have a small positive WTP, just one much smaller than the bid amount they were asked to pay. To ascertain if protesting respondents completely rejected the public program (for example, ineffectiveness) or the means of payment, or felt government wasted money, we asked respondents who voted against the program at their initial bid amount, whether they would pay $1. This approach is in the spirit of Collins and Rosenberger (2007) who indicate that some protest respondents in their payment card CVM did have small positive values. In our study, if respondents said 'No' to the $1 and wrote down a reason suggesting a protest, they were classified as protests in this second approach. Conversely if they would pay the $1, this suggests the respondent did have a positive value for the program, but just less than their bid amount, and their rejection may have been related to the amount of money being asked to pay for the program. Thus adding the follow-up question on whether those responding 'No' to their bid would pay $1 helps the researcher to determine if the 'No' votes at the random bid indicates no value and complete rejection of the constructed market or whether they do hold positive values for the public good.

To test whether the traditional versus new increased information treatment of protests has a statistically significant effect on median WTP, we test the null hypothesis of:

$$\text{Ho: WTP}_{\text{traditional protest}} = \text{WTP}_{\text{increased info protest}} \qquad (6.4)$$

WTP MODEL

Hanemann (1984) views a person responding to a dichotomous choice or voter referendum format WTP question as evaluating the difference in utility associated with the status quo versus paying some amount ($X) to have the program. If the difference in utility is positive for the program, the individual would respond 'Yes'. If the difference in utility is distributed logistically, a logit model can be used to estimate the parameters and allow for calculation of WTP.

$$\ln \{[\text{Prob}(Y = 1)] / [1 - \text{Prob}(Y = 1)]\} = \beta_0 + \beta_1(\$X_1) + \beta_2 X_2$$

$$+ \beta_3 X_3 + \ldots \beta_n X_n \qquad (6.5)$$

where β_1 is the coefficient on the dollar amount households were asked to pay, and $\beta_2 \ldots \beta_n$ are coefficients on the other explanatory variables.

The log of the odds ratio is linear in the coefficients and the independent variables. Two goodness-of-fit measures are typically used for evaluating the logit model: the McFadden R-squared and the likelihood ratio (LR) statistic. For a given logit regression equation, the LR ratio statistic tests the null hypothesis of whether collectively all the coefficients in the logistic regression are, as a group, statistically different from zero.

Median willingness to pay is calculated as:

$$\text{Median WTP} = ((\beta_o + \beta_2 X_2 + \beta_3 X_3 + \ldots \beta_n X_n)/|\beta_1| \qquad (6.6)$$

where β_0 is the constant term, and $\beta_2 \ldots \beta_n$ are the other non bid coefficients.

DATA

Phone Survey–Booklet and Video Design

The public program used to compare video and phone–mail booklet–phone interviews was forest fire prevention in California. The survey booklet and videotape were developed in conjunction with forestry professionals in California and described the acreage that is burned by wildfires in an average year as well as the typical number of houses lost to wildfire each year. The current situation (the without program) was illustrated with a colour drawing refined through several focus groups. Next, a program increasing the use of prescribed fire or controlled burning in California was described. Specifically, respondents were told that the prescribed burning fuel reduction program would reduce potential wildfire fuels through periodic controlled burning. It was acknowledged that prescribed burning does create some smoke, although far less than a wildfire. A similar drawing showing that prescribed burning has lower flame length, slower rate of fire spread along with fire crews standing by was used to illustrate the public prescribed burning program. Then the respondent was provided additional information and drawings contrasting wildfire and prescribed fire. The cost of financing this program of prescribed burning was described as a cost-share program between the state of California and the county of residence of the individual. Respondents were told the new program would be implemented only if a majority of county residents voted in favour of the program.

The WTP elicitation wording was:

> California is considering using some state revenue as matching funds to help counties finance fire prevention programs. If a majority of residents vote to pay the county share of this program, the Expanded California Prescribed Burning program would be implemented in your county on federal, state, and private forest and rangelands. Funding the Program would require that all users of California's forest and rangelands pay the additional costs of this program . . . If the Program was undertaken it is expected to reduce the number of acres of wildfires from the current average of 362,000

acres each year to about 272,500 acres, for a 25 per cent reduction. The number of houses destroyed by wildfires is expected to be reduced from an average of 30 a year to about 12. Your share of the Expanded California Prescribed Burning program would cost your household $X a year. If the Expanded Prescribed Burning Program were on the next ballot would you vote __In favour ___Against?

The $X was replaced with one of 10 different bid amounts developed from previous fire prevention surveys in Florida (Loomis et al., 2002) and ranged from $10 to $470. The exact bid amounts were $10, 20, 40, 60, 90, 120, 160, 250, 350 and 470 having been selected based on pre-testing and prior fire surveys.

The basic format of the survey booklet and script had previously been through several focus groups in two different states. In the first treatment, the survey was conducted through a phone–mail booklet–phone process. To obtain a representative sample of households, random digit dialling of the households living in a sample of California counties was performed. The counties were selected so there was a mix of counties that frequently experience wildfires, counties that occasionally experience wildfires, and counties that almost never experience wildfires. Once initial contact was established, we elicited initial attitude and knowledge of wild and pre-scribed fire, followed by the scheduling of appointments with individuals for detailed follow-up interviews. During the interim time period, a colour survey booklet was mailed to the household.

The 15-minute videotape was designed to follow closely the layout of the booklet, the same two colour drawings, and the question order of the phone interview. First, a script was created by adhering to the exact wording of the survey booklet and interviewer script used in the first phone interview. The video was simple and included only a headshot of the narrator, the same two still graphics in the booklet and occasional written text on the screen including the wording of the questions. In order to focus solely on the survey mode effects, the video did not deviate from the booklet or phone script. Thus, we did not take full advantage of the dynamic nature of video to be consistent with the visuals in the booklet. The video, like the booklet, begins by defining important fire management terms like 'prescribed fire' and 'wildfire'. Then, the narrator continues to describe the current problem and suggested solution in detail. Ultimately, respondents were asked questions about whether or not they agree with the proposed solution and whether or not they would be willing to pay a certain dollar amount for the solution to be implemented. The script and video were edited and revised slightly following two focus groups.

The initial contact of potential households for the videotape was much like the phone-interview process. To obtain a representative sample,

Table 6.1   Response rates for video and phone–mail–phone surveys

	Video	Phone	Total
First wave – RDD screener			
Total initial sample contacted	1261	794	2055
Completed initial	588	328	916
1st wave response rate	46.6%	41.31%	
Chi-square			2.158
Second wave – In-depth interview/returned			
Net sample for second wave	588	257	845
Completed	174	187	361
2nd wave response rate	29.6%	72.76%	
Chi-square			49.73***

random digit dialling of the households was used in the same counties that were used in the phone survey. A videotape or DVD, answer sheet, and postage-paid self-addressed envelope were mailed to individuals who agreed to participate in the survey. Follow-up contact was made with non-respondents, including sending a replacement videotape if necessary.

The relative cost of the two approaches should be noted. The upfront cost of the video production is fairly expensive (about $15 000) but the cost per unit is pretty small ($7 per unit-videotape and mailing costs). The phone–mail booklet–phone survey was contracted via a survey research centre and averaged about $75 per completed interview. Thus, if more than 200 surveys are planned it may be cheaper to use the video.

Comparison of Survey Response Rates

Because the survey was conducted in two waves, we compare the response rates from the initial random digit dial phone survey and the follow-up in-depth interviews separately in Table 6.1. We obtained 46.6 per cent in the initial phone contact in the video survey and 41.3 per cent with the initial phone contact in the phone–mail booklet–phone interview, a response rate not statistically different at the 5 per cent level using a chi-square test (calculated χ^2 of 2.158 versus critical of 3.84 with one degree of freedom). However, response rates to the follow-up were higher for the phone–mail booklet–phone at nearly 73 per cent as compared with the 30 per cent for the video. The direction of the difference is surprising as one would have expected the more novel video survey would have yielded a higher response rate. The difference is statistically significant at the 1 per cent level (calculated χ^2 is 49.73). Perhaps, having a preset appointment with

Table 6.2   Reasons why respondent would not pay for the program by survey mode

Valid reasons	Video	Phone	Total
No value/No benefits	7	1	8
Cannot afford	4	3	7
Total	11	4	15
Protest reasons			
Taxes already too high	*1*	*2*	*3*
Should be paid for with existing taxes	*1*	*4*	*5*
Government wastes money	*2*	*0*	*2*
Those that live in WUI/forest should pay	*1*	*0*	*1*
Don't trust government	*4*	*0*	*4*
Program won't work	*2*	*0*	*2*
Government should pay	*2*	*0*	*2*
Other	*8*	*1*	*9*
Total	*21*	*7*	*28*
Per cent of 'No' responses that are protests	*66%*	*64%*	
Overall survey protest rate	*12%*	*4%*	

Note: Italicized considered protest responses for purposes of the chi-square analysis.

the phone interviewer calling back and recording responses, with nothing for the respondent to have to initiate or mail back is an advantage to the phone–survey booklet approach over the video.

Comparing Reasons Why Households Would Not Pay for the Program by Survey Mode

Table 6.2 presents the analysis of refusals to pay, that is, individuals who indicated they would neither pay their initial bid amount nor the $1 in the follow-up willingness to pay question (our increased information screening). Table 6.2 lists the reasons why a person would not pay using Jorgensen and Syme's (2000) classification. The first two reasons listed in Table 6.2 are not considered protest responses because having no value for the program or receiving no benefits from the program, as well as not being able to afford to pay, are valid reasons for zero WTP. However, the other categories of responses (italicized in Table 6.2) are considered protests because they were frequently prefaced with, 'I am in favour of program' or 'I'm all for it, but I think the program should be paid for by those living in the forests or with existing taxes'.

The overall protest rate for the phone–mail booklet–phone is 4 per cent. The video protest rate is 12 per cent, while three times larger than the phone–mail booklet–phone, is still low compared to protest rates reported in the literature (see Collins and Rosenberger 2007). The calculated chi-square of protest refusals to pay versus non-protest refusals to pay for video versus phone is 0.014 so we accept the null hypothesis that there is no statistical difference between the two survey modes in terms of non-protest and protest reasons for not paying. As can be seen at the bottom of Table 6.2, the percentage of respondents giving protest 'No' responses is nearly identical between the video and the phone-mail booklet-phone interview.

LOGIT REGRESSIONS RESULTS

Comparison of Phone–Mail Booklet–Phone and Video Logit Regression Results

Tables 6.3a and 6.3b presents the logit regression result for the phone–mail–phone survey mode and the video survey mode, respectively. For comparison of survey mode, both logit regression samples include all observations, including about seven protest responses in the phone–mail–phone and 21 protest responses in the video. As can be seen in Tables 6.3a and 6.3b, the bid slope coefficients are statistically different from zero at conventional levels (1 per cent for the phone–mail–phone and 5 per cent for the videotape) for both types of survey administration. The sign on the bid coefficient is negative, indicating the higher the cost to the household, the less likely a household would agree to pay for the program. The likelihood ratio statistic indicates that both overall logit models are statistically significant at the 1 per cent level.

WTP RESULTS

Comparing Median WTP for Video and Phone–Mail Booklet–Phone

Median willingness to pay for the video survey was $323 while for the phone–mail–phone was $423, a 24 per cent difference between the two survey modes. Confidence intervals (CI) were calculated using a technique developed by Park et al. (1991). The 90 per cent CI for the phone–booklet–phone is $337 to $598. For the video survey the confidence interval is larger, spanning from $234 to $510. Given the overlapping CI's there is no

Table 6.3a   Phone–mail–phone interview results and no protests dropped

Dependent variable: VOTE RX BURN
Observations: 263

Variable	Coefficient	Std. error	z-statistic	Prob.
Constant	1.7442	0.2966	5.8800	0.0000
BIDRX	−0.0041	0.0010	−4.0822	0.0000
RXHEALTHPROB	−0.0822	0.4493	−0.1829	0.8548
WITNESSFIRE	0.0252	0.2985	0.0846	0.9326
Mean dependent var	0.7452	S.D. dependent var		0.4365
Log likelihood	−140.59	Restr. log likelihood		−149.251
LR statistic (3 df)	17.312	Probability(LR stat)		0.00061
		McFadden R-squared		0.0579
N with dependent = 0	67	Total N		263
N with dependent = 1	196			

Table 6.3b   Video logit results and no protests dropped

Dependent variable: VOTE RX BURN
Observations: 156

Variable	Coefficient	Std. error	z-statistic	Prob.
Constant	−3.5766	1.5290	−2.3391	0.0193
RXBIDAMT	−0.0040	0.0012	−3.2536	0.0011
RXHEALTHPROB	1.9810	0.6607	2.9982	0.0027
WITNESSFIRE	0.7970	0.4032	1.9765	0.0481
Mean dependent var	0.6474	S.D. dependent var		0.4793
Log likelihood	−87.911	Restr. log likelihood		−101.247
LR statistic (3 df)	26.671	Probability(LR stat)		6.90E-06
		McFadden R-squared		0.1317
N with dependent = 0	55	Total N		156
N with dependent = 1	101			

statistical difference between the two mean willingness to pay estimates, despite the 24 per cent difference in mean WTP. Thus, it appears there is no statistical difference between the new videotape/DVD approach and more traditional phone–booklet–phone yield. Therefore, the choice between the two methods can be based on selecting the mode that best matches the complexity of the good to be valued and the cost relative to the target number of surveys.

Comparison of Different Protest Identification Procedures Logit Regression Results

Table 6.2 previously presented the classification of protest 'No' responses in the two surveys using the increased information procedure or what we called 'No–No' protests. These responses are classified as protests if the respondent not only voted against their random bid amount but also voted against paying $1, and then cited one of the protest reasons listed in Table 6.2. Because this procedure uses information on two dichotomous choice responses to two different bid amounts, it helps identify individuals that have a positive WTP, but a WTP less than the random bid amount. This procedure identified the 21 protest responses shown for the video survey in Table 6.2. These 21 observations were dropped from the logit regression, and the estimation results are shown in Table 6.4a. In this logit regression the bid amount is negative and statistically significant, but the other two variables are not individually significant at conventional levels. However, the likelihood ratio statistic (LR Statistic) indicates that as a group, all three of these variables are statistically different from zero at the 1 per cent level.

In contrast to this newer approach of identifying protests, the standard protest classification in many dichotomous choice studies is to ask those who will not pay their bid amount why they would not. Using the same protest categories in Table 6.2, but ignoring individual's response to the $1 bid, we find a total of 32 protests in our logit regression data, representing an additional 11 protest responses over the No–No approach. These additional protests are concentrated in Table 6.2 protest categories of 'Taxes already too high', 'Government wastes money', 'Those living in the forest should pay', and a few more in the 'Other' protest category. Dropping these 32 responses from the full data-set yields 124 complete observations and the estimation results presented in Table 6.4b.

In this logit regression, as in the newer approach, the bid amount is negative and statistically significant, but the other two variables are not individually significant at conventional levels. However, the likelihood ratio statistic (LR statistic) indicates that as a group, all three of these variables are statistically different from zero at the 1 per cent level.

Testing the Robustness of Median WTP to Different Treatment of Protests

The second main thrust of this chapter is to compare the effect of three treatments of protest responses on median WTP. The $323 median WTP from the video survey noted above was estimated including protest responses to the hypothetical voter referendum (as would be done in a

Table 6.4a   Increased information 'No–No' protest analysis

Dependent variable: VOTE RX BURN
Observations: 135

Variable	Coefficient	Std. error	z-statistic	Prob.
Constant	0.60716	1.9644	0.3090	0.7573
RXBIDAMT	−0.00481	0.0014	−3.4329	0.0006
RXHEALTHPROB	0.3967	0.8858	0.4455	0.6559
WITNESSFIRE	0.3767	0.4373	0.8615	0.3890
Mean dependent var	0.7462	S.D. dependent var		0.4367
Log likelihood	−68.912	Restr. log likelihood		−75.897
LR statistic (3 df)	13.969	Probability(LR stat)		0.0029
		McFadden R-squared		0.0920
N with dependent = 0	34	Total obs		135
N with dependent = 1	101			

Table 6.4b   Dropping standard protest responses

Dependent variable: VOTE RX BURN
Observations: 124

Variable	Coefficient	Std. error	z-statistic	Prob.
Constant	0.6031	2.0138	0.2995	0.7645
RXBIDAMT	−0.0055	0.0015	−3.4489	0.0006
RXHEALTHPROB	0.9575	0.8595	1.1140	0.2652
WITNESSFIRE	0.0390	0.5148	0.0758	0.9395
Mean dependent var	0.813008	S.D. dependent var		0.391500
Log likelihood	−50.89464	Restr. log likelihood		−59.26529
LR statistic (3 df)	16.74130	Probability(LR stat)		0.000799
		McFadden R-squared		0.141240
N with dependent = 0	23	Total obs		124
N with dependent = 1	101			

real election). However, it is common in many CVM surveys, particularly those conducted for benefit–cost analysis, to identify and drop protest responses (Mitchell and Carson 1989).

Applying just the standard verbal responses to the question of why they would not pay their bid amount resulted in dropping about 21 per cent of the respondents (32 individuals) who would not pay their bid amount. Removing these 21 per cent of full sample observations increases the video median WTP from \$323 to \$454 for a 29 per cent increase in WTP. Using the double criteria for identifying protest responses works particularly well for overcoming the inability of the standard binary dichotomous choice question to identify protest zero WTP. This 'increased information' approach combines the traditional open-ended statements along with a follow up WTP question regarding whether respondents would pay $1 for the program. To be classified as a protest by this method requires that respondents not only give a protest reason for their refusal to pay their bid amount, but also indicate they would **not** vote for the program even at $1 (what we call 'No–No' protesters). This double protest screening criteria identifies fewer protest responses (12 per cent), and yields a median WTP of $392. This WTP of $392 is in between the WTP from dropping all those that gave a written protest response ($454) and the WTP from including all respondents ($323). The absolute magnitude of the differences in WTP is 18 per cent (no protests dropped versus the 'No–No' protesters) as compared to a 29 per cent difference between not dropping any protests and dropping all respondents who give written responses objecting to paying for the program at their bid amount. However, given the overlapping confidence intervals around these three median WTP estimates, there appears to be no statistical difference in WTP estimates to treatment of protest responses. Our empirical result of robustness may be due to our relatively low protest rate (12 per cent to 21 per cent, depending on which of the two methods is used to classify protesters). For example, Collins and Rosenberger (2007) had 118 out of their 296 observations or 40 per cent protest zero WTP responses to their payment card. Given this large protest rate, how protests were treated in their survey makes a statistically significant difference in WTP estimates. Dropping protest respondents increased mean WTP from $60 to $98, a 39 per cent increase. This high percentage of protest zero responses is not unusual (Jorgenson et al., 1999; Lindsey, 1994) and Stevens et al. (1991) recorded protest rates of 50 per cent. In these cases, treatment of protests can substantially affect WTP.

Thus, four recommendations arise from our findings and the findings of others. The first, and most preferred, is to conduct a sufficient number of focus groups and extensive pretesting to uncover protest responses and redesign the survey to minimize them. While some respondents will always object to realistic payment vehicles and provision mechanisms, there are ways to counter this. For example, if respondents distrust government to provide the good, an independent citizen advisory board to approve government expenditures or even an independent non-profit trust to administer the program can be established. Second, is for social scientists to develop a more theoretical basis for including or rejecting protests (Boyle and Bergstrom, 1999). Third, is to develop professionally agreed standards for how to classify and treat protest responses. This would at least provide comparability in relative WTP values that would enhance the ability to rank public programs by their relative benefits. Finally, and perhaps the most controversial, is that economists could abandon their sole reliance on obtaining values from individuals answering in isolation of one another. Since economists are often asked to value public programs, several authors have suggested group valuation, sometimes called discursive ethics (Haddad and Howarth, 2006), deliberative valuation or values juries to reach an informed and acceptable group valuation.

CONCLUSION

The overall equivalency of results between the two survey modes is encouraging. The videotape/DVD survey costs more for the initial production, but is less expensive per unit than the follow-up phone interviews. The videotape technology also offers the potential to present actual fire footage and more dynamic images, something we did not undertake in this study to maintain consistency with the original booklet. However, the phone–booklet approach offers a live interviewer, which may result in a more engaged respondent even if the interaction is only audio. Further research investigating the convergent validity of video versus a pure mail and in-person interviews is warranted to evaluate the full potential of using videotape to present information about public goods and eliciting willingness to pay.

The results regarding the robustness of WTP to treatment of protest responses is encouraging, as there were no statistically significant differences in WTP across approaches for dealing with protest responses. Despite the lack of statistical significance the 29 per cent difference in WTP for including all protests versus dropping all suspected protests is undesirably high. However, this difference in WTP is lower than many CVM surveys, we suspect in part due to the other surveys' higher protest rate. Thus, to increase the robustness of CVM WTP results to how protests are treated substantial effort must be expended in the focus group and pretest phases to design CVM surveys that minimize protest responses to begin with.

NOTE

1. We wish to thank Hayley Hesseln, University of Saskatchewan for her assistance in pretesting the video survey. Funding for this study was provided by the Joint Fire Sciences Program and USDA Forest Service. The Survey Research at University of California-Riverside collected the videotape data collected in this research. The Survey Research Center that was formerly at California State University-Chico collected the phone–mail–phone data used in this research. The analysis of this data was supported by the W2133 Regional Research project of the Colorado Agricultural Experiment Station.

REFERENCES

Arrow, K., R. Solow, P. Portney, E. Leamer, R. Radner and H. Schuman (1993), 'Report of the NOAA Panel on Contingent Valuation. U.S. Department of Commerce', *Federal Register*, **58** (10), 4602–14.

Banzhaf, H.S., D. Burtraw, D. Evans and A. Krupnick (2006), 'Valuation of natural resource improvements in the Adirondacks', *Land Economics*, **82** (3), 445–64.

Barro, S., M. Manfredo, T. Brown and G. Peterson (1996), 'Examination of the predictive validity of CVM using attitude behavior framework', *Society and Natural Resources*, **9** (2), 111–24.

Berrens, R.P., A.K. Bohara, H.C. Jenkins-Smith, C.L. Silva and D.L. Weimer (2004), 'Information and effort in contingent valuation surveys: application to global climate change using national internet samples', *Journal of Environmental Economics and Management*, **47** (2), 331–63.

Bishop, R. and T. Heberlein (1979), 'Measuring values of extra-market goods: are indirect measures biased?', *American Journal of Agricultural Economics*, **61** (5), 926–30.

Boyle, K. (2003), 'Contingent valuation in practice', in P. Champ, K. Boyle and T. Brown (eds), *A Primer on Nonmarket Valuation*, Boston, MA: Kluwer Academic, pp. 111–70.

Boyle, K. and J. Bergstrom (1999), 'Doubt, doubts, and doubters: the genesis of a new research agenda', in I. Bateman and K. Willis (eds), *Valuing Environmental Preferences*, Oxford: Oxford University Press, pp. 183–206.

Brookshire, D., W. Schulze, M. Thayer and R. d'Arge (1982), 'Valuing public goods: a comparison of survey and hedonic approaches', *American Economic Review*, **72** (1), 165–77.

Carson, R. (1991), 'Constructed markets', in J. Braden and C. Kolstad (eds), *Measuring the Demand for Environmental Quality*, Amsterdam: North Holland, pp. 121–62.

Carson, R.T., R.C. Mitchell, M. Hanemann, R.J. Kopp, S. Presser and P.A. Ruud (2003), 'Contingent valuation and lost passive value: damages from the Exxon Valdez oil spill', *Environmental and Resource Economics*, **25**, 257–86.

Collins, A. and R. Rosenberger (2007), 'Protest adjustments in valuation of watershed restoration using payment card data', *Agricultural and Resource Economics Review*, **36** (2), 321–35.

Davis, R. (1963), 'Recreation planning as an economic problem', *Natural Resources Journal*, **3** (3), 239–49.

Haddad, B. and R. Howarth (2006), 'Protest bids, commensurability, and substitution: contingent valuation and ecological economics', in A. Alberini and J. Kahn (eds), *Handbook on Contingent Valuation*, Cheltenham, UK and Northampton, MA: Edward Elgar, pp. 133–52.

Hammack, J. and G. Brown (1974), *Waterfowl and Wetlands: Toward Bioeconomic Analysis*, Baltimore, MD: Johns Hopkins University Press for Resources for the Future.

Hanemann, M. (1984), 'Welfare evaluations in contingent valuation experiments with discrete responses', *American Journal of Agricultural Economics*, **66** (3), 332–41.

Hanemann, M., J. Loomis and B. Kanninen (1991), 'Statistical efficiency of double-bounded dichotomous choice contingent valuation', *American Journal of Agricultural Economics*, **73** (4), 1225–63.

Jorgensen, B., G. Syme, B. Bishop and B. Nancarrow (1999), 'Protest responses in contingent valuation', *Environmental and Resources Economics*, **14** (1), 131–50.

Jorgensen, B. and G. Syme (2000), 'Protest responses and willingness to pay: attitude toward paying for stormwater pollution', *Ecological Economics*, **33** (2), 251–65.

Lindsey, E. (1994), 'Market models, protest bids, and outliers in contingent valuation', *Journal of Water Resources Planning and Management*, **120** (1), 121–9.

Loomis, J. (1987), 'Balancing public trust resources of Mono Lake and Los Angeles' water right: an economic approach', *Water Resources Research*, **23** (8), 1449–56.

Loomis, J. and M. King (1994), 'Comparison of mail and telephone-mail contingent valuation surveys', *Journal of Environmental Management*, **4** (4), 309–24.

Loomis, J., L. Bair and A. González-Cabán (2002), 'Language related differences in a contingent valuation study: English versus Spanish', *American Journal of Agricultural Economics*, **84** (4), 1091–102.

Mitchell, R. and R. Carson (1989), *Using Surveys to Value Public Goods: The Contingent Valuation Method*, Washington, DC: Resources for the Future.

Morrison, M.D., R.K. Blamey and J.W. Bennett (2000), 'Minimizing payment vehicle bias in contingent valuation studies', *Environmental and Resource Economics*, **16** (4), 407–22.

Murphy, J., P. Allen, T. Stevens, D. Weatherhaead (2005), 'A meta-analysis of hypothetical bias in stated preference valuation', *Environmental and Resource Economics*, **30** (3), 313–25.

Park, T., J. Loomis and M. Creel (1991), 'Confidence intervals for evaluating benefit estimates from dichotomous choice contingent valuation studies', *Land Economics*, **67** (1), 64–73.

Randall, A., B. Ives and C. Eastman (1974), 'Bidding games for valuation of aesthetic environmental improvements', *Journal of Environmental Economics and Management*, **1**, 132–49.

Stevens, T., J. Eschewerria, R. Glass, T. Hager and T. Moore (1991), 'Measuring existence value of wildlife: what do the estimates really show?', *Land Economics*, **67**, 390–400.

Walsh, R., J. Loomis and R. Gillman, (1984), 'Valuing option, existence and bequest demands for wilderness', *Land Economics*, **60** (1), 14–29.

7 Consequentiality and contingent values: an emerging paradigm

Gregory L. Poe and Christian A. Vossler

In recent years a new paradigm has emerged with respect to the concept of 'hypothetical bias' in contingent valuation. Following Bohm's (1972) seminal public goods experiments, empirical criterion validity tests of contingent valuation have sought to compare hypothetical ('stated') survey responses against the criterion of actual ('revealed') economic commitments to public goods: 'Hypothetical bias is said to exist when values that are elicited in a hypothetical context, such as a survey, differ from those elicited in a real context, such as a market' (Harrison and Ruström, 2008, p. 752). Whereas occasional research has found that hypothetical, stated values can be lower than actual commitments, reviews of hypothetical versus actual public goods contributions (for example, Harrison and Ruström, 2008; Murphy and Stevens, 2004) and meta-analyses of these data suggest 'that people tend to overstate their actual willingness to pay in hypothetical situations' (List and Gallet, 2001, p. 241; see also Little and Berrens, 2004; Murphy et al., 2005). These conclusions translate into what appears to be the conventional wisdom regarding contingent valuation (CV): 'A fundamental concern of any CV study is hypothetical bias. Respondents have a well-established tendency to state willingness to pay values that are significantly greater than those revealed in real-market interactions' (Aadland et al., 2007).

In a series of conference presentations, working papers, and a journal article, Richard Carson and Theodore Groves and co-authors (for example, Carson and Groves, 2007; Carson et al., 1997, 1999) present an alternative paradigm for conceptualizing the relationship between stated preference survey responses and real economic commitments to private and public goods. To paraphrase Kuhn (1970, p. 81), in his influential treatise, *The Structure of Scientific Revolutions*, these authors have looked at the same stated preference data, but placed them in a new set of relations with one another by giving them a different framework. Specifically, they argue that the bifurcation of data into purely hypothetical responses and real actions is misplaced and uninformative from an economic perspective. Whereas psychologists have developed theories of hypothetical responses (for example, Kahneman et al., 1982), 'economic theory has nothing to say about . . . purely hypothetical questions' (Carson et al., 2004). Building on the mechanism design literature, economic theory does, however, offer a predictive, theoretical framework for interpreting responses that have the potential to influence agency action.

In this chapter, we summarize the theoretical arguments of Carson and Groves et al. and assemble early empirical evidence that comports with this theoretical framework. In doing so, we argue that redefining criterion validity in terms of consequentiality offers the potential for a fundamental paradigm shift in the Kuhnian sense. That this shift has yet to be fully incorporated into the contingent valuation literature reflects the nascent state of this paradigmatic challenge as well as the continued inertia of the dominant hypothetical bias paradigm. Further, empirical support for Carson and Groves et al.'s consequentiality arguments have emerged in a somewhat piecemeal manner, spread across a diverse set of journal articles and unpublished manuscripts.

CONSEQUENTIALITY: CONCEPTUAL FRAMEWORK

In this section we liberally draw from two sets of papers that lay the conceptual foundations of the consequentiality framework to criterion validity in contingent valuations (Carson and Groves, 2007; and Carson et al., 1997, 1999, 2004). The critical component of these is captured in the following comparative definitions:

> **Consequential survey questions:** If a survey's results are seen by the agent as potentially influencing an agency's actions and the agent cares about the outcomes of those actions, the agent should treat the survey questions as an opportunity to influence those actions. In such a case, standard economic theory applies and the response to the question should be interpretable using mechanism design theory concerning incentive structures.
> **Inconsequential survey questions:** If a survey's results are not seen as having any influence on an agency's actions or the agent is indifferent to all possible outcomes of the agency's actions, then all possible responses by the agent will be perceived as having the same influence on the agent's welfare. In such a case, economic theory makes no predictions. (Carson and Groves, 2007, p. 183)

The authors argue that in responding to a consequential survey question 'a rational economic agent will take the incentive structure of a consequential survey into account in conjunction with information provided in the survey and beliefs about how that information is likely to be used' (Carson and Groves, 2007, p. 204). Cover letters accompanying surveys typically stress that everyone's response matters, in part to maximize response rates. Survey instruments generally suggest that responses will inform the policy process, and increase realism by, for example, providing reminders of substitute goods and budget constraints. This does not imply that respondents to a consequential survey, however, will necessarily reveal their true preferences. Indeed they may respond strategically if the question format is not incentive compatible, for example, if it is an open-ended format. Also, even with an incentive-compatible elicitation, if respondent beliefs about the proposed outcome or its cost upon implementation differ from what is stated in the survey, the analyst will not be able to recover the respondent's true preferences without knowledge of these beliefs. In this case, at least theoretically, the elicitation yields a truthful response but to a different proposal.

FOUNDATIONS: INCENTIVE COMPATIBILITY AND DEMAND REVELATION OF BINARY REFERENDUM QUESTIONS

The incentive structure used in a survey question is therefore critical to the theoretical formulation and empirical evaluation of consequentiality. When moving from theoretical conceptualizations to empirical explorations, it is useful to distinguish between the theoretical notion of incentive compatibility and the empirical notion of demand revelation. In many presentations these concepts have been used interchangeably (for example, Cummings et al., 1995; Taylor et al., 2001) with the lack of clarity being a source of confusion. Here we are explicit in our terms. An incentive-compatible mechanism is a theoretical concept, meaning that a respondent has an incentive to truthfully reveal his preferences. Demand revelation is an empirical concept, providing a measure of how well decisions correspond with true, underlying values. If other conditions are not satisfied, it is possible that a theoretically incentive-compatible mechanism is not demand revealing, and vice versa.

Building upon mechanism design theory, most specifically what is referred to as the Gibbard–Satterthwaite theorem (Gibbard, 1973; Satterthwaite, 1975), Carson et al. (2004) argue that binary referenda can be incentive compatible under the following conditions.

Proposition 1: A binding (binary) referendum vote with a plurality aggregation rule is incentive compatible in the sense that truthful preference revelation is the dominant strategy when the following additional conditions hold: (a) the vote is coercive in that all members of the population will be forced to follow the conditions of the referendum if the requisite plurality favours its passage and (b) the vote on the referendum does not influence any other offer [that] might be made available to the relevant population.

Four recent studies (Burton et al. 2007; Collins and Vossler, 2009; Taylor et al., 2001; Vossler and McKee, 2006)[1] have used induced value laboratory experiments to explore the demand revelation characteristics of referenda that correspond with Carson et al.'s (2004) proposition 1. Following Smith (1976), assuming that individuals abide by the postulate of non-satiation and are otherwise rational, experimental preferences can be achieved in a controlled economic laboratory setting by using a reward structure to induce prescribed monetary value on actions. The basic idea is that given the opportunity to choose between two alternatives, 'identical except that the first yields more of the reward medium (usually currency) than the second, the first will always be chosen (preferred) over the second' (Smith, 1976, p. 275). Building on this idea, the common framework for exploring demand revelation in these experiments is that individuals are offered the opportunity to vote for a public good that will be provided to all individuals in the group if a specified voting threshold is surpassed. The public good has value in the sense that it provides personal monetary rewards to each individual i in the group. If the provision rule is met individuals have to pay a specified cost, C_i, for its provision and each individual receive his or her induced value, V_i.[2] If the voting threshold is not achieved, no one receives any payment and no one incurs any cost: the public good is not provided. As an example, Taylor et al. replicate the Carson et al. (2004) proposition 1 conditions in a secret ballot, majority rule referendum which they describe as follows:

> If it passed, each subject in the room would pay \$5 (regardless of whether they voted yes or no) and in return, they received 'the good', which was simply the amount of money that would be paid to them at the end of the experiment. If it did not pass, no one paid \$5 and no one received the good, regardless of how they voted . . . They were instructed to vote 'yes' if they would like the referendum to pass, and 'no' if they did not want the referendum to pass.(Taylor et al., 2001, p. 63)

Participants were informed of their personal induced value and told that not everyone had the same value. They were not however informed of the range of values or how the values were distributed across other participants.

In the Taylor et al. experiment, the personal induced value of the good varied across participants, while all individuals paid the same cost (that is, $C_i = 5$ for all i). Experiments 1 and 2 of the Burton et al. study follow a similar design.[3] The other induced-value experiments varied both costs

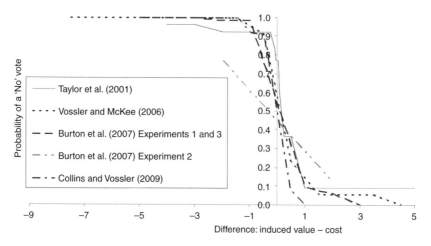

Figure 7.1   Proportion of 'No' respondents, difference value

and benefits: Vossler and McKee used induced values over the range from $1.50 to $9.50, in $1 increments, and costs of $1, $3, $5, $7 and $9; in Burton et al.'s induced values in experiment 3 were $4 and $8 while costs were $3, $5, $7 or $9; for the dichotomous choice component of the Collins and Vossler study, induced values range from −$1 to $10.50, in $0.50 increments, with associated costs of $2, $3, $4 and $5. While the underlying experimental designs vary across the four studies, a common feature is that each can be represented in terms of the distribution of 'No' responses as a function of induced personal value minus personal costs (that is, $V_i - C_i$).

The $V_i - C_i$ reverse cumulative distribution functions (CDFs) for the five groups of experiments are presented in Figure 7.1.[4] If the referendum mechanism is perfectly demand revealing, we expect 100 per cent 'Yes' votes for negative difference values and zero per cent 'Yes' votes for positive difference values. In other words there would be single step from 100 to zero per cent at $V_i - C_i = 0$. It is evident from the graphs that perfect demand revelation is not observed in any of the four studies. The four studies combined yield 556 of 603, or 92 per cent, of votes consistent with induced preferences. As a test of demand revelation, we use one-sample Kolmogorov–Smirnov (K–S) tests to test the null hypothesis that the empirical and theoretical difference value CDFs are equal.[5] This null hypothesis is rejected at the five per cent level for three of the five data sets, Taylor et al., Burton et al. (experiment 2) and Collins and Vossler. However, for two of the three studies where K–S tests reject the hypothesis of perfect demand revelation the 'mis-votes' or digressions from induced-preferences at the source of the rejection occur at rather small difference values: for Taylor et al. this is between −$0.10 and $0.50; for Vossler and McKee this is between $0 and $0.50. As Taylor et al. argue, it may be that 'rewards and penalties of less than $1 may not have been salient' (2001, p.65). Similarly, along the line of thought underlying random utility modelling, the assumption that utility is driven by induced values may only capture the true underlying utility comparison with some degree of unobservable error. For example, social preferences may play a role. Models relying only on induced values do not capture possible altruism or alternative forms of other-regarding preferences participants may have. We do not, however, believe that these arguments carry over to the level of 'mis-votes' observed in the Burton et al. experiment 2 for more salient difference values of −$2 and $2. For the moment at least, this experiment appears to be an unexplained outlier, in which behaviour for this group of students seems to differ considerably and significantly from economic predictions as well as from the results of the body of experiments in this area.

We further note that although there are some systematic differences between empirical and theoretical difference-value distributions, this does not necessarily translate into biased willingness-to-pay (WTP) distributions. That is, it may be the case that at a particular cost amount that 'Yes' and 'No' 'mis-votes' cancel each other out to a large degree. We turn to an analysis of 'aggregate' demand revelation below.

In a similar fashion to our analysis of difference values, we compare empirical and theoretical WTP CDFs using K–S tests for the Vossler and McKee and the Collins and Vossler studies.[6,7] To be clear, these CDFs are constructed from the proportion of 'No' responses to each cost amount, rather than the proportion of 'no' responses to each difference value. We fail to reject the null hypothesis of equality between empirical and theoretical WTP distributions in both studies.

Taken together, we interpret the results from the above tests as indicative that decisions are consistent with aggregate demand revelation, but there are some deviations from induced preferences at particular dollar values. Most of the deviations from induced preferences occur for small differences between induced value and cost. As mentioned above, uncontrolled social preferences may explain at least some of these decisions.

DEMAND REVELATION IN BINARY REFERENDUM WITH UNCERTAINTY IN VALUES

To this point, our discussion has only reported results from demand revelation studies in which the induced values are certain. It has, however,

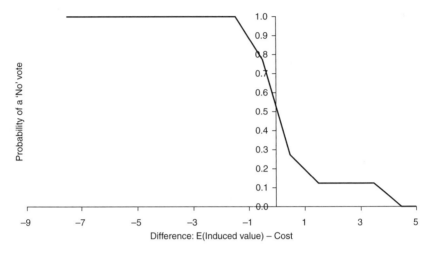

Figure 7.2   Proportion of 'No' respondents, expected difference value,
Vossler and McKee (2006)

long been recognized (for example, Dubourg et al., 1994; Opaluch and
Segerson, 1989; Ready et al., 1995) that rather than having a single point
estimate of the value for the environmental or public good, contingent
valuation respondents may instead have a distribution or range of possible WTP values. To explore the effect of uncertainty on demand revelation of the binary referendum mechanism, Vossler and McKee built upon
their previously discussed experimental design by inducing uncertainty in
values as follows:

> For value certainty treatments, induced values across group members are uni-
> formly distributed over the range of $1.50 to $9.50, in $1 increments. For uncer-
> tain value treatments, participants are given a $2 range of possible values. These
> ranges are constructed by adding/subtracting $1 from the set of certain values.
> This range is wide relative to the value distribution. Participants are instructed
> that each value in the range (in 25-cent increments) has an equal chance of
> being selected. After all the [voting] decisions are made, the exact value for each
> participant is determined through a die roll. (2006, p. 142)

Under the assumption that individuals are expected utility maximizers
who base their voting decisions on the expected difference value, $E[V_i - C_i] = E[V_i] - C_i$, Figure 7.2 plots the distribution of 'No' responses across
expected induced difference values using the methods described above.
Using a K–S test, we reject the null hypothesis of equal empirical and theoretical difference-value functions at the 5 per cent level. Note, however,

that this rejection is driven by votes made under expected differences of −$0.50 and $0.50, both of which lie within the range of induced uncertainty. Arguably, if respondents invoke decision heuristics other than expected value maximization, it is not valid to assume that these represent errors. The null hypothesis of equality between the theoretical and empirical distributions cannot be rejected when differences from −$0.50 to $0.50 are excluded. Similar to the above results with certain values, we do not find any bias between the theoretical and empirical WTP functions. While the evidence regarding uncertain induced values is limited to one study, these results are consistent with the notion that the demand revelation characteristics of the incentive-compatible consequential binary referendum carry over to cases for which induced values are uncertain.

FRAMED FIELD EXPERIMENTS: HOMEGROWN VALUES AND CONSEQUENTIALITY

While induced-value laboratory experiments provide critical information about the demand revelation characteristics of consequential, incentive-compatible value elicitation mechanisms for public goods, contingent valuation is inherently a field method to elicit 'homegrown values' that an individual might have for a non-market environmental or public good. 'Homegrown value', 'refers to a subject's value that is independent of the value which an experimenter might "induce" (see Vernon L. Smith, 1976). The idea is that homegrown values are those that the subject brings *to* an experiment' (Cummings et al., 1995, p. 260, original emphasis).

Researchers have used framed field experiments, which differ from a conventional laboratory experiment in a number of ways, to further explore consequentiality. As defined by Harrison and List (2004) laboratory experiments conventionally use a standard participant pool of students, frame the decision abstractly and impose a set of rules. A framed field experiment instead uses a non-standard participant pool with a 'field context in either the commodity, task, or information set that the subjects can use' (Harrison and List, 2004, p. 1014).

Landry and List (2007) and Carson et al. (2004) undertake a series of framed field experiments using participants from a well-functioning marketplace – the floor of a sports card show in Tucson, Arizona. Participants were recruited as they entered the show for a public goods experiment run in a separate room in the same building. The public good is the provision of *n* identical pieces of sports memorabilia if the majority of *n* participants votes to fund 'Mr. Twister.' An excerpt from Landry and List describes the good.

Welcome to Lister's Referendum. Today you have the opportunity to vote on whether 'Mr. Twister,' this small metal box, will be 'funded.' If 'Mr. Twister' is funded, I will turn the handle and *n* (the amount of people in the room) ticket stubs dated October 12, 1997, which were issued for the game in which Barry Sanders passed Jim Brown for the number 2 spot in the NFL all-time rushing yardage, will be distributed – one to each participant (illustrate). To fund 'Mr. Twister,' *all* of you will have to pay $*X*. (2007, p. 423, original emphasis)

The $X values were $5 and $10 in Landry and List. In the Carson et al. (2004) study, 'Mr. Twister' distributed Kansas City Royal game ticket stubs dated 14 June 1996, which were issued for admission to the baseball game in which Cal Ripken Jr broke the world record for consecutive games played. The cost to each individual of funding 'Mr. Twister' was $10.

We report on three treatments here. First, in what we label as the 'baseline' treatment the ticket stubs were provided and everyone paid the indicated costs if the majority of the participants voted to fund 'Mr. Twister'. If 50 per cent or less of the participants voted to fund 'Mr. Twister', no one paid the fee and no one received a ticket stub. The 'probabilistic referenda' was the same as the baseline treatment, with the following exception. If the majority voted to fund 'Mr. Twister', then a second step, a coin flip, would be used to determine if the funding decisions would be binding. The funding decision was binding if the coin flip turned up heads, a 50 per cent probability. To impose other probabilities, a ten-sided die was used in Carson et al. (2004). If, for example, a 20 per cent chance was being used, and the die turned up one or two, the ticket stubs would be provided and all participants would have to pay the specified amount. If the die turned up a value between three and ten, 'Mr Twister' would not be funded. In the 'hypothetical' treatment, 'passive language was used so that subjects understood that their vote would not induce true economic consequences – i.e. no money would change hands' (Landry and List, 2007, p. 423).

Referring back to the consequential/inconsequential definitions, and proposition 1 above, the baseline treatment and the probabilistic referenda satisfy the conditions for an incentive-compatible elicitation mechanism. However, in contrast with the induced-value laboratory experiments it is not possible to test for demand revelation by comparing induced-value and cost distributions. Instead, with homegrown-value criterion validity studies, a common approach is to use results from an incentive-compatible elicitation as a benchmark from which to compare treatments intended to more closely capture the contingent valuation setting. As a result, the relevant null hypothesis here is simply that each of the probabilistic treatments results in vote proportions that are equal

Table 7.1 Field tests of consequentiality: percentage 'Yes' (number of observations)

Description	Consequential Real	Probabilistic % chance of being binding			Inconsequential Hypothetical
		0.80	0.50	0.20	
Landry and List	33	n.a.	32	n.a.	84
(2007), $5	(64)		(59)		(64)
Landry and List	19	n.a.	20	n.a.	75
(2007), $10	(64)		(59)		(64)
Carson et al.	46	41	48	44	60
(2004), $10	(96)	(46)	(52)	(50)	(58)

to those in the baseline, binding referenda. In contrast, the hypothetical treatment is inconsequential and hence, we are unable to formulate economic-theoretic expectations of voting patterns vis-à-vis the baseline and probabilistic referenda.

Selected relevant results from these two studies are reported in Table 7.1. Examination of the table suggests that there is little difference in the voting behaviour between the baseline treatment and the probabilistic referenda. However, the proportion of 'Yes' votes in the hypothetical treatment is considerably higher than the consequential treatments. Statistical tests of the hypotheses confirm that the distribution of voting decisions is equal among the consequential treatments, that is, the null hypothesis of equality cannot be rejected. However, the equality of the voting behaviour between the consequential and inconsequential (that is, hypothetical) treatments can be rejected. Interestingly, the difference in distributions appears to be 'knife-edged': even low-probability referenda provide similar values as the baseline treatments.

The lesson from these data is best summarized by Landry and List:

> . . . we find experimental evidence that suggests responses in hypothetical referenda are significantly different from responses in real referenda. This result is in accordance with many of the studies that have examined hypothetical and real statements of value. Yet, we do find evidence that when decisions *potentially* have financial consequences, subjects behave in a fashion that is consistent with behaviour when they have consequences with certainty. Our results furthermore suggest that estimates of the lower bound of mean WTP derived from 'consequential' referenda are statistically indistinguishable from estimates of the actual lower bound of WTP. (2007, p. 427, original emphasis)

ADVISORY REFERENDA

The framed field test experiments support the hypothesis that as long as decisions can probabilistically influence an outcome, individuals have incentives to respond as if the referenda were binding. This notion of probabilistic referenda, however, deviates from the situation presented in most contingent valuation studies. Rather, 'cover letters for SP studies often state that the survey results will be shared with state or local officials . . . Survey instruments generally provide additional signals that respondents should take seriously the valuation exercise' (Vossler and Evans, 2010). In this manner, the aspect of potential consequentiality is stressed, but not probabilistically. Rather, the survey responses are presented as being advisory to decision-makers. That such efforts by survey researchers are effective is evidenced in a recent contingent valuation study of willingness to vote in favour of a referendum to improve water quality at an Iowa lake by Herriges et al. (2010). This survey included a Likert-scale question to measure the respondents' beliefs about the likelihood that survey results would affect policies related to water quality in Iowa lakes. A 'one' response indicated 'no effect at all' and a 'five' response denoted 'definite' effects. Less than 7 per cent of those returning a survey reported a value of one, suggested that only a small proportion of respondents regarded the survey as being inconsequential.

Carson et al. (2004) address this advisory nature of contingent valuation research in a separate proposition:

Proposition 2: changing from a binding referendum to an advisory referendum doesn't alter the incentive structure as long as the decision maker is more likely to undertake the referendum proposed outcome if the specified plurality favours it. This proposition follows from noting that it is the nature of the influence on the decision . . . not the binding nature of the referendum that matters.

In general, incentive compatibility in the advisory referendum will be based on the respondents' perceived influence on the outcome.

In a homegrown value laboratory experiment, Vossler and Evans used a split sample design to compare responses to binding, advisory and hypothetical referenda. Student participants were asked to vote in a referendum on whether everyone in the group (session) would fund the provision and administration of one on-campus, classroom recycling container at a particular cost. Consistent with proposition 1(a), the funding mechanism was coercive. In addition, there was no clear venue for which students themselves can purchase recycling containers (and have them maintained by the university), such that the binding and advisory referenda are likely to also satisfy proposition 1(b).

The binding referendum, as in the prior studies, serves as a baseline for comparison. It involved a referendum with majority-vote implementation rule, which has already been noted to be incentive compatible and demonstrated to be demand revealing in induced-value experiments. In the advisory referendum, which Vossler and Evens refer to as an 'implicit advisory referendum', efforts were made to make the instructions as close as possible to a field contingent valuation survey in which there is no direct signal on exactly how responses will be used in a policy decision. In this treatment, participants were given the following information.

> Passage of the referendum will not solely be determined by how you and the other participants vote. In particular, we, the experiment coordinators, will use your votes as *advice* on whether or not to pass the referendum. While you will not be told how we came to a decision, know that the likelihood the referendum is passed increases with the number of YES votes cast. (Vossler and Evans, 2010, p. 341, original emphasis)

In actuality, unknown to the participants, the decision rule used was identical to the baseline, that is, a majority-rule vote with no experiment coordinator votes. The hypothetical treatment framed a referendum similar to the baseline, but with slightly different language to make clear that the vote was inconsequential.

The results of the three treatments are provided in Figure 7.3, which depicts the probability of a 'Yes' response for costs of $1, $3, $6 and $8. As depicted, the distribution of votes in the hypothetical treatment lies to the right of the other two treatments. Using two-sample K–S tests, the null hypothesis of equal WTP distributions is marginally rejected between the hypothetical and baseline treatment ($D = 0.231$, $p < 0.10$) and between the hypothetical and advisory vote ($D = 0.231$, $p < 0.10$). The null hypothesis of equality between the baseline and the advisory distributions cannot be rejected ($D = 0.104$, $p > 0.10$).[8] These results are only suggestive however, as with homegrown values there is no guarantee that the underlying true WTP distribution is the same across treatments. Using parametric models that account for whether the student has a class in the building designated as the location of the proposed recycling container, and socio-economic variables, the authors find that elicited WTP in the hypothetical referendum is statistically different, and is roughly 100 per cent higher, than in the baseline. Yet there is no statistical difference in elicited WTP between baseline and advisory referenda.

Based on their statistical analyses, Vossler and Evans (2010, p. 344) conclude that the results of their experiments 'designed to capture key

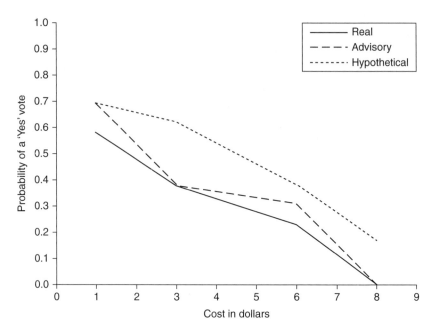

Figure 7.3   Real, advisory and hypothetical voting distributions, Vossler and Evans (2009)

characteristics of a SP survey for a proposed environmental program, provide support for the theoretical predictions regarding voter behaviour in advisory referenda'. This conclusion is further supported in the Herriges et al. (2010) comparison of the estimated WTP distributions of respondents who indicated that the Iowa lake survey was inconsequential and respondents who indicated otherwise: 'we find support for the equality of WTP distributions among those believing the survey is at least minimally consequential, while those believing the survey will have no effect on policy have statistically different distributions associated with WTP' (Herriges et al., 2010, p. 30). These results are consistent with the 'Mr Twister' framed field experiments.

A CONTINGENT VALUATION CRITERION VALIDITY TEST

The last empirical piece of evidence in support of the Carson and Grove et al.'s theory of consequentiality is a contingent valuation criterion validity test conducted by Johnston (2006), which compares:

genuine discrete choice CV responses to aggregated votes in a subsequent, binding public referendum. The assessment is designed to be unambiguous and simple. Hypothetical and actual choice contexts are parallel and consequential, and address the provision of an identical quasi-public good (i.e., the provision of public water to the Village of North Scituate, Rhode Island). Respondents are drawn from the same well-defined population. No re-coding or transformation of survey responses is required, no cheap-talk or certainty adjustments are applied, and a 'one vote per survey' format eliminates the need to adjust for correlation or sequence effects among responses. (p. 470)

The contingent valuation study was conducted to assist the village committee assess the public support for a public water provision project. The intention was to use survey methods to determine if there should be an officially sanctioned referendum on the project, as required by the State of Rhode Island. Sanctioning, promoting, scheduling and implementating a referenda incurs significant costs. Johnston continues:

Although the survey instrument noted the possibility of a public vote as a possible subsequent step in the process of establishing the water supply project, this was the first indication that any official referendum might be forthcoming. As the survey was designed as a means to assess public preferences – before the official vote was approved or scheduled – it provides a nearly ideal context in which to assess the validity of hypothetical survey responses in a genuine CV context. (2006, p. 472).

Based on the contingent valuation study, the village decided to pursue a real referendum, wherein the quarterly cost per household was estimated to be $250.

The results from this comparison of an advisory contingent valuation survey and a real vote are consistent with the previously discussed laboratory and field experiments. As depicted in Figure 7.4, the contingent valuation response distribution across a number of possible costs closely predicts the actual proportion of 'Yes' responses to $250 in the real referendum. The null hypothesis of equality between the contingent valuation (48.4 per cent) and the actual (45.7 per cent) 'Yes' vote percentage at $250 cannot be rejected ($p = 0.69$). As in Vossler and Evans (2010), these results are further supported by parametric estimations of the contingent valuation WTP distribution.

DISCUSSION

With few exceptions, conclusions from past criterion validity studies cast contingent valuation in a much different light than studies that focus on other aspects of validity. First, there is strong evidence of construct

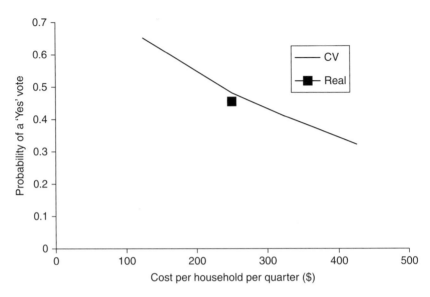

Figure 7.4   Contingent valuation and real referendum comparison, Johnston (2006)

validity: consistent with consumer demand theory, elicited contingent values vary with factors such as income and scope, and elicited willingness to accept exceeds WTP (see Carson, 1997; Carson et al., 2001). Second, there is strong evidence of convergent validity: estimates of value from contingent valuation studies approximate those from revealed preference studies (see Carson et al., 1996). This suggests that, at least for eliciting use values, contingent valuation may be appropriate. Third, there are persistent elicitation effects demonstrating that, consistent with expectations from mechanism design theory, the mechanism used to elicit contingent values matters. In particular open-ended elicitation questions lead to lower estimates of value than does dichotomous choice (for example, Cameron et al., 2002). These elicitation effects provide further evidence of construct validity.

So, then, why is there a divergent conclusion from the majority of criterion validity studies? We hypothesize that reliance on using a purely inconsequential decision setting as the analogue to a stated preference survey is at least a partial explanation. Based on the results from the studies highlighted in this chapter, if survey respondents perceive their decisions to be consequential, then this motivates responses that are quite different from those in inconsequential settings. As such, placing the results of criterion validity studies in their proper context of consequentiality can help reduce misinterpretations. On a related note, criterion validity studies that compare *consequential* surveys with actual behaviour need also cast results in their proper context by drawing on the foundations put forth by Carson and Groves et al. In many cases, for example, these studies compare voluntary contributions with consequential surveys cast in a similar context (for example, Champ et al., 1997). In such a framing, proposition 1(b) is likely to be violated and hence, as argued by Carson and Groves, those in the contingent setting should overstate their value if they believe doing so will increase the chance of an actual fundraising campaign being implemented. On the other hand, as shown in Poe et al. (2002), the voluntary nature of the actual contributions in such comparisons will engender free riding, further muddying any efforts to compare actual contributions and purely inconsequential survey responses. Rather than providing a test of criterion validity, the observed deviation in response patterns, if they are consistent with mechanism design theory, may be construed as empirical evidence of construct validity rather than as evidence that contingent valuation lacks criterion validity.

Our discussion is not meant to imply that we should reject the accumulated, sizable literature that explores hypothetical bias. As suggested by the Herriges et al. (2010) study, where there was a history of similar surveys affecting public policy, not all respondents indicated that they perceived the survey to be consequential. In other settings, such as one where respondents would question the ability of the authority to coercively collect payment, they perceived that the agency would place zero weight on public opinion or, for what appears to be a purely academic study, there is likely to be a much higher proportion of respondents for which consequentiality does not hold.

Assuming there is a suitable way to separate respondents into consequential and inconsequential camps, researchers are still charged with the task of uncovering the demand of those in the latter group. Cheap-talk scripts, alternative elicitation formats and/or calibration methods will continue to be essential in this regard. Justification for continued reliance on these approaches include minimizing possible sample selection bias that may otherwise arise, as well as the maximizing the number of useful surveys collected for a given budget.

We further note that there may be a connection between consequentiality and various aspects of survey design, including the use of cheap talk and language in cover letters. For instance, cheap-talk scripts serve to emphasize the importance of obtaining accurate signals of value, and may hence increase the proportion in the consequential camp. On a related note, consequentiality may confound split-sample field survey comparisons if there is uncontrolled correlation between treatment and consequentiality. As such, this is yet one more reason why the development and use of questions to elicit perceptions about consequentiality remain an important area of research.

From the scant number of methodological studies that are grounded in mechanism design theory, it is clear that there is an abundance of additional, fundamental research questions that remain. First, with the exception of Johnston, past research on consequentiality has been comprised of very controlled studies with attributes that differ from the field survey environment, making further field research a priority. Within the laboratory setting the experimental design may be modified to invoke closer correspondence with the field survey setting. Further, given that many researchers, usually out of concern for statistical efficiency or scenario plausibility, continue to use alternatives to the referendum elicitation format, sometimes with a voluntary contributions payment vehicle, exploration of these formats in controlled but consequential decision settings is warranted.

On a final note, there is a very pragmatic reason for redefining criterion validity in terms of consequentiality: we, as stated preference researchers, have been our own worst enemy in the debate over the criterion validity of contingent values. Stated preference researchers who cast surveys as purely inconsequential exercises are providing the impetus to other economists, academics and policy-makers to dismiss results from our work. By grounding our work in mechanism design theory we, like many other economists, would have theoretical justification for what we do as well as a framework from which to undertake empirical tests. Pursuing this path will no doubt lead to theoretical refinements that will not only inform stated preference research, but more broadly the economics profession in areas such as decision-making under uncertainty and voting. Further, shifting to the consequentiality paradigm should serve to increase the demand for stated preference research in the private and public sectors.

NOTES

1. In the analysis that follows, we use data from Vossler and McKee's dichotomous choice 'real, certainty' treatment, Burton et al.'s 'consequential' treatment for the three experiments they report on, and the dichotomous choice 'plurality' treatment data from Collins and Vossler.
2. Collins and Vossler's experiment is couched in a choice experiment elicitation framework. To make these data compatible with the other studies, the cost is taken to be the net benefits associated with the status quo choice or 'No' vote whereas the value is the net benefits associated with the alternative choice or 'Yes' vote.
3. Burton et al. conduct three experiments 'using two very different participant groups (cadets at a US military academy and university students in Northern Ireland' (2007,

     pp. 518–19), and report finding different behaviours across the two groups. On this basis we group experiments 1 and 3, conducted using cadets from the US military academy, and treat experiment 2, with the university students from Northern Ireland, separately. The basic findings reported in the text for this grouping hold for the alternate in which each experiment is treated separately.

4. To obtain a valid CDF we imposed a monotonicity constraint following the approach described by Haab and McConnell (1997).

5. The D-statistic corresponding with the K–S goodness of fit test is the absolute value of the maximum difference between the theoretical and empirical distributions. For a large sample, the critical value for this test associated with a five per cent significance level is approximately $1.36\sqrt{n}$, where n is the sample size of the empirical distribution.

6. An alternative to the approach used in the text would be to estimate mean and median values for the difference distributions presented in Figures 7.1 and 7.2, and to compare these estimates with the theoretical prediction that the mean and median values of the $V_i - C_i$ distribution are equal to zero. Rejection of this test would suggest that errors are systematic in one direction relative to $V_i - C_i = 0$. We do not adopt this approach here because the validity of the test would rest on the assumption that the V_i and C_i are not correlated. Based on our personal knowledge of the Vossler and McKee study, this is not the case. In the Vossler and McKee study the V_i and C_i values were deliberately correlated. Personal communication with Mike McKee indicates that the V_i to C_i relationship in the Taylor et al. study was specifically structured so that it was unlikely that the referenda would pass, thus facilitating more rapid pay-outs in classroom experiments.

7. The Taylor et al. and experiments 1 and 2 of Burton et al. have a single cost. The values and costs of the third experiment in Burton et al. had value to cost relationships that were, for some costs only one-sided, not allowing for a two-sided error distribution. For these reasons we judged that the data from these studies were not amenable to estimating willingness-to-pay distributions.

8. In their paper, Vossler and Evans (2010) test whether the overall proportion of 'Yes' responses are equal across treatments using Fisher exact tests, which yields stronger evidence of hypothetical bias.

REFERENCES

Aadland, D., B. Anatchkova, B. Grandjean, J.F. Shogren, B. Simon and P.A. Taylor (2007), 'Valuing access to our public lands: a unique public good pricing experiment', selected paper presented at the American Agricultural Economics Association meetings, Portland, Oregon, July.

Bohm, P. (1972), 'Estimating demands for public goods: an experiment', *European Economic Review*, **3**, 111–30.

Burton, A.C., K.S. Carson, S.M. Chilton and W.G. Hutchinson (2007), 'Resolving questions about bias in real and hypothetical referenda', *Environmental and Resource Economics*, **38** (4), 513–25.

Cameron, T.A., G.L. Poe, R.G. Ethier and W.D. Schulze (2002), 'Alternative non-market value-elicitation methods: are the underlying preferences the same?', *Journal of Environmental Economics and Management*, **44**, 391–425.

Carson, R.T. (1997), 'Contingent valuation surveys and tests of insensitivity to scope', in R.J. Kopp, W. Pommerhene and N. Schwartz (eds), *Determining the Value of Non-Marketed Goods: Economic, Psychological, and Policy Relevant Aspects of Contingent Valuation Methods*, Boston, MA: Kluwer, pp. 127–63.

Carson, R.T and T. Groves (2007), 'Incentive and informational properties of preference questions', *Environmental and Resource Economics*, **37** (1), 181–210.

Carson, R.T., N.E. Flores and N.F. Meade (2001), 'Contingent valuation: controversies and evidence', *Environmental and Resource Economics*, **19** (2), 173–210.

Carson, R.T., N.E. Flores, K.M. Martin and J.L. Wright (1996), 'Contingent valuation and revealed preference methodologies: comparing the estimates for quasi-public goods', *Land Economics*, **72** (1), 80–99.
Carson R.T., T. Groves and M.J. Machina (1997), 'Stated preference questions: context and optimal response', paper presented at the National science foundation preference elicitation symposium, University of California, Berkeley.
Carson R.T., T. Groves and M.J. Machina (1999), 'Incentive and informational properties of preferences questions', plenary address, European Association of Environmental and Resource Economists, Oslo, Norway.
Carson, R., T. Groves, J. List and M. Machina (2004), 'Probabilistic influence and supplemental benefits: a field test of two key assumptions underlying stated preferences', unpublished draft manuscript.
Champ, P.A., R.C. Bishop, T.C. Brown and D.W. McCollum (1997), 'Using donation mechanisms to value non-use benefits from public goods', *Journal of Environmental Economics and Management*, **33** (2), 151–63.
Collins, J.P. and C.A. Vossler (2009), 'Incentive compatibility tests of choice experiment value elicitation questions', *Journal of Environmental Economics and Management*, **58** (2), 226–35.
Cummings, R.G., G.W. Harrison and E.E. Rustrom (1995), 'Homegrown values and hypothetical surveys: is the dichotomous choice approach incentive compatible?', *American Economic Review*, **85** (1), 260–66.
Dubourg, W.R., M.W. Jones-Lee and G. Loomes (1994), 'Imprecise preferences and the WTP-WTA disparity', *Journal of Risk and Uncertainty*, **9**, 115–33.
Gibbard, A. (1973), 'Manipulation of voting schemes: a general result', *Econometrica*, **41** (3), 587–602.
Haab, T.C. and K.E. McConnell (1997), 'Referendum models and negative willingness to pay: alternative solutions', *Journal of Environmental Economics and Management*, **32** (2), 251–70.
Harrison, G.W. and J.A. List (2004), 'Field experiments', *Journal of Economic Literature*, **42**, 1009–55.
Harrison, G.W. and E. Rustrom (2008), 'Chapter 81: experimental evidence on the existence of hypothetical bias in value elicitation methods', *Handbook of Experimental Economics*, **1**, 752–67.
Herriges, J., C. Kling, C-C Liu and J. Tobias (2010), 'What are the consequences of consequentiality?', *Journal of Environmental Economics and Management*.
Johnston, R.J. (2006), 'Is hypothetical bias universal? Validating contingent valuation responses using a binding public referendum', *Journal of Environmental Economics and Management*, **52** (1), 469–81.
Kahneman, D., P. Slovic and A. Tversky (1982), *Judgment under Uncertainty: Heuristics and Biases*, New York: Cambridge University Press.
Kuhn, T.S. (1970), *The Structure of Scientific Revolutions*, 2nd edn, Chicago, IL: University of Chicago Press.
Landry, C.E. and J.A. List (2007), 'Using *ex ante* approaches to obtain credible signals for value in contingent markets: evidence from the field', *American Journal of Agricultural Economics*, **89** (2), 420–29.
List, J.A. and C.A. Gallet (2001), 'What experiential protocol influence disparities between actual and hypothetical stated values: evidence from a meta analysis', *Environmental and Resource Economics*, **20** (3), 251–4.
Little, J. and R. Berrens (2004), 'Explaining disparities between actual and hypothetical stated values: further investigations using meta analysis', *Economics Bulletin*, **3** (6), 1–13.
Murphy, J.J., P.G. Allen, T.H. Stevens and D. Weatherhead (2005), 'A meta-analysis of hypothetical bias in stated preference valuation', *Environmental and Resource Economics*, **30** (3), 313–25.
Murphy, J.J. and T.H. Stevens (2004), 'Contingent valuation, hypothetical bias, and experimental economics', *Agricultural and Resource Economics Review*, **33** (2), 182–92.

Opaluch, J.J. and K. Segerson (1989), 'Rational roots of "irrational" behavior: new theories of economic decision-making', *Northeastern Journal of Agricultural and Resource Economics Review*, **18** (2), 81–95.

Poe, G.L., J.E. Clark, D. Rondeau and W.D. Schulze (2002), 'Provision point mechanisms and field validity tests of contingent valuation', *Environmental and Resource Economics*, **23** (1), 105–31.

Ready, R.C., J.C. Whitehead and G.C. Blomquist (1995), 'Contingent valuation when respondents are ambivalent', *Journal of Environmental Economics and Management*, **29** (2), 181–6.

Satterthwaite, M. (1975), 'Strategy-proofness and arrow conditions: existence and correspondence theorems for voting procedures and welfare functions', *Journal of Economic Theory*, **10** (2), 187–217.

Smith, V.L. (1976), 'Experimental economics: induced value theory', *American Economic Review*, **66** (2), 274–9.

Taylor, L.O., M. McKee, S.K. Laury and R.G. Cummings (2001), 'Induced-value tests of the referendum voting mechanism', *Economics Letters*, **71**, 61–5.

Vossler, C.A. and M. McKee (2006), 'Induced value tests of contingent valuation elicitation mechanisms', *Environmental and Resource Economics*, **35**, 137–68.

Vossler, C.A. and M.F. Evans (2010), 'Bridging the gap between the field and the lab: environmental goods, policy maker input, and consequentiality', *Journal of Environmental Economics and Management*, **58** (3), 338–45.

8 Decision versus experienced utility: an investigation using the choice experiment method

Dugald Tinch, Sergio Colombo and Nick Hanley[1]

EMPIRICAL CONTEXT

The upland areas of the UK are replete with rich and varied landscapes. Few of these are 'wild' landscapes; most are managed in some way, and can at best be described as semi-natural. Management is vital for maintaining these semi-natural upland landscapes. However, many land management practices, and in particular agricultural activity, are currently uneconomic, making a loss net of subsidy payments (Peak District Rural Deprivation Forum, 2004). Therefore, the maintenance of landscape quality is at least in part dependent upon funding from agri-environmental schemes. An analysis of preferences for upland management intensity is therefore indicated as it provides a useful tool for analysis of appropriate agri-environmental policies from an economic efficiency standpoint.

In his seminal 1967 paper on non-use values, Krutilla identified landscape quality as being an important source of utility for individuals, making up a significant part of 'real income'. This, he suggested, argued for an increase in attempts to value the environment. There has been much research on the topic of environmental resources since Krutilla wrote his article but the central tenet, that environmental goods should be considered in the decision-making process as they have significant value, remains the same. Given that government spending decisions are increasingly being made on a cost–benefits basis there is a further requirement that environmental goods are quantified in such a way as to be included in this structure, that is, a monetary value of the benefits be calculated. For these reasons environmental valuation, while at times flawed and inaccurate, has become central to the decision-making process to the extent that major rural policies such as the Water Framework Directive now require that social costs and benefits be considered (Hanley and Barbier, 2009).

Current policy involves expenditure on the management of the UK uplands through agri-environmental schemes, which provide additional financial support to farmers in return for undertakings regarding management actions thought to lead to an increased supply of public, environmental goods. In this chapter, we use choice experiments to measure the benefits (or costs) of potential changes in public good supply in the uplands in the future, using different approaches to the measurement of underlying utility change.

DECISION VERSUS EXPERIENCED UTILITY

In recent years, Daniel Kahneman and others have called for the Benthamite (Bentham, 1789) approach to utility to become central to economics again. Kahneman and Sugden (2005) note that nineteenth-century economics employed a concept of hedonic utility based on an absolute measure of pleasure and pain. Bentham argued that utility, which he identified as the amount of pleasure or pain associated with an event, was quantifiable and additive. He related levels of utility to the drivers of probability, intensity, duration and extent. Edgeworth (1879) referred to absolute measures of pleasure and pain from which overall happiness measures should be calculated over some time period. The idea of utility as a momentary measure of hedonic experience has become referred to as *experienced utility*. However, as Kahneman and Sugden (2005) point out, economics retreated from this concept of utility around the end of the nineteenth century. Later economists argued that utility could only be measured by backward induction from observed behaviour (the notion of revealed preference). Marshall (1920) stated that quantification of desires or their outcomes was impossible (bk 3, ch. 3, para. 2). Utility became viewed as something which indexed the preferences of individuals and explained how they chose (thus the term *decision utility*), and therefore could be interpreted in a positive manner, in contrast to the normative concept of experienced utility. However, Kahneman and others have argued, based upon insights from behavioural economics and psychology, that this (now traditional) Marshallian approach to utility is flawed and that a return to the ideology of Bentham was one approach to deal with the issues of a reliance upon decision utility which is not supported by observed behaviour (Kahneman et al., 1997). Examples of this literature include Kahneman and Thaler (2006), Bateman et al. (2000), Tversky et al. (2000), Kahneman (2003), Kahneman and Sugden (2005), Loomes (2006) and Beshears et al. (2008). Such an approach is called for, they argue, as 'anomalies' in individual behaviour mean that the idea of individual rationality within a decision utility context seems a shaky foundation on which to build public policy analysis through, for example, the use of stated preference methods (Hanley and Shogren, 2005).

Kahneman and others' normative approach to consideration of utility is that 'instant utility' gives a measure of the utility (pleasure or pain) we are experiencing at any moment. A summation of instant utility gives us a measure of 'experienced utility' for a given period of time. Either concept may be measured in a number of ways, including the experience sampling method (Stone et al., 1999), and the day reconstruction method (Kahneman et al., 2004).

However, most economic analysis of the past 100 years has made use of the concept of decision utility (Kahneman and Sugden, 2005), even though observed behaviour consumption choices are based upon the anticipation of utility gained. For decision- and experienced-utility measures to be equivalent, individuals must be affective forecasters, accurately predicting the consequences of their actions in terms of the consequences for their well-being. A growing body of research would suggest this is not the case (Kahneman et al., 1999; Gilbert and Ebert, 2002; Gilbert et al., 2004). For example, Dunn et al. (2003) find errors in how much happier students think they will be if they succeed in their preferred choice of university accommodation. Reasons for divergence between predicted well-being, and actual well-being, once experienced, include a failure of affective forecasting (the ability of people to correctly anticipate the consequences of events on their well-being in future states), adaptation to changes over time in the absolute level of consumption, and focusing effects. Kahneman and Sugden (2005) suggest that experienced utility may be a more appropriate measure upon which to base economic policy evaluation than the standard economic concept of decision utility, since the problems of affective forecasting means that people's *ex ante* choices or preferences may be biased indicators of actual well-being. They, however, accept that the measurement of experienced utility is difficult. Moreover, based on findings reported in Dunn et al. (2003), we might expect the relationships between variables thought to determine the satisfaction of certain outcomes and a measure of such satisfaction or well-being to differ according to whether people are making predictions about how a particular choice will impact on their well-being in the future, relative to how a choice actually impacts on their well-being as measured at the moment of consumption. Dunn et al. (2003) found that the factors explaining predicted happiness from choice of housing were different to those explaining variations in actual reported happiness after housing had been allocated.

Two particular issues arise from the literature which are relevant to distinctions between valuation exercises based on experienced rather than decision utility. These are the ideas of adaptation and representative moments. The idea of an adaptation level was first proposed by Helson (1964) and extended by Scitovsky (1976). An alternative view point with similar implications is that of projection bias (Loewenstein et al., 2003). In summary, the issue is that the overall satisfaction individuals anticipate from a particular outcome or situation tends not to equate to the final satisfaction they report once a change has occurred. For instance, individuals get used to a new situation (such as higher disposable income), and factor this into their measures of well-being. Well-being increases due to rising incomes are thus temporary. This has been referred to as the 'hedonic treadmill' (Brickman and Campbell, 1971). Several examples are provided in Kahneman and Sugden (2005).

However, not all goods or experiences are susceptible to similar degrees of adaptation. Scitovsky (1976) identified two types of goods, *pleasures* and *comforts.* Pleasures are goods to which individuals do not adapt, the suggestion being that consumption should concentrate on pleasures (that is, goods to which one will not adapt) as buying comforts is a waste of money. However, this leaves a question of how one goes about distinguishing between comforts and pleasures in making 'purchase' decisions. In the context of this chapter, Kahneman and Sugden (2005) note that it is unlikely that individuals adapt to beautiful landscapes which may suggest that household expenditure on non-market environmental resources is a valuable way to increase utility. However, the overall point remains that experienced utility may differ from decision utility, owing to adaptation.

A second issue concerns possible differences between momentary measures of well-being and remembered measures. Redelmeier and Kahneman (1996) identified that there was a benefit associated with extending the length of colonoscopies since a period of lesser discomfort at the end of the treatment increased patients' willingness to undergo additional treatments. This was explained by individuals placing additional emphasis on the last moments of an experience when that experience is remembered, rather than on average or cumulative measures of experience. Work on pleasurable experiences reported in Do et al. (2008) suggest that intensity of pleasure is more important than length of experience, and that addition of less positive (but still positive) experience could reduce overall utility even if it increased total worth of the experience. Given these factors it is likely that experienced utility will vary according to when it is measured.

The above arguments suggest that measures of welfare (in our case, willingness to pay) based on experienced utility should differ from those based on decision utility, and that welfare measures elicited at the 'moment of consumption' will differ from those elicited based on the memory of that experience. In this chapter, we attempt to compare decision utility-based measures of economic value for upland landscapes with a number of measures of value based on experienced utility. Our interest is in whether decision utility-based measures are equivalent to experienced utility based measures, and also in how these experienced-based measures evolve over time.

STUDY AREA AND DESIGN

The Peak District National Park lies within an hour's drive of a third of the UK's population. As a multifunctional, semi-natural upland landscape it is valuable because of the ecosystem services which it provides. A particular focus for this research was the impact of management change on recreational use, non-use and biodiversity values of the area. Management intensity changes can impact upon other ecosystem functions, in particular water quality, flood protection and revenues from consumptive recreational use such as grouse hunting. However, these were specifically not included in the experimental design. We focused on the values of changes in ecosystems to individuals living near, but not within, the Peak District National Park itself (for reasons that will become apparent). The choice experiments were applied through a workshop approach (Alvarez-Farizo and Hanley, 2006) with three locations being chosen for sampling as representative of the local area. Individuals were chosen who lived relatively close to the workshop locations through mail shots, telephone calls, leaflet drops and advertisements in local shops. The choice of locations was constrained by the need to be close to a site in the Peak District National Park which contained landscapes representative of the management intensities being considered. The communities chosen for recruiting participants were Stannington, a large village on the outskirts of Sheffield; Stocksbridge, a former steel and mining town; and Penistone, a market town. The site chosen for the second experimental treatment (experienced utility) was on the Strines Moor Road, selected because it gave views of all relevant representative land management regimes. Participants were paid £25 for participation in the first workshop and £50 for participation in a second workshop. In total 52 participants took part. Workshops were run in October 2007 and January 2008.

It was necessary to ask participants to complete a large number of choice cards. However, respondent fatigue[2] was identified as a possibility and participants were encouraged throughout to consider carefully every choice they were making. From observations at the time of the experiment it was clear that most if not all of the participants were paying attention to each choice and referencing the additional material provided at regular intervals. As each of the experiments contained 16 choice cards, this gave in the region of 800 choices for each experiment upon which to run analysis.

The choice experiment was developed with colleagues from the Department of Animal and Plant Sciences Sheffield University who provided inputs on the likely impacts of management change on the Peak District National Park. This information was based upon data collected and experience developed through a wider project investigating the likely impacts of changes to agri-environmental schemes on management practices and the resultant impacts on bird species diversity. In order to simplify the experiment, a series of ranking exercises were run in a pilot study. The ranking exercise allowed two candidate attributes, sheep numbers and employment, to be dropped as explicit factors of the experiment, although they were included in the information given to participants. All policies under consideration were changes to agri-environmental schemes to reduce or increase management intensity, but not to abandon farmland. In relation to biodiversity impacts, respondents were told that less intensive management would lead to a greater variety of habitats and species. It was made clear to participants that more species did not mean a greater number of total birds, or any greater chance of seeing birds.

CHOICE EXPERIMENT ATTRIBUTES

The choice experiment included five choice attributes: intensity of management in three habitat areas – moorland, moorland fringe and valley bottom farmland; footpath network quality; and annual household tax increases. These attributes were explained to respondents at the start of treatment 1.

Moorland management intensity was set at three possible levels (More intensive, No change in intensity, Less intensive). The intensity of management on the moorland areas currently varies across the national park. More intensive moorland management was represented by increased numbers of sheep and moorland burning. Burning of moorland encourages young shoots to grow which also leads to increased numbers of grouse for shooting. Less intensive management was depicted as having the opposite impacts. Representative moorland bird species selected to be shown to respondents in the survey materials were: the golden plover (*pluvialis apricaria*), merlin (*falco columbarius*), dunlin (*calidris alpine*) and short-eared owl (*asio flammeus*).

Moorland fringe management intensity also took three levels (More intensive, No change in intensity, Less intensive). More intensively managed moorland fringe can basically become resemblant of farmland, with sufficient fertilizer input producing lush green fields, additionally increased sheep numbers would be present. Less intensive management leads to more scrubby appearance with occasional shrub-like plants. The moorland fringe area is relatively important for biodiversity since it is a transitional zone providing resources to both moorland and farmland species in addition to habitat specific and generalist species. Representative moorland fringe bird species used were: the reed bunting (*emberiza schoeniclus*), stone chat (*saxicola torquata*), wheatear (*oenanthe oenanthe*) and lapwing (*vanellus vanellus*).

Valley bottom farmland management intensity – three levels were again used (More intensive, No change in intensity, Less intensive). These valley bottom farmlands in the Peaks are the 'traditional' green fields of the English countryside, found in the Peak District at lower altitudes bordered by dry stone walls. More intensive management results in greener fields with more sheep, with less intensive management having the opposite impact. It was made clear that field boundaries and buildings would continue to be maintained whatever the management regime adopted. Representative bird species used were the yellow hammer (*emberiza citrinella*), linnet (*carduelis cannabina*), redstart (*phoenicurus phoenicurus*) and pied flycatcher (*ficedula hypoleuca*).

Footpath network quality also took three levels (Improved, No change, Degraded). The quality of the footpath network with a degraded state was represented by an increase in the length of footpaths with more degraded sections (eroded and muddy) and an improvement represented by an increase in the number of paths managed to prevent degradation.

Tax – six levels were selected based on average council tax in the areas, shown as additional tax burden to the household per year.

A business-as-usual baseline based upon likely future levels was adopted. Estimates of the impacts on the park, if no additional money is made available, identify the likelihood of an increased management intensity in all areas and a degradation of the footpath network. As such the 'do nothing' (zero cost) option available to participants for every choice-set presented was increased management intensity of all landscape areas (moorland, moorland fringe and farmland), a worsened footpath network and zero additional tax cost. The choices this was set against were developed using a fractional factorial orthogonal design, with two alternative choices being presented on each choice card (see Table 8.1 for a sample choice card).

Additional verbal information was given at the start of each workshop, detailing the information presented above, and individuals were encouraged to ask questions in order to clarify the information they had

Table 8.1   Sample choice card

	A	B	Do nothing
Moorland – intensity of management	Less intensive – less sheep and burning. More bird species	No change in intensity	More intensive – more sheep and burning
Moorland fringe – intensity of management	Less intensive – less sheep and burning. More bird species	Less intensive – less sheep and burning. More bird species	More intensive – more sheep, fertilizer and drainage
Valley bottom farmland – intensity of management	No change in intensity	Less intensive – less sheep and fertilizer. More bird species	More intensive – more sheep and fertilizer
Footpath network	Improved	Degraded	Degraded
Tax cost	£5	£55	£0
Please tick the option you prefer.			

received. In order that participants were familiar with the process involved in making a choice, a series of practice sample choices were presented and explained prior to undertaking the first choice tasks.

RESULTS

Initial analysis of results was conducted using a multinomial logit specification. Some models, however, failed the Hausman test for independence of irrelevant alternatives (IIA), so an alternative specification was sought. It was found that both the nested logit model and error component model provided good model fit, and that model specification did not alter the sign (or relative size) of the coefficients. The error component model is in essence an evolution of the nested logit model and the results of this specification are presented here (although the results with either specification were essentially the same). The error component model allows flexible patterns of substitution via an induced correlation across utilities which relaxes the identically and independently distributed (IID) assumption of the multinomial logit specification.

It is important to note that the results presented below are derived from the same participants responding to the same choices in repeated experiments. Standard theory would suggest that any differences in preference estimates which arise across sessions would be due to either increased information or learning with respect to task complexity. For a learning effect to exist, then a change in estimated preferences would be expected between treatment 1 and treatment 2, but not between treatment 2 and treatment 3.

Treatment 1 (decision utility) gives our baseline estimate of willingness to pay for different levels of management of the Peak District National Park; this experiment was run in a local hall prior to the visit to the national park. This treatment represents the value estimated in most choice experiments (and other stated preference techniques), since it is based on information given to participants through description, visual images and orally. It is not, however, provided at the 'point of consumption'.

Treatment 2 (experienced utility) aims to identify the impact of the moment of experience of landscape on values, and was conducted on site where a representative series of landscapes could be seen. Participants were driven to the park and shown the landscape characteristics which they were valuing in the choice experiment. Individuals could identify the impacts of management changes without needing to rely on their own anticipation of changes and (to some extent) anticipation of adaptation to landscape changes. Participants were shown landscape features characteristic of each proposed level for each attribute, and were asked to identify those features relevant to the combinations presented in the choice before them. The only landscape type not visible at this stage was a freshly burnt heather moorland but this landscape had been identified to participants one or two minutes prior to arrival on site and a second year[3] burnt area was visible from the selected site.

The two adjacent fields[4] to the site involved intensive and extensive moorland fringe management practices whilst areas of intensively and extensively managed moorland backed onto these fields. Below the site was a panorama showing intensive and extensive management of farmland rising across the valley to additional examples of moorland fringe and moorland management. There was a steep area adjacent to the site which displayed a dominance of fern species which was used as an example of the possible management actions being required to prevent fern dominance under certain management alternatives.

The third treatment (remembered 1) was conducted upon return to the village hall on the same day as the site visit. The fourth treatment (remembered 2) was administered during a second workshop held four months after the first.

Table 8.2 shows estimate coefficients for each treatment, Table 8.3 identifies the coding used and Table 8.4 shows implicit prices calculated

Table 8.2 *Error component logit model coefficients for each treatment (coefficients found to be statistically significant at the 95 per cent level are indicated in bold)*

Treatment	Decision		Experienced		Remembered 1		Remembered 2	
	Coef.	*S.e.*	*Coef.*	*S.e.*	*Coef.*	*S.e.*	*Coef.*	*S.e.*
Mean values								
Const	**−1.538**	0.628	−0.854	0.692	−0.837	0.617	**−1.533**	0.693
MoorLI	−0.066	0.167	**−0.454**	0.179	−0.081	0.164	−0.137	0.260
MoorMI	**−0.820**	0.230	**−0.441**	0.195	**−0.606**	0.231	**−0.994**	0.333
FringeLI	**−0.552**	0.176	**−0.584**	0.218	−0.270	0.157	−0.442	0.240
FringeMI	−0.245	0.174	−0.147	0.173	−0.292	0.218	−0.210	0.259
FarmLI	**−0.778**	0.188	−0.342	0.206	−0.432	0.237	**−0.839**	0.246
FarmMI	**−1.135**	0.210	**−0.576**	0.206	**−0.744**	0.266	**−1.121**	0.323
PathD	**0.337**	0.134	0.175	0.154	**0.336**	0.138	0.151	0.177
PathI	**0.469**	0.212	−0.015	0.212	0.415	0.265	0.310	0.300
TAX	**−0.013**	0.001	**−0.013**	0.001	**−0.013**	0.001	**−0.014**	0.001
INCOME	−0.017	0.015	−0.020	0.015	−0.019	0.015	−0.018	0.015
FEMALE	**2.369**	0.462	**2.354**	0.456	**2.367**	0.458	**2.379**	0.457
LOCAL	−0.299	0.473	−0.275	0.454	−0.273	0.459	−0.304	0.483
NA	0.246	0.305	0.289	0.304	0.246	0.301	0.270	0.308
NC	−0.170	0.204	−0.147	0.198	−0.169	0.200	−0.146	0.204
OM	0.845	0.547	0.819	0.544	0.856	0.554	0.845	0.555
AGE	**0.035**	0.011	**0.033**	0.011	**0.033**	0.011	**0.033**	0.011
Error component								
Sigma	**2.590**	0.203	**2.554**	0.198	**2.572**	0.201	**2.587**	0.202
Pseudo R^2	0.22		0.22		0.22		0.22	

for each treatment. It should be noted that it is not possible to compare coefficient estimates across different choice models as they are scaled with an unknown scale parameter. To compare across coefficient estimates is equivalent to setting the scale parameter equal to 1 which assumes that all individuals have the same scale parameter, however it is possible to compare across willingness-to-pay (WTP) since the scale parameter cancels out of the implicit price calculations (Scarpa et al. 2008).

It is interesting to note that all significant management change WTPs are negative. The analysis calculates a shift away from the current management system (no change in management intensity) however this was not the zero cost option presented to participants. The results suggest that individuals are willing to pay in order to avoid a future level of management which is more intensive in character, except in the moorland fringe area where the estimate is never significant. This is perhaps down to the

Table 8.3   Explanation of variable abbreviations and coding in Table 8.2

Const	Constant term (= 0 for baseline zero cost, = 1 for option A or B)
MoorLI	Shift to less intensive moorland management
MoorMI	Shift to more intensive moorland management
FringeLI	Shift to less intensive moorland fringe management
FringeMI	Shift to more intensive moorland fringe management
FarmLI	Shift to less intensive valley bottom farmland management
FarmMI	Shift to more intensive valley bottom farmland management
PathD	Degraded footpath network
PathI	Improved footpath network
TAX	Tax increase to the household indicated in pounds
INCOME	Household income
FEMALE	Gender (Female = 1, Male = 0)
LOCAL	Whether respondent considers themselves as a local of the national park (Yes = 1, No = 0)
NA	Number of adults in the household
NC	Number of children in the household
OM	Whether other household member is a recreational user of the national park (Yes = 1, No = 0)
AGE	Respondent's age in years

Table 8.4   WTP for a change from the current level of provision

Variable	Predicted	Experienced	Remembered 1	Remembered 2
Moor LI	−£4.88	−£36.43	−£6.13	−£9.95
	(£12.40) (NS)	(£14.54)**	(£12.45) (NS)	(£18.80)(NS)
Moor MI	−£60.93	−£35.34	−£45.81	−£71.95
	(£17.45)***	(£15.85)**	(£17.67)***	(£24.65)***
Fringe LI	−£41.05	−£46.85	−£20.39	−£32.00
	(£13.31)***	(£17.96)***	(£11.94)*	(£17.41)*
Fringe MI	−£18.24	−£11.77	−£22.03	−£15.18
	(£13.03) (NS)	(£13.92) (NS)	(£16.67) (NS)	(£18.83)(NS)
Farm LI	−£57.80	−£27.46	−£32.62	−£60.74
	(£14.92)***	(£16.84) (NS)	(£18.40)*	(£18.49)***
Farm MI	−£84.34	−£46.15	−£56.25	−£81.14
	(£16.48)***	(£21.73)**	(£20.48)***	(£23.45)***
Path degraded	£25.07	£14.00	£25.43	£10.95
	(£10.46)**	(£12.57) (NS)	(£11.01)**	(£12.89)(NS)
Path improved	£34.87	−£1.21	£31.33	£22.43
	(£15.95)**	(£17.00) (NS)	(£20.15)(NS)	(£21.67)(NS)

Note: Figures in brackets are standard errors, *** = significant at the 99 per cent level, ** = 95 per cent, * = 90 per cent.

nature of fringe areas as transitional habitats which through more intensive management can be made to resemble farmland. Additionally, individuals are also willing to pay (in general) to avoid a less intensive management regime in the habitats, although this is not significant for moorland habitats, with the exception of the second experiment. The implication for policy is that in the case of locals living close to the national park there appears to be a significant status quo preference. Individuals living near the national park would be willing to pay in order to maintain the current levels of management intensity. Also it is perhaps worth noting that the number of significant estimates is highest in the first treatment. Once experience of the landscape has occurred, some attributes lose significance for the rest of the experiment. This may suggest a prominence effect or could be seen as an indicator of a focusing effect in the first experiment which was mitigated by experience.

It can be seen from the results that experience and memory appear to have an impact on the WTP for landscape management change and the significance of variables. Owing to a relatively low sample size and the resultant standard errors, it is not clear in statistical terms whether the change in estimates between experiments are significant. However, there is a distinct trend in estimated coefficients between the treatments: willingness to pay is typically high in treatment 1, falls in treatment 2 and then rises again. The trend in means between experiment 1 and 2 does not continue into experiments 3 and 4, which shows that a learning effect is unlikely to be having a major impact on results, since otherwise we would expect the means in treatment 3 to be very close to those in treatment 2 (no new information was available between these treatments).

Treatment 1 – Decision Utility

Individuals have the highest WTP to avoid more intensive management in the moorland areas and value bottom farmland habitats. This is perhaps unsurprising as while valley bottom farmland makes up a relatively small proportion of the park (as opposed to moorland habitats) most roads in the park run through valley bottoms and this landscape is seen from representative images presented of the national park on tourism websites to be archetypal of the Peak District National Park.

Treatment 2 – Experienced Utility

The results of the second treatment show the value associated with WTP for maintenance of the current management level falling, with the exception of less intensive management of moorland and fringe habitats.

Picking out the values associated with more intensive moorland and farmland habitats the mean WTP values fell by 42 per cent and 45 per cent respectively. Although a statistically significant trend cannot be identified, due in part to the small sample size, there appears to be a trend none the less: willingness-to-pay amounts are lowest when using the experienced utility concept to measure values.

Treatments 3 and 4 – Remembered Utility

So what of the impact of memory? With the exception of less intensive fringe management, all WTP for management variables increase in terms of preference for current management levels in the third treatment. By the fourth treatment these mean WTP estimates have returned to essentially the same level as in the first treatment, again with the exception of non-significant estimates and less intensive management of moorland fringe habitats.

One unexpected result is the positive value associated with a degraded footpath network. At first it was difficult to determine why such a result would be found. However, upon re-analysis of the individuals involved in this survey it was noted that participants chosen were non-users of the national park despite their close proximity. It could be concluded that these individuals see the footpath network, among other attributes, as what attracts visitors to the national park. Given that a relatively small area is one of the most visited national parks in the UK, indeed it is claimed to be the second most visited national park in the world, visitation rate must have a significant impact on those living in proximity to the park and reliant upon the trunk roads running through the park for daily access to resources. Congestion in the park has been identified as significant during periods of peak visitation (the idea of the first rural congestion charge was put forward for the Peak District in 2004). It is possible that those living on the boundaries of the park identify elements of park management which increase visitation (and that they make no use of) as having a negative impact upon their own utility due to vehicular congestion caused by sight-seeing tourists. The alternative explanation is that, despite significant effort on the part of the researchers, during the experimental design the dominance of management variables over footpath network variables was not avoided.

A range of socio-economic factors were included in the analysis. Sex and age, however, were the only characteristics significant in any models (and were significant in all treatments). These suggest that women in particular, and to a lesser extent older individuals, are more likely to choose either option A or B over the status quo.

CONCLUSIONS

The proposition of the New Benthamites such as Kahneman is that the moment of experience impacts on the utility associated with consumption. They suggest that individuals are inefficient in determining utility maximizing consumption behaviour *ex ante*, as they are poor at forecasting the utility that will be experienced from a decision. They propose that an analysis of experienced utility gives a better measure of happiness than one based on decision utility. Experienced utility is put forward as a preferable basis for assessing the public values of changes in environmental goods (although not, it should be admitted, by asking people their willingness to pay for changes in experienced utility).

This chapter aims to identify if the moment of experience impacts on individual's preferences for environmental goods, such that environmental values differ according to which concept or utility is used: *ex ante* decision utility, or 'moment of consumption' experienced utility. Additionally, we examine the effects of memory on willingness to pay. It was not possible to make definitive statements about the changes in preferences between treatments due to a relatively small sample size and the possibility of divergent preferences between participants, resulting in relatively high standard errors. There appears to be consistency in the results found between an initial WTP (first treatment) and a final (fourth treatment) WTP, which to all intents and purposes remained the same. Memory leads to a shift in mean willingness to pay to an intermediary level between the second and third treatments in the short term and between the third and fourth treatments in the longer term. In our case, this seems to mitigate the impact of experience altogether. The one exception is in the value associated with less intensive moorland fringe habitats. These are probably the most unfamiliar habitats to the average person on the street. The implication is that where there is limited prior exposure to an environmental good, experience can alter long-term preferences, while familiar attributes are valued similarly in both 'decision utility' and 'remembered utility' terms.

We noted the finding by Dunn et al. (2003) that the relationships between possible determinants of well-being and a measure of such satisfaction or well-being are likely to differ according to whether people are making predictions about how a particular choice will impact on their well-being, or whether their well-being is measured at the moment of consumption. This would suggest that the estimated parameters relating choices to landscape attribute levels should vary across treatments 1 and 2. However, we find relatively little evidence to support this finding, based on the results reported in Table 8.2.

Finally, we note that we have not controlled for changes in information which individuals hold between treatments 3 and 4: individuals may have been exposed to many more environmental 'good causes' or learnt more about the Peak District in the period between the sessions, which caused them to revise their preferences or attitudes. Both additional information and 'time to think' have been shown to change WTP in other workshop approaches to environmental valuation (MacMillan et al., 2003, 2006).

One question which is raised from the research is whether the fourth (remembered utility) and first (decision utility) treatments are relatively similar because the initial level is based upon remembered experience prior to the workshop; whether over time the impact of experience is negated and an individual's preferences returns to the same level; or whether the level with no experience of the landscape (in terms of the questions being asked) is by chance convergent with a fully informed remembered level of WTP. We also note that while the values obtained in treatment 2 are at the 'point of consumption' in terms of the levels of each attribute in the choice experiment, they do not relate to real outcomes where individuals have paid a higher tax, and then waited for different environmental qualities to emerge. In this sense, our measures based on experienced utility are not really equivalent to what Kahneman advocates in his experience sampling or day reconstruction approaches, since we are still dealing with hypothetical choices, even if the context is real. Behavioural psychologists might thus find problems with our approach.

In terms of policy implications, Loomes (2006) and Kahneman and Sugden (2005) note that experienced utility does not necessarily give results consistent with the dynamics of the decision-making process. Decision at the landscape scale are made at a governmental level, and assuming that the government aims to provide socially optimal levels of public goods, then preferences of individuals (once identified) should inform policy. But the measure of utility which is most relevant in terms of winning votes is decision utility. This will be the value in an individual's mind at the time of voting. Loomes (2006) suggests that this may lead to a policy which makes people better off in the long term not being implemented as it is not a 'recipe for electoral success' (p. 734).

NOTES

1. We thank the Economic and Social Research Council and the Natural Environment Research Council for funding this work under the 'Rural Environment and Land Use' research programme.
2. Risk of invalid response due to excessive demands being placed upon the research participants.
3. Assuming the burn took place in autumn the previous year, although it may have taken

place in the same or previous year as an early season burn. However, it was clearly not a new burn.

4. While field seems the most appropriate term in respect to moorland fringe this is not agricultural land in the same way as the valley bottom area. However, boundaries are present – for ownership demarcation or stock management.

REFERENCES

Alvarez-Farizo, B. and N. Hanley (2006), 'Improving the process of valuing non-market benefits: combining citizens' juries with choice modelling', *Land Economics*, **82** (3), 465–78.

Bateman, I., A. Munro, B. Rhodes, C. Starmer and R. Sugden (2000), 'A test of the theory of reference-dependent preferences' in D. Kahneman and A. Tversky (eds), *Choices, Values and Frames,* Cambridge: Cambridge University Press, pp. 180–201.

Bentham, J. (1789), *An Introduction to the Principles of Morals and Legislation*, available at: http://www.econlib.org/library/Bentham/bnthPML2.htm (accessed February 2010).

Beshears, J., J.J. Choi, D. Laibson and B.C. Madrian (2008), 'How are preferences revealed?', *Journal of Public Economics*, **92**, 1787–94.

Brickman, P. and D. Campbell (1971), 'Hedonic relativism and planning the good society', in M.H. Apley (ed.), *Adaptation Level Theory: A Symposium*, New York: Academic Press, pp. 287–302.

Do, A.M., A.V. Rupert and G. Wolford (2008), 'Evaluation of pleasurable experiences: the peak – end rule', *Psychonomic Bulletin and Review*, **15** (1), 96–8.

Dunn, E., D. Gilbert and T. Wilson (2003), 'Location, location, location: the misprediction of satisfaction in housing lotteries', *Personality and Social Psychology Bulletin*, **29** (11), 1421–32.

Edgeworth, F.Y. (1879), 'The hedonical calculus', *Mind*, **4** (15), 394–408.

Gilbert, D.T. and J.E.J. Ebert (2002), 'Decisions and revisions: the affective forecasting of changeable outcomes', *Journal of Personality and Social Psychology*, **82**, 503–14.

Gilbert, D.T., M.D. Lieberman, C.K. Morewedge and T.D. Wilson (2004), 'The peculiar longevity of things not so bad', *Psychological Science*, **15**, 14–19.

Hanley, N. and E. Barbier (2009), *Pricing Nature: Cost–Benefit Analysis and Environmental Policy*, Cheltenham, UK and Northampton, MA, USA: Edward Elgar.

Hanley, N. and J. Shogren (2005), 'Is cost–benefit analysis anomaly-proof?', *Environmental and Resource Economics*, **32** (1), 13–34.

Helson, H. (1964), *Adaptation-Level Theory: An Experimental and Systematic Approach to Behavior*, New York: Harper and Row. s

Kahneman, D. (2003), 'Maps of bounded rationality: psychology for behavioural economics', *The American Economic Review*, **93** (5), 1449–75.

Kahneman, D. and R. Sugden (2005), 'Experienced utility as a standard of policy design', *Environmental and Resource Economics*, **32**, 161–81.

Kahneman, D. and R. Thaler (2006), 'Anomalies: utility maximisation and experienced utility', *Journal of Economic Perspectives*, **20** (1), 221–34.

Kahneman, D. and A. Tversky (2000), 'Choices, values and frames', in D. Kahneman and A. Tversky (eds), *Choices, Values and Frames*, Cambridge: Cambridge University Press, pp. 17–43.

Kahneman, D., A. Kreuger, D. Schkade, N. Schwarz and A. Stone (2004), 'A survey method for characterizing daily life experience: the day reconstruction method', *Science*, **306**, 1776–80.

Kahneman, D., I. Ritov and D. Schkade (1999), 'Economic preferences or attitude expressions? An analysis of dollar responses to public issues', *Journal of Risk and Uncertainty*, **19** (1–3), 203–35.

Kahneman, D., R. Sarin and P. Wakker (1997), 'Back to Bentham? Explorations of experienced utility', *Quarterly Journal of Economics*, **112** (2), 375–405.

Krutilla, J.V. (1967), 'Conservation re-considered', *American Economic Review*, **47**, 777–86.
Loewenstein, G., T. O'Donoghue and M. Rabin (2003), 'Projection bias in predicting future utility', *The Quarterly Journal of Economics*, **118** (4), 1209–48.
Loomes, G. (2006), '(How) Can we value health, safety and the environment', *Journal of Economic Psychology*, **27** (6), 713–36.
MacMillan, D., N. Hanley and N. Lienhoop (2006), 'Contingent valuation: environmental polling or preference engine?', *Ecological Economics*, **60** (1), 299–307.
MacMillan, D., L. Philip, N. Hanley and B. Alvarez-Farizo (2003) 'Valuing non-market benefits of wild goose conservation: a comparison of interview and group-based approaches', *Ecological Economics*, **43**, 49–59.
Marshall, A. (1920), *Principles of Economics*, 8th edition, London: Macmillan, available at: http://www.econlib.org/library/Marshall/marP11.htm (accessed January 2010).
Peak District Rural Deprivation Report (2004), *Hard Times*, available at: www.pdrdf.org.uk (accessed January 2010).
Redelmeier, D.A. and D. Kahneman (1996), 'Patients' memories of painful medical treatments: real-time and retrospective evaluations of two minimally invasive procedures', *Pain*, **66**, 3–8.
Scarpa, R., M. Thiene and K. Train (2008), 'Utility in WTP space: a tool to address confounding random scale effects in destination choice to the Alps', *American Journal of Agricultural Economics*, **90**, 994–1010.
Scitovsky, T. (1976), *The Joyless Economy: The Psychology of Human Satisfaction*, Oxford: Oxford University Press.
Stone, A.A., S.S. Shiffman and M. DeVries (1999), 'Rethinking self-report assessment methodologies', in D. Kahneman, E. Diener and N. Schwarz (eds), *Well-Being: The Foundations of Hedonic Psychology*, New York: Cambridge University Press, pp. 26–39.
Tversky, A., S. Sattath and P. Slovic (2000), 'Contingent weighting in judgement and choice', in D. Kahneman and A. Tversky (eds), *Choices, Values and Frames*, Cambridge: Cambridge University Press, pp. 503–17.

9 Bioindicator-based stated preference valuation for aquatic habitat and ecosystem service restoration[1]

Robert J. Johnston, Eric T. Schultz, Kathleen Segerson and Elena Y. Besedin

INTRODUCTION

Because human welfare derived from the restoration of aquatic ecological systems can include non-use components, applications of stated preference (SP) valuation such as choice experiments are often required for comprehensive welfare evaluation. Many recent studies apply SP techniques to assess willingness-to-pay (WTP) for policies that affect the ecology of aquatic systems (for example, Bateman et al., 2006; Birol et al., 2008; Boyer and Polasky, 2004; Do and Bennett, 2009; Flores and Shafran, 2006; Hanley et al., 2006; Holmes et al., 2004; Johnston et al., 2002; Loomis et al., 2000; Milon and Scrogin, 2006; Morrison and Bennett, 2004; Morrison et al., 2002). In these and other studies, the validity of resulting welfare estimates depends on an appropriate integration of ecological and economic information (Johnston et al., 2002).

To date, the integration of ecological information within SP methods has been limited. Despite substantial attention among natural scientists to the properties of ecological indicators used to characterize ecosystem function and change, SP surveys often communicate such information using ecologically ambiguous, ad hoc descriptors. Measures of change in aquatic living resources presented in SP surveys, for example, are rarely developed within the context of established models or formal indicators from the ecological literature, and are frequently based on imprecisely defined measurement units. Common examples in the broader valuation literature include frequent use of terms such as low, medium or high biodiversity (for example, Birol et al., 2008; Carlsson et al., 2003), with little ecological detail supporting such categories. Although representations of ecological change within SP surveys should reflect the cognitive capacity of survey respondents, consistency with ecological science ensures that commodities valued by respondents have precise ecological meaning. The issue is more fundamental than a simplification of complex ecological concepts such as biodiversity so that they may be more easily understood (Christie et al. 2006; Czajkowski et al. 2009). Rather, it concerns a tendency to present ecological concepts at such a high level of abstraction and ambiguity that, at least as presented on the survey page, they may have no clear ecological meaning that can be understood, even by experts.

This chapter introduces a variant of SP valuation designed to address these and other criticisms related to the integration of ecology and economics. This approach, which we call bioindicator-based stated preference valuation (BSPV), is distinguished by guidelines that, among other things, inform the structure and use of ecological indicators to define policy scenarios in valuation surveys. Specifically designed for applications to ecological systems, the guidelines underlying BSPV promote ecological clarity and closer integration of ecological and economic information. The approach begins with a formal basis in ecological science and extends to relationships between attributes in respondents' preference functions and those used to characterize policy outcomes. The resulting welfare measures are designed to be unambiguously linked to models and indicators of ecosystem function, grounded in measurable ecological outcomes, and more easily incorporated into benefit–cost analysis. These methods also provide a means to estimate values for ecological outcomes that individuals might value, even though they may not fully understand all relevant ecological science.

Performance of the developed methods is illustrated through an application to migratory (diadromous) fish passage restoration in a Rhode Island watershed.[2] Results provide sometimes unexpected insights into public preferences for aquatic ecosystem restoration, many of which might be obscured by more traditional stated preference approaches to welfare evaluation. These and other findings suggest that less structured treatments of ecological change within SP surveys can omit information that is both essential for the estimation of nonuse or indirect use values and relevant to respondents when determining WTP.

VALUATION OF ECOLOGICAL RESTORATION: CONCEPTUAL AND THEORETICAL CHALLENGES

Stated preference methods, including choice experiments, use carefully designed surveys to estimate public, often non-market values for well-defined changes in the quantity or quality of a bundle of goods and services. Choice experiments present individuals with an opportunity to select one out of a set of available multi-attribute options or to reject all of the presented options in favour of the status quo (Adamowicz et al., 1998; Louviere et al., 2000). Choice data over many sets of possible choice options, where each option is defined by component attribute levels, enables the probability of choice to be modelled as a function of attribute levels (Bennett and Blamey, 2001).[3] Model results reveal trade-offs made by respondents when choosing over options; respondents' willingness to trade off non-monetary attributes (for example, ecological attributes) for changes in household cost provides the theoretical and empirical basis for WTP estimation.

To yield valid estimates of value, SP surveys and estimation methods must have certain methodological features (Bateman et al., 2002; Bennett and Blamey, 2001; Louviere, 2001; Louviere et al., 2000). For example, individuals can only make well-informed choices if provided with sufficient information (Hanemann, 1994). In the context of ecological protection or restoration, welfare estimates are contingent upon information that allows respondents to predict the expected influence of ecological changes on their welfare (Bergstrom et al., 1990; Bingham et al., 1995). One of the associated challenges in the design of surveys for valuation of aquatic ecosystem restoration is characterization of the condition and change in ecosystem function and related impacts on valued goods and services (Flores and Shafran, 2006).

Within the following discussion, we distinguish between two terms. The term 'attribute' here refers either to an argument in a utility function or to a corresponding element characterizing a stated preference choice option. The term 'ecological indicator,' in contrast, refers to a measure that characterizes, and may be used to communicate, the condition of an ecosystem or one of its components (Jackson et al., 2000).

While not made explicit in most SP studies,[4] ecological change is most often communicated through indicators. That is, ecological indicators – either formal or ad hoc – are often used as attributes in choice experiments. Ecologists have developed numerous indicators such as ecological diversity and integrity indices, among many others, to represent the status and function of natural systems (Bortone, 2005; Davis and Simon, 1995; Jorgensen et al., 2004).[5] Within SP valuation, the role of such indicators is to communicate changes in welfare-relevant qualities or quantities, so that meaningful expressions of value can be elicited (Spash and Hanley, 1995). This ecological information must not only be placed in a format that is readily understood by respondents, but that also provides an accurate representation of the change being valued. As stated by Schiller et al. (2001, p. 19), 'effective communication of ecological indicators involve[s] more than simply transforming scientific phrases into easily comprehensible words. [It requires] language that simultaneously fit[s] within both scientists' and nonscientists' . . . frames of reference, such that resulting indicators [are] at once technically accurate and understandable'.

In contrast to the attention devoted to indicator development and interpretation in the ecological literature, indicators used in SP surveys often lack documented reference to empirical findings regarding ways in which natural systems respond to changes or stresses, and have often limited grounding in prior ecological research. As a result, indicators of ecological change presented in SP surveys: (1) rarely correspond to formal indicators presented in the published ecological literature, (2) are often ambiguously linked to quantifiable policy impacts, (3) are often based on imprecise measurement units, and (4) have often incomplete or ambiguous links to ecosystem goods or services valued by respondents. Among the most common shortcomings are in ecological accuracy and measurability – limitations that can be difficult to avoid given the challenges of ecological prediction and the communication to non-expert respondents. Such challenges are often recognized explicitly and can occur in carefully designed studies that are acknowledged for methodological rigour. Holmes et al. (2004, p. 23), for example, use a good–poor categorical scale of ecosystem service provision to 'obviate problems associated with characterizing an exact change in ecosystem services that could be expected'. Similarly, when describing scenarios used to characterize effects on river ecology, Hanley et al. (2006, p. 186) state, 'none of these attributes are necessarily consistent with what an ecologist would choose in terms of either indicators of the ecological health of a waterbody, or underlying factors driving changes in ecological status: they merely represent the characteristics of "water quality" as perceived by the general public'.

Surveys that provide extensive, ecologically grounded and quantitative characterization of aquatic ecological outcomes are relatively uncommon. Examples include surveys that characterize effects using the number of native species present, a measurable and relatively precise indicator (for example, Do and Bennett, 2009; Morrison and Bennett, 2004). Others report the presence, absence or abundance of indicator species to reflect ecosystem quality or to characterize ordinal scales of biodiversity, ecosystem condition or other policy effects (for example, Bateman et al., 2006; Hanley et al., 2006; Milon and Scrogin, 2006). These mirror approaches found in the ecological literature. Even many of these studies, however, rely on some ecologically imprecise elements to ease information burden on respondents.

Even when well defined ecologically, indicators used in surveys may have incomplete or ambiguous linkages to commodities valued by respondents. For example, SP studies often define policy changes solely in terms of convenient units such as the number of organisms or acres of habitat affected. While descriptions such as these may relate to welfare-relevant attributes in direct or indirect ways, it is unlikely that such characterizations by themselves promote valid expressions of welfare. For example, it is not clear whether, when answering valuation questions of this type, respondents are directly valuing the commodity over which they have preferences. Do respondents care directly about the loss of a specific number of fish, birds or other organisms, or do they instead care about other environmental attributes or outcomes, such as ecosystem condition or biodiversity, and use the number of fish or birds as a proxy for the attributes or outcomes of real concern? In the latter case, respondents might assume ecological production function relationships that do not correspond with those quantified by ecologists. For example, respondents might use presented information on organism numbers, habitat area or iconic species to make speculative inferences regarding other omitted but welfare-relevant ecological attributes (Jacobsen et al., 2008).

A related criticism of SP methods, and economic valuation in general, is that lay individuals might not understand or appreciate fully the ecological importance of certain species or processes, and hence estimated economic values will not reflect the true value of these ecological changes (see, for example, US EPA 2009). This is most likely to be a concern for non-use values or use values for which the implications for use are very indirect, such as values stemming from contributions of microorganisms or insects to soil formation, primary productivity and overall ecological integrity or condition (for example, Nichols et al., 2008; Weslawski et al., 2004).[6] Such contributions are often captured poorly if at all by the types of ecological variables often included in SP studies, such as changes in water quality, acreage of wetlands or habitat, or even species abundance. Unless such contributions can be expressed in terms that survey respondents can understand and value, and that are consistent with ecological science, welfare estimates will not reflect the full range of potential values derived from ecological systems.[7]

Ambiguous correspondence between SP survey attributes and measurable policy impacts can also render welfare estimates of limited use for policy evaluations. Ecological outcomes of policy implementation are quantified – both in *ex ante* predictions and *ex post* evaluations – through effects on measurable outcomes, often called measurement endpoints (US EPA 1998). An emerging literature discusses ways in which these endpoints correspond to well-defined ecosystem services and other valued outputs (Boyd and Banzhaf, 2007). Survey-based valuation, in contrast, often derives welfare estimates as a function of attribute levels that have little or no systematic relationship to measurable outcomes. As noted above, the use of ecologically ambiguous descriptors such as 'unique wildlife habitat', 'high quality groundwater' or 'high biodiversity' is widespread among SP surveys in the literature. A common consequence is that associated welfare estimates cannot be integrated into benefit–cost analyses without ad hoc and often questionable assumptions required to reconcile ecologically ambiguous SP attributes with measurable policy outcomes.[8]

The Theoretical Issue

As with all economic values, WTP estimated using SP methods is contingent upon the information available to respondents – either as provided by the survey or derived from other sources (Bergstrom and Stoll, 1989; Bergstrom et al., 1989; Cameron and Englin, 1997; Hoehn and Randall, 2002). In the view of many ecologists and economists, SP survey instruments often fail to provide sufficient information to enable respondents to understand potential effects of ecological change on welfare (Spash and Hanley, 1995).

In formal neoclassical economic terms, the question regards the content and structure of the utility function. For example, assume that respondent i's utility is of the form $U_i(E(X))$, where $E(\cdot)$ is ecosystem integrity, biodiversity or some other valued ecological outcome and X is the number of migratory fish passing upstream, or some other quantifiable measure. If the respondent cares about X solely because of its impact on $E(\cdot)$, then a valuation question framed solely in terms of X effectively asks the respondent to directly value changes in the *input* rather than changes in the *output* that directly influences utility. This is akin to asking an individual to value a change in the labour or capital that is used in the production of a good or service, rather than a change in the output of the good or service that results from the input change (Boyd and Banzhaf, 2007).

The first implication of this is a potential for bias. A preference function of the form $U_i(E(X))$ can be *mathematically* collapsed to $U_i(X)$. However, if individuals value $E(\cdot)$ directly, the specification of valuation scenarios solely in terms of X will likely lead to biased WTP estimates, because this requires respondents to assume their own (almost certainly incorrect) ecological production function (that is, to assume a relationship between X and E). As noted by Carson (1998, p. 23), '[r]espondents will tend to fill in whatever details are missing in the . . . survey with default assumptions. These may differ considerably from what the researcher perceives'. This is particularly true for ecological resources and functions, for which respondents often have little baseline information (for example, Carson, 1998; Christie et al., 2006; Spash and Hanley, 1995).

The potential for bias is compounded if utility takes a more complex form such as $U_i(E(X), H(X), X)$, where $H(X)$ represents a second valued ecological outcome influenced by X. For example, $H(\cdot)$ might represent expected quality of recreational fishing for non-diadromous species (for example, largemouth bass), where diadromous fish could have a positive $(\partial H(\cdot)/\partial X > 0)$ or negative $(\partial H(\cdot)/\partial X < 0)$ marginal effect on recreational fisheries, depending on ecological relationships.[9] Here, X influences utility directly, as well as indirectly through its influence on both $E(X)$ and $H(X)$. Moreover, the indirect effects may not be universally positive. In this context, appropriate modelling of utility is critical to obtaining understanding and unbiased estimates of values for policies that influence X, $E(X)$ and $H(X)$.

The situation is further complicated if one cannot observe ecological outcomes directly. Assume, for example, that ecologists have developed multimetric indicators of overall ecosystem condition that are designed to proxy for true underlying ecosystem condition, $E(\cdot)$, that we assume influences individuals' well-being. As a simple illustration, assume that the multimetric indicator W is a formal indicator or measure of $E(\cdot)$ developed by ecologists. However, the survey designer, concerned that respondents will not be able to understand W (or unaware of the appropriate ecological literature), instead uses a simplified, ad hoc indicator (for example, high, medium, low), which we denote $\widetilde{W}$. In this case, respondents must infer $E(\cdot)$ based on $\widetilde{W}$. with no provided function or information to make this inference; there is no quantitative relationship between $\widetilde{W}$ and either W or $E(\cdot)$.[10] Hence, the model estimates WTP for a derived indicator, $\widetilde{W}$, which has no formal ecological interpretation or link to measurable policy outcomes.

The remainder of this chapter presents and illustrates the use of a variant of the SP method designed to ameliorate these limitations. In particular, it allows for the incorporation of indicators designed to capture non-use or indirect use values in a manner that is both grounded in the relevant ecological science and able to distinguish among the various ways in which ecological changes influence respondents' welfare.[11]

STRUCTURED USE OF ECOLOGICAL INDICATORS WITHIN STATED PREFERENCE VALUATION

Outcomes of ecological restoration may be measured and represented using ecological indicators developed by natural scientists. Some of these indicators may be simple and direct, such as the use of laser/optical fish counter data to measure the number of fish passing upstream through a fish ladder. Others are more complex, less direct and can require additional interpretation. For example, the ecological literature offers numerous integrative, multimetric indicators that formally assimilate multiple ecosystem components and are widely used as indicators of ecosystem health or condition (for example, Bortone, 2005; Davis and Simon, 1995; Jorgensen et al., 2004). These indicators (for example, Index of Biotic Integrity (IBI) and the Estuarine Biotic Integrity Index (EBI)) are calculated from ecological data and provide a quantitative, if sometimes controversial, means to characterize changes in ecosystem condition (Bortone, 2005; Karr, 1981, 1991).

In contrast to traditional SP valuation that has no formal guidelines for the use and presentation of ecological information, BSPV employs a more structured use of ecological indicators to characterize and communicate welfare-relevant changes. Specific guidelines ensure that survey scenarios and resulting welfare estimates are characterized by (1) a formal basis in established and measurable ecological indicators, (2) a clear structure linking indicators to attributes influencing individuals' well-being, (3) consistent and meaningful interpretation of ecological information, and (4) a consequent ability to link welfare measures to measurable and unambiguous policy outcomes. Specific guidelines to ensure (1) through (4) include:

1. *Indicators used within BSPV survey scenarios must be associated with specific and well-defined ecological changes over which respondents express preferences.* Results of preliminary research such as focus groups and cognitive interviews (Johnston et al., 1995; Kaplowitz et al., 2004; Powe, 2007) should be combined with findings from the relevant ecological literature first to determine a comprehensive set of ecological outputs with potential influences on respondents' utility, then to identify ecological indicators best able to characterize those outputs. This requires differentiation between intermediate ecological changes valued solely as inputs into other final ecological outcomes versus those valued at least in part due to direct influences on utility (Boyd and Banzhaf, 2007). Resulting information is then used to provide a one-to-one match between ecological indicators (serving as attributes) in SP scenarios and final welfare-relevant ecological outputs. This guideline requires mapping of relationships between underlying ecological changes, formal indicators of those changes and attributes in respondents' utility functions.

2. *Indicators used within BSPV survey scenarios must have a systematic relationship to ecological field data or quantitative model results.* All indicators within survey scenarios should reflect a measure that is empirically quantifiable, for example, as the output of a recognized ecological model or standard field measurement. If ordinal categories (for example, high, medium, low) are used to represent ecological change, the empirical basis for these categories must be defined

quantitatively and presented to survey respondents. In addition, there must be justification for the applied categorization within the ecological literature. That is, survey attributes must be traceable to unambiguous ecological measurements.

3. *The quantitative basis for survey attributes must be understandable to respondents and meaningful to scientists.* Survey pre-testing must ensure that respondents understand the units and definition of ecological indicators included in survey scenarios, and that these correspond to meaningful outcomes from the perspective of individual utility. Respondents' understandings of indicator units, definitions and interpretations must coincide, at least broadly, with those of natural scientists.

4. *Indicators used within BSPV survey scenarios should be specified such that respondents can identify baselines (that is, status quo), reference conditions (that is, the best possible outcome or level of the indicator in an undisturbed system), and changes in both relative and cardinal units where applicable.* Findings from the valuation literature demonstrate that WTP often depends on available (or visible) choice sets, reflecting the full set of policy options possible within a given choice experiment or policy context (Bateman et al., 2004). Similarly, ecological reference conditions may be thought of as characterizing the range of possible substitute goods or policy outcomes that might be available, regardless of whether these are available in presented survey scenarios. Reference conditions also provide a means to interpret quantities such as '200000 birds' that might be otherwise largely meaningless to lay respondents (for example, Desvousges et al., 1993; see also comments by Hanemann, 1994). The communication of ecological information in this more comprehensive manner provides respondents with an increased capacity to comprehend policy scope and to anticipate effects on welfare.

5. *Indicators used within BSPV survey scenarios must be described so that respondents can understand potential linkages between ecological attributes and how these are, or are not, captured in illustrated scenarios.* To prevent respondent speculation regarding ecological production functions and implications for valued ecological outputs, surveys should provide sufficient information regarding relationships between ecological functions, for example, as inputs and outputs according to ecological production functions. This, together with other BSPV guidelines, can help prevent problems in which, for example, respondents' choices reflect a speculated (likely incorrect) value for an omitted ecological outcome $E(X)$ caused by a presented change in X.

6. *Indicators used within BSPV survey scenarios must provide a*

comprehensive perspective on welfare-relevant policy outcomes, including both direct and indirect effects. As noted above, incomplete coverage of welfare-relevant outcomes in survey scenarios can encourage respondents to speculate regarding omitted outcomes. For the case of complex ecological systems, such speculation will almost certainly lead to incorrect assumptions regarding the value of these outcomes. For many restoration policies this guideline requires specification of outcomes (using appropriate ecological indicators) at three levels: (1) the direct effect of proposed policies on targeted species or habitats (for example, an increase in the number of fish able to travel upstream to spawning areas due to fish run restoration); (2) resulting indirect effects on other specific ecosystem commodities or human uses (for example, indirect effects of fish passage on other wildlife species); (3) broader indirect effects on ecosystem condition (for example, as might be measured using a multimetric index of biotic integrity). The inclusion of ecological changes at these three levels also provides a basis for investigating the structure of preferences. For example, it allows a test of whether utility takes the form $U(E(X), X)$ or simply $U(E(X))$. That is, it allows for a distinction between utility gained from specific elements of the ecological system and utility associated with overall system condition, the latter of which may be a source of perhaps substantial non-use values.

As noted above, there are many examples of SP survey instruments addressing aquatic restoration that incorporate ecological indicators – either simple or complex – in a less structured manner. Some of these surveys may have generated valid welfare estimates. However, the lack of a clear framework specifying linkages among different types of ecological impacts, well-defined ecological indicators and the structure of respondents' utility can lead to ambiguity regarding the interpretation of model results and potential bias in welfare estimates. Bioindicator-based stated preference valuation is designed at least partially to ameliorate these concerns and thereby promote valid estimates of non-market values.

Random Utility Model

The theoretical model for the present application is adapted from a standard random utility specification (Hanemann, 1984). We assume that the utility of household h from ecological restoration program k (U_{hk}) is given by

$$U_{hk}(\mathbf{X_k}, \mathbf{W_k}(\mathbf{X_k}), Y_h - C_{hk}) = v_{hk}(\mathbf{X_k}, \mathbf{W_k}(\mathbf{X_k}), Y_h - C_{hk}) + e_{hk} \quad (9.1)$$

where:

$\mathbf{X_k} =$ vector of indicators characterizing *direct* ecological outcomes of program k;

$\mathbf{W_k}(\cdot) =$ vector of indicators characterizing *indirect* ecological outcomes of program k (outcomes related to direct outcomes $\mathbf{X_k}$);

$Y_h =$ disposable income of household h;

$C_{hk} =$ mandatory cost to the respondent of preservation plan k;

$v_{hk}(\cdot) =$ function representing the empirically measurable component of utility;

$e_{hk} =$ unobservable component of utility, modelled as econometric error.

Given the above specification, household h chooses among three policy plans, ($j = A, B, N$). The household may choose option A, option B, or may reject both options and choose the status quo (neither plan, $j = N$). A choice of neither plan would result in no restoration and zero household cost, $C_{hk} = 0$. The model assumes that household h assesses the utility that would result from choice options ($j = A, B, N$) and chooses that which offers the greatest utility. That is, given equation 9.1, household h will choose plan A if

$$U_{hA}(\mathbf{X_A}, \mathbf{W_A}(\mathbf{X_A}), Y_A - C_{hA}) \geq U_{hz}(\mathbf{X_z}, \mathbf{W_z}(\mathbf{X_z}), Y_z - C_{hz}) \text{ for } z = B, N,$$
$$(9.2)$$

so that

$$v_{hA}(\mathbf{X_A}, \mathbf{W_A}(\mathbf{X_A}), Y_A - C_{hA}) + \varepsilon_{kA} \geq v_{hz}(\mathbf{X_z}, \mathbf{W_z}(\mathbf{X_z}), Y_z - C_{hz}) + \varepsilon_{kz}.$$
$$(9.3)$$

If the ε_{hk} are assumed independently and identically drawn from a type I extreme value distribution, the model may be estimated as a conditional logit (CL) model (Maddala, 1983). The mixed logit (ML) model applied here is a generalization allowing alternative error structures, a relaxation of certain assumptions imposed by the CL model, and expanded possibilities to model response heterogeneity (Train, 2009).

EMPIRICAL APPLICATION AND DATA

The SP methods outlined above were developed for a case study addressing public preferences for the restoration of migratory fish passage in the

Pawtuxet and Wood-Pawcatuck watersheds of Rhode Island. The present illustration is drawn from a subset of surveys addressing restoration of the Pawtuxet Watershed. The Pawtuxet Watershed currently provides no spawning habitat for migratory fish; access to all 4347 acres of potential habitat is blocked by 22 dams and other obstructions (Erkan, 2002). The choice experiment questionnaire 'Rhode Island Rivers: Migratory Fishes and Dams' estimated willingness to pay of Rhode Island residents for options that would provide fish passage over dams and access to between 225 and 900 acres of historical, but currently inaccessible, habitat. Choice scenarios and restoration options were informed in part by data and restoration priorities in the *Strategic Plan for the Restoration of Anadromous Fishes to Rhode Island Coastal Streams* (Erkan, 2002). Additional information was drawn from the ecological literature on fish passage restoration, interviews with ecologists and policy experts, and other sources described below. Consistent with the strategic plan, the choice experiment addressed restoration methods that neither require dam removal nor would cause appreciable changes in river flows; considered options included fish ladders, bypass channels and fish lifts.

The SP questionnaire was developed and tested over two and a half years through a collaborative process involving interactions of economists and ecologists; meetings with resource managers, natural scientists and stakeholder groups; and 12 focus groups with 105 total participants. In addition to survey development and testing in focus groups, individual interviews were conducted with both ecological experts and non-experts. These included cognitive interviews (Kaplowitz et al., 2004), verbal protocols (Schkade and Payne, 1994) and other pre-tests conducted to gain additional insight into respondents' understanding and interpretation of the questionnaire.[12] Careful attention to development and testing helped ensure that the survey language and format would be easily understood by respondents, that respondents would have similar interpretations of survey terminology and scenarios, and that the survey scenarios captured restoration outcomes viewed as relevant and realistic by both respondents and natural scientists. In all cases, survey development paid particular attention to the use and interpretation of ecological indicators and related information in the survey instrument.

The choice experiment asked respondents to consider alternative options for the restoration of migratory fish passage in the Pawtuxet Watershed. Respondents were provided with two multi-attribute restoration options, 'Restoration Project A' and 'Restoration Project B,' as well as a status quo option that would result in no policy change and zero household cost. Prior to administration of choice experiment questions, the survey provided information (1) describing the current status of Rhode Island river ecology and migratory fish compared with historical baselines, (2) characterizing affected ecological systems and linkages, (3) describing the methods and details of fish passage restoration, and (4) providing the definitions, derivations and interpretations of ecological indicators used in survey scenarios, including the reason for their inclusion. All survey language and graphics were pre-tested to ensure respondent comprehension.

Using Ecological Indicators to Characterize Restoration Outcomes

As noted above, the primary distinguishing feature of BSPV is the set of guidelines for the use and structure of ecological indicators within survey scenarios. Here, survey choice options are characterized by seven attributes (Table 9.1). These include five ecological indicators, one attribute characterizing public access, and one attribute characterizing unavoidable household cost. Table 9.2 illustrates associated attribute levels included in the choice experiment design.

Ecological indicators included in each choice option characterize:

1. The quantity of river habitat accessible to migratory fishes (*acres*), based upon restorable Pawtuxet habitat acreage in Erkan (2002).
2. The probability that the restored fish run will exist in 50 years, reflecting numerical results that could be made available through population viability analysis (*PVA*).[13]
3. The abundance of fish suitable for recreational harvest (*catch*), reflecting abundance measures available from ongoing statewide river sampling.[14]
4. The abundance of fish-dependent wildlife (*wildlife*), reflecting the common appearance of identifiable species within restored areas.
5. Overall ecological condition (*IBI*), reflecting the output of a multimetric aquatic ecological condition score (that is, an Index of Biotic Integrity).

Following BSPV guidelines, all indicators have a systematic linkage to ecological field data or quantitative model results. Attribute levels (within the experimental design) are grounded in feasible restoration outcomes identified by ecological models, field studies or expert consultations. Choice scenarios represent each ecological attribute in relative terms with regard to upper and lower reference conditions (that is, best and worst possible in the Pawtuxet) as defined in survey informational materials. Scenarios also present the cardinal basis for relative scores where applicable.[15] Relative scores represent per cent progress towards the upper reference condition (100 per cent), starting from the lower reference condition (0 per cent). This also implies bounds on the potential attribute levels that

Table 9.1   Choice experiment variables and descriptive statistics

Variable	Definition	Mean (Std. dev.)[a]
acres	The number of acres of river habitat accessible to migratory fish, presented as a percentage of the reference value for the watershed (Erkan, 2002). Range 0–100.	8.1794 (8.1550)
PVA	Population viability analysis (PVA) score: Estimated probability, in percentage terms, that migratory species will migrate the river in 50 years. Reference condition is estimated based from surveys of experts in fish restoration. Range 0–100.	33.4413 (28.1265)
access	Binary (dummy) variable indicating whether the restored area is accessible to the public for walking and fishing; a value of 1 indicates that the public can access the area. Range 0–1.	0.3296 (0.4702)
IBI	Index of biotic integrity (IBI) score: A linear multimetric index of aquatic ecological condition, reflecting the similarity of the restored area to the most undisturbed watershed area in Rhode Island. Index components include overall fish abundance, number of mussel species, number of native species, number of sensitive species, number of feeding types, percentage of native individuals, percentage of migratory individuals, and percentage of fish that are tumor free. Presented as a percentage of the reference condition. Range 0–100.	71.6978 (6.0762)
cost	Household annual cost, described as the mandatory increase in annual taxes and fees required to implement the restoration plan. Household cost for the status quo is zero. Range 0–25.	11.9762 (14.1019)
neither	Alternative specific constant (ASC) associated with the status quo, or a choice of neither plan.	0.3333 (0.4715)
catch	The number of catchable-size fish in restored areas, measured as the number of fish per hour caught by scientific sampling crews. Presented as a percentage of the reference value for the watershed, defined as the highest average level sampled in any Rhode Island river (from Rhode Island Department of Environmental Management sampling data). Range 0–100.	79.9087 (7.5807)
wildlife	Number of fish-eating species that are common in restored areas, such as egrets, osprey, otters, eagles, turtles and mink. Presented as a percentage of the reference value for the watershed, quantified from surveys of regional experts in wildlife biology. Range 0–100.	65.0125 (10.3920)

Note: [a] Means and standard deviations include status quo option of no restoration.

Table 9.2   Attribute levels in choice experiment design

Variable	Levels
acres	0% (0 acres accessible to fish)[a]
	5% (225 acres accessible to fish)
	10% (450 acres accessible to fish)
	20% (900 acres accessible to fish)
PVA	0% (probability of 50 year fish run survival)[a]
	30% (probability of 50 year fish run survival)
	50% (probability of 50 year fish run survival)
	70% (probability of 50 year fish run survival)
access	Public Cannot Walk and Fish in Area[a]
	Public Can Walk and Fish in Area
IBI	65% (aquatic ecological condition score)[a]
	70% (aquatic ecological condition score)
	75% (aquatic ecological condition score)
	80% (aquatic ecological condition score)
cost	$0 (cost to household per year)[a]
	$5 (cost to household per year)
	$10 (cost to household per year)
	$15 (cost to household per year)
	$20 (cost to household per year)
	$25 (cost to household per year)
catch	70% (102 fish/hour sampling abundance)
	80% (116 fish/hour sampling abundance)[a]
	90% (130 fish/hour sampling abundance)
wildlife	55% (20 species common)[a]
	60% (22 species common)
	70% (25 species common)
	80% (28 species common)

Note: [a] Status quo value.

might occur in choice questions, following guidance in the literature to provide visible choice sets (Bateman et al., 2004).

Consider, for example, the aquatic ecological condition score (*IBI*), described in the survey as '0–100 score representing how close a river is to the most natural, undisturbed area found in Rhode Island'. This indicator was included following guidance from preliminary focus groups suggesting that respondents would be willing to pay to restore overall ecological condition in the Pawtuxet Watershed, above and beyond WTP related to all other identifiable restoration outcomes (guideline 1 above). Prior to the illustration of *IBI* scores in choice questions, the survey described the calculation and quantitative basis for this multimetric indicator, including characterization of the eight component unimetric indicators included within the combined *IBI* score (guideline 2). Also included were descriptions of ecological linkages through which the restoration of fish passage influences ecological condition (guideline 5). Each choice question specified the status quo level for this indicator (65 per cent) calculated to reflect current watershed conditions, as well as the maximum possible value in the watershed (100 per cent) (guideline 4). Focus groups and pretests were used to ensure shared and accurate interpretation of this information among potential respondents, and that respondents' interpretations of this indicator were broadly similar to those of policy experts and scientists (guideline 3). Survey pre-tests and verbal protocols (Schkade and Payne, 1994) were also used to ensure correspondence between the presented *IBI* and the associated welfare-relevant policy outcome (that is, the effect of restoration on overall ecological condition), and that this outcome was not confused with other restoration outcomes (guideline 6). Parallel guidelines were applied to all ecological indicators used within choice questions.

Survey Implementation

From choice attributes (Table 9.1) and levels (Table 9.2), a fractional factorial experimental design was created using a D-efficiency criterion for main effects and selected two-way interactions, resulting in 180 profiles optimally blocked into 60 booklets (Lusk and Norwood, 2005). Figure 9.1 illustrates a sample survey scenario and choice question. Each respondent was provided with three choice experiment questions and was instructed to consider each as an independent, non-additive choice. Detailed instructions were also provided, including reminders to consider budget constraints and statements highlighting survey consequentiality (Carson and Groves, 2007).

Surveys were implemented using a dual wave phone–mail approach during June, July and August 2008. An initial random digit dial (RDD) sample of Rhode Island households was contacted via telephone and asked to participate in a survey addressing Rhode Island 'environmental issues and government programs'. Those agreeing to participate were sent the questionnaire via postal mail, with repeated follow-up mailings as suggested by Dillman (2000) to increase response rates. A total of 2400 surveys were mailed to Rhode Island residents; 1157 surveys were returned (48.2 per cent response rate). Of the total surveys mailed, 600 addressed restoration in the Pawtuxet watershed.[16] The following analysis is based on the 277 usable returns for the Pawtuxet questionnaire, providing 803 completed responses to choice questions.

Question 5. Projects **A** and **B** are possible restoration projects for the Pawtuxet River, and the **Current Situation** is the status quo with no restoration. Given a choice between the three, how would you vote?

Effect of Restoration	Current Situation (no restoration)	Restoration Project A	Restoration Project B
Fish Habitat	**0%** 0 of 4347 river acres accessible to fish	**5%** 225 of 4347 river acres accessible to fish	**20%** 900 of 4347 river acres accessible to fish
Population Survival Score	**0%** Chance of 50-year survival	**30%** Chance of 50-year survival	**30%** Chance of 50-year survival
Catchable Fish Abundance	**80%** 116 fish/hour found out of 145 possible	**70%** 102 fish/hour found out of 145 possible	**70%** 102 fish/hour found out of 145 possible
Fish-Dependent Wildlife	**55%** 20 of 36 species native to RI are common	**80%** 28 of 36 species native to RI are common	**60%** 22 of 36 species native to RI are common
Aquatic Ecological Condition Score	**65%** Natural condition out of 100% maximum	**70%** Natural condition out of 100% maximum	**80%** Natural condition out of 100% maximum
Public Access	Public **CANNOT** walk and fish in area	Public CANNOT walk and fish in area	Public **CAN** walk and fish in area
$ Cost to your Household per Year	**$0** Increase in Annual Taxes and Fees	**$15** Increase in Annual Taxes and Fees	**$25** Increase in Annual Taxes and Fees
HOW WOULD YOU VOTE? (CHOOSE ONE ONLY)	☐ I vote for **NO RESTORATION**	☐ I vote for **PROJECT A**	☐ I vote for **PROJECT B**

Figure 9.1   Sample choice experiment question

EMPIRICAL MODEL

Over the past decade choice experiment research has increasingly applied mixed logit (ML) models of choice among discrete alternatives, replacing traditional conditional logit models (Hensher and Greene, 2003; Train,

2009). Mixed logit models allow for coefficients on attributes to be distributed across sampled individuals according to a set of estimated parameters and researcher-imposed restrictions. While such models require a greater number of choices regarding model specification, they have greater flexibility and can approximate any random utility model (Hensher and Greene, 2003).

The random utility model is estimated here using maximum likelihood mixed logit with Halton draws in the likelihood simulation. Coefficients on *acres*, *PVA*, *access* and *IBI* are specified as random with normal distributions. The coefficient on annual household cost (*cost*) is specified as random with a lognormal distribution, ensuring a positive marginal utility of income. Sign-reversal is applied to the cost variable prior to estimation (Hensher and Greene, 2003). Coefficients on other variables are specified as fixed. These include the coefficients on the alternative specific constant (*neither*), *catch* and *wildlife*. The final model was chosen after the estimation of preliminary models with varying specifications of fixed and random coefficients. Preliminary models show a high degree of robustness to variations in model specification.

RESULTS

Model results are reported in Table 9.3. ML estimates suggest good model fit. Estimated coefficients are jointly significant at $p < 0.0001$ (-2 log likelihood $\chi^2 = 537.18$; df $= 13$), with a pseudo-R^2 of 0.31. Seven out of eight model coefficients are statistically significant at $p < 0.10$; six of these are significant at $p < 0.01$. Estimated standard deviations of all random parameter distributions are statistically significant, suggesting that a ML specification is warranted. Results of log-likelihood tests of conditional (suppressed for conciseness) versus mixed logit results yield the same conclusion at $p < 0.0001$ ($\chi^2 = 118.08$; df $= 5$). Signs of estimated coefficients match prior expectations.

Even before welfare estimates such as WTP are calculated, the model specification provides a convenient means to interpret and contrast results. As detailed in Table 9.1, all model variables except *access* and *cost* represent percentage progress towards the upper reference condition (100 per cent). Hence, model coefficients may be directly compared as the relative weight (or marginal utility) given to a one percentage point change in each attribute. Viewed from this perspective, marginal utility is greatest (per percentage point change) for increases in restored acres (*acres*) and changes in overall ecological condition in the restored area (*IBI*).[17] Changes in marginal utility associated with the probability of fish

Table 9.3   Mixed logit results: Pawtuxet restoration choice experiment

Variable	Coefficient	Std. error	Pr > |t|
Random parameters			
acres	0.0520	0.0150	0.0005
PVA	0.0196	0.0067	0.0035
access	1.2435	0.2354	0.0001
IBI	0.0525	0.0219	0.0163
cost (lognormal)	−2.9738	0.1724	0.0001
Fixed parameters			
neither	−1.7598	0.5038	0.0005
catch	0.0027	0.0105	0.7957
wildlife	0.0275	0.0099	0.0057
Standard deviations of random parameter distributions			
std_acres	0.1089	0.0257	0.0001
std_PVA	0.0452	0.0083	0.0001
std_access	1.3564	0.4572	0.0030
std_IBI	0.1531	0.0380	0.0001
std_cost (lognormal)	0.8351	0.2347	0.0004
−2 log likelihood χ^2	537.18		0.0001
Pseudo-R^2	0.31		
Observations (*N*)	803		

run survival (*PVA*) and increases in the number of fish-dependent wildlife species (*wildlife*) are statistically significant and roughly half the size of those associated with *acres* and *IBI*. Marginal utility is lowest – and not statistically significant – for changes in the abundance of catchable fish (*catch*).

These results are mirrored by WTP estimates derived from model results. Because the ML model includes random coefficients, we estimate WTP using the welfare simulation approach of Johnston and Duke (2007, 2009) following the framework illustrated by Hensher and Greene (2003). The procedure begins with a parameter simulation following the parametric bootstrap of Krinsky and Robb (1986), with $R = 1000$ draws taken from the mean parameter vector and associated covariance matrix. For each draw, the resulting parameters are used to characterize asymptotically normal empirical densities for fixed and random coefficients. For each of these R draws, a coefficient simulation is then conducted for each random coefficient, with $S = 1000$ draws taken from simulated empirical densities.[18] Welfare measures are calculated for each draw, resulting in a combined empirical distribution of $R \times S$ observations from which summary statistics are derived. The resulting empirical distributions

Table 9.4   Marginal willingness-to-pay estimates (implicit prices): empirical distributions[a]

Variable	WTP	Standard deviation	Skewness	Kurtosis	Percentiles (1%, 99%)	$Pr > |t|$[b]
acres	0.7841	0.2658	0.37	3.17	(0.23, 1.44)	<0.01
PVA	0.2881	0.1143	0.39	3.34	(0.05, 0.58)	<0.01
access	19.9620	4.5110	0.53	3.59	(10.71, 33.46)	<0.01
IBI	0.7916	0.3749	0.28	3.52	(−0.03, 1.70)	0.02
catch	0.0497	0.2109	−0.32	3.61	(−0.52, 0.53)	0.76
wildlife	0.5489	0.2024	0.20	3.12	(0.12, 1.04)	<0.01

Notes:
[a]   Results reflect the mean over the parameter simulation of median WTP over the coefficient simulation (see text). Estimates are per household, per year. For all variables except *access*, estimates represent WTP for a 1 percentage point increase.
[b]   P-values are two-tailed, for the null hypothesis of zero mean of median WTP, calculated directly from percentiles in simulated empirical WTP distributions (see text).

accommodate both the sampling variance of parameter estimates and the estimated distribution of random parameters.

Using this procedure, we simulate WTP associated with each restoration policy attribute. While the lognormal distribution of the program cost coefficient in this case ensures a negative impact of cost on utility, and hence is the most commonly chosen distribution for SP payment vehicle parameters, it can also lead to unrealistic mean WTP estimates over simulated distributions (Hensher and Greene, 2003; Train and Weeks, 2005). Accordingly, we follow Hu et al. (2005) and Johnston and Duke (2007, 2009) and simulate welfare estimates as the mean over the parameter simulation of median WTP calculated over the coefficient simulation (that is, mean of median WTP).

Resulting WTP distributions are summarized in Table 9.4, along with p-values for the null hypothesis of zero (mean of median) WTP. For all attributes except *access*, results are interpreted as WTP for a marginal, one percentage point increase in the indicator, holding all else constant. For *access*, results indicate WTP for the provision of public access in the restored area, relative to the default of no access. Statistical significance levels (*p*-values) reported in Table 9.4 are determined through reference to the percentiles on the empirical distributions (Poe et al., 2005).

Welfare estimates may be interpreted in either relative (that is, per percentage point increase in the indicator) or cardinal terms. For example, the reported welfare results in Table 9.4 imply that mean of median, per household annual WTP for a one percentage point increase in river acres accessible to migratory fish is $0.78. Given that each percentage increase in *acres* within the Pawtuxet watershed represents 43.47 cardinal acres restored,[19] marginal WTP per acre is $0.018, *ceteris paribus*. In contrast, annual WTP for a 1 percentage point increase in the probability of 50-year fish run survival is $0.29, while that for a 1 percentage point increase in the aquatic ecological condition index (*IBI*) is $0.79. Based on simulated empirical welfare distributions (Poe et al., 2005), all WTP estimates except that on *catch* are statistically significant.

Estimated welfare measures demonstrate that respondents were able to distinguish between anticipated welfare effects of different ecological outcomes, with WTP higher for some outcomes (for example, increases in ecosystem condition) than for others (for example, increases in catchable fish abundance). Results suggest substantial WTP both for restoration outcomes that are straightforward and direct (for example, the number of acres accessible to migratory fish), as well as more complex and indirect (for example, effects on ecological condition). Moreover, while public access (*access*) to restored areas is valued highly, the relationship of ecological outcomes to human uses is not sufficient to guarantee non-zero WTP. Changes in catchable fish abundance (*catch*), for example, are not associated with statistically significant WTP. Taken together, results suggest that respondents are able to make systematic choices over complex restoration possibilities, and that the design of restoration options can have non-trivial impacts on public welfare.

IMPLICATIONS AND DISCUSSION

Results presented in this chapter suggest that ad hoc, oversimplified representation of ecological outcomes is not a compulsory aspect of survey-based welfare estimation; SP choice experiment scenarios can use indicators that are meaningful from both ecological and economic perspectives. More complete, structured specifications of ecological outcomes within SP questionnaires – while demanding greater attention to survey design and testing – can provide welfare results that are both more comprehensive from a utility perspective and more easily linked to measurable policy outcomes.

Model results for the case study discussed here – that of migratory fish passage restoration in Rhode Island watersheds – provide considerable insight into ways in which respondents value outcomes of aquatic ecosystem restoration. Survey responses suggest nuanced preferences for aquatic ecosystem change among the Rhode Island public. Welfare estimates reveal clear differences in WTP across distinct restoration attributes.

Interestingly, some of the more direct effects of fish passage restoration, such as increases in the probability of fish run survival (PVA), are associated with modest WTP compared to some indirect restoration effects. This suggests that past surveys in which policy effects have been characterized solely in terms of the direct effects on individual species might have omitted some of the primary outcomes through which ecological restoration influences utility.

For example, SP survey scenarios often omit effects on overall ecosystem condition,[20] as measured here using an index of biotic integrity. In the present study, this indicator has a larger associated marginal welfare estimate than any other ecological attribute (Table 9.4). These results suggest that respondents can gain significant utility from changes in overall ecosystem condition, even after one holds constant effects on other primary restoration outcomes. Welfare evaluations should therefore consider the possibility that ecosystem condition can yield significant non-market values that are distinct from the values of ecological attributes or outcomes that might influence that condition (such as species abundance). Model results also imply that some past SP surveys in the literature may have suppressed exactly the type of information that is most relevant to respondents when determining WTP for ecological restoration.

Model results also raise the prospect – following similar findings of Bulte et al. (2005) and Johnston and Duke (2007) – that respondents may have well-defined WTP for an attribute reflecting the status of an ecological *process* (the condition of a functioning ecological system), apart from the outcomes of that process. Some economists might argue that the condition of an ecosystem represents the status of an ecological process that should only be valued in as much as it contributes to other valued outputs. Others, however, might interpret ecological condition as an output that can be valued apart from other ecosystem services or outputs. While results here cannot resolve this debate, they do indicate clearly that respondents are willing to pay for improvements in ecological condition, holding other outputs constant. From an empirical perspective, respondents view ecological condition as directly welfare relevant.

Results also suggest the potential hazards in less comprehensive coverage of ecological outcomes in SP scenarios. For example, contingent valuation and choice experiment surveys often emphasize direct or indirect effects on recreational fishing, sometimes with relatively sparse descriptions of other ecological outcomes. Associated models frequently estimate statistically significant WTP for improvements in recreational fishing. In contrast, results here suggest that if one accounts for other ecological impacts, respondents may not always express a significant WTP for recreational fishery improvements (that is, the coefficient on *catch* is not statistically significant). This raises the possibility that the incorporation of recreational fishery effects in SP scenarios that omit other related ecosystem effects might cause respondents to use fishery impacts as a proxy for other welfare-relevant ecological outcomes.

At a minimum, results here suggest that WTP for aquatic ecosystem restoration can reflect a wide range of direct and indirect effects. In the absence of details on such effects and related ecosystem services, respondents might 'fill in whatever details are missing . . . with default assumptions' (Carson, 1998, p.23). Some of these default assumptions might involve erroneous speculations regarding ecological production functions, with a concomitant likelihood of bias in survey responses and welfare estimates. Avoidance of such speculation requires careful survey and model development to ensure a comprehensive perspective on welfare-relevant ecological outcomes.

CONCLUSION

Stated preference valuation methods may in some cases provide insufficient ecological information to enable meaningful, unbiased WTP estimation. While there are exceptions (for example, Horne et al., 2005), the large number of valuation surveys implemented with ad hoc treatments of ecological outcomes suggests the need for more structured guidance on the use of ecological information within non-market valuation. The research presented above illustrates a method that addresses the need for a more systematic treatment of ecological indicators within SP valuation and related structural linkages between ecological and economic frameworks. Despite prior efforts to merge ecological and economic information for economic valuation, SP valuation still commonly retains ad hoc treatments of ecological information, with little reference to the extensive work by ecologists to model and measure ecosystem condition and function.

The broader purpose of the research presented in this chapter is to better ground SP welfare evaluation in the types of ecological indicators and models developed within the ecological sciences, as well as in measurable data available to policy-makers. This chapter formalizes an approach to SP valuation characterized by a set of guidelines and criteria for use of ecological indicators within models and surveys. These guidelines promote a more defensible structure for ecological valuation and a more comprehensive representation of ecological change within SP scenarios, yielding more valid welfare estimation.

Despite the promising findings of this study, it addresses only a few of the many challenges involved in the coordination of economics and ecology for welfare estimation. Reported findings are limited by the policy case study from which they are drawn, and additional verification in other valuation contexts will be required to assess the broader applicability of the proposed methods. These limitations aside, results presented here suggest the potential benefits of closer and more meaningful collaboration among natural and social scientists. Potential benefits for economists include enhanced validity and relevance of welfare estimates, increased ability to link non-market values to measurable policy outcomes and improved validity of results.

NOTES

1. This research is supported by the EPA Science to Achieve Results (STAR) program, Grant number RD 83242001. Opinions and findings are those of the authors, and do not imply endorsement of the funding agency.
2. Affected species include river herring (blueback herring and alewife), shad and American eel.
3. For example, respondents might select among different options for coastal wetland restoration, each with distinct effects on wetland attributes, related ecosystem services and household costs (Johnston et al., 2002).
4. For an exception, see Holmes et al. (2004).
5. For example, population viability analysis (PVA) is an approach that yields benchmarks on the status of individual species in the system. Population viability analysis is a process wherein demographic features (abundance, population structure), genetic characteristics, and environmental variability are modelled to yield predictions of the probability that a population will persist for a specified period of time under different scenarios, bounded by 0 and 1 (Boyce, 1992). Indices of Biotic Integrity (IBIs) provide comparable benchmarks on a system-wide level representing ecological condition; they are conventionally scaled relative to least-impacted, relatively pristine reference sites (Jackson et al., 2000). While some have advocated widely used bioindices such as the IBI (for example, Jordan and Smith, 2005), critiques have pointed out the limitations of such metrics, regarding the above-mentioned criteria as well as the core concept of ecological integrity (for example, Suter, 2001).
6. Many of these fall under the category of 'supporting services' in the typology of ecosystem services used in the Millennium Ecosystem Assessment (2005).
7. An alternative approach would be to educate the survey respondents about the relevant ecological science. However, the ability to do this within the confines of a survey is limited.
8. For example, in the absence of other defining information, WTP for attainment of 'high' biodiversity cannot be linked to measurable policy outcomes without assumptions regarding the combinations of observable conditions, or measurement endpoints, that one might associate with this otherwise ambiguous descriptor.
9. For example, some species of diadromous fish compete with juveniles of valued recreational species and also are prey for the adult stages of the same species. The balance of such positive and negative effects depend on other factors (Yako et al., 2000).
10. This lack of formalized relationship may be realized at either the researcher level (that is, researchers have not specified any formal relationship) or at the respondent level (that is, researchers may have specified a relationship), but this is unknown or poorly understood by respondents.
11. While not explored here, the proposed method also has the potential to expand possibilities for benefit transfer. Consider, for example, a utility function of the form $U(E(X,$

Y)), where *E* is an ecological outcome determined by two (or more) relevant variables *X* and *Y*. Suppose that in a given context a change in *X* leads to a change in *E*, and this change in *E* is valued using the illustrated methods. Provided the affected population is sufficiently similar, this value could then be transferred and used in a context where *E* changes as a result of a change in *Y* rather than a change in *X*. This would be valid provided that individuals care only about the change in *E* and not independently about the source of any change in *E*, as posited in a utility function of this form. Whether utility, in fact, takes this form is an empirical question, which the present methods can help to answer.

12. No formal count was made of individual interviews used in survey design, but we approximate that a minimum of 60 in-person and telephone interviews were conducted with expert and non-expert respondents between September 2005 and June 2008.

13. For an illustration of population viability analysis applied to diadromous fish, see Lee and Rieman (1997).

14. This reflects the effect of fish passage on the abundance of other recreationally harvested fish such as largemouth bass (Yako et al., 2000).

15. For example, river acres available to fish migrations (*acres*) are presented both as a cardinal number of acres and as a percentage relative to historical habitat available in the watershed.

16. Other versions of the survey included variations in the definition or set of included ecological indicators or addressed restoration in other Rhode Island watersheds.

17. This excludes *access*, which is measured as a dummy variable and is hence not comparable in this manner.

18. Because the coefficient on *cost* is specified with a lognormal distribution, an exponential transformation is required subsequent to the coefficient simulation to obtain a simulated empirical density for the coefficient itself (Hensher and Greene, 2003).

19. There are 4347 total acres of potential river habitat in the watershed, of which zero are currently accessible to migratory fish.

20. For an exception, see Jakus and Shaw (2003).

REFERENCES

Adamowicz, W., P. Boxall, M. Williams, and J. Louviere (1998), 'Stated preference approaches for measuring passive use values: choice experiments and contingent valuation', *American Journal of Agricultural Economics*, **80** (1), 64–75.

Bateman, I.J., B.H. Day, S. Georgiou and I. Lake (2006), 'The aggregation of environmental benefit values: welfare measures, distance decay and total WTP', *Ecological Economics*, **60** (2), 450–60.

Bateman, I.J., R.T. Carson, B. Day, M. Hanemann, N. Hanley, T. Hett, M. Jones-Lee, G. Loomes, S. Mourato, E. Ozdemiroglu, D.W. Pearce, R. Sugden and J. Swanson (2002), *Economic Valuation with Stated Preference Surveys: A Manual*, Northampton MA: Edward Elgar.

Bateman, I.J., M. Cole, P. Cooper, S. Georgiou, D. Hadley, and G.L. Poe (2004), 'On visible choice sets and scope sensitivity', *Journal of Environmental Economics and Management*, **47** (1), 71–93.

Bennett, J. and R. Blamey (2001), 'Introduction', in J. Bennett and R. Blamey (eds), *The Choice Modelling Approach to Environmental Valuation*, Cheltenham, UK and Northampton, MA, USA: Edward Elgar.

Bergstrom, J.C. and J.R. Stoll (1989), 'Application of experimental economics concepts and precepts to CVM field survey procedures', *Western Journal of Agricultural Economics*, **14** (1), 98–109.

Bergstrom, J.D., J.R. Stoll and A. Randall (1989), 'Information effects in contingent markets', *American Journal of Agricultural Economics*, **71** (3), 685–91.

Bergstrom, J.D., J.R. Stoll and A. Randall (1990), 'The impact of information on environ-mental commodity valuation decisions', *American Journal of Agricultural Economics*, **72** (3), 614–21.

Bingham, G., R. Bishop, M. Brody, D. Bromley, E. Clark, W. Cooper, R. Costanza, T. Hale, G. Hayden, S. Kellert, R. Norgaard, B. Norton, J. Payne, C. Russell and G. Suter, (1995), 'Issues in ecosystem valuation: improving information for decision making', *Ecological Economics*, **14** (1), 73–90.

Birol, E., P. Koundouri and Y. Kountouris (2008), 'Using the choice experiment method to inform river management in Poland: flood risk reduction versus habitat conservation in the Upper Silesia Region', in E. Birol and P. Koundouri (eds), *Choice Experiments Informing Environmental Policy: A European Perspective*, Cheltenham, UK and Northampton, MA, USA: Edward Elgar, pp. 271–91.

Bortone, S.A. (ed.) (2005), *Estuarine Indicators*, Boca Raton, FL: CRC Press.

Boyce, M.S. (1992), 'Population viability analysis', *Annual Review of Ecology and Systematics*, **23**, 481–506.

Boyd, J. and S. Banzhaf (2007), 'What are ecosystem services? The need for standardized environmental accounting units', *Ecological Economics*, **63** (2–3), 616–26.

Boyer, T. and S. Polasky (2004), 'Valuing urban wetlands: a review of non-market valuation studies', *Wetlands*, **24** (4), 744–55.

Bulte, E., S. Gerking, J.A. List and A. de Zeeuw (2005), 'The effect of varying the causes of environmental problems on stated WTP values: evidence from a field study', *Journal of Environmental Economics and Management*, **49** (2), 330–42.

Cameron, T.A. and J. Englin (1997), 'Respondent experience and contingent valuation of environmental goods', *Journal of Environmental Economics and Management*, **33** (3), 296–313.

Carlsson, F., P. Frykblom and Carolina Liljenstolpe (2003), 'Valuing wetland attributes: an application of choice experiments', *Ecological Economics*, **47** (1), 95–103.

Carson, R.T. (1998), 'Valuation of tropical rainforests: philosophical and practical issues in the use of contingent valuation', *Ecological Economics*, **24** (1), 15–29.

Carson, R.T. and T. Groves (2007), 'Incentive and informational properties of preference questions', *Environmental and Resource Economics*, **37** (1), 181–210.

Christie, M., N. Hanley, J. Warren, K. Murphy, R. Wright and T. Hyde (2006), 'Valuing the diversity of biodiversity', *Ecological Economics*, **58** (2), 304–17.

Czajkowski, M., M. Buszko-Briggs and N. Hanley (2009), 'Valuing changes in forest biodi-versity', *Ecological Economics*, **68** (2), 2910–17

Davis, W.S. and T. P. Simon (eds) (1995), *Biological Assessment and Criteria: Tools for Water Resource Planning and Decision Making*, Boca Raton, FL: Lewis.

Desvousges, W.H., F.R. Johnson, R.W. Dunford, K.J. Boyle, S.P. Hudson and K.N. Wilson, (1993), 'Measuring natural resource damages with contingent valuation: tests of validity and reliability', in J.A. Hausman (ed.), *Contingent Valuation, A Critical Assessment*, Amsterdam: Elsevier, pp. 91–164.

Dillman, D.A. (2000), *Mail and Internet Surveys: The Tailored Design Method*, New York: John Wiley and Sons.

Do, T.N. and J. Bennett (2009), 'Estimating wetland biodiversity values: a choice modelling application in Vietnam's Mekong river delta', *Environment and Development Economics*, **14** (2), 163–86.

Erkan, D.E. (2002), *Strategic Plan for the Restoration of Anadromous Fishes to Rhode Island Coastal Streams*, Wakefield, RI: Rhode Island Department of Environmental Management, Division of Fish and Wildlife.

Flores, N.E. and A. Shafran (2006), 'A review of studies valuing ecosystem improvements and restoration', Annual USDA W-1133 Meetings, San Antonio, TX.

Hanemann, W.M. (1984), 'Welfare evaluations in contingent valuation experiments with discrete responses', *American Journal of Agricultural Economics*, **66** (3), 332–41.

Hanemann, W.M. (1994), 'Valuing the environment through contingent valuation. *Journal of Economic Perspectives*, **8** (4), 19–43.

Hanley, N., R.E. Wright and B. Alvarez-Farizo (2006), 'Estimating the economic value of improvements in river ecology using choice experiments: an application to the water framework directive', *Journal of Environmental Management*, **78** (2), 183–93.

Hensher, D.A. and W.H. Greene (2003), 'The mixed logit model: the state of practice', *Transportation*, **30** (2), 133–76.

Hoehn, J.P. and A. Randall (2002), 'The Effect of resource quality information on resource injury perceptions and contingent values', *Resource and Energy Economics*, **24** (1), 13–31.

Holmes, T.P., J.C. Bergstrom, E. Huszar, S.B. Kask and F. Orr, III (2004), 'Contingent valuation, net marginal benefits, and the scale of riparian ecosystem restoration', *Ecological Economics*, **49** (1), 19–30.

Horne, P., P.C. Boxall and W.L. Adamowicz (2005), 'Multiple-use management of forest recreation sites: a spatially explicit choice experiment', *Forest Ecology and Management*, **207**, 189–99.

Hu, W., M.M. Veeman and W.L. Adamowicz (2005), 'Labeling genetically modified food: heterogeneous consumer preferences and the value of information', *Canadian Journal of Agricultural Economics*, **53** (1), 83–102.

Jacobsen, J.B., J.H. Boisen, B.J. Thorsen and N. Strange (2008), 'What's in a name? The use of quantitative measures versus 'iconised' species when valuing biodiversity', *Environmental and Resource Economics*, **39** (3), 247–63.

Jackson, L.E., J.C. Kurtz and W.S. Fisher (eds) (2000), 'Evaluation guidelines for ecological indicators', EPA/620/R-99/005. Washington, DC: US EPA.

Jakus, P.M. and W.D. Shaw (2003), 'Perceived hazard and product choice: an application to recreational site choice', *Journal of Risk and Uncertainty*, **26** (1), 77–92.

Johnston, R.J. and J.M. Duke (2007), 'Willingness to pay for agricultural land preservation and policy process attributes: does the method matter?', *American Journal of Agricultural Economics*, **89** (4), 1098–1115.

Johnston, R.J. and J.M. Duke (2009), 'Willingness to pay for land preservation across states and jurisdictional scale: implications for benefit transfer', *Land Economics*, **85** (2), 217–37.

Johnston, R. J., G. Magnusson, M. Mazzotta and J.J. Opaluch (2002), 'Combining economic and ecological indicators to prioritize salt marsh restoration actions', *American Journal of Agricultural Economics*, **84** (5), 1362–70.

Johnston, R.J., T.F. Weaver, L.A. Smith and S.K. Swallow (1995), 'Contingent valuation focus groups: insights from ethnographic interview techniques', *Agricultural and Resource Economics Review*, **24** (1), 56–69.

Jordan, S.J. and L.M. Smith (2005), 'Indicators of ecosystem integrity for estuaries', in S.A. Bortone (ed.), *Estuarine Indicators*, Boca Raton, FL: CRC Press, pp. 467–80.

Jorgensen, S.E., R. Costanza and F. L. Xu (2004), *Handbook of Ecological Indicators for Assessment of Ecosystem Health*, Boca Raton, FL: CRC Press.

Kaplowitz, M.D., F. Lupi and J.P. Hoehn (2004), 'Multiple methods for developing and evaluating a stated-choice questionnaire to value wetlands', in S. Presser, J.M. Rothget, M.P. Coupter, J.T. Lesser, E. Martin, J. Martin and E. Singer (eds), *Methods for Testing and Evaluating Survey Questionnaires*, New York: John Wiley and Sons, pp. 503–24.

Karr, J.R. (1981), 'Assessment of biotic integrity using fish communities', *Fisheries*, **6** (6), 21–7.

Karr, J.R. (1991), 'Biological integrity: a long-neglected aspect of water resource management', *Ecological Applications*, **1** (1), 66–84.

Krinsky, I. and A.L. Robb (1986), 'On approximating the statistical properties of elasticities', *Review of Economics and Statistics*, **68** (4), 715–19.

Lee, D.C. and B.E. Rieman (1997), 'Population viability assessment of salmonids by using probabilistic networks', *North American Journal of Fisheries Management*, **17** (4), 1144–57.

Loomis, J., P. Kent, L. Strange, K. Fausch, and A. Covich (2000), 'Measuring the total economic value of restoring ecosystem services in an impaired river basin: results from a contingent valuation survey', *Ecological Economics*, **33** (1), 103–17.

Louviere, J.J., D.A. Hensher and J.D. Swait (2000), *Stated Preference Methods: Analysis and Application*, Cambridge: Cambridge University Press.

Louviere, J.J. (2001), 'Choice experiments: an overview of concepts and issues', in J. Bennett and R. Blamey (eds), *The Choice Modelling Approach to Environmental Valuation*, Cheltenham, UK and Northampton, MA, USA: Edward Elgar, pp. 13–36.

Lusk, J.L. and F.B. Norwood (2005), 'Effect of experimental design on choice-based conjoint valuation estimates', *American Journal of Agricultural Economics*, **87** (3), 771–85.

Maddala, G.S. (1983), *Limited Dependent and Qualitative Variables in Econometrics*, Cambridge: Cambridge University Press.

Millennium Ecosystem Assessment (2005), *Ecosystems and Human Well-being: Synthesis*, Washington, DC: Island Press.

Milon, J.W. and D. Scrogin (2006), 'Latent preferences and valuation of wetland ecosystem restoration', *Ecological Economics*, **56**, 162–75

Morrison, M. and J. Bennett (2004), 'Valuing New South Wales rivers for use in benefit transfer', *Australian Journal of Agricultural and Resource Economics*, **48** (4), 591–611.

Morrison, M., J. Bennett, R. Blamey and J. Louviere (2002), 'Choice modelling and tests of benefit transfer', *American Journal of Agricultural Economics*, **84** (1), 161–70.

Nichols, E., S. Spector, J. Louzada, T. Larsen, S. Amezquita, M.E. Favila and the Scarabaeinae Research Network (2008), 'Ecological functions and ecosystem services provided by Scarabaeinae dung beetles', *Biological Conservation*, **141** (6), 1461–74.

Poe, G.L., K.L. Giraud and J.B. Loomis (2005), 'Computational methods for measuring the difference in empirical distributions', *American Journal of Agricultural Economics*, **87** (2), 353–65.

Powe, N.E. (2007), *Redesigning Environmental Valuation: Mixing Methods within Stated Preference Techniques*, Cheltenham, UK and Northampton, MA, USA: Edward Edgar.

Schiller, A., C.T. Hunsaker, M.A. Kane, A.K. Wolfe, V.H. Dale, G.W. Suter, C.S. Russell, G. Pion, M.H. Jensen and V.C. Konar (2001), 'Communicating ecological indicators to decision makers and the public', *Conservation Ecology*, **5** (1), 19.

Schkade, D.A. and J.W. Payne (1994), 'How people respond to contingent valuation questions: a verbal protocol analysis of willingness to pay for an environmental regulation', *Journal of Environmental Economics and Management*, **26** (1), 88–109.

Spash, C.L. and N. Hanley (1995), 'Preferences, information and biodiversity preservation', *Ecological Economics*, **12** (3), 191–208.

Suter, G.W., II (2001), 'Applicability of indicator monitoring to ecological risk assessment', *Ecological Indicators*, **1** (2), 101–12.

Train, K.E. (2009), *Discrete Choice Methods with Simulation*, Cambridge: Cambridge University Press.

Train, K.E. and M. Weeks (2005), 'Discrete choice models in preference space and willing-to-pay space', in R. Scarpa and A. Alberini (eds), *Applications of Simulation Methods in Environmental and Resource Economics*, Dordrecht: Springer, pp. 1–16.

US Environmental Protection Agency (EPA) (1998), 'Guidelines for ecological risk assessments', Washington, DC: Risk Assessment Forum, April, EPA/630/R-95/002F.

US Environmental Protection Agency (EPA) (2009), 'Valuing the protection of ecological systems and services: a report of the EPA Science Advisory Board', May, EPA/SAB/09/012.

Weslawski, J.M., P.V.R Snelgrore, L.A. Levin, M.C.V. Austin, R.T. Kneib, T.M. Iliffe, J.R. Garey, S.J. Hawkins and R.R. Whitlatch (2004), 'Marine sedimentary biota as providers of ecosystem goods and services', in D.H. Wall (ed.), *Sustaining Biodiversity and Ecosystem Services in Soils and Sediment*, Washington, DC: Island Press, pp. 73–98.

Yako, L.A., M.E. Mather and F. Juanes (2000), 'Assessing the contribution of anadromous herring to largemouth bass growth', *Transactions of the American Fisheries Society*, **129** (1), 77–88.

10 Efficiency versus bias: the role of distributional parameters in count contingent behaviour models

Jeffrey Englin, Arwin Pang and Thomas Holmes[1]

INTRODUCTION

One of the challenges facing many applications of non-market valuations is to find data with enough variation in the variable(s) of interest to estimate econometrically their effects on the quantity demanded. A solution to this problem was the introduction of stated preference surveys. These surveys can introduce variation into variables where there is no natural variation and, as a result, natural experiments are not possible. The problem of no or insufficient variation in naturally occurring data to estimate the effects of interest has led to a large literature on stated preference methods.

Among the methods developed, two can be linked directly to observed behaviour. Unlike contingent valuation questions, these approaches key off of actual choices that individuals have made in the past or are contemplating in the future. Consequently, the consistency of these choices with the responses to stated preference questions can be examined. The two methods are those based upon random utility theory and those based upon demand theory. While the two can be linked theoretically in practice, one either adopts a random utility framework or a demand framework. The demand framework, adopted here, is frequently identified as a 'contingent behaviour' approach.

The contingent behaviour method was proposed by Englin and Cameron (1996). Their paper suggests focusing on the number of trips an individual might make under different situations rather than how a single choice might vary (random utility model) under different situations. The advantage of the contingent behaviour model is that it includes both the intensive and the extensive margin while the random utility approach focuses solely on the intensive margin. As a result, the contingent behaviour approach can capture improvements with the extensive margin as well as quality reductions on the intensive margin.

While considerable effort has been expended examining the functional form, parametric specifications and distributional assumptions used in contingent behaviour studies, no effort has been spent examining the role of heteroscedasticity. Cameron and Englin (1997) provided the first analysis of the role that systematic differences between respondents may play in generating heteroscedasticity in a stated preference analysis. Their work examined the role of experience in the variance of dichotomous choice WTP survey responses. The analysis in this chapter examines the relationship between demographic characteristics and potential heteroscedasticity in contingent behaviour studies.

The analysis is important because of the relationship between distributional shape parameters and the demand shift parameters. The intuition of OLS models fails in the case of many count models. Unlike OLS models where simple algebra can be used to calculate the parameters and standard errors of a regression *ex post*, count models must be estimated using maximum likelihood methods and the distributional shape parameter(s) and demand parameters must be estimated simultaneously. If the shape parameters are correlated with the demand shift variables and the relationship is not properly specified, mis-specification has been introduced into the model and the demand shift parameters will be biased. This results in both a possible bias in the parameter on the travel cost variable as well as an inability to recover the mean dependent variable of the data. Subsequent estimates of welfare measures will suffer from the effects of biased parameters.

In this chapter, these methods are illustrated using data on off highway vehicle (OHV) riders in North Carolina, USA. While OHV riding generates economic benefits for riders, they also generate negative externalities. The externalities include smoke, noise, disturbed trail conditions and the presence of large machines (Jakus et al., 2008; Priskin, 2003). The combination of benefits and external costs make OHV riding a useful activity to examine. Several studies have applied travel cost models to examine the value of OHV riding. Bergstrom and Cordell (1991) apply a national zonal travel cost model to examine values and find that daily values of about $21 in 2005 US dollars. Bowker et al. (1997) suggest that consumer surplus in fee based sites in Florida to range between $14.60 and $80.32 in 2005 US dollars. Englin et al. (2006) estimated a demand system for the same four OHV sites in North Carolina used in this analysis and found consumer surplus to be between $25.51 and $131.58.

The remainder of the chapter is structured in the following way. The next section presents count models of recreational site demand that are used in this study. The third section outlines the data collection procedures and the data used in the analysis. The fourth section provides the results, and the final section provides a discussion of the limitations of the analysis and suggestions for future research.

COUNT MODELS OF RECREATIONAL SITE DEMAND

Count models have become a very popular application of the traditional travel cost model. Traditional OLS models suffered from a number of issues including negative and fractional trip forecasts. In the last decade or so count distributions have been widely applied to model this relationship. Count distributions are attractive because they naturally handle both the integer and non-negative characteristics of recreation demand. Specifically, the demand for a site is:

$$Y = f(tc, d) \tag{10.1}$$

where $f()$ is the exponential function, Y is the number of trips, tc is the travel cost to the site and d is the demographic variables that characterize the respondents.

In the case of pooled sites, the demand equation must be expanded to include site characteristics. The specification of the demand is given by:

$$Y_i = f(tc_{ij}, d_i, x_j) \tag{10.2}$$

where $f( )$ is the exponential function, i denotes individuals and j denotes sites, tc_{ij} is the travel cost for individual i to site j, d_i is the demographic variables that characterize the respondents, and x_j is the characteristics of the sites contained in the pooled data. The estimated per trip consumer surplus for the individual i is simply $\int Q^*(.) \, dp$, or $1/\beta_p$ where β_p is the parameter on the price variable. This is clearly the 'average site' in the sample and corresponds to the value at the intensive margin. To calculate values at the extensive margin or, more simply, allowing the number of trips to change, one needs to estimate the change in the number of trips. Quantity demanded for a particular site is simply found by substituting the site attributes into the demand equation. Changes in quantity that result from changing site attributes is found by substituting the new site attributes into the demand equation forecasting the new quantity demanded. Dividing the change in trips by the parameter on travel cost, β_p, gives the change in value for the extensive and intensive margins. Traditionally this calculation is performed for each respondent and the resulting mean consumer surplus and standard error are reported.

The Poisson Model

The most basic count travel cost demand is the Poisson model. The Poisson model provides an excellent reference point because it does not contain any shape parameters to be estimated. This makes it one of the distributions that is a member of the linear exponential family (Gourieroux et al., 1984). The Poisson regression model specifies that each y_i is drawn from a Poisson distribution with parameter, λ_i. The predictive variables are linked to the latent λ using an exponential link function, $\lambda_i = \exp(tc_{ij}, d_j, x_j)$ where i denotes individuals and j denotes sites. The probability mass function for the Poisson is

$$\text{Prob}(Y_i = y_i|x_i) = \frac{e^{-\lambda_i}\lambda_i^{y_i}}{y_i!}, \, y_i = 0, 1, 2, \ldots \tag{10.3}$$

where x_i now includes both demographic and site variables. The expected number of y_i (trips) and the variance of trips are both given by

$$E[y_i|x_i] = Var[y_i|x_i] = \lambda_i = e^{x_i\beta} \tag{10.4}$$

While the Poisson has the unattractive property that the mean equals the variance, it does retain the attractive linear exponential property that the parameters are unbiased as long as the underlying relationship is linear exponential. One way to address the heteroscedasticity that is usually inherent with the Poisson is to use White's (1982) standard errors with the Poisson parameter estimates. Another approach is to adopt a distributional specification that allows for more heterogeneity in the variance and presumably provides more efficient estimates.

The Negative Binomial Generalization

A popular generalization of the Poisson is the negative binomial. The negative binomial is found by mixing a gamma density with mean 1 and variance $1/\alpha$ with the Poisson. The likelihood for the negative binomial distribution is:

$$\text{Prob}(Y_i = q) = \frac{\Gamma(q + \frac{1}{\alpha})}{\Gamma(q + 1)\Gamma(\frac{1}{\alpha})}(\alpha\lambda_i)^q[1 + \alpha\lambda_i]^{-\left(q + \frac{1}{\alpha}\right)} \tag{10.5}$$

where q is the number of trips taken by individual i and α is the over-dispersion parameter. Notice that this likelihood collapses to the Poisson if α equals zero. An important point to notice is that in empirical work the α parameter is estimated from the data. As a result the distribution loses the attractive linear exponential properties held by the Poisson. The expected number of y_i (trips) is given by

$$E[y_i|x_i] = \lambda_i = e^{x_i'\beta} \tag{10.6}$$

while the variance of trips is given by

$$V[y] = \lambda(1 + \lambda\alpha) \tag{10.7}$$

Note that when α is zero, the expression collapses to the Poisson moments. The expectation is that relaxing the equivalence between the mean and variance will result in improved efficiency.

The Gaussian Random Effects Poisson Generalization

Terza (1998) suggested introducing normally distributed heterogeneity to the Poisson model. Cameron and Trivedi (1998) called this density a Gaussian Random Effects Poisson. Terza utilized a two-stage method of moments estimator to avoid the full information maximum likelihood's (FIML) computational burden. In the Gaussian Random Effects Poisson the random effects follow the normal distribution. Following Terza, y_{it} are assumed to be iid $P[\exp(u_i + x_{it}'\beta)]$ where the random effect u_i is iid $N[0, \sigma_u^2]$:

$$y_{it} \sim P[\alpha_i \exp(x_{it}'\beta)] \tag{10.8}$$

and $\alpha_i = \exp u_i$
  The joint density is:

$$\Pr(y_{it}) = \int_{-\infty}^{\infty} \left[\prod_{t=1}^{T} \left(\frac{e^{-\lambda_{it}}\lambda_{it}^{y_{it}}}{y_{it}!} \right) \frac{e^{-\frac{1}{2}u^2}}{\sqrt{2\pi}} \right] du \tag{10.9}$$

where $\lambda_{it} = \exp(x_{it}\theta + \sigma u)$.
  The expected number of trips is given by:

$$E[Y] = \exp(\mu + 0.5\sigma^2) \tag{10.10}$$

and the variance is given by:

$$V[y] = \exp(x_i'\beta + 0.5\sigma^2) + (\exp(2\lambda + \sigma^2)(\exp(\sigma^2) - 1) \tag{10.11}$$

Note that when σ^2 is zero the expressions again collapse to the Poisson moments. From a conceptual viewpoint the expectation is that loosening the equivalence between the mean and the variance will result in improved efficiency. Of course, the Gaussian Random Effects Poisson takes a very different approach to relaxing this restriction.

Heteroscedasticity and the Negative Binomial and Gaussian Random Effects Models

Failure to model heteroscedasticity can lead to a variety of issues. There are the conventional problems with model testing but there are also problems which can affect the welfare results. This section provides a framework for modelling heteroscedasticity in negative binomial and Gaussian random effects Poisson models.

Modelling heteroscedasticity is accomplished by developing a relationship between the over-dispersion parameters and exogenous variables that could underlay the pattern of over-dispersion. In this case, the two over-dispersion parameters that are of interest are α from the negative binomial and σ^2 from the Gaussian random effects Poisson model. In each case an exponential link function between the over-dispersion parameters and the exogenous variables is used. An exponential link function assures that the predicted over-dispersion parameters will be positive (which is a requirement).

The exponential link function is a second equation that links the over-dispersion parameters to a set of exogenous variables. The equation for the negative binomial can be represented by:

$$\alpha_i = \exp(z_i'\delta) \tag{10.12}$$

where α is the negative binomial over-dispersion parameter, the δ are parameters to be estimated and the z's are exogenous variables. The equation for the Gaussian Random Effects Poisson can be represented by:

$$\sigma_i^2 = \exp(z_i'\rho) \tag{10.13}$$

where σ^2 is the Gaussian random effects Poisson shape parameter, the ρ are parameters to be estimated and the z is exogenous variables.

The introduction of a parameterized shape parameter for α in the negative binomial and σ^2 in the Gaussian random effects Poisson model provides a way to enrich the specification of the distributional shape parameter. Clearly, if only the constant in the function is significantly different from zero then the traditional methods are perfectly adequate. If, however, other variables are significantly affecting the shape parameter then the system of two equations for each model will be mis-specified if only a constant is used. The goal is to enjoy the increased efficiency of the negative binomial or the Gaussian random effects Poisson without incurring the bias that comes from mis-specifying the shape parameter.

DATA

The study area included four US Forest Service OHV areas in western and central North Carolina, USA during the summer of 2000. These included Upper Tellico, Wayehutta, and Brown Mountain in the Southern Appalachian Mountains and Badin Lake in the Uwharrie Mountains. The areas include some of the most attractive OHV areas of southeastern USA.

Surveys were administered by volunteers from local riding clubs. The volunteers were especially helpful due to their understanding of the nuances of the sites and the types of riders that frequented each site as well as their ability to maintain a cooperative ambiance throughout the data collection process. Although the sample was a convenience sample, an attempt was made to obtain data from a diverse array of riders. Only one rider per party was asked to respond to the survey. The goal was to obtain at least 100 completed surveys per site.

The survey consisted of an eight-page booklet consisting of 25 questions. To elicit the recreation count data, respondents were presented with a table and asked to enumerate the total number of trips made to each of the four OHV sites during each of the previous three years. Although this procedure may induce some degree of recall bias, respondents commonly left blank cells for some locations and years, suggesting a possible response strategy for those who could not recall the requested information. However, it is anticipated that some respondents may have made a best (but inaccurate) guess, inducing heteroscedasticity in the responses.

In addition, respondents were presented with three contingent behaviour questions. These questions asked how many trips would have been taken if the characteristics of the sites were changed from their current level. The characteristics chosen for inclusion in the contingent behaviour questions were attributes under consideration by US Forest Service recreation managers at the four OHV sites. In particular, the site characteristics that were varied included the number of parking spaces (Parking); the trail mileage (Trail); and whether or not alcohol consumption was allowed on-site (Alcohol). The level of these characteristics was varied using a fractional factorial experimental design. Data used for analysis included only the reported actual and contingent number of trips for the site at which the survey was administered based on the rationale that those responses would be most accurate. Thus, if respondents answered all visitation questions, six observations per respondent were available for analysis. Some respondents answered fewer questions, so their panel of responses is reduced. The survey also elicited a suite of demographic variables that could be included in the analysis. For the analysis here, the age (Age), income (Income), and gender (Male = 1, Female = 0) of the respondent were included in the model specifications.

RESULTS

Table 10.1 presents the econometric results. The first column presents the Poisson parameter estimates while columns two and three present the partially parameterized and fully parameterized specifications of the negative binomial model, respectively. Columns four and five present the partially parameterized and fully parameterized versions of the Gaussian random effects Poisson, respectively. Standard errors are shown in parentheses beneath the respective parameter estimates.

Each equation satisfies the basic expectation of a downward sloping demand curve (all of the estimates of β_p are negative and statistically significant at conventional levels). The parameter estimates on the miles of trail (Trail) are consistently positive across all model specifications, as one would expect – more trails to ride increases visitation. However, there is inconsistency among the influence of other site attributes on visitation with the Poisson and negative binomial providing consistent signs on the parameter estimates and the Gaussian random effects Poisson parameter estimates telling a slightly different story. The Poisson and negative binomial models suggest that having a greater number of parking spaces (Parking) decreases visitation and that allowing alcohol consumption on site (Alcohol) also decreases visitation – both of which are somewhat counter intuitive. The Gaussian random effects Poisson model suggests that a greater number of parking spaces increases visitation (which is logical) and that allowing alcohol consumption also increases visitation (which is at least plausible.) The Poisson regression provides unbiased, although inefficient, estimates of the demand parameters. The other models should provide more efficient estimates of the parameters. The issue at hand is the utility of different methods of handling the specification of the distributional parameters.

The second and third columns provide some insight into the negative binomial model. The second column provides the standard negative binomial specification. The usual test of the desirability of the negative

Table 10.1 OHV demand parameter results

Variables	Poisson	Negative binomial		Gaussian random effects Poisson	
		Partially parameterized	Fully parameterized	Partially parameterized	Fully parameterized
Constant	0.9786***	0.9297***	0.7939***	0.0330	−0.5250***
	(0.0736)	(0.3783)	(0.3664)	(0.4505)	(0.3561)
Tc	−0.0027***	−0.0016***	−0.0015***	−0.0028***	−0.0023***
	(0.0002)	(0.0004)	(0.0004)	(0.0002)	(0.0002)
Parking	−0.0078***	−0.0086***	−0.0082***	0.0034***	0.0043***
	(0.0008)	(0.0036)	(0.0037)	(0.0005)	(0.0004)
Trail	0.0106***	0.0116***	0.0122***	0.0155***	0.0124***
	(0.0012)	(0.0063)	(0.0063)	(0.0009)	(0.0010)
Alcohol	−0.0598***	−0.0534	−0.0503	0.0778***	0.0594***
	(0.0307)	(0.1304)	(0.1324)	(0.0149)	(0.0147)
Age	−0.0030***	−0.0061	−0.0042	−0.0113***	−0.0052
	(0.0014)	(0.0075)	(0.0072)	(0.0102)	(0.0083)
Income (in 100s)	0.0001***	0.0001	0.0002	0.0003	0.0005***
	(5.01E−05)	(0.0002)	(0.0002)	(0.0004)	(0.0002)
Male	0.0243***	0.0872	0.0899	−0.1003	0.1239
	(0.0242)	(0.2073)	(0.2124)	(0.3664)	(0.2936)
α		7.5047***			
		(0.3696)			
α_constant			4.4646***		
			(1.61)		
α_revealed			−0.3737		
			(0.7743)		

Table 10.1 (continued)

Variables	Poisson	Negative binomial		Gaussian random effects Poisson	
		Partially parameterized	Fully parameterized	Partially parameterized	Fully parameterized
α_age			0.0950*** (0.0343)		0.0981 (0.2951)
α_male			−0.1845 (1.2069)		0.1255*** (0.0129)
σ^2				1.0159*** (0.0671)	0.0195*** (0.0052)
σ^2constant					0.2592 (0.2607)
σ^2revealed					
σ^2age					
σ^2male					
Log-likelihood	−9501.4	−3693.9	−3689.6	−7698.4	−7692.6

Note: *** Significant at 1 per cent level.

binomial specification is the *t*-statistic on the over-dispersion parameter, α. The value of the test statistic is over 20, signifying that the negative binomial is the superior specification. The question remains, however, whether a simple linear specification of the dispersion parameter is, in fact, a good enough specification. Column three provides the parameter estimates for a specification that fully parameterizes α.

For the purposes of illustrating the methodology, the over-dispersion parameter is modelled with a constant and three variables. These include whether the observation is a revealed (α_revealed = 1) or stated (α_revealed = 0) observation, the age of the respondent (α_age) and the gender of the respondent (α_male). It is interesting to observe that the parameter estimates indicate that there is no (statistically significant) difference between the revealed and stated observations. Nor does gender play a role in the degree of dispersion. There remains a fixed effect but the *t*-statistic is now on the order of three instead of 20 which suggests that the constant in the simple negative binomial specification is trying to capture a great deal of variation. Age is now a statistically significant determinant with older people displaying more dispersion around the mean number of trips than younger people. In addition, the likelihood ratio test is 8.6 with three degrees of freedom which is significantly different from zero at the 5 per cent level.

The effect of multicollinearity is also clear in the results. The partially parameterized effect of male gender on demand is 0.0872 while in the fully parameterized model it is 0.0899, virtually the same. This would be expected since male gender is not a significant determinant of α. Age, however, does affect α. The partially parameterized value is -0.0061 while in the fully-parameterized model the value is -0.0042. If the shape parameter α is not fully parameterized, the regression is forced to put the net effect of age into the demand shift variable rather than apportion it among the demand shift effect and the heteroscedasticity effect.

A similar exercise is conducted with the Gaussian random effects Poisson model. The standard approach is to estimate the model by only partially parameterizing σ^2 – the fifth column reports the results for the partially parameterized model. Note that the parameter on σ^2 is very accurately measured with a *t*-statistic over 10. As noted above, the parameters on Parking, Trails and Alcohol are all positive and significant at the 1 per cent level. Age has a significant negative affect and the parameter on Income remains insignificant.

The last column shows the model with a fully-parameterized σ^2. For purposes of comparison, the parameterization is the same as the one used in the negative binomial model. This specification indicates that the revealed preference data have greater variance than the contingent behaviour responses, and that Age also significantly increases the variation

Table 10.2   Welfare estimates for each model*

Poisson	Negative binomial		Gaussian random effects Poisson	
	Partially parameterized	Fully parameterized	Partially parameterized	Fully parameterized
$370	$625	$667	$372	$435
($45)	($273)	($313)	($42)	($63)

Note: * 10 per cent confidence interval in parentheses.

around the mean number of trips. Neither the constant nor being male has a significant effect on σ^2.

Further, it is important to note the effect of fully-parameterizing σ^2 on the demand shift variables. The parameter on Age in the demand equation is roughly halved – to −0.0052 – relative to the partially parameterized model. Being Male remains insignificant and the estimates from columns four and five remain about the same. Of particular note, the Income parameter is now statistically significant, suggesting that the partially parameterized σ^2 was correlated with the income level. This correlation may have been through the Age variable, where older people earn higher salaries. In any case, fully parameterizing σ^2 results in an equation that fits better than the base case. The likelihood-ratio test statistic is 11.6 with three degrees of freedom, which is significant at the 0.05 level.

As discussed above the estimated per trip consumer surplus for the individual i is simply $\int Q^*(.) dp$. One is also interested in the variance around the welfare measures so that welfare measures can be meaningfully compared. Following Englin and Shonkwiler (1995) the variance of the per trip consumer surplus estimates can be calculated as:

$$Var\left(\frac{1}{\beta_{tc}}\right) = \frac{V}{\beta_{tc}^4} + 2\frac{V^2}{\beta_{tc}^6} \qquad (10.14)$$

Table 10.2 provides the per trip consumer surplus for each model and the associated 10 per cent confidence interval. For example, the 10 per cent confidence interval around the Poisson welfare measure of $370 is $370 plus or minus $45. As can be seen in the table there is a wide variation in the welfare measure and the respective confidence intervals. Some observations about the results include the relatively high values yielded by the negative binomial models. These also have quite large confidence intervals and as a result they encompass every other model including each other. The other models are more precise and more interesting to explore.

The welfare and confidence intervals around the Poisson and the partially parameterized Gaussian random effects Poisson are remarkably close. While the partially parameterized Gaussian random effects Poisson sharply outperforms the Poisson in terms of fit, the welfare estimates are indistinguishable. The fully parameterized Gaussian random effects Poisson shows an increase in value of about a quarter. The partially parameterized Gaussian random effects Poisson and the Poisson welfare estimates are at the ragged edge of the bottom of the confidence interval around the fully parameterized Gaussian random effects estimate. The superiority of fit of the fully parameterized Gaussian random effects Poisson and the precision of the model seem to suggest that modelling the shape parameter of a Gaussian random effects Poisson provides the best approach to characterizing these data.

SUMMARY

An avenue of analysis that has not received attention to date is the role that shift variables play in the degree of homogeneity that is found in contingent behaviour data. This analysis presented a framework within which one can explore the importance of fully specifying distributional shape parameters. The evidence, which is not surprising upon reflection, is that there are systematic influences on distributional shape parameters that can be captured in a multi-equation framework as suggested in this chapter.

In each case, the effect of demographic or survey design variables was found to be a significant determinant of the shape parameters and, importantly, to affect the demand parameters and the resulting welfare measures. This is important because failure to capture the separate effects of an explanatory variable on demand and the imposed distributional shape parameter assures a bias in the shape parameter and in the one place the demand parameter appears. Clearly, more work remains to be done to understand the role that different demographic variables or survey designs have on demand and distributional shape parameters. One can easily consider survey complexity and respondent burden in a framework such as the one described here.

NOTE

1. The authors acknowledge the invaluable assistance provided by Scott Shonkwiler and USDA Forest Service employees Bonnie Amaral, Chad Boniface, Jake Cebula, Bill

Champion and Kathy Ludlow. Research partially supported by USDA Forest Service and the Nevada Agricultural Experiment Station.

REFERENCES

Bergstrom, J.C. and H.K. Cordell (1991), 'An analysis of the demand for and value of outdoor recreation in the United States', *Journal of Leisure Research*, **23** (1), 67–86.

Bowker, J.M., M.P. Miles and E.J. Randall (1997), 'A demand analysis of off-road motorized recreation', in *Expanding Marketing Horizons into the 21st Century: Proceedings of Association of Marketing Theory and Practice*, Annual Conference, Jekyll Island, Georgia, March, pp. 387–93.

Cameron, C. and P. Trivedi (1998), *Regression Analysis of Count Data*, New York: Cambridge University Press.

Cameron, T. and J. Englin (1997), 'Respondent experience and environmental valuation', *Journal of Environmental Economics and Management*, **33**, 296–313.

Englin, J. and T. Cameron (1996), 'Enhancing travel cost models with multiple-scenario contingent behavior data: Poisson regression analysis with panel data', *Environmental and Resource Economics*, **7**, 133–47.

Englin, J. and J.S. Shonkwiler (1995), 'Modeling recreation demand in the presence of unobservable travel costs: toward a travel price model', *Journal of Environmental Economics and Management*, **29**, 368–77.

Englin, J., T. Holmes and R. Niell (2006), 'Alternative models of recreational off-highway vehicle site demand', *Environmental and Resource Economics*, **35**, 327–38.

Gourieroux, C., A. Montfort and A. Trognon (1984), 'Pseudo maximum likelihood methods: applications to Poisson models', *Econometrica*, **52**, 701–20.

Jakus, P.M., J.E. Keith and L. Liu (2008), 'Economic impacts of land use restrictions on OHV recreation in Utah', report for the Utah Governor's Public Lands Policy Coordination Office, Utah State University, Department of Applied Economics, Logan, UT.

Priskin, J. (2003), 'Physical impacts of four-wheel drive related tourism and recreation in semi-arid, natural coastal environment', *Ocean and Coastal Management*, **46** (1–2), 127–55.

Terza, J. (1998), 'Estimating count data models with endogenous switching: sample selection and endogenous treatment effects', *Journal of Econometrics*, **84**, 129–54.

White, H. (1982), 'Maximum likelihood estimation of mis-specified models', *Econometrica*, **50**, 1–16.

11 Estimation of household water demand with merged revealed and stated preference data
Jeremy Cheesman and Jeff Bennett

INTRODUCTION

The practice of merging revealed preference (RP) and stated preference (SP) data in order to estimate demand and non-market values has gained credence in the resource and environmental economics literature since the approach was first used in Cameron (1992) and Adamowicz et al. (1994). The merging of RP and SP data provides several advantages to the researcher (Whitehead et al., 2008)

- SP data can be used to extend RP datasets to situations that have not been observed previously.
- merging SP and RP data can alleviate estimation issues of multicollinearity and endogeneity that may confound econometric estimation when only RP data is used (von Haefen and Phaneuf, 2008).
- a panel dataset is created when the RP data of an individual is merged with at least one SP observation from the same individual. This Merging generally improves estimation efficiency, all other factors constant.
- RP data can be used to identify and control response bias in SP data through the identification of whether the individual has used the same underlying preference structure in their observed behaviour, and in the formation of their stated preferences.
- Studies that have combined stated and revealed preference data come predominantly from the literature on the estimation of recreation travel demand, marketing, and the valuation of environmental services. Whitehead, et al. (2008) provide a comprehensive synthesis of this research. Resource and environmental economics literature that merges RP and SP data generally concentrates on how historical and hypothetical exogenous variations in the quantity or quality of an environmental good or service affect individual demand for that good or service (von Haefen and Phaneuf, 2008; Whitehead et al., 2000).

In this chapter, we estimate household water demand in the Central Highlands region of Vietnam using a merged RP and SP dataset. The SP data are obtained via survey using the contingent behaviour approach. The contingent behaviour method (CBM) is fundamentally similar to the contingent valuation method (CVM), but differs in the response elicited from respondents. Whereas in the CVM respondents are asked whether they would be willing to pay or accept compensation for some change in the supply or a good or service, the CBM asks respondents how they would change their behaviour if a certain state of the world occurred. That is, while the CVM elicits a value statement from the respondent, the CBM elicits a stated behavioural response in the level of use of a good or service, which can then be used to value the good or service of interest.

Here, the contingent behaviour of a household is modelled from statements of how, in response to hypothetical changes to the water price, the household would alter its water consumption in seven main usages (1) bathing and washing, (2) meal preparation, (3) drinking, (4) cleaning, (5) laundry, (6) outside (generally gardening), and (7) home business.

The merged RP/SP approach surmounts key challenges to the estimation of household water demand in developing countries. In many developing countries, households that receive municipal water supplies are charged either at a single volumetric rate, or a volumetric rate with an increasing block tariff that results in most households falling in the first or second tariff block (Whittington, 2002). In these situations, the lack of observed variation in price is a fundamental problem to the estimation of empirical household water demand functions and price elasticities. Merging RP and SP data of household water consumption overcomes this issue. Moreover, households in developing countries often consume water from multiple non-municipal sources, such as household and municipal wells, river systems and rainwater tanks. Water from these non-municipal sources is often unpriced, and is at risk of being ignored in demand estimation. Household demand substitution between water sources is an important issue of economic and water planning however, meaning a system of conditional household water demands should be estimated in this situation. The construction of shadow prices for non-priced water sources enables an understanding of the demand effects of these substitution patterns to be clarified.

To our knowledge, the study reported in this chapter is only the second to have merged RP and SP data to estimate household water demand functions and cross-price elasticities in a less developed country (LDC). Acharya and Barbier (2002) merged contingent behaviour and RP data to measure household water demand in Nigeria. Our approach differs from that of Acharya and Barbier in that we estimate household water demand by (1) having household respondents estimate their water consumption in the seven household water usages, (2) confirming the accuracy of the household water consumption estimates against the most recent water bill of the household, and (3) using the water consumption profile of the household as an anchor from which the household could evaluate how they would practically go about altering their water consumption in response to price changes. In contrast, the approach of Acharya and Barbier required that respondents stated how much they would change total household water consumption in response to price changes, but not how they would have gone about achieving this change. Our approach is therefore more closely aligned to that of Thomas and Syme (1988), who estimated own and cross-price elasticity of household water demand in Perth, Western Australia. These authors first developed a baseline water consumption profile of each household they interviewed that concentrated on the behavioural and technical features of household water use in the bathroom, toilet, laundry, kitchen and outdoors. Then, in the contingent behaviour stage, respondents were required to identify, with the assistance of the enumerator, the specific technical and behavioural changes they would make in order to change water consumption.

The remainder of this chapter is organized as follows. First, the conceptual model of household water demand is developed in the next section, followed by the econometric specification of household water demand in section three. The fourth section deals with the empirical application, and the fifth section the results. The sixth section is devoted to a discussion of the findings, and the final section concludes.

SPECIFICATION OF THE HOUSEHOLD WATER DEMAND FUNCTION

Acharya and Barbier (2002) characterize the decision framework of water demand when the household has access to two water sources. Water from one source comes at the opportunity cost of the labour input that is required to obtain the water. Water from the second source is conventionally priced and does not require labour input. This arrangement is typical of a household that has access to piped municipal water in the house, and uses labour to draw water from an unpriced source such as a public well.

The objective of the household is to maximize its utility from water consumption, given the water sources and subject to household constraints of income and labour. The household water demand function is:

$$Q_j = Q_j(p_p, s_c, \mathbf{A}_p, \mathbf{A}_c, \mathbf{Z}) \tag{11.1}$$

Q_j is the quantity of water consumed from source j, p_p is the price of purchased water, and s_c is the shadow price of the non-priced water, being the marginal opportunity cost of foregone work income. $\mathbf{A}_p$, $\mathbf{A}_c$ are vectors of the attributes of the water by source. These attributes may include turbidity, smell, taste, delivery pressure and seasonal reliability. The vector $\mathbf{Z}$ defines household-specific characteristics, including income and labour capacity.

If water from the two sources is identical, that is, if $\mathbf{A}_p = \mathbf{A}_c$, the household maximizes utility by consuming water from both sources until the marginal rate of substitution of water purchases and water collection are equal. At this point, the marginal opportunity cost of foregone work income equals the marginal water price. The household decision framework includes two corner solutions. When the opportunity cost of forgone work income incurred by water collection always exceeds the marginal price of water, the household will only consume priced water. Moreover, when the marginal water price is always greater than the marginal opportunity cost of household labour, the household will always collect water.

ECONOMETRIC ESTIMATION OF HOUSEHOLD WATER DEMAND

We evaluate the water demands of two categories of households: those that consume water from a single source only, and those that consume water from two sources. Assume households that consume water from a single source pay a volumetric price for this water. Households that consume water from two sources take water from the priced source and from a second source with a shadow price defined by the opportunity cost of labour. Separate demand functions are estimated for each of these subgroups.

It is possible that households consuming water from two sources differ systematically, albeit in unobserved ways, from households that consume water from only one source. Consistency of econometric estimation is based on the assumption that the chance that a household belongs to one subsample is random. If the process by which a household comes to belong to one subgroup is not random, a sample selection problem arises. The parameters of an estimated econometric model that does not control for this sample selection will be biased due to violation of the Gauss–Markov assumption of zero correlation between independent variables and the error term.

Household Consumption from Multiple Sources

The two-stage estimation procedure of Heckman (1979) is used to control for potential sample selection bias. The Heckman approach involves the construction of an explanatory variable in the equation of interest that captures unobserved but systematic heterogeneity that would otherwise be included in the error term.

In the first stage of the Heckman approach, a regression for observing a positive outcome of the dependent variable is modelled with a probit model:

$$\Pr(d_i = 1) = \Pr(\mathbf{x}_i\beta < u_i) = \Phi(\mathbf{x}_i\beta) \tag{11.2}$$

where d_i is the binary dependent variable, $\mathbf{x}_i$ is a vector of household explanatory variables, β a vector of unknown coefficients to be estimated, u_i the error term, which is assumed to be distributed *iid* $N(0, \sigma^2)$, and $\Phi(\mathbf{x}_i\beta)$ is the cumulative normal distribution.

The estimated parameters of the probit model are used to calculate the inverse Mill's ratio, which is the ratio of the probability density function $\phi(\mathbf{x}_i\hat{\beta})$ over the cumulative distribution function:

$$M_i = \frac{\phi(\mathbf{x}_i\hat{\beta})}{[1 - \Phi(\mathbf{x}_i\hat{\beta})]} \tag{11.3}$$

The inverse Mill's ratio is included as an explanatory variable in the equation of interest.

Conditional Household Water Demand Functions

The demand of households that consume water from a single water source is assumed to take the functional form:

$$\ln(Q_m) = c_1 + a_1 \ln(p_m) + a_2\mathbf{Z} + \varepsilon_1 \tag{11.4}$$

Those households that consume water from two sources are assumed to have the conditional water demand functions:

$$\begin{cases} \ln(Q_m) = c_2 + b_{m1} \ln(p_m) + b_{m2} \ln(s_w) + b_{m3}\mathbf{Z} + \varepsilon_2 & (11.5) \\ \ln(Q_w) = c_3 + b_{w1} \ln(p_m) + b_{w2} \ln(s_w) + b_{w3}\mathbf{Z} + \varepsilon_3 & (11.6) \end{cases}$$

The water price of the first source is p_m, s_w is the shadow price of water of the second source, $\mathbf{Z}$ describes household socio-economic characteristics, taken to include household water supply infrastructure and the inverse Mill's ratio, and ε_i is the error term, which is *iid* $N(0, \sigma^2)$.

EMPIRICAL APPLICATION

Study Region

Buon Ma Thuot (BMT) is the capital city of Dak Lak Province in the Central Highlands of Vietnam, and is located in the middle of the Dak Lak Plateau. The Dak Lak Plateau is characterized by intensive agricultural production, primarily of Robusta coffee destined for international export markets. Sustained growth in the regional population and in intensive agriculture has contributed towards the region facing increasingly severe dry season water shortages. The effective management of the scarce water resources of the plateau is therefore of key importance to being able to sustain economic growth of the region over the long run.

Households in BMT that are connected to the municipal water system pay a non-tiered tariff of VND2250 per cubic metre of water supplied. This tariff falls below the long run marginal supply cost of municipal water, which is estimated to be around VND4000 per cubic metre. Household consumption of municipal water is metered, and households receive monthly water bills.

Many households connected to the municipal water supply system also draw water for household usage from at least one other source, typically a private household well, or from water vendors. Prior to this study, little was known about household water consumption external to the municipal supply system, nor why households chose to consume water from sources other than the municipal system. These water substitution strategies of households carry important implications for economic and water planning in the Dak Lak Plateau.

Household Survey Procedure

The merged RP and SP dataset was obtained via a household survey. The RP data were the observed water consumptions of households, taken from monthly household water bills. The SP data were obtained using a CBM approach in which households were asked how they would alter their monthly water consumptions in seven household usages following the introduction of a hypothetical (shadow) water price.

The objective of the first stage of the survey interview was to develop the household profile of water consumption behaviour, and technology used to deliver and consume water in the household for seven main usages: bathing and washing, meal preparation, drinking, cleaning, laundry, outside (mainly gardening) and home business. To do this, the enumerator walked through the household and identified with the respondents: (1) where activities that consumed water occurred; (2) the technology used in the water consuming activity (if any); and (3) where the water came from. Following this initial identification, the enumerator worked with respondents to estimate the amount of water consumed in each of the seven main household usages during a normal day. As different household members are generally responsible for specific water using activities, both the male and female household heads were asked to participate in the survey when available. Having both household heads responding may reduce the potential for strategic behaviour, because respondents audited each other and there was open discussion on points of difference. The household members estimated their daily water consumption mainly by demonstration. For water usages that were not daily, weekly consumption figures were estimated.

After the daily or weekly water consumption of the household was estimated in the seven usages, the enumerator extrapolated these data to estimate the monthly water consumption and expenditure profile of the household, by water source and by usage. This was compared to the most recent water bill on hand to check how accurately respondents had estimated their household water consumption.

The same procedure was followed to calculate the monthly cost of private well water by household usage. The opportunity cost of household well water was assumed to be VND450 per cubic metre, which was the average opportunity cost of households that participated in the pre-testing stage. While it would have been preferable to calculate and use household specific shadow prices of well water, pre-testing indicated this approach was prohibitively time consuming, caused distraction and often resulted in the enumerators estimating an incorrect shadow price.

After the enumerator confirmed that the respondents understood their monthly water cost by the seven household usages by source, this water usage and expenditure profile was used as the anchoring point for the CBM scenarios. In the CBM scenarios, respondents were presented with a hypothetical change in either the price of municipal or well water, while the price of water from the second source was held constant. Each household received one price below the VND2250 tariff (VND500, VND1000 or VND1750) and one higher hypothetical price (VND5000, VND7500, VND10000, VND15000 or VND25000). The same approach was followed to obtain monthly well water consumption contingent on hypothetical well water shadow prices. Hypothetical prices were VND100, VND250, VND1000, VND1500, VND2000, VND2500, VND3000, VND4500, or VND7500.

Using the hypothetical price, the enumerator first calculated the new total cost of monthly household water under the assumption that monthly water consumption did not change. This total water cost to the household was separated into the cost components of the seven household usages. The approach enabled respondents to understand how their total monthly water expenditure was distributed between the seven usages by source. Respondents were then asked whether they would alter their household water consumption in any way as a result of their new water budget. Households that stated they would change their water consumption were asked to describe or show the enumerator how they would change their water consumption patterns across the seven usages. While respondents could employ behavioural, technical or structural means to alter their water consumption, most respondents focused on short-term behavioural adjustments. These behavioural adjustments generally involved changing the amount of water consumed, or the substitution of water from one source to the second. After respondents had revised their household water consumption, the enumerator recalculated the water consumption and expenditure profile of the household. Respondents who were satisfied with the profile proceeded to the next scenario, while dissatisfied households iterated the process until they were satisfied.

The household survey was undertaken in mid-2006 and obtained 291 usable responses.

RESULTS, DISCUSSION AND POLICY IMPLICATIONS

Household Profiles

Table 11.1 summarizes key statistics of the households surveyed. Approximately 55 per cent of the households participating in the survey consumed municipal water only. A further 32 per cent consumed municipal water and household well water, and the remainder consumed municipal water and water from various other sources. The daily per capita consumption of households that consumed only municipal water was 120 litres. Households that consumed municipal and household well water consumed around 70 litres of municipal water per capita per day. Of households consuming municipal water solely, the municipal water bill accounted for less than 1.5 per cent of monthly household income; in the case of households that drew water from two sources the figure was 0.8 per cent.

Almost nine out of ten households had some form of in-house water

Table 11.1   Household descriptive statistics

Variable	Unit	Obs.	Mean	SD	Min.	Max.
Basic household information						
Household size	Number	291	4.66	2.30	1	21
Main occupation is farming	Yes = 1	291	0.10	–	0	1
Household income	VND Mil	291	3.29	2.27	0.25	20.00
Operate a home business	Yes = 1	291	0.28	–	0	1
Household water consumption						
Sources used by the household						
Municipal water only	Yes = 1	291	0.56	–	0	1
Household monthly usage	m^3	163	15.98	15.19	4.02	123
Per capita daily usage	Lt	163	120.06	105.88	14.81	841.53
Municipal water expenditure as a per cent of household income	%	119	1.37	1.67	0.04	17.33
Municipal water and private well	Yes = 1	291	0.32	–	0	1
Household monthly municipal water usage	m^3	94	9.12	9.53	1	58
Per capita daily municipal water usage	Lt	94	70.22	65.97	4.68	316.93
Municipal water expenditure as a per cent of household income	%	92	0.81	0.75	0.05	4.05
Water storage tank situation						
Have in house water storage tank	Yes = 1	257	0.81	–	0	1
Average storage tank capacity	m^3	208	2.41	1.86	0	16
Household knowledge of municipal water tariff						
Municipal water tariff correctly described	Yes = 1	291	0.15	–	0	1

storage infrastructure, mainly to stock against intermittent water supply shortages. Cement water storage tanks were the most prevalent form of storage infrastructure, being installed in eight of every ten households surveyed. The average storage capacity of the cement storage tanks was 2.4 cubic metres. This is a sufficient storage capacity to supply the average household with 4.5 days of water at 120 litres per capita per day. Approximately 85 per cent of those households that used household wells drew water using motorized pumps. Notably, only 15 per cent of households surveyed knew the municipal water tariff.

More detailed descriptive analyses are provided in Cheesman et al. (2007).

Accuracy of Households' Own Estimates of Water Consumption

The accuracy of the econometric estimates of household water demand rely on the ability of the households surveyed to estimate accurately their water consumption, and then estimate how household water consumption would change in response to the hypothetical price changes. To evaluate the ability of households to estimate their existing household water consumption, pair-wise correlations were constructed of the actual monthly municipal water consumption of the household from the most recent municipal water bill on hand, and the household municipal water consumption that was estimated by the household with assistance of the enumerator.

The pair-wise correlation of these covariates for households that only consumed municipal water was 0.86. The pair-wise correlation of the covariates for households that consumed municipal and household well water was 0.93. Both correlations were significant at the 1 per cent level. These pair-wise correlations suggest that the participating households were able to estimate their household water consumption with reasonable accuracy. Further, the accuracy of the estimates suggest that households drawing well water are likely to consume around 100 litres of household well water per capita per day. These estimates suggest that those households consuming both well and municipal water had a combined per capita consumption of 170 litres per day, on average.

Estimates of Household Water Demand

Consistency of RP and SP preferences

A dummy variable approach was used to test the assumption that households used the same underlying preference structure in the formation of their RPs and SPs. This involved the inclusion of a dummy variable in the system of demand equations to test the null hypothesis of the equivalence of the RP and SP data. Equivalence was not rejected in any of the demand equations.

Water demand of households using municipal water only

The water demand of those households that solely consumed municipal water was estimated by random effects generalized least squares. The balanced panel dataset contained 390 observations, comprising two contingent behaviour responses and one revealed preference response per each of the 130 households that consumed only municipal water.[1]

Several functional forms were evaluated and only the best fitting model is reported here:

$$\ln (Q_{m,i,t}) = c_1 + a_1 \ln (p_{m,i,t}) + a_2 D_{know_m,i} + a_3 \ln (p_{know_m,i,t}) + a_4 \ln (inc_i)$$
$$+ a_5 \ln (hhsize_i) + a_6 D_{store,i} + a_7 \ln (store_i)$$
$$+ a_8 farm_i + a_9 own_i + a_{10} mills_i + w_{i,t} \tag{11.7}$$

(i) is the household observation number, (t) the elicited observation, ln denotes logarithms to base e, and Q_m is the dependent variable, which is the monthly municipal water consumption of the household, measured in cubic metres. Variables used to explain household water consumption are the municipal water price (p_m), a dummy variable (D_{know_m}) that differentiated those respondents who knew the municipal water price and those respondents who did not, an interaction variable that measured the partial effect of knowing the municipal water tariff on demand elasticity (p_{know_m}), income (inc), household size ($hhsize$), which we measured as the number of people who lived in the household for more than five months each year in order to account for itinerant labour, a dummy variable to differentiate between households with in-household water storage (D_{store}) from those who did not; household water storage capacity, measured in cubic metres ($store$), dummy variables to distinguish between farming and non-farming households ($farm$), and those households with home businesses (own), and the inverse Mill's ratio calculated from the probit estimate ($mills$) (Table 11.2).

The additive composite error (w) includes a term for individual specific unobserved heterogeneity (u), and the usual idiosyncratic disturbance term (e). Individual specific unobserved heterogeneity and the random disturbance term are assumed to be uncorrelated, and *iid* $N(0, \sigma^2)$. The approach in Battese (1997) was used to code the dummy and interaction variables to identify those respondents who knew the municipal water tariff and their marginal price elasticity, and also for the subgroup of households with in-household water storage and their storage capacity. The Battesse approach overcomes potential estimation bias that may result from assigning small values to observations with a value of zero prior to these data being transformed to natural logarithms.

Water storage infrastructure was assumed to be exogenous to present water consumption as the majority of households had water storage in place prior to a substantial upgrade to the municipal supply system in 2003.

Table 11.2   Household well status, probit model results

	Coefficient	z-ratio
Dependent variable: probability of having a household well		
Monthly household income	−1.52e−07***	−2.92
	(5.20e−08)	
In-house water storage (1 = Yes)	0.318	−1.21
	(0.262)	
In-house water storage capacity in cubic metres	−0.002	−0.51
	(0.003)	
Farming is main household employment (1 = Yes)	0.723**	2.40
	(0.300)	
Self-employment is main household employment	0.246	1.19
(1 = Yes)	(0.207)	
Constant	−0.161	−0.57
	(0.284)	
Log likelihood	−138.890***	
Likelihood ratio chi2(5)	19.89	
Pseudo R^2	0.07	
Percentage correct predictions (overall)	65	
Observations	220	

Notes: *, ** and *** denote statistical significance at the 0.10 level, 0.05 and 0.01 level respectively. Numbers in parentheses are asymptotic standard errors.

Table 11.3 summarizes the estimated municipal water demand function. A Hausman test confirmed the orthogonality conditions imposed by the random effects estimator were not violated. A Breusch-Pagan Lagrange multiplier test rejected the null hypothesis that the variance of u_i was equal to zero, and thereby demonstrated that significant individual effects existed in the demand equation.

Own price elasticity of household water consumption was −0.06, significant at the 1 per cent level. Those households that knew the municipal water tariff had marginally more elastic demand for water, at −0.08. Income elasticity is significant at the 10 per cent level, and shows that a 10 per cent increase in monthly household income increases consumption of household water by 1.4 per cent, on average. Monthly household municipal water consumption increases as the number of household residents increases, at a rate of around 50 per cent per individual.

The significant dummy variable for in-household storage shows that households with water storage infrastructure consumed more water than households without storage, irrespective of the total storage capacity.

Table 11.3   Random effects water demand estimates for households using municipal water only

	Coefficient	z-ratio
Dependent variable: log of total municipal water usage per month, m³		
Municipal price per cubic meter (VND) (log)	−0.059***	−12.71
	(0.005)	
Know water tariff (1 = No, Yes = 0)	−0.096	−0.72
	(0.134)	
Municipal price per cubic metre (VND)	−0.022*	1.71
(log) – households knowing water tariff	(0.013)	
Monthly household income (VND) (log)	0.141*	1.66
	(0.085)	
Household size (log)	0.507***	5.91
	(0.086)	
In-house water storage (1 = No Yes = 0)	−0.144^	−1.57
	(0.092)	
In-house water storage capacity in cubic	0.110**	2.17
metres (log)	(0.051)	
Farming (1 = Yes, No = 0)	−0.016	−0.10
	(0.153)	
Operate a home business (1 = Yes, No = 0)	0.101	1.28
	(0.079)	
Mills ratio	0.086	0.57
	(0.150)	
Constant	0.161	0.14
	(1.139)	
Wald chi²(9)	294.24	
Adjusted R-square	0.43	
Observations	390	
Groups	130	
Hausman test for random effects		
Ho: difference in coefficients not systematic.		
chi²(2)	0.10	
Prob > chi²	0.95	
Breusch and Pagan Lagrangian multiplier		
test for random effects:		
H0: Var(u) = 0		
chi²(1) =	349.19	
Prob > chi²	0.00	

Notes: ^, *, ** and *** denote statistical significance at 15, 10, 5 and 1 per cent level respectively. Numbers in parentheses are asymptotic standard errors.

Moreover, the significant elasticity estimate of water storage capacity shows that as the water storage capacity of the household increases, so does municipal water consumption. Estimated coefficients of the variables for operating a home business, operating a farm and the inverse Mills ratio are insignificant. The lack of significance of the inverse Mill's ratio suggests household well status does not suffer from selection bias.

Conditional water demand of households using municipal and well water

The conditional water demands of the 90 households that consumed municipal and well water were estimated with an unbalanced panel dataset of 357 observations. The conditional household demand functions were estimated using seemingly unrelated estimation (SUE). Seemingly unrelated estimation combines the parameter estimates, the variance and covariance matrices of the separately estimated municipal and well water demand equations into a robust single parameter-vector and simultaneous variance covariance matrix. Estimation using yields the same coefficients as seemingly unrelated regression (SUR). Seemingly unrelated estimation is less efficient than SUR, but is robust to cross-equation correlation and between group heteroskedasticity, which is likely present in this dataset.

Household demand for municipal and well water was defined to be a function of the same explanatory covariates:

$$\ln(Q_{j,i,t}) = c_j + b_{j1} \ln(p_{m,i,t}) + b_{j2} D_{know,i} + b_{j3} \ln(p_{knowm,i,t}) + b_{j4} \ln(s_{w,i,t})$$
$$+ b_{j5} \ln(inc_i) + b_{j6} \ln(hhsize_i) + b_{j7} pc_i + b_{j8} D_{store,i}$$
$$+ b_{j9} \ln(store_i) + b_{j9} farm_i + b_{j10} own_i + b_{j11} mills_i + e_{j,i,t} (11.8)$$

$s_{w,i,t}$ is the shadow price of household well water, pc denotes the horsepower of the household well pump. The other variables of the equation have already been defined. We assumed that water storage infrastructure and pump capacity were exogenous in the demand system for the same reasons cited as those households that solely consumed municipal water.

Table 11.4 presents the estimation results of the conditional household demand functions. The estimated own price elasticity of municipal water is −0.51, and the own price elasticity of well water −0.44. Both estimates are significant at the 1 per cent level. The cross price elasticity of municipal water is 0.49, and 0.34 for household well water, significant at the 1 per cent level. The result confirms that municipal and well water are substitutes.

Tests of the cross-equation equality of the own and cross-price elasticity coefficients show that the ratio of these elasticities for municipal water were statistically equal to −1. In other words, when a household reduces municipal water consumption by a given percentage in response to an

Table 11.4 Seemingly unrelated water demand estimates for households using municipal and private well water

	Coefficient	t-ratio
Dependent variable: household municipal water usage per month (log)		
Municipal price per cubic metre (log)	−0.509***	−8.82
	(0.058)	
Know water tariff (1 = Yes, No = 0)	−0.562	−0.67
	(0.845)	
Municipal price per cubic metre (VND)	−0.112	−1.03
(log) – households knowing water tariff	(0.119)	
Well opportunity cost price per cubic	0.347***	5.59
metre (log)	(0.062)	
Monthly household income (log)	0.003	0.06
	(0.057)	
Household size (log)	0.192	1.08
	(0.178)	
Well pump capacity (HP)	−0.171^	−1.56
	(0.110)	
In-house water storage (1 = No Yes = 0)	−0.155	−1.02
	(0.153)	
In-house water storage capacity in cubic	0.065	0.44
metres (log)	(0.155)	
Farming (1 = Yes, No = 0)	−0.174	−0.69
	(0.252)	
Operate a home business (1 = Yes,	0.130	0.72
No = 0)	(0.181)	
Mills ratio	0.531*	1.77
	(0.30)	
Constant	3.40**	2.25
	(1.513)	
$F(12, 89) =$	16.91	
Adjusted R-square	0.35	
Dependent variable: household well water usage per month (log)		
Municipal price per cubic metre (log)	0.456***	7.48
	(0.061)	
Know water tariff (1 = Yes, No = 0)	1.533	1.41
	(1.079)	
Municipal price per cubic metre (VND)	0.209^	1.46
(log) – households knowing water tariff	(0.144)	
Well opportunity cost price per cubic	−0.441***	−6.38
metre (log)	(0.069)	
Monthly household income (log)	0.186***	3.24
	(0.058)	

Table 11.4   (continued)

	Coefficient	*t*-ratio
Household size (log)	0.401	1.39
	(0.289)	
Motorised well pump capacity (HP)	0.633***	3.95
	(0.160)	
In-house water storage (1 = No, Yes = 0)	0.036	0.16
	(0.227)	
In-house water storage capacity in cubic	0.120	0.73
metres (log)	(0.164)	
Farming (1 = Yes, No = 0)	0.685***	2.35
	(0.291)	
Operate a home business (1 = Yes,	0.633***	3.15
No = 0)	(0.201)	
Mills ratio	−0.063	−0.16
	(0.386)	
Constant	−4.786***	2.88
	(1.659)	
F(12, 89) =	17.44	
Adjusted R-square	0.39	
Observations	357	
Clusters	90	

Notes: *, ** and *** denote statistical significance at the 0.10 level, 0.05 and 0.01 level respectively. Numbers in parentheses are asymptotic standard errors.

increase in the price of municipal water, they substitute consumption by increasing well water consumption by an equal percentage. On the other hand, an increase in the shadow price of household well water was found to result in a larger percentage shift out of well water than was substituted into municipal water.

Household income elasticity of well water consumption was 0.19, significant at the 1 per cent level. The income elasticity of municipal water consumption was insignificant.

The estimates suggest that pump capacity is the main infrastructure determinant of the volume of well versus municipal water consumed. Each additional horsepower of capacity in the household well pump causes municipal water consumption to fall by approximately 15 per cent, and well water consumption to increase by 88 per cent. Household water storage capacity was not a significant determinant of the monthly consumption of municipal or well water of the household.

Households whose main occupation was farming, and those households who operated a home business, consume a larger quantity of well water than otherwise similar households, but have the same consumption levels of municipal water as otherwise comparable households. Farming households consume approximately double the amount of well water per month than an otherwise comparable household, while the well water consumption of home businesses is approximately 90 per cent greater that an otherwise identical household. For farming households, these results may indicate differences in local municipal or well water quality, and also potentially some mixing of household and farm production usages. Descriptive analysis shows households operating home businesses use most additional water in their business operations.

DISCUSSION

Compared to estimates of household water demand in LDCs from other studies, in this study the own price elasticity of households that only consumed municipal water is highly inelastic. In their review of the literature on household water demand in LDCs, Nauges and Whittington (2008) concluded that most estimates of own price elasticity of water from private connections fell within a range of −0.3 to −0.6, which is consistent with own price elasticities of household water demand observed in industrialized countries. In comparison, the own price elasticity of households that consumed only piped water in this study was −0.06. The own and cross-price elasticities of the households in our study that drew municipal and well water align with elasticity estimates of earlier studies. While the elasticity estimates are consistent, the substitution effects of the cross-price elasticities means that these households also did not reduce total household water consumption to any great degree in response to price changes. Rather, they simply substituted water from one source for the other.

However, the extent to which cross-LDC comparisons of household water demand can be relied upon to make conclusions about the veracity and implications of a particular set of observed price elasticity estimates is limited. It is reasonable to assume in the cross-country comparison of the water demands of households in industrialized nations that municipal water supplies are relatively homogenous in terms of potability, supply reliability, delivery pressure, and so on The same assumption cannot be made of piped water supplies in LDCs. As a result, it is unclear whether estimates of household water demand across LDCs are for directly comparable goods. Moreover, households in developed economies are typically homogenous in the sense that they consume the bulk of their water from a municipal source only, and would not substitute with other sources in response to price changes. The same cannot be assumed for households in LDCs. The possibility that household water demand studies in LDCs do not identify all water source substitutions in their demand specification also exists.

Households in our survey that used municipal water only consumed approximately 120 litres per capita per day (l/c/d) on average, and households consuming municipal water and well water around 190 l/c/d. These quantities are well above the 20 l/c/d minimum water requirement for human hygiene set by the WHO and UNICEF (WHO/UNICEF, 2000). The daily per capita consumption of households is also near or above estimates of the per capita household water requirement for economic and sustainable development, which is around 135 l/c/d (Chenoweth, 2008). In other words, the observed inelasticity of demand of households in our study cannot be attributed to households already being very low per capita water users. Thus, some other factor must be at play.

One potential reason for the relatively inelastic demand of households that consumed municipal water only is the small impact that the raising of municipal water prices had on the total household budget. The hypothetical municipal water prices used in the survey were 2.2, 3.1, 4.4, 6.7 and 11 times the existing tariff of VND2250. The average income of households in the survey that used municipal water only was 20 per cent higher than that of all other households (VND3.6 million versus VND2.9 million). The average of monthly water consumption of households using municipal water only was 15.98 cubic metres, and the own price elasticity −0.06. Adjusting the total monthly household water consumption of the average household for own price elasticity means that for the price scenarios considered the water bill of households that consumed municipal water only is always less than 4 per cent of household income. Thus, one potential explanation is that the hypothetical price changes of the contingent behaviour scenarios may not have caused a sufficient impact on the household budget to induce a substantial change in consumption behaviour.

Nevertheless, the highly inelastic demand of households in this survey, especially those consuming municipal water only, is deserving of further consideration. Several further paths of research exist. These include the estimation of separate arc elasticities between the RP/SP price points, estimation of the household water demand relationship using a more flexible functional specification, and estimation of the own and cross-price elasticities of specific household water usages.

Our estimates of household water demand in BMT have ramifications for the water supply planners of BMT, and for regional water management by implication. The first ramification is that the pricing of municipal water in BMT cannot be used to manage household water consumption, at least over the short term. For the minimum 40 per cent of households in BMT that use municipal water exclusively, increases in the municipal water tariff over the range considered in this research appear to have little impact on household water consumption. Moreover, for the minimum 25 per cent of households in BMT that augment municipal water with well water, increasing the municipal water tariff would cause these households to substitute water consumption between sources, but not reduce total consumption. Second, the result observed that households knowing the municipal water tariff have more elastic demand than households that do not know the water tariff is consistent with that of Gaudin (2006), who found that increases in the price information content of domestic water bills increased own price elasticity of demand by 30 per cent. These results, in combination with the fact that 85 per cent of respondent households were unaware of the domestic water tariff, suggests that one pathway to strengthen the ability of water authorities to effect demand management would be to make households more aware of the price of municipal water.

CONCLUSION

This research contributes to the limited but growing body of studies that have merged stated preference and revealed preference data to estimate household water demand. The chapter also contributes to the growing body of literature on the estimation of household water demand in LDCs. The results of the study suggest that the novel household water activity budget approach used to estimate household water consumption, and then to predict how households would alter their water consumption behaviour in response to hypothetical changes in the water price, can be used to estimate the (shadow) price elasticity of household water demand from municipal and non-municipal supply sources. One strength of the contingent behaviour method is that household responses to hypothetical changes in the water price were anchored in the respondents' understanding of how the household actually used water in various activities. This approach may reduce the potential for hypothetical response bias.

Limitations of the research approach should be noted. The low percentage of respondents who knew the municipal water tariff a priori shows that most respondents learnt the water tariff and their preferences for water consumption as a function of price from the survey. By implication, if this situation did not change and a new municipal water tariff was implemented in BMT, then the majority of households would not alter water consumption. The artifice of the shadow price of household well water used in the study is a second limitation. Because the cost of household well water will differ between households, the use of a common shadow price may have sacrificed some incentive compatibility. If this is the case, then respondents could have simply been playing by the rules of the game in the estimation of their demand for household well water.

ACKNOWLEDGEMENTS

The authors gratefully acknowledge the Australian Center for International Agricultural Research (ACIAR) for project funding. The authors also thank, without implication, Céline Nauges, Truong Dang Thuy and Vo Duc Hoang Vu, Tran Ngoc Kham, and the graduate students at Ho Chi Minh City University of Economics and Tay Nguyen University who were survey enumerators.

NOTE

1. Comparison of the household descriptive statistics and the results of the contingent behaviour scenarios revealed that a number of households who reported not having access to a private well stated that they would draw water from a private household well if the municipal water price were to increase. In the estimation of water demand, households that stated they would use a household well in at least one of the contingent behaviour scenarios where categorized as being dual access households. Moreover, households that only drew from the municipal source in the contingent behaviour scenarios were categorized as single (municipal) source households. The categorization resulted in a subgroup of 133 households using municipal water exclusively, and a subgroup of 92 households using municipal and well water. The remaining 66 households that drew water from other secondary sources were excluded from the demand analysis due to small subgroup numbers. Removal of influential outlier observations reduced the municipal water subgroup to 130 observations, and the dual source subgroup to 90 observations.

REFERENCES

Acharya, Gayatri and Edward Barbier (2002), 'Using domestic water analysis to value groundwater recharge in the Hadejia-Jama'are Floodplain, Northern Nigeria', *American Journal of Agricultural Economics*, **84** (2), 415–26.
Adamowicz, Wiktor, Jordan Louviere and Michael Williams (1994), 'Combining revealed and stated preference methods for valuing environmental amenities', *Journal of Environmental Economics and Management*, **26**, 271–92.
Battese, George E. (1997), 'A note on the estimation of Cobb-Douglas production functions when some explanatory variables have zero values', *Journal of Agricultural Economics*, **48** (2), 250–52.
Cameron, Trudy (1992), 'Combining contingent valuation and travel cost data for the valuation of nonmarket goods', *Land Economics*, **68**, 302–17.

Cheesman, Jeremy, Tran Vo Hung Son, Tuong Dang Thuy, Vo Duc Hoang Vu and Jeff W. Bennett (2007), 'The marginal economic value of household water in Buon Ma Thuot, Viet Nam,' *Managing Groundwater Access in the Central Highlands of Viet Nam*, Canberra: Australian National University.

Chenoweth, Jonathan (2008), 'Minimum water requirement for social and economic development', Desalination, 229 (1–3), 245.

Gaudin, S. (2006), 'Effect of price information on residential water demand', *Applied Economics*, 38 (4), 383–93.

Heckman, James R. (1979), 'Sample selection bias as a specification error', *Econometrica*, 47 (1), 153–61.

Nauges, Celine and Dale Whittington (2008), 'Estimation of water demand in developing countries: an overview', working Papers 08.20.264, LERNA, University of Toulouse.

Thomas, J.F. and G.J. Syme (1988), 'Estimating residential price elasticity of demand for water: a contingent valuation approach', *Water Resources Research*, 24, 1847–57.

Von Haefen, Roger H. and Daniel J. Phaneuf (2008), 'Identifying demand parameters in the presence of unobservables: a combined revealed and stated preference approach', *Journal of Environmental Economics and Management*, 56 (1), 19.

Whitehead, John C., Subhrendu K. Pattanayak, George Van Houtven and Brett R. Gelso (2008), 'Combining revealed and stated preference data to estimate the nonmarket value of ecological services: an assessment of the state of the science', *Journal of Economic Surveys*, 22 (5), 872–908.

Whitehead, John C., Timothy C. Habb and Jikun Huang (2000), 'Measuring recreation benefits of quality improvements with revealed and stated behavior data', *Resource and Energy Economics*, 22, 339–54.

Whittington, Dale (2002), *Municipal Water Pricing and Tariff Design: A Reform Agenda for Cities in Developing Countries*, Washington DC: Resources for the Future.

World Health Organization/United Nations Children's Fund (WHO/UNICEF) (2000), 'Joint monitoring programme for water supply and sanitation, global water supply and sanitation assessment 2000 report', Washington, DC.

12 Preference heterogeneity and non-market benefits: the roles of structural hedonic and sorting models

H. Allen Klaiber and V. Kerry Smith*

I INTRODUCTION

Simple descriptions of the equilibria we attribute to ideal markets make it easy to overlook the complexities underlying these outcomes. Aggregate demand and supply functions do not require the micro elements of each function's characterization of a component of the market's interactions to be known in order for the aggregate structure to be identified. Our ideal market metaphor, for a simple, identical commodity, assures that price signals harmonize heterogeneous agents' behaviour. When we relax these assumptions, as would be routine for environmental applications that exploit spatial heterogeneity in the non-market attributes of locations, the models must describe more fully the interactions that give rise to equilibria with heterogeneous goods and agents. The hedonic model has been the 'workhorse' for these situations.[1] As Rosen (1974) first described the model, markets seemed capable of revealing a great deal of information about preferences. Few analysts would debate that what seemed to be a simple estimation task in using the hedonic model for applications with housing prices, turned out to be much more complex. As a result there has been an explosion of literature on hedonic and structural models for describing heterogeneous households' choices. The latter models exploit the heterogeneity in household preferences as well as the properties implied by a sorting equilibrium. Incorporating features of the sorting equilibrium in the estimation process has allowed these models to be used for a type of general equilibrium policy analysis where households re-sort following exogenous interventions.

These are not the only areas where there has been a significant research response to the need to measure the tradeoffs people would make for spatially delineated amenities. The most active alternative type of application involves what has been referred to as quasi-random experiments or program evaluation. This approach recognizes that household sorting can confound the ability of the simple hedonic to estimate the effect of spatially delineated amenities. People are at locations *because* they have the attributes analysts wish to consider in measuring economic tradeoffs. They are not randomly assigned. Estimating the roles for the attributes in motivating these choices as distinct from other considerations requires exogenous information. The importance of these confounding influences is application specific. A discussion of them is beyond the scope of this chapter.[2]

This chapter has three objectives. First, after a very brief review of conventional hedonic models, we describe the 'new' structural hedonic models that offer the potential for simulating market equilibrium. Second, we describe the basic components of locational sorting models, focusing on the distinctions in the economic assumptions that are important for their use in evaluating economic policies in a special type of general equilibrium setting. Finally, we discuss how these models can be used for policy evaluation and the new research opportunities ahead. While our discussion of applications is limited to environmental examples, the opportunities are equally relevant that involve policy questions that would arise in the applications of labour, public, transportation or urban economics.

Before 'getting down to business,' some motivation to readers for going further might be in order. We take as a given that anyone looking at this volume likes to learn (otherwise each of us would have selected some other job). Nonetheless, we all realize in reading technical material that there is too much to master and too little time to do it. So a couple of examples might help to convince readers it is worth the effort to learn about sorting models. Three examples may provide such motivation: sorting and the 'catch-22' of protecting open space, gentrification and environmental policy, and general equilibrium model validation.

Walsh (2007) estimated a sorting model to describe residential land markets in Wake County, North Carolina. Open space was treated as a public good available by selecting one of 91 neighbourhoods in the model. It was defined as the total amount of public, protected, open space *and* the private, undeveloped, land relative to the land area in each neighbourhood. This partitioning of open space allowed him to ask the 'catch-22' question – can we buy private land to protect it and realize an equilibrium sorting of households that actually has *less* open space in the areas where the private land was removed from the market and protected? The answer – yes! Without a locational sorting model we could not describe spatially delineated land acquisition policies and analyse them in a realistic setting that allows this question to be considered.

Banzhaf and Walsh (2008) provide an example addressing the second issue. They considered whether locationally targeted improvements to local public goods can create situations where the disadvantaged group, that these measures seek to help, winds up with lower levels of the public goods. Their analysis uses a sorting model to explain how this is possible and to formulate hypotheses to test it. Their result can arise when the households involved have strong preferences for being part of an ethnic or racial group. In these circumstances, sorting can lead to what appears to be endogenous preferences for segregated communities that lead to less of the local public good available to the targeted groups because they move to be with their counterparts. Under these conditions the policy that sought to enhance their levels of public goods raises prices and forces them to select less desirable locations in order to cluster.

Finally, our last motivational example arises in the area of model validation. There is widespread acceptance of what might be described as 'Tiebout-tendencies' in some areas of public and environmental economics. That is, these arguments suggest that with enough time, large changes in local conditions induce households to change their preferred communities. The quantitative importance of this tendency is difficult to test. Later we summarize a validating cross-check that Sieg et al. (2004) used to evaluate their model of the role of air pollution for choices in the South Coast Air Basin. Here we just offer the short version of this longer story. Their model requires price indexes for housing that adjust for housing attributes and reflect the effects of locally delineated public goods. To evaluate the model as an integrated description of household sorting these authors estimated community price indexes based on housing sales between 1989 and 1991 with corresponding ozone conditions and then used their sorting model for two tasks: (a) to predict what the equilibrium prices would be for 1990, the middle year of their sample, and (b) to estimate what prices should be in 1995 based on 1995 ozone conditions (a year outside the model's sample period). The first task sought to gauge the model as an integrated whole using within sample criteria. The second sought to gauge indirectly the importance of Tiebout tendencies by comparing the model's predictions with estimates for the price index based on a hedonic model fit to actual sales prices for the 1995 time interval. Their findings suggest the computed prices tend to match the results estimated based on actual sales for 1995. Hopefully, this selection of applications has enticed readers to endure and go further.

II   MODELLING CONSUMER CHOICE

The primary distinction between hedonic and sorting model's descriptions of consumer choice arises from the specification of the constraint set. For a hedonic model the household maximizes utility subject to a non-linear budget constraint. The price function for a differentiated good describing how prices vary with characteristics is the source of this nonlinearity in the budget constraint. For applications to housing this is usually assumed to be the house price (expressed as an annual rental rate). Its arguments include the housing attributes and the locational features conveyed by selecting a specific location of a house. The price function defines the market equilibrium and is exogenous from the individual's perspective. More formally, equation (12.1) assumes utility is a function of a vector of housing characteristics, c, locationally delineated public goods, q, a numeraire good, χ, and one or more unobserved household preference parameters described by the vector, β.

$$U = U(c, q, \chi, \beta) \tag{12.1}$$

Behavior is assumed to be capable of being described from the outcomes suggested by maximizing (12.1) subject to the budget constraint given in (12.2), with, m, the income, $p(c,q, \varphi)$ the hedonic price function for a house, and φ an indicator for unobserved locational attributes. The price of χ is normalized to unity.

$$m = p(c, q, \varphi) + \chi \tag{12.2}$$

Now we come to distinguishing the assumptions of the various modelling strategies.

Conventional hedonic models assume $p(.)$ is continuous. They add observable attributes of households, together with unobservable characteristics (from the analyst's perspective) to $U(.)$, and then use either assumptions about the structure of $U(.)$ or exploit the variations in $p(.)$ across markets to identify and estimate the model's parameters. Convincing estimates require careful attention to selecting instruments for identification. The point of itemizing these details is that the process requires sufficient information to distinguish the features of preferences from the properties of the equilibrium price function, $p(.)$. We explain these issues more specifically in the next sections of the chapter.

There are two approaches to adding structure that have been considered in this analysis. The first involves assuming the preference function has a specific functional form and it is that functional structure combined with the specification of the hedonic price function that distinguishes preferences from the equilibrium price function (see Chattopadhyay, 1999, as an example of this logic). A second approach assumes there is a continuous choice set in order to satisfy the conditions for a Lipschitz continuous price function (see Apostol, 1957, pp. 87–8, for discussion of the assumptions associated with this concept of continuity).

It is possible to exploit the assumed continuity in the choice set provided we assume a somewhat different structure for preferences. Bajari and Benkard [2005] have used this logic. They assume the preference parameters (β) vary with each household. Each household winds up with a different choice from the continuous set. With well behaved preferences we can use the choice set continuity to recover what the unobserved β must be. This process estimates the parameter as the value that rationalizes the observed choice. To illustrate this logic, these authors use both a simple first order approximation for $U(.)$ and a Cobb Douglas specification. For example, if we assume that (12.1) is defined by equation (12.3),

$$U = \beta_{i1}\log(c_{j1}) + \beta_{i2}\log(c_{j2}) + \ldots + \beta_{ik}\log(c_{jk}) + \beta_{i\chi}\log\chi_i \quad (12.3)$$

the first order conditions for household i's choice of house j are given by equation (12.4a).

$$\left.\frac{\partial U}{\partial c_1}\right|_j = \frac{\beta_{i1}}{c_{j1}} - \lambda\frac{\partial p}{\partial c_{j1}} = 0 \quad (12.4a)$$

Using the numeraire, χ, we have $\lambda = +\beta_{i\chi}/\chi_i$. Substituting the normalized value of β_{i1} (that is, expressed in terms of the numeraire), $\overline{\beta}_{i1}$ is measured by the adjusted marginal price as in (12.4b).

$$\overline{\beta}_{i1} = \frac{\beta_{i1}}{\beta_{i\chi}} = \left(\frac{c_{j1}}{\chi_i}\right)\frac{\partial p}{\partial c_{i1}} \quad (12.4b)$$

Equation (12.4b) suggests we can measure each individual's marginal willingness-to-pay for each housing attribute *from a single choice!*[3] This result arises from the continuity in the choice set and the assumptions about how preferences vary across people.

As Bishop and Timmins (2008) note, the Bajari and Benkard (BB) framework must assume constant (or very specifically restricted, as in the case of Cobb-Douglas) marginal rates of substitution, MRS, (or equivalently the structure for the marginal willingness-to-pay) for the attributes. These can vary across households but generally not with the amount of each attribute or with levels of other attributes (this is one of the key implications of the separability assumption). This constancy can imply the second order conditions for some households will be violated.[4]

When we consider sorting models, by contrast, whether vertical or horizontal, we alter the budget constraint to accommodate a discrete choice set and we also assume that tastes vary across households in specific ways (giving rise to the vertical and horizontal nomenclature). The choice set is finite, so there is a fixed number of neighbourhoods or types of houses. The household's choice is often described (to help motivate a mixed discrete/continuous logic) as one that involves selecting among a set of optimized outcomes. That is, the choice of a type of house or neighbourhood within a selected area is conditional on other optimal decisions given that choice. This logic allows the problem to be described in terms of indirect utility functions, $V(.)$, as in equation (12.5).

$$Max \ V(c_j, 1, m - p_j, \beta), j \in set \ of \ alternatives \qquad (12.5)$$

The '1' is in (12.5) to recognize the normalized price for χ. Recall in our description χ is the only good assumed available in continuous quantities. The consumer can only select different mixes of attributes through the selection of one of the discrete set of alternatives. As Kuminoff (2009) notes, sorting models rely on two types of restrictions to isolate preferences. One of these restrictions stems from the selection of a specific functional form for the indirect utility function. The second is the characterization of a distribution for the heterogeneity in consumer preferences.

To illustrate his logic we separate the preference parameters into two groups: parameters assumed to be constant for all households and those varying based on a distributional assumption. The latter are associated with locationally delineated public goods (and environmental amenities).

The logic of revealed preference implies that choices give us an ordering of the selected alternative as superior to all the other possibilities (that is, if k is the selected alternative $V_k \geq V_l \forall l = 1, 2, \ldots J$). The vertical model assumes all households evaluate public goods in the same way. Thus, if we partition c into attributes of houses independent of location, c_h, and those conveyed with location, c_a, this framework assumes the subset of β associated with location is reduced to one parameter, say β_0. This parameter varies across households and the remaining parameters, describing how the c_a variables influence decisions, are the same for everyone. For a given income level, each household's choice bounds the values for β_0. That is, revealed preference isolates a range for the values of β_0 that are consistent with an observed selection of each choice alternative (that is, community or neighbourhood). When we have a discrete choice set, the information provided by these choices is not enough to pin down the parameter. For example, when either the lowest ranked alternative or the highest ranked alternative is selected the implied boundary values for the parameters are unbounded from below and above respectively. This limitation is usually resolved by assuming a distribution for the parameter β_0. With this added assumption the framework transforms the estimation problem to one of characterizing the parameters of that distribution, rather than finding each household's value for β_0.[5] More generally, this result for the discrete case illustrates the 'cost' of discreteness. In the case of the BB framework, the value of the parameter was what rationalized the choice given all the other parameters (and the assumed separability of preferences).

Horizontal models allow the weights attributed to each locationally delineated good to vary across households. For a given income there is a region for each set of parameters that would be consistent with selecting each neighbourhood (community or type of house). By restricting all but one of these weighting parameters, the vertical model isolates a preference set that is a subset of what is implied with the horizontal. The economic implication of this condition is that it imposes a restriction on substitution relationships among choice alternatives. For the vertical model, the substitutes are defined by the ordering of choice alternatives. So those neighbouring alternatives immediately above and below the selected location are substitutes. With horizontal models, the number of substitutes depends on the count of choice alternatives compared with the number of locationally specific goods.[6]

Kuminoff's logic also allows the sorting models to be related, at least heuristically, to the BB logic. The BB approach uses restricted preference structures (usually assuming separability of the contributions of both the choice alternatives and their attributes to household well-being), together with the assumed continuity in the hedonic price function to point identify a separate parameter for each household and attribute. Sorting models assume there is a discrete set of prices but allow continuity in different sets of the preference parameters used to describe household heterogeneity.

For our purpose here, what is important is the way heterogeneity is conveyed to the model. Bajari and Benkard assume a continuous array of choice alternatives in observed attributes and at least one unobserved attribute for the choice alternatives. This structure implies (by their theorem 1) that the hedonic price function is continuous, so with a separable and restricted (usually with constant MRS) preference specification they can point identify estimates for household preference parameters.

Sorting models assume a discrete set of choice alternatives and thus have a finite set of prices, each with a vector of attributes that is specific to each alternative. Revealed preference, given knowledge of the levels of the attributes, prices and household income can establish bounds for sets of the parameters. What is actually estimated are the parameters of the continuous distributions used to describe household heterogeneity. These models also differ in the ways they use the properties of the market equilibrium as we explain further in sections IV and V.

The discussion in this section has been fairly general, describing the conceptual relationship, especially the assumptions being made about preferences in the three methods that are the primary focus of this chapter.[7] The next three sections consider in more detail the implementation issues with each of the methods and how they bear on the interpretation and use of each in partial and general equilibrium benefit measurement. After that we provide some specific discussion of examples (as promised at the outset) and conclude with discussions of future research opportunities.

III HEDONIC MODELS

The broad appeal of the conventional hedonic method stems from its ability to 'reveal' the tradeoffs households make for environmental amenities through observable choices *and* its apparent success in a wide array of applications. There are, of course, numerous qualifications and limitations to existing estimates. Nonetheless, if one has ever presented empirical measures of economic tradeoffs to non-economists, evidence based on the prices of homes in different locations in a metropolitan area is usually viewed as a plausible basis for uncovering these connections.[8] Applications of the hedonic method are diverse. The most frequent early application to environmental issues involved the impacts of air quality on housing values. More recently, hedonic studies have considered a wide range of land uses including the impacts of landfills with hazardous substances, past hurricanes as signals of future risks, and open space on nearby property values.

As we noted earlier, the model assumes heterogeneous households, i, sort across a differentiated set of products (in this case the houses), j, each containing a bundle of attributes, c. The ability of the hedonic model to measure non-market benefits arises through the inclusion of measures for the non-market services as elements in c. We highlighted this group by labelling them as q in the discussion in section II. As a rule, these measures are proxy variables. Usually we do not know how households conceptualize the services each receives from these spatially delineated environmental resources whether the services are associated with open space, access to a watershed or wetlands, or the ambient concentration of specific pollutants. When we measure the effects of changes in any of these proxy variables we assume there is a consistent link to changes in the underlying perceived services.

The hedonic price schedule for the houses in a housing market defines the market equilibrium – a matching of buyers and sellers so none of them has an incentive to change their respective decisions. In practice, this equilibrium is assumed to be 'defined' by the sales prices of the homes sold (and their structural characteristics and locational attributes) in the market during the time period used in each application to approximate the 'market period.' As we noted, Bajari and Benkard's model induces a continuous distribution for the price function by assuming household preferences are continuous in observed and unobserved housing attributes, and that all pairs of the differentiated prices can be used to define an arbitrage condition that is consistent, in the limit, with Lipschitz continuity of the price function. Thus, as they acknowledge, there is no restriction imposed on the supply process. Their result will hold for a wide array of supply processes. Products must exist and in the limit they span the space of c and the unobserved attribute(s), φ, that define the price function $P(c, q, \varphi)$. These prices are assumed to be exogenous from the perspective of each household. That is, while households 'determine' the price once a house is selected based on the levels of the characteristics they pick and the price function, their actions alone cannot change the equilibrium price schedule.

While the theoretical underpinnings of the hedonic are well established, econometric estimation raises several challenges. First, the theoretical derivation of the hedonic provides no guidance on the actual functional form for the price schedule. The lack of an explicit functional form has given rise to a variety of functional forms, including non-parametric approaches for estimating the price function. A second challenge involves the difficulty in recovering underlying demand curves for characteristics. This feature was highlighted by Brown and Rosen (1982). Without structural restrictions or the ability to observe the 'same' (or equivalent) households in different markets (or times), Brown and Rosen argue that the hedonic is ill-suited to evaluate how non-marginal changes in the attributes of the houses (or in the public goods conveyed with them) influence prices in a specific application.

The key issue raised by Brown and Rosen is the inability to identify Rosen's second stage marginal rate of substitution functions using the logic he described. That is, using a single market there is simply not enough information, without making arbitrary functional form assumptions, to identify these marginal willingness-to-pay (or equivalently MRS) functions. To address this problem, they propose using data from multiple-markets that would offer additional points along the inverse demand curve, provided the households in these markets were the 'same' or, if different, we have observable measures for the sources of these differences and can distinguish the parameters of the MRS functions that are constant across markets and the ones that vary with the observable variables.[9] Identification alone does not address the endogeneity of attribute levels selected and marginal prices that confounds estimation. Brown and Rosen also argued that suitable instruments were unlikely to exist. Bartik (1987) later presented some further reasons to accept this conclusion.

With little insight available from theory on the form of hedonic price functions, applications have tended to select specifications that are easy to work with and seem to fit the sales records for the application being studied. This practice is usually conditioned by considering the economic implications of a specification. For example, a linear price function assumes all attributes could be readily re-packaged and thus any configuration of attributes is feasible. This is simply not true.

Even when we apply the Tinbergen (1956)/Epple (1987) logic to derive the hedonic price function as a quadratic function of housing attributes, the marginal price measures something akin to a *conditional mean* household willingness to pay.[10] It is not the marginal willingness-to-pay for the jth household in the selected house but rather what we would expect it to be, if we know the population means of the taste parameter distribution, the population mean for the distribution of attributes available in houses, and the corresponding covariance matrices of taste parameters and attributes of houses available. This feature is important because the Bajari and Benkard strategy assumes we can estimate values for each household's preference parameters by assuming there is a finite set of households observed. In the case of the analytical derivation of the hedonic, the model explicitly parameterizes the distributions for preference parameters and the marginal price measures a type of mean marginal willingness-to-pay for a household that would select the observed house based on its attributes. This point is important to the derivation and interpretation of partial and general equilibrium measures of willingness to pay using sorting models.

One of the most influential papers on the practice of hedonic modelling is the work by Cropper et al. (1988). In it, the authors compare the accuracy of a variety of parametric specifications in the presence of omitted variables. Their evaluation strategy compares hedonic price equilibrium by solving an assignment problem using a sample of homes from Baltimore and a set of different specifications for the 'true' unknown preference function. These authors found that omitted variable bias is greatest in more complex functional forms such as the quadratic Box-Cox compared with simpler linear approximations. As a result of this judgment, the majority of hedonic papers rely on fairly simple specifications that are generally linear in parameters.

Addressing the endogeneity concerns and the lack of valid instruments, Ekeland et al. (2004) argue that non-linearities in the hedonic price function provide opportunity for instruments created from non-linear transformations of exogenous variables. Chattopadhyay (1999) uses a different instrument selection strategy by including household specific characteristics which he argues are uncorrelated with unobservable components, but correlated with housing characteristics. This approach relies much more heavily on assumptions of exogeneity than the approach outlined by Ekeland et al. (2004), but nevertheless is an interesting early attempt to address the problem.

While some promising approaches have emerged to estimate the second-stage of hedonic models, challenges still exist. The remainder of this section examines the functional form approach of Chattopadhyay (1999) and both the parametric and non-parametric approaches of Ekeland et al. (2004). A key difference between these approaches is the notion of economic consistency. That is, we use economic consistency to consider the question of whether a modelling strategy relies on a small set of assumptions derived from economic theory versus the case where it uses algebraic assumptions that must be maintained but where the specifics usually have little relation to economic theory. The functional form assumptions employed by Chattopadhyay (1999), while convenient, are an example of the algebraic strategy. By contrast, the Ekeland et al. (2004) methods are shown to be derived directly from theory and thus represent the first consistent treatment of second stage estimation.

To see the logic behind the algebraic approach to identification, recall the first order conditions for household optimization together with the assumption that the price function is invariant from the household perspective. These imply the well-known relationship given in equation (12.6).

$$\frac{U^i_{c_k}}{U^i_\chi} = \frac{\partial P}{\partial c_k} \tag{12.6}$$

This relationship equates marginal price of a characteristic, c_k, to the MRS between c_k and the numeraire. By specifying non-linear functional forms for both the hedonic price function and the underlying utility function, identification is derived from the differences in the non-linear functional forms implied by these specifications.

In his application of this logic, Chattopadhyay uses a variety of Box-Cox hedonic price specifications along with both Translog and Diewert (or generalized Leontief) utility functions to 'identify' and estimate the preference parameters. He finds the estimates for the marginal willingness-to-pay for his air quality measures are robust to specification changes. To instrument for endogenous characteristics in the hedonic second-stage, he uses variables derived from household specific attributes. He argues this strategy relies on the fact that consumption decisions are correlated with household characteristics, but these characteristics are uncorrelated with the error term.[11]

The second strategy (due to Ekeland et. al.) relies primarily on the assumptions we can deduce form the economic characterization of the hedonic equilibrium. It uses semi-parametric and non-parametric methods to avoid the selection of a specific function for the hedonic price function used in the hedonic equilibrium. To illustrate this logic, consider a general form for a semi-parametric specification of the price equation as in (12.7) where the housing attributes, c, are treated parametrically and the measures for non-market goods and services are described as making non-parameter contributions to price.

$$P(c, q) = c\beta + G(q) + \eta \tag{12.7}$$

To estimate the model, the researcher usually relies on a kernel, often chosen to be a normal density function of the form $f(P, c)$, as well as a bandwidth determining the dispersion of the kernel. With $\hat{G}(q_0)$ it is possible to recover marginal willingness to pay for non-market goods with numerical approximations.[12]

IV   VERTICAL SORTING MODEL

In explaining the origins of the estimation strategy used in the vertical model to classes, the second author describes it as an example of how a decade of research found analytical structures that conclusively describe the predictable implications of Tiebout sorting models. When this was established, Epple and Sieg (1999) realized that there was an additional insight from this research program. The structure that had been developed also offered a new direction for estimating household preferences for local public goods. More specifically, Epple and Platt (1998) explained the rationale for this line of research noting that models seeking to integrate mobility among local jurisdictions with mobility within jurisdictions found that households perfectly stratified along the dimension in which they differed. To establish this finding, the models assumed the marginal rate of substitution between locally provided public goods, q, (usually the object of choice provided with the voting mechanism in these models) and the price of housing, P_h, in each jurisdiction

$$\left(-\frac{V_q}{V_{P_n}} = \frac{dP_h}{dq} \right)$$

was monotone in income. This result was inconsistent with the patterns of sorting we actually observe.

Households are not perfectly stratified by income. Hence the search for a structure that was capable of producing equilibrium sorting that does not perfectly stratify. Epple and Platt (1998) introduce an unobserved taste parameter for the local public good. With more than one public good the vertical model as we observed in section II assumes all households evaluate all local public goods in the same way. Each household is allowed to have a different taste for them – but in judging amounts – all households 'agree.'

The point of the second authors' story is that the analytical models *predicted* income distributions for each jurisdiction. Epple and Sieg (1999) exploited this outcome proposing that if the analytical sorting models have 'enough' structure to predict this observable outcome then with the observable outcomes (income distributions) across jurisdictions we should be able to go backwards! That is, income distributions in each community, along with price indexes for housing, and measures of local public goods should allow us to estimate the parameters of preferences, including the parameters describing the distribution of the unobserved taste parameter for local public goods.

This interpretation is somewhat different from what we emphasized at the outset. They are not in conflict.[13] In introducing the logic for the sorting models at the outset of this chapter, we followed Kuminoff's interpretation of the vertical and horizontal models. He emphasized how each formulation of the sorting problem added information to the basic insights that could be recovered to identify preference parameters from revealed preference choices alone. In each case he describes how a composite of the revealed preference data, theoretical restrictions on preferences, and the assumptions about distribution contribute to identification. These features could readily distinguish a discrete choice random coefficients model applied to micro choices of houses or neighbourhoods. One would restrict parameters in a specific way. Another would not.

Here we pursue the analysis of the vertical model a step further. The single crossing condition introduced in this literature by Ellickson (1971) allowed Epple and Sieg (1999) to pursue a different information source to estimate preferences and to explicitly use properties of the sorting equilibrium in the process. Locational choices in equilibrium will satisfy three conditions: boundary indifference, stratification and ascending bundles. To consider how each relates to the Epple–Sieg estimator we discuss each in turn. Beginning with the last, ascending bundles; this property 'implies' if we order communities from the lowest price to the highest and the index of public goods from lowest to highest, in equilibrium the two orderings of communities will be the same. This condition implies boundary indifference can be used to establish a relationship between equilibrium prices in adjacent communities. More specifically, the households indifferent between community j and $j + 1$ satisfy equation (12.8).

$$V(q_j, P_j, m, \beta) = V(q_{j+1}, P_{j+1}, m, \beta) \tag{12.8}$$

Notice that with a finite set of communities (or neighbourhoods) the price function is no longer a continuous function of c and q. Instead, we will assume P_j is a price index for community j that is for a standard home (that is, with a given vector of housing attributes). Sieg et al. (2004) use a variant of a CES indirect utility function for V as given in (12.9).

$$V_j = \left[\beta q_j^\rho + \left[e^{\frac{m^{1-\eta}-1}{1-\eta}} e^{\frac{-aP_j^{\varepsilon+1}-1}{1+\varepsilon}} \right]^\rho \right]^{\frac{1}{\rho}} \tag{12.9}$$

Substituting in equation (12.8) for V_j and V_{j+1} using equation (12.9) we have equation (12.10).

$$\beta q_j^\rho + \left[e^{\frac{m^{1-\eta}-1}{1-\eta}} e^{\frac{aP_j^{\varepsilon+1}-1}{\varepsilon+1}} \right]^\rho = \beta q_{j+1}^\rho + \left[e^{\frac{m^{1-\eta}-1}{1-\eta}} e^{\frac{aP_{j+1}^{\varepsilon+1}-1}{\varepsilon+1}} \right]^\rho \tag{12.10}$$

Rearranging terms and taking logs of both sides we have the basis for linking the observed distribution of income in each community to the parameters of preferences.

$$\ln(\beta) - \rho \left(\frac{m^{1-\eta}-1}{1-\eta} \right) = \ln \left(e^{\frac{-\rho a P_{j+1}^{\varepsilon+1}-1}{\varepsilon+1}} - e^{\frac{-\rho a P_j^{\varepsilon+1}-1}{\varepsilon+1}} \right) - \ln(q_j^\rho - q_{j+1}^\rho) \tag{12.11}$$

Notice that the right side of equation (12.11) allows the definition of households who will be in community j or lower. Ascending bundles allows communities to be ordered by prices. So for all households whose values of $\ln(\beta) - \rho((m^{1-\eta}-1)/(1-\eta))$ lies between bounds defined by the q_{j-1} and the P_{j-1} and the q_{j+1} and P_{j+1} we know they would sort into community j in equilibrium. The lower bound is

$$LB_j = -\ln(q_{j-1}^\rho - q_j^\rho) + \ln \left(e^{\frac{-\rho a P_j^{\varepsilon+1}-1}{\varepsilon+1}} - e^{\frac{-\rho a P_{j-1}^{\varepsilon+1}-1}{\varepsilon+1}} \right) \tag{12.12a}$$

and the upper bound compared P and q for j to the next highest community as follows:

$$UB_j = -\ln(q_j^\rho - q_{j+1}^\rho) + \ln \left(e^{\frac{-\rho a P_{j+1}^{\varepsilon+1}-1}{\varepsilon+1}} - e^{\frac{-\rho a P_j^{\varepsilon+1}-1}{\varepsilon+1}} \right) \tag{12.12b}$$

Household heterogeneity is described through the specification of a joint distribution for ρ and m.

The actual implementation of the estimator relies on defining expressions for measures of the distribution of income and housing expenditure in each community as functions of the models' parameters. These could be percentiles or quartiles. The model estimates the preference parameters to match these observed values across communities. These can be used to define a generalized method of moments estimator as explained in Sieg et al. (2004). Some specifics of this process are not fully discussed in that paper so we will highlight a few of the ones most relevant to estimating the model here. Some of the omitted details are also important to understanding how to use the model for policy analyses

Price Indexes

The model assumes housing is homogeneous within a community. The only reasons for differences arise with the location specific public goods in each community. Sieg et al. (2002) developed price indexes assuming housing attributes make a separable contribution to the sales price function for housing. As the authors explain, the fixed effects defined for each community in hedonic price equations, estimated with housing sales prices, offer ideal community price indexes provided housing attributes are separable from local public goods in their effects on preferences.

Indexes for local public goods

The equilibrium conditions for the vertical model (given the single crossing property and the assumed joint distribution for tastes and income) imply a logic to sort households among communities. Equation (12.13) defines a measure for the 'number' of households in each community.

$$H_j(N_j) = \int_{-\infty}^{+\infty} \int_{LB_j + \rho[(m^{1-\eta}-1)/(1-\eta)]}^{UB_j + \rho[(m^{1-\eta}-1)/(1-\eta)]} f(\ln(\beta), \ln(m)) \, d\ln(\beta) \ln(m) \qquad (12.13)$$

where $H_j(N_j)$ designates a measure of the jth community's size.[14]

To fix ideas about what the logic of the equilibrium implies, each household is defined by what might be labelled a preference index of $\ln(\beta) - \rho[(m^{1-\eta} - 1)/(1 - \eta)]$. We order households from lowest to highest values of this index. The bounds defined by the boundary indifference condition imply an allocation of households to each community and (12.13) adds them up. Our index of the public good q_j can now be rewritten using θ as our index for each household. Given equilibrium Ps, sorting implies a relationship between qs that is a recursive rule as in equation (12.14),

$$q_j = q_1^\rho - \sum_{k=2}^{K} \exp(\theta_{k-1}) \, (\exp(\rho(1 - aP_k^{\varepsilon+1})/(1 + \varepsilon)$$
$$- \exp(\rho(1 - aP_{k-1}^{\varepsilon+1})/(1 + \varepsilon))) \tag{12.14}$$

where K = the number of communities and θ_{k-1} is the value of the preference index for the 'last' household in community $(k - 1)$. So if one were implementing this rule numerically – each community is 'filled-up' with households in order of their θs until each $H_j(N_j)$ is reached with given prices. Equation (12.14) tells us for a normalized value of q_1 in the first community what the $(K - 1)$ qs must be for consistency between the allocation of households and the index of prices for the K communities. By replacing q_j with an expression in terms of the location specific public goods, Z_s, (that is, $q_j = \Sigma_s \gamma_s \cdot Z_{s_j} + e_j$) we have a two step estimator. Recover parameter estimates for $a, \eta, \varepsilon, \rho$ and the parameters of the joint distribution of $\ln(\beta)$ and $\ln(m)$ and then use them to construct the right side of equation (12.14) and we have (for a normalizing value of q_1) a means to estimate the γs and thus the remaining qs consistent with the equilibrium. To exactly match the households in each community implies a contraction mapping similar to the Berry et al. (2004) logic that derives a latent value for contributions to q that exactly reconciles estimates for the γs, Ps, and the measure of the share of the households assigned to each community.

This logic is important because we can reverse the causality in (12.14) and, for given parameter values and changes in one or more of the Zs resort the households until prices normalized by the recursive rule implied by (12.14) exactly allocate all households to a community. This re-sorting provides the basis for general equilibrium benefit analysis.

V HORIZONTAL SORTING MODEL

While one could envision estimating a vertical model with micro data, this is simply a special case of the horizontal model with restrictions on the parameters. Since the horizontal specification is a more general form, a vertical format is usually not considered.[15] The horizontal model is based on the discrete choice random utility maximization framework (RUM) of McFadden (1978).

A distinguishing feature of the horizontal model compared to conventional RUM specifications is the inclusion of a complete set of alternative specific constants (ASCs) intended to reflect the unobservable attributes of choices – houses or communities in most sorting applications. These are unknown to the econometrician, but observable to decision-making agents. Including a complete set of alternative specific constants in the specification of a conditional logit model results in perfect prediction of observed choices. Similar to the contraction mapping we cited earlier, Berry (1994) introduced a contraction mapping algorithm that greatly improves estimation speed for problems having large numbers of alternatives. The validity of the contraction mapping equating predicted choice probabilities to observed behaviour arises as a result of optimizing behaviour.

The basic setup of the model consists of a set of decision-making agents, $i = 1 \ldots N$, choosing from a choice set of discrete alternatives, $j = 1 \ldots J$. In our case we have labelled the agents as households. The choice alternatives in the vertical model were communities or neighbourhoods. For the horizontal model we can consider a more disaggregate specification of the choice set. Usually the lowest level considered is classes of houses. Klaiber and Phaneuf's (2010) horizontal model defines choice alternatives by location, housing size, and the time period of the purchase with utility given in equation (12.15),

$$U_j^i = X_j b^i + a^i P_j + \xi_j + \mu_j^i$$
$$b^i = b_0 + b_1 l^i$$
$$\alpha^i = \alpha_0 + \alpha_l l^i$$
$$\mu_j^i \sim iid\ extreme\ value\ error \tag{12.15}$$

where ξ_j is a choice specific unobservable and l^i are observable household characteristics. The decomposition of the parameters b^i and α^i into a common component (denoted with a 0 subscript) and a component varying by observable characteristics (denoted by a 1 subscript) introduces preference heterogeneity into the model. The inclusion of a choice specific fixed effect captures components of utility unobservable to the econometrician, but observable to the decision making agent.

Including an unobserved utility component at the choice level precludes identification of all parameters in a single estimation stage. To avoid the identification problem, estimation is divided into two stages by rearranging utility from equation (12.15) into two components, (12.16a) and (12.16b)

$$U_j^i = \delta_j + X_j^i I^i b_1 + P_j I^i \alpha_1 + \mu_j^i \tag{12.16a}$$

$$\delta_j = \beta_0 X_j + \alpha_0 P_j + \xi_j \tag{12.16b}$$

where δ_j is an alternative specific constant. As we noted in equation (12.15), the error term is typically assumed to follow a type I extreme value distribution yielding the log-likelihood in equation (12.17),

$$\ln L = \sum_i \sum_j Y_j^i \ln (\mathrm{Pr}_j^i) \tag{12.17}$$

where the logit probabilities are given by equation (12.18).

$$\mathrm{Pr}_k^i = \frac{e^{\delta_k + X_k^i I'b_1 + P_k I'\alpha_1}}{\sum_j e^{\delta_j + X_j^i I'b_1 + P_j I'\alpha_1}} \tag{12.18}$$

The structure of the multinomial logit model together with the market equilibrium condition allows the mean parameters, δ_j, to be estimated using the contraction mapping routine introduced by Berry (1994). More specifically, the equilibrium concept employed in the horizontal model is not an allocation equilibrium per se, but an aggregative equilibrium formed by summing probabilities. To see the motivation for this strategy, it is useful to examine the first order conditions of the log-likelihood function with respect to each δ_j as in (12.19)

$$\frac{\partial \ln L}{\partial \delta_j} = \sum_{i \in j} \frac{\partial \ln (\mathrm{Pr}_j^i)}{\partial \delta_j} + \sum_{i \notin j} \frac{\partial \ln (\mathrm{Pr}_j^i)}{\partial \delta_j} = W_j - \sum_i \mathrm{Pr}_j^i = 0 \tag{12.19}$$

where W_j is the observed share of agents choosing alternative j. These first order conditions together with market clearing in the aggregate imply that the observed share of agents choosing alternative j must perfectly match the sum of the agent probabilities for choosing the same housing type.[16] Using this result, it is possible to recover δ_j indirectly within the maximum likelihood routine using the contraction mapping in equation (12.20) where s indexes the iteration of the contraction mapping.

$$\delta_j^{s+1} = \delta_j^s - \ln \left(\sum_i \left[\left(\frac{\mathrm{Pr}_j^i}{W_j} \right) \right] \right) \tag{12.20}$$

A key assumption required to consistently estimate the second stage is that the recovered alternative specific constant is the true value, without estimation error. Berry, et al. (2004) have shown the asymptotic requirements for consistent second stage estimation that essentially require the number of agents to grow large relative to the number of alternatives. Developing benefit measures from this model, given this condition, imposes restrictions on the choice set. In the context of housing this assumption requires that houses be aggregated into neighbourhoods or at least that an assumption that well defined and recognized neighbourhoods exist in the area be maintained.

VI   BENEFIT MEASUREMENT AND POLICY APPLICATIONS OF SORTING MODELS

There are many 'flavours' of general equilibrium models for benefit measurement. Under ideal conditions, one would like a fully dynamic, economically consistent model of household and firm behaviour that allowed evaluation of the market (that is, considering price and income changes) and non-market effects of exogenous policy interaction. To our knowledge, a framework to address policy issues with this level of detail does not as yet exist.[17]

For most environmental problems three considerations are especially important in selecting a model for evaluating a large-scale policy change: (1) the ability to include spatial variation in environmental conditions and household adjustments to them; (2) non-separability of market goods and environmental amenities; and (3) recognition of the physical/economic processes for non-market feedbacks influencing market choices and thus general equilibrium outcomes.

Sorting models address all of these concerns in a specialized way within a static setting. Both vertical and horizontal models allow for spatial heterogeneity and the feedback effects of household adjustment on their respective housing price indexes. To date they have not allowed for full income adjustment in response to policy. Kuminoff's (2009) joint housing and job market model allows the equilibrium wage effects of policy change to be considered.[18] His dual-market structure links non-market amenities and house locations so that these components are *not* separable. However, the amounts of housing attributes and other non-housing goods are assumed to be separable decisions. Nevertheless, this approach offers some initial insights into the importance of non-market general equilibrium responses to large policy interventions.

The remainder of this section is divided into four parts. The first defines partial equilibrium (PE) and general equilibrium (GE) welfare measures at a general level and discusses some of the key issues in measuring them with vertical and horizontal sorting models. The next three subsections briefly summarize applications of the sorting logic to air pollution and calibration questions for a vertical model (based on Sieg et al., (2004); open space policy – based on Walsh (2007) and Klaiber and Phaneuf (2010) to compare a vertical and horizontal analysis of the issue in different locations; and the role of endogenous taste outcomes and sorting for measuring marginal willingness to pay, based on Banzhaf and Walsh's (2008) recent vertical models.

Partial and General Equilibrium Benefit Concepts

Equations (12.21a) and (12.21b) provide the general definitions for Hicksian willingness-to-pay used in the Sieg et al. (2004) partial (WTP_{PE}) and general (WTP_{GE}) equilibrium measures for community (or choice alternative j and in the GE case j and k), with q_j^k the new level of air quality at location j.

$$V(\beta, m - WTP_{PE}, q_j^k, p_k) = V(\beta, m, q_j, p_j) \qquad (12.21a)$$

$$V(\beta, m - WTP_{GE}, q_k, p_k) = V(\beta, m, q_j p_j) \qquad (12.21b)$$

There are several aspects of these expressions that differ with the interpretation used in the Klaiber and Phaneuf (2010) welfare analysis in a horizontal framework. Equations (12.21a) and (12.21b) adopt an *ex post* perspective for the GE measures. A household's objective function in the Sieg et al. (2004) model is described in equation (12.22).

$$\underset{j \in K}{Max} V_j(\beta, m, p_j, q_j) \qquad (12.22)$$

Sieg et al. do not consider the expected value of (12.22). All unobserved heterogeneity is assumed to be due to household tastes and the welfare analysis is simulated with the 'households' simulated as assigned to each community treated as non-stochastic. One could envision numerically computing a conditional mean over multiple replications of households identified in each community to smooth the estimates derived by (12.21a) and (12.21b). This would *not* be an *ex ante* welfare measure. It would recognize that one of the identifying assumptions of the vertical model is the normality of the joint distribution for $(\ln \beta, \ln m)$. Averaging across replications would reduce the impact of extreme draws of pseudo-random numbers that can exaggerate the effects of PE/GE distinctions.

By contrast, the Klaiber and Phaneuf (2010) welfare analysis defines the welfare measure in *ex ante* terms. It is based on the expected value of the maximum utility from the choices under each set of conditions. As with the vertical model, the policy change and ability for households to adjust requires that prices adjust to meet the equilibrium condition. With the vertical model this is based on treating the amount of housing in each community as an exogenous supply that is taken as given in the baseline conditions (or it is assumed to adjust with an exogenously specified simple supply process); households move based on their preference ordering implied by their β and income according to the recursive updating relationship based on equation (12.14) (solving in terms of price updating given the q_js). For the horizontal model, the market equilibrium is the matching of sample average probabilities as Klaiber and Phaneuf explain for a given set of prices.[19]

The difference between PE and GE measures for the vertical model are readily displayed in (12.21a) and (12.21b). Partial equilibrium 'holds' each household in their initial community (choice alternative) and evaluates what they would give up to obtain the exogenous change in the q for the community. For the GE case, households can move so what they experience depends *both* on the exogenous changes in q and the new locations they select based on the adjusted prices. This point is more difficult to detect in the horizontal model because there is no 'selection' of a choice alternative. In this case it is a change in probabilities.

Finally, the qs in equation (12.21b) can also be made endogenous to the household choice of community. Walsh's (2007) discussion of open space is such an example. He defines open space to be a composite of protected open space that is determined exogenously and undeveloped vacant land. The latter depends on how many households select a community. Thus, increases in protected open space could attract enough households to a community that the aggregate open space measure declines endogenously in the communities where policy sought to increase open space.

This diversity in characterizations of the responses in the model and in interpretations of the agents in the model implies there are many options for interpreting results. For example, the benefit computation can identify households' locations before a policy change and we can ask what happened to households in communities experiencing improvements versus not, or what happened to households who adjusted or not. Smith et al. (2004) examine the effects by income group and community. In our brief summary of three examples we will not consider methodological issues such as the proper interpretation of these measures as random variables. The preference parameters are estimates. The computed general equilibrium is therefore an estimate, including any assumed non-market adjustment. No one has considered these issues as yet. In addition, there is no protocol as yet for averaging the results from simulated equilibrium, aside from the issues associated with the estimates as random variables. As Kuminoff (2009) and other authors (notably Klaiber and Phaneuf, 2010 and Walsh, 2007) have noted, there has been little work on the consequences of the computed equilibrium.[20] Our objective here is to motivate

Table 12.1 *Estimates for annual benefits of ozone reductions, 1990 to 1995*

	Proportionate change in ozone based on selected Community	WTP_{PE}	WTP_{GE}	Proportionate change in prices
Study area as a whole	0.193	1210	1371	0.002
Orange County	0.180	901	1391	−0.009
Riverside County	0.207	834	372	0.058

Source: Sieg et al. (2004).

attention to these technical issues by illustrating the interesting range of applications these models can address.

Air Quality and Calibration

Sieg et al. (2004) were the first to use sorting models for GE welfare assessment.[21] The issue was to compare PE and GE measures of the benefit derived from actual improvement in ozone in five counties in Southern California around Los Angeles (Orange, Los Angeles, San Bernadino, Riverside and Ventura counties).

Table 12.1 extracts from the Sieg et al. results presented in their table 4 a few illustrative results. Overall the ozone concentrations declined between 1990 and 1995 by 18.9 per cent. The cases we selected illustrate that differences in average PE and GE for households who *initially resided* in these counties can be ordered in two different ways based on the change in housing prices or compared to their realized improvement in ozone after adjusting (in the GE case).[22]

An issue the authors considered but did not report is also of interest. How well does the equilibrium model reproduce prices that would have been estimated based on actual sales in 1995? Figure 12.1b compares 1995 prices with computed GE prices using the new ozone conditions. Suppose a hedonic price function was used to estimate the price indexes based on actual data – how would the model be judged? Figure 12.1a compares the model as an integrated whole for the central year (1990) of the transactions used to estimate it. With the exception of some very high income communities the fit is quite good. In 1995 (shown in Figure 12.1b) it is even better and in some sense – this 'prediction' is closer to the logic used in calibrating models in other contexts.

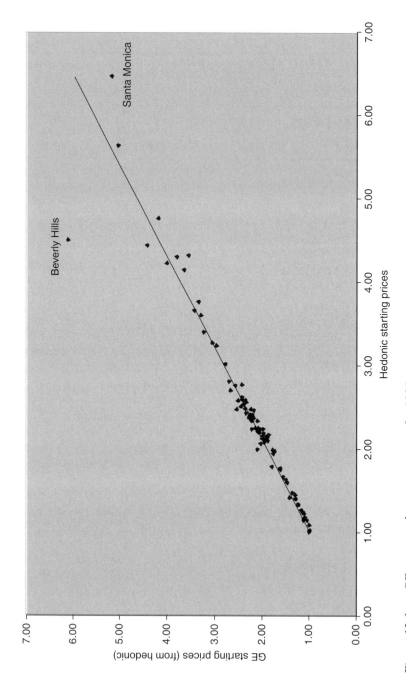

Figure 12.1a   GE computed versus estimate for 1990

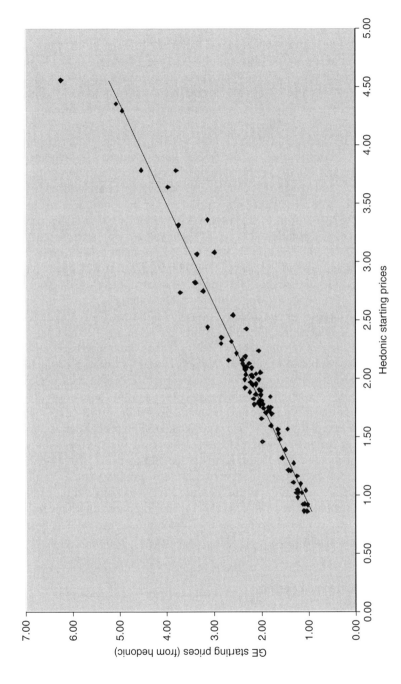

Figure 12.1b   GE computed versus estimate for 1995

Open Space

This example has both a vertical model for Wake County, North Carolina and a horizontal model for Minneapolis–St. Paul, Minnesota. The Walsh (2007) model has one type of open space and focuses on the feedback effects of displacing vacant private land in response to household adjustment. These are quite different urban areas and the models are different, so specific comparison of estimates makes little sense. This is especially true when we acknowledge that Walsh's model treats all open space as homogeneous in its contribution to the public good element of preferences, while Klaiber and Phaneuf can distinguish a rich array of different types of open space and the distinctions are important to household choices. When we compare somewhat comparable scenarios – additions to open space in the urban centres of the metropolitan areas, we find Klaiber and Phaneuf can consider different types of open space – non-park protected land versus small conservation easements. Comparing households initially located in areas targeted by policy, the difference in types of open space affect the PE–GE relationships and the levels of computed benefits for the two types of open space are quite different. The differences in PE and GE measures are largest for the affected households but at 10 to 30 per cent even for households whose initial location was not in an affected area. As expected, as the size of intervention decreases the difference between PE and GE measures becomes smaller. Walsh's model for additions to urban open space also finds large differences in PE and GE benefit measures for household in areas where the change takes place and for those households in areas where they do not. In both models, the GE measures are *smaller* in affected areas relative to PE. For the Walsh (2007) model the opposite ranking is true for an area where the policy does not affect protected open space. This is not the case in the Klaiber-Phaneuf analysis. The direction of difference between PE and GE is the same. A possible explanation for this difference is due to the welfare measure itself – a change in the choice set (and the probabilities of alternatives) rather than a change in what is selected.[23] Thus, careful consideration of the characterization of equilibrium should be undertaken when using the two types of models in benefits transfers.

Social Interaction and Sorting

The last example is a recent paper by Banzhaf and Walsh (2008). They caution analysts in using quasi-experimental results because sorting can undo estimates for the effect of policy changes in a public good if households also care about who their neighbours are. In short, the feedback loop need not be a change in the public good like Walsh's open space measure. It can be another attribute of a neighbourhood that is a summary of who lives there, but not directly related to the public good. Exogenous improvements in the levels of public goods can change community composition – undoing the motivation for the intervention. To the extent we attempt to interpret capitalization estimates after the fact – the sorting process potentially undermines hypotheses that poor or any other specific groups are under provided some public goods.

Hopefully, these examples convince readers there are a rich array of policy analyses that are enabled by these models and a large set of questions to consider in asking how we should perform applied welfare analysis. It is clear spatial detail makes a difference and sorting models are here to stay as methods for helping us understand its role for economic analysis of households' (and ultimately firms') choices.

VII   CHALLENGES AHEAD

No doubt a reader who has reached this point feels there is a long list of qualifications to these models. However, we hope our discussion has prompted interest in working to resolve them. This section picks three areas where we feel special attention would help to take these models to a new level of 'usefulness.' They are: (1) models of supply; (2) what is the extent of the market – both in terms of choice set for each household and households who are 'new' consumers (that is, new entrants into a metropolitan area); and (3) should we deal more explicitly with homes as assets. This last point is not simply a call for an inter-temporal life-cycle model, as Epple et al. (2010) have recently outlined, but in addition dealing more specifically with the household budget constraint for housing as one of a set of assets that reflect past choices, credit conditions and current portfolio decisions. We close by suggesting a few issues on each that are relevant to environmental uses of these types of models.

Bajari and Benkard remarked that the absence of supply from their derivation could be viewed as a strength. This may well be the case when applications are confined to differentiated goods that do not have a long 'temporal shadow.' History matters in land use, and to understand the capitalization of amenities into land values as well as the effects of large-scale changes in land use we must describe how supply changes. Consider the case of a rapidly developing area like Maricopa County, Arizona. Table 12.2 describes the duration of land exchanges, time between sales and holding time of parcels before residential development of vacant land that was both privately and publicly held. This table displays the average

Table 12.2   Time to residential sale from initial land acquisition

Developer size (quantile)	No. of transactions	Time (months)			
		Mean	Std.	Min.	Max.
0–10	10 543	19.59309	14.75074	0	120
10–25	15 378	19.64098	12.63312	0	116
25–50	25 624	21.26186	11.44954	0	120
50–75	26 519	22.82326	10.85266	0	105
75–90	15 429	24.77549	10.05885	0	67
>90	9 419	25.80582	10.16669	1	74

number of months between first purchase of undeveloped land and the sale of residential structures. We grouped this summary of land (and finally land and structure) sales by one measure of the size of the developer. Here we use the number of times the developer appears in our records of sales from 1993 to 2006 as a gauge of size. Larger developers plan ahead and are able to hold land longer. There is clearly much more to learn to characterize the linkages in these transactions. Understanding the sources for these differences is essential for describing how new policy will affect people's behaviour and the gains and losses from intervention.

Rhodes and Strumpf (2003) reminded Tiebout enthusiasts that most people move for jobs – not local public goods. Equally important, there are significant costs to moving and most sorting models either do not deal with these costs or fail to use them in considering the definition of the choice set. Kuminoff has demonstrated we can expand the choice set to include communities and jobs and that this extension matters for the results. Bayer et al. (2009) have demonstrated migration costs experienced by households make differences to benefit measures we attribute to air quality policy compared to hedonic models that ignore them. How do we decide the complexity of the choice set and the extent of the market? Perhaps we need to revisit the role of weak complementarity in modelling migration and the definition of the choice set for sorting models.

It is difficult to move beyond static models without a panel framework that provides household information as well as housing information. Right now confidentiality concerns compromise progress. Bishop and Timmins (2008) and Murphy (2010) have initiated some creative efforts at constructing panels after the fact by linking repeat sales when buyers and sellers can be identified. We need to consider ways in which analyses can demonstrate the importance of temporal and spatial linkages in a panel setting. Hopefully this chapter has encouraged newcomers to this topic and they will want to jump in!

NOTES

*   Partial support for this research was provided to both authors by the Decision Center for a Desert City and, for the second author, by US Environmental Protection Agency (EPA) under STAR grant RD-83159502-0. The research has not been subjected to EPA review and therefore does not necessarily reflect the views of the Agency, and no official endorsement should be inferred. Thanks are due Michael Kaminsky for excellent research assistance and to Jon Valentine for helping to prepare this chapter from a diverse array of drafts.

1. Hedonic models are also relevant to applications to labour markets. In this case the heterogeneity can also be spatial and across sectors. See Palmquist (2005a) for a review of both types of applications and Viscusi and Aldy (2003) for applications to job risk and the measurement of risk tradeoffs.

2. See Kuminoff et al. (2010) for a review, Kuminoff and Pope (2009) and Klaiber and Smith (2009) for discussion of the relationships between quasi-experimental estimates using hedonic applications with housing prices and measures of willingness to pay.

3. It is important to acknowledge that we have not described the challenges in estimating p(.) when we assume the cs can be correlated with the errors due to unobserved attributes that are omitted from p(.).

4. See Bishop and Timmins (2008) for further discussion.

5. We describe how this is done in section IV.

6. See Kuminoff (2009) for further discussion.

7. For a more detailed discussion of the theoretical properties and estimation of sorting models see Kuminoff et al. (2009).

8. This observation was true before the meltdown in many US housing markets. Even for the worst of these markets hedonic price analyses are still believed as benchmarks for evaluating the relative values of some housing and locational characteristics.

9. This is the logic first used by Palmquist (1984) and later used in an environmental application by Boyle et al. (1999).

10. This interpretation follows from Epple (1987, pp. 62–3). Kuminoff and Pope (2009) also use this relationship to describe hedonic difference models before and after an exogenous shock. As Epple explains, preference heterogeneity is introduced into the model by assuming a vector of parameters in the quadratic utility function are drawn from a multivariate normal distribution with specified expected values and a given covariance structure. The marginal willingness-to-pay (MWTP) for an individual in the conventional interpretation of this logic would be based on one draw from this distribution. Epple's analysis argues the hedonic measures the MWTP implied for a individual with parameter values that correspond to the conditional mean, given we observe the individual selecting a house with specific attributes. These are not the same, and to our knowledge this distinction has not been appreciated in the literature.

11. In practice omitted household attributes or housing characteristics could easily confound this approach. He does not report tests or alternatives to this approach to evaluate its importance for his findings. Nonetheless, the application is one of the first complete applications of the algebraic strategy for structural modelling. At one level it is akin to Bajari and Benkard, except in their case they do not restrict how the estimates for each household's preference parameters relate to those of other households. In addition, in applications of the logic to housing markets considerable attention is focused on the definition of instruments, see Bajari and Kahn (2005) as an example.

12. To date, the use of semi-parametric and non-parametric estimation methods is limited in the context of non-market benefit analysis. For a further description of non-parametric estimation in the context of housing see Pace (1995).

13. This description highlights how the information available can be used consistently with a revealed preference logic even though we may not observe individual choices.

14. Notice that in practice we assumed the distribution of the taste parameter and income was expressed in log terms.

15. Kuminoff's (2008) generalization of the vertical model following Epple et al. (2005) is an intermediate case.
16. The validity of the contraction mapping routine arises from properties of the linear exponential family of distributions and does not necessarily generalize to other distributions.
17. There are variations on computable general equilibrium models that include a time separable, approximation to a dynamic model. See Pattanayak et al. (2009). Their adaptation of the RTI Adage model developed by Ross (2007) treats environmental services as separable to consumer preferences. Adage is a detailed, multi-sector, multi-period model that could otherwise be adapted to meet most of these needs. Non-separability is however a serious limitation and a large challenge for a model at this scale. Carbone and Smith (2008) demonstrate it can have a marked impact on general equilibrium analyses, even with modest assumptions about the importance of non-market resources to household well-being.
18. Hallstrom and Smith (2003) also considered the possibility in their simulations of households to experience gains or losses in their existing locations, due to a policy as part of the delineation of general equilibrium.
19. To solve for a new price equilibrium following a policy shock the following algorithm is used. For $iter - 1, 2, 3 \ldots$ complete the following steps:

   - Calculate $s_h^{d,iter}$, the aggregate housing demand for house type h following the policy intervention, using for all h the sample average probabilities and prices ρ_h^{iter}. For iter = 1 use the observed equilibrium price.
   - For each housing type, determine if excess demand or excess supply exists by comparing $s_h^{d,iter}$ to the exogenously given supply of housing, s_h^{s}.
   - Incrementally increase prices for housing types with excess demand and decrease prices for housing types with excess supply to generate a new set of housing prices, ρ_h^{iter+1}.
   - Continue iterating until housing demand equals supply for all housing types.

   To implement the above steps, it is necessary to smooth the price changes at each iteration. To accomplish this updated prices are a weighted average of current and previous iterations' prices.
20. Bayer and Timmins [2005] have discussed existence and related issues within a narrow class of horizontal models.
21. Smith et al. (2004) was published before this paper but was actually undertaken after the research by Sieg et al. (2004) was completed.
22. These estimates treat all households as renters and do not consider income gains or losses in price of their initial housing.
23. An alternative explanation is that the partial equilibrium measure in the horizontal model relaxes the Supply = Demand relationship imposed in the GE model, further changing the nature of the choice set.

REFERENCES

Ackerberg, Daniel A., C. Lanier Benkard, Steven Berry and Ariel Pakes (2007), 'Econometric tools for analyzing market outcomes', in J.J. Heckman and E.E. Leamer (eds), *Handbook of Econometrics*, vol. 6A, Amsterdam and Oxford: North-Tolland, pp. 4171–276.
Apostol, Tom M. (1957), *Mathematical Analysis*, Reading, MA: Addison Wesley.
Bajari, Patrick and C. Lanier Benkard (2005), 'Demand estimation with heterogeneous consumers and unobserved product characteristics: a hedonic approach', *Journal of Political Economy*, **113** (6), 1239–76.
Bajari, Patrick and Matthew E. Kahn (2005), 'Estimating housing demand with an

application to explaining racial segregation in cities', *Journal of Business and Economic Statistics*, **23** (1), 20–33.

Banzhaf, H. Spencer and Randall P. Walsh (2008), 'Do people vote with their feet? An empirical test of Tiebout's mechanism', *American Economic Review*, **98** (3), 843–63.

Bartik, Timothy J. (1987), 'The estimation of demand parameters in hedonic price models', *Journal of Political Economy*, **95** (1), 81–8.

Bayer, Patrick and Christopher Timmins (2005), 'On the equilibrium properties of locational sorting models', *Journal of Urban Economics*, **57** (3), 462–77.

Bayer, Patrick, Nathaniel Keohane and Christopher Timmins (2009), 'Migration and hedonic valuation: the case of air quality', *Journal of Environmental Economics and Management*, **58** (1).

Berry, Steven (1994), 'Estimating discrete choice models of product differentiation', *Rand Journal of Economics*, **25** (Summer), 242–62.

Berry, Steven, James Levinsohn and Ariel Pakes (2004), 'Differentiated products demand systems from a combination of micro and macro data: the new car market', *Econometrica*, **112** (1), 68–105.

Bishop, Kelly and Christopher Timmins (2008), 'Simple, consistent estimation of the marginal willingness to pay function: recovering Rosen's second stage without instrumental variables', mimeo.

Boyle, Kevin, Joan Poor and Laura Taylor (1999), 'Estimating the demand for protecting freshwater lakes from eutrophication,' *American Journal of Agricultural Economics*, **81** (5), 1118–22.

Brown, James N. and Harvey S. Rosen (1982), 'On the estimation of structural hedonic price models', *Econometrica*, **50** (3), 765–8.

Carbone, Jared C. and V. Kerry Smith (2008), 'Evaluating policy interventions with general equilibrium externalities', *Journal of Public Economics*, **92** (June), 1254–74.

Chattopadhyay, Sudip (1999),'Estimating the demand for air quality: new evidence based on the Chicago housing market', *Land Economics*, **75** (1), 22–38.

Cropper, Maureen L., Leland B. Deck and Kenenth E. McConnell (1988), 'On the choice of functional form for hedonic price functions', *Review of Economics and Statistics*, **70** (4), 668–75.

Ekeland, Ivar, James J. Heckman and Lars Nesheim (2004), 'Identification and estimation of hedonic models', *Journal of Political Economy*, **112** (1), S60–S109.

Ellickson, Bryan (1971), 'Jurisdictional fragmentation and residential choice', *American Economic Review*, **61** (2), 334–9.

Epple, Dennis (1987), 'Hedonic prices and implicit markets: estimating demand and supply functions for differentiated products', *Journal of Political Economy*, **95** (1), 59–80.

Epple, Dennis and Glenn J. Platt (1998), 'Equilibrium and local redistribution in an urban economy when households differ in both preferences and incomes', *Journal of Urban Economics*, **43** (1), 23–51.

Epple, Dennis and Holger Sieg (1999), 'Estimating equilibrium models of local jurisdiction', *Journal of Political Economy*, **107** (4), 645–81.

Epple, Dennis, M. Peress and H. Sieg (2005), 'Identification and semiparametric estimation of equilibrium models of local jurisdiction', unpublished manuscript.

Epple, Dennis, Richard Romano and Holger Sieg (2010), 'The intergenerational conflict over the provision of public education', Carnegie Mellon University, working paper.

Greenstone, Michael and Justin Gallagher (2008), 'Does hazardous waste matter? Evidence from the housing market and the superfund program', *Quarterly Journal of Economics*, **123** (3), 951–1003.

Hallstrom, Daniel and V. Kerry Smith (2003), 'Habitat protection policies and open space: a general equilibrium analysis of "takings" and "givings"', unpublished paper presented to AERE workshop, June.

Klaiber, H. Allen and Daniel J. Phaneuf (2010), 'Valuing open space in a residential sorting model of the twin cities', *Journal of Environmental Economics and Management*, **60** (2), 57–77.

Klaiber, H.A. and V. Kerry Smith (2009), 'Evaluating Rubin's causal model for measuring the capitalization of environmental amenities', NBER Working Paper no. 14957.

Kuminoff, Nicolai V. (2008), 'Recovering preferences from a dual-market locational equilibrium', ASU unpublished working paper, November.

Kuminoff, Nicolai V. (2009), 'Decomposing the structural identification of nonmarket values', *Journal of Environmental Economics and Management*, **57** (2), 123–39.

Kuminoff, Nicolai V. and Jaren C. Pope (2009), 'Capitalization and welfare measurement in the quasi-experimental hedonic model', mimeo.

Kuminoff, Nicolai V., Christopher F. Parmeter and Jaren C. Pope (2009), 'How much should we trust hedonic estimates to evaluate public policy?', mimeo.

Kuminoff, Nicolai V., Christopher F. Parmeter and Jaren C. Pope (2010), 'Which hedonic models can we trust to recover the marginal willingness to pay for environmental amenities?', *Journal of Environmental Economics and Management*, **60** (November): 145–60.

McFadden, Daniel (1978), 'Modelling the choice of residential location', in A. Karlqvist, L. Lundqvist, F. Snickars and J. Weibull (eds), *Spatial Interaction Theory and Planning Models*, Amsterdam: North Holland, pp. 75–96.

Murphy, Alvin (2010), 'A dynamic model of housing supply', Washington University, unpublished working paper.

Pace, R.K. (1995), 'Parametric semiparametric, and nonparametric estimation of characteristic values with mass assessment and hedonic pricing models', *Journal of Real Estate Finance and Economics*, **11** (3), 195–217.

Palmquist, Raymond B. (1984), 'Estimating the demand for the characteristics of housing', *Review of Economics and Statistics*, **66** (3), 394–404.

Palmquist, Raymond B. (2005a), 'Property value models,' in Karl-Göran Mäler and Jeffery Vincent (eds), *Handbook of Environmental Economics*, Vol. 2, Amsterdam: North Holland Press, pp. 763–820.

Palmquist, Raymond B (2005b), 'Weak complementarity, path independence, and the intuition of the Willig condition', *Journal of Environmental Economics and Management*, **49** (1), 103–15.

Pattanayak, Subhrendu K., Martin T. Ross, Brooks M. Depro, Simone C. Bauch, Christopher Timmins, Kelly J. Wendland and Keith Alger (2009), 'Climate change and conservation in Brazil: CGE evaluation of health and wealth impacts', *The B.E. Journal of Economic Analysis & Policy*, Berkeley Electronic Press, **9** (2) (Contributions), art. 6, 1–42.

Rhodes, Paul W. and Koleman S. Strumpf (2003), 'Assessing the importance of Tiebout sorting: local heterogeneity from 1850 to 1990', *American Economic Review*, **93** (5), 1648–77.

Rosen, Sherwin (1974), 'Hedonic prices and implicit markets: product differentiation in pure competition', *Journal of Political Economy*, **82** (1), 34–55.

Ross, Martin T. (2007), 'Documentation of the applied dynamic analysis of global economy model', (ADAGE) Working Paper 07-02, RTI International, April.

Sieg, Holger, V. Kerry Smith, H. Spencer Banzhaf and Randy Walsh (2002), 'Interjurisdictional housing prices in location equilibrium', *Journal of Urban Economics*, **52** (1), 131–53.

Sieg, Holger, V. Kerry Smith, H. Spencer Banzhaf and Randy Walsh (2004), 'Estimating the general equilibrium benefits of large changes in spatially delineated public goods', *International Economic Review*, **45** (4), 1047–77.

Smith, V. Kerry and H. Spencer Banzhaf (2004), 'A diagrammatic exposition of weak complementarity and the Willig condition', *American Journal of Agricultural Economics*, **86** (2), 455–66.

Smith, V. Kerry, Holger Sieg, H. Spencer Banzhaf and Randy Walsh (2004), 'General equilibrium benefits for environmental improvements: projected ozone reductions under EPA's prospective analysis for the Los Angeles air basin', *Journal of Environmental Economics and Management*, **47** (3), 559–84.

Tinbergen, Jan (1956), 'On theory of income distribution', *Weltwirtschaftliches Archiv*, **77**, 155–75. Reprinted in 1959.

Viscusi, W. Kip and Joseph E. Aldy (2003), 'The value of a statistical life: a critical review of market estimates throughout the world', *Journal of Risk and Uncertainty*, **27** (3), 239–56.
Walsh, Randall P. (2007), 'Endogenous open space amenities in a locational equilibrium', *Journal of Urban Economics*, **61** (2), 319–44.

13 Dealing with scale and scope issues in stated preference experiments[1]

John Rolfe and Xuehong Wang

1 INTRODUCTION

The application of stated preference techniques such as contingent valuation (CV) and choice modelling (CM) involves a constructed market setting where respondents are asked to identify how they would choose between a single trade-off (CV) or for several repeated trade-offs (CM). The analyst designing these applications typically has some discretion over the size and complexity of trade-offs that will be offered in the choice alternatives (Carson et al., 1994). In most cases the analyst balances the desire to make the choice task realistic against the desire to minimize choice complexity. Important decisions thus need to be made about the scope of the trade-off that will be presented to respondents, the actual quantities involved and the way in which those trade-offs are framed.

As stated preference experiments can be replicated with the trade-offs constructed in different ways, it is relatively easy to test how changing the trade-offs can influence the choices made by respondents, and hence the subsequent values that are assigned. There was early evidence with the CV method that respondent choices were insensitive to changing the dimensions of the trade-off on offer, contrary to expectations from economic theory. This insensitivity to smaller and larger trade-offs became known as part-whole bias (Mitchell and Carson, 1989) or scope insensitivity (Arrow et al., 1993), and has generated heated and divergent views about the usefulness of the CV method (Schulze et al., 1998).

An example of scope insensitivity was reported by Desvousges et al. (1993) where they reported that the average willingness-to-pay (WTP) to clean up oil-filled lakes in Ontario and prevent migratory birds from dying in them was the same when 2000 birds were saved as when 20000 or 200000 birds were prevented from dying. These results imply that the marginal WTP for an increase in the number of birds saved is zero, which is clearly at odds with the standard economic maxim that more of some good is generally preferred to less (apart from when satiation is reached). Attention on scope insensitivity intensified with the embedding hypothesis of Kahneman and Knetsch (1992), which held that scope insensitivity was caused by the purchase of 'moral satisfaction'. The hypothesis was that respondents gained utility from the satisfaction of giving to a worthy cause rather than from the specific environmental improvements that were on offer.

The concerns about what trade-offs were being assessed with the CV method became prominent in the USA after some of the damages arising from the 1989 *Exxon Valdez* oil spill were assessed with the CV method, leading to widespread debate about its appropriateness (Portney, 1994). An inquiry was conducted by a panel of experts for the National Oceanic and Atmospheric Administration to assess the validity of the technique (Arrow et al., 1993). Similar concerns were raised in Australia following the use of CV to ascertain the non-use values of potential environmental damage at Coronation Hill, a proposed mining site in a conservation zone adjacent to Kakadu National Park. There was widespread criticism of the subsequent results and the methodology of the CV study, and partly as a consequence, CV has never been accepted in Australia to the same extent that it was in the USA and Europe (Bennett, 1996).

The panel of experts that reviewed CV in the USA concluded that the technique was reliable enough to generate estimates of value, but identified scoping problems as 'perhaps the most important internal argument against the reliability of the CVM approach' (Arrow et al., 1993, p. 4607). The panel also outlined a number of guidelines for future use of CV, including the conduct of a scope test to ensure that respondents understood the scenarios accurately (Portney, 1994). In Australia and elsewhere attention turned to the development of the CM technique because of its built-in tests of scope sensitivity (Hanley et al., 1998). In CM, the use of attributes to represent choice dimensions means the amenity of interest can be framed within a pool of substitutes, while variation in attribute levels means that respondents are automatically aware that different amounts are available (Rolfe et al., 2000).

The use of application guidelines with CV and the development of CM have addressed many issues relating to minor changes in the amount and dimensions of the amenity to be valued. However, a number of issues still remain, as demonstrated by difficulties in transferring values accurately between source valuation studies and target applications where the dimensions of the trade-offs vary. A number of reviews of benefit transfer applications involving stated preference techniques (for example, Bergland et al., 2002; Brouwer, 2000; Rolfe and Bennett, 2006) have noted that tests of convergent validity are difficult to satisfy even when there are only modest differences between source and target sites. This suggests that the way that values change when there are variations in the dimensions of the good to be valued are still not always well understood.

The primary goal of this chapter is to clarify the description and treatment of choice dimensions in stated preference experiments. In the CV literature, variations in the dimensions of the choice task and the quantities involved are described together as changes in 'scope'. However this treatment is problematic because responses to differences in choice dimensions may be confounded with variations in the amount on offer. As a consequence, CM researchers (for example, Mazur and Bennett, 2009) distinguish the CV 'scope' concept into two separate categories. *Scope* refers to the context of value estimates, best described in terms of the elements of the choice task being presented. *Scale* refers to the quantity of changes being considered within those choice elements.

These issues are reviewed within this chapter in the following order. A historical overview of the identification of 'scope' effects (the encompassing CV version) is provided in the next section, followed by a precise categorization of scale and scope effects in section three. A review of scale and scope issues relevant to the CM technique is provided in sections four and five, followed by final conclusions.

2   THE HISTORICAL TREATMENT OF SCOPE AND SCALE ISSUES IN STATED PREFERENCE EXPERIMENTS

Historically, problems of 'scope' have been taken to encompass situations where respondents are insensitive to both the dimensions of the choice task and the amount of the environmental amenity being offered. Problems of 'scope' have been used to argue that CV does not meet requirements of rational choice, and that the resulting WTP amounts are not consistent with economic theory (Diamond and Hausman, 1994). Arguments such as the embedding hypothesis (Kahneman and Knetsch, 1992), the good cause dump (Harrison, 1992), and the warm glow effect (Diamond and Hausman, 1994) imply that any constructed markets are problematic because respondents will react to the opportunity to signal their support for a cause rather than trade-off the quantities on offer.

The responses to the significant challenge to CV of 'scope' insensitivity and embedding effect arguments can be classified into three groups. In the first are the theoretical arguments explaining why some level of 'scope' insensitivity can be expected in stated preference studies. These arguments encompass both changes in the quantity of the environmental good involved (a scale issue), and the dimensions of the trade-offs being offered (a scope issue), helping to illustrate why it is important to distinguish between these effects.

The theoretical argument relating to scale is that increasing amounts of an environmental asset are likely to be associated with diminishing marginal utility, implying that willingness to pay is not a linear function of the amount of the amenity on offer (Randall, 1997). Smith and Osbourne conclude that the only bound on the CV scope test that can be consistently used is that 'a larger amount of an object of choice should have a larger WTP than a smaller amount' (1996, p. 289), while Carson and Mitchell (1995) note that CV scope tests are only valid when respondents view different amounts of a good as meaningful. A second theoretical argument is that apparent insensitivity to scope can arise because of a sequencing effect (Randall and Hoehn, 1996). This relates to the situation where the value of an item changes according to whether it is offered first or alone, as against later in a long list of choices. Thus the position of an amenity in a queue of choices can influence values. Furthermore, a sub-additivity effect can be generated according to whether an amenity is framed by itself or within a group (Bateman et al., 1997; Hanemann, 1994; Randall, 1997). Values can be sensitive to the way that a good is framed against both context and substitutes.

The second group of responses incorporate the more practical options for identifying and dealing with 'scope' issues. A number of apparent problems of 'scope' have been shown to be the result of poor design and definition of contingent markets (Carson and Mitchell, 1995). In many cases the effects occur because of amenity mis-specification problems, particularly when respondents focus on a more inclusive good than the one nominated by the researcher (Carson and Mitchell, 1995). Methodological issues and inappropriate statistical analysis can also cause apparent 'scope' problems (Hanemann, 1994; Harrison, 1992). A number of meta-analyses of CV method studies have identified that the technique can capture differences in choice dimensions and quantities on offer (Loomis and Ekstrand, 1997; Smith and Osbourne, 1996), suggesting that careful framing of the contingent market and performance of stated preference surveys can address most of the more critical concerns about embedding and 'scope' issues.

The third group of responses to issues of 'scope' insensitivity has been to design better ways of internalising differences within contingent markets. The CM technique has advantages in this respect because variations in choice about potential improvements are automatically offered to respondents in CM experiments (Hanley et al., 1998, Rolfe et al., 2000). As well, the CM technique frames the trade-offs more precisely to respondents through a focus on selected attributes, forcing some internal consistency of valuation (Rolfe et al., 2000). If respondents do not differentiate between different amounts of a good on offer, then this is reflected in the insignificance of different attributes in subsequent models of choice processes.

Application of the CM technique typically involves the selection of key attributes to describe the trade-off of interest (Rolfe et al., 2002). Other potential factors can be held constant across choice tasks as part of the frame of the choice experiment, but may be varied across split-sample experiments (Rolfe et al., 2002). This means that potential changes to the scope and scale of the amenity involved can be considered both within the choice sets and external to the choice sets. The internal scope tests involve consideration of how respondents have viewed the different attributes, while the internal scale tests identify how they have made decisions about the different quantities on offer. The latter can be classified as a weak CV 'scope' test, as it is limited to the internal variations in quantity offered within each attribute (Rolfe et al., 2002). The external scope tests, sometimes nominated as framing effects, identify how changes in other factors may influence value estimation. External scale tests would identify how larger changes in quantities can impact on marginal values.

Evidence from a number of studies (for example, Bennett and Blamey, 2001) indicates that respondents do distinguish internal quantity variations (scale), identifying compliance with a weak CV 'scope' test. The significant coefficients for attributes in many CM experiments suggest that internal scope is generally present, although evidence of decision heuristics (for example, Blamey et al., 2002) and studies of attribute non-attendance (for example, Scarpa et al., 2009) suggest that respondents may not consider all attributes in every choice task. Wider split-sample experiments (for example, Rolfe et al., 2002) show that changing the way that the choice trade-offs are framed can have significant impacts on value estimates.

A number of benefit transfer studies that have been conducted with CM experiments also provide some indication of where there are similarities in framing, scope and scale between split-sample experiments (Brouwer and Spaninks, 1999; Rolfe and Bennett, 2006). Particular advantages of using CM for this purpose is that it is possible to transfer benefit functions rather than point value estimates so as to systematically account for differences between source and target sites (Brouwer and Spaninks, 1999), and to identify where transfer errors may be occurring (Rolfe, 2006). Results of benefit transfer tests suggest that there are often substantial errors involved, even when variations in site and population differences are taken into account (Bergstrom and Taylor, 2006; Brouwer, 2000; Brouwer and Spaninks, 1999; Rolfe and Bennett, 2006).

Bergstrom and Taylor (2006) describe the difficulties of ensuring commodity consistency between source and target sites, where it may be difficult to ensure that amenities in two different sites provide similar services. Key differences can emerge in relation to spatial and temporal factors, where variations in value can be expected for amenities that are offered at different geographic contexts or over different periods of time. Differences can also be expected for amenities where there are very different ranges of quantity being offered. Evidence of this is provided by van Bueren and Bennett (2004), who identified significantly different values for the protection of environmental assets and country communities in Australia according to whether they were valued in a national or regional context.

This brief review shows that issues of general 'scope' effects in stated preference experiments are difficult to resolve. While there is substantial evidence from research on CV studies that the technique can identify value increments between scenarios that offer more or less environmental improvements, there is no strong theoretical basis to identify the extent of value changes that can be expected with variations in quantity or choice dimensions (Heberlein et al., 2005). In applications of CM where there is more ability to control and test for variations between split sample experiments, the evidence to reject scope-insensitivity is weaker. To identify the reasons for this, the focus turns to defining the effects more precisely and then exploring scale and scope issues with CM experiments.

3   CATEGORIZING SCOPE, SCALE AND FRAMING

The CV literature around 'scope' insensitivity was focused on broad changes in the amount of the amenity on offer, where the amount encompassed both quantity and context factors. For example, Mitchell and Carson (1989) categorized part-whole bias (the most relevant of the scope-related issues) as possibly occurring in three formats, relating to variations in geography, benefits and public policy. This meant that respondents might confuse different scopes if they found it difficult to isolate a particular geographical area from others, if it was difficult to differentiate between benefit sub-components, or if they treated the particular issue at hand as symbolic of a wider group of public actions. Over time though 'scope' issues became simply associated with changes in the quantity of the amenity on offer (issues of scale), particularly after the split-sample form of CV dichotomous choice models became prevalent (Randall, 1997).

The use of the term 'scope' to represent quantity changes is also occurring in descriptions of CM experiments. For example Goldberg and Roosen (2007) use 'scope' to identify different quantities of risk and 'embedding' to represent insensitivity to risk over different diseases.

While the term 'scope' has continued to be used in the CV literature to represent changes in both context (scope) and quantity (scale), the ability of the CM technique to distinguish different effects much more accurately means that this general typology is not appropriate. In this section the concepts of scope and scale are defined more precisely to distinguish clearly between them. The applications are based on the precise meanings of the words,[2] where:

- scale – a sequence of regular intervals used as a reference in making measurements
- scope – range of view, or area covered by an activity or topic.

In a similar manner, Mazur and Bennett (2009) draw on the production economics literature to define scale as the quantity of production, and scope as the variety of products being generated. These definitions mean that scale relates to the measurement of quantities involved, while scope relates more to the coverage of the concept.

Key tasks in the design of an experiment are to define the scope, scale and frame of the trade-offs that will be presented to respondents. The following definitions are offered to clarify the concepts involved: the *scope* of a good involved in a stated preference experiment refers to the dimensions used to define the good and the trade-offs involved, the *scale* refers to the quantities involved, and the *framing* to the context in which the choices are made. Scale and scope issues are often intertwined, because increasing amounts of an environmental good often involve both changes in the quantity (scale) and extent of the good (scope). To identify this relationship more completely for CM applications, scope is defined in three dimensions, with a summary provided in Figure 13.1.

In a CM experiment the scope of the trade-off, or extent of the contingent market considered in a choice set, can be defined in three important ways. *Geographic scope* identifies the geographical setting of the trade-offs (for example, at local, regional, national or international levels), while *policy scope* refers to the type of trade-off or policy option that is used to describe how choice alternatives can vary between each other. In a choice experiment, policy scope can be varied by using policy labels or descriptors of different alternatives, or by describing how varying management and policy options can lead to specific attribute combinations. *Attribute scope* refers to the dimensions of the good being considered, which is normally defined by the selection of attributes to build choice alternatives. Attribute scope can be varied by changing the number and definitions of attributes used in choice sets.

Within a choice set, *attribute scale* describes the levels of the attributes,

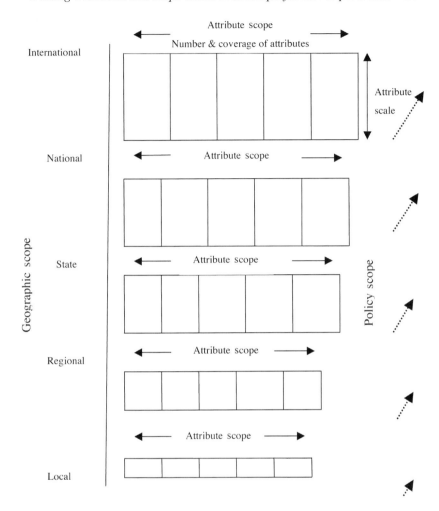

Figure 13.1   Scale and scope options in CM experiments

capturing variations in the quantity involved. The selection of different scope and scales to create a choice experiment is not independent, as attribute scope and policy scope may correlate to changes in geographic scope, and ranges in attribute scale may be set by different scope factors. These interdependencies are summarized in Figure 13.1. As geographic scope diminishes, the extent of attribute scope and policy scope is reduced, reflecting the more specific trade-offs that are available. In a similar way, attribute scale also diminishes with geographic scope, reflecting the smaller quantities of different attributes that are involved.

In addition to deciding the scope and scale at which trade-offs should be presented, the analyst designing a CM experiment also has to decide how trade-offs should be framed. Framing refers to the context in which trade-offs are made, and is related to the institutional and policy setting where the choice alternatives become possible and the payment mechanisms are realistic. There is often some interplay between the way a CM study is framed and the decisions regarding appropriate scope and scale. For example, if a policy issue is framed as a national government responsibility then the scale and scope of trade-offs in the contingent market need to relate to the institutional context.

These definitions reveal that the scope test in CV as defined by Arrow et al. (1993) was poorly labelled because it was typically focused on changes in the quantity being offered rather than changes in the type of trade-off being considered. It could be more accurately described as a 'scale' test.

4   SCALE DIFFERENCES IN CHOICE MODELLING

Much of the attention in stated preference experiments on scale and scope dimensions has focused the quantity of the good involved. The key issue relating to scale in designing a CM application is how the marginal trade-offs within a CM experiment vary as different quantities of attribute levels are presented. In many cases the potential for diminishing marginal utility is considered to be low, so only linear parameter estimates are generated for each attribute. The challenges here are to identify when respondents treat changing quantities of an attribute in more complex ways and the appropriate design and analysis responses.

There is potential for changes in scale to affect value estimates though the effect of diminishing marginal utility. This is particularly likely across geographic scale differences. As the frame in which a trade-off is scoped varies from smaller to a larger scale, then the marginal effects of a one-unit change become smaller (Rolfe and Windle, 2008). For this reason, trade-offs framed at a larger geographic or policy scope (that is, nationally) can be expected to have lower marginal values than trade-offs framed at a smaller scale (that is, locally) (Bergstrom and Taylor, 2006; Mazur and Bennett, 2009; van Bueren and Bennett, 2004). These issues may be enhanced or offset to some extent by other factors such as familiarity, loyalty, proximity, perceptions of responsibility and perceptions of institutional arrangements. The variation of diminishing marginal utility across different scales of presentation, both across and within CM studies, is likely to vary with the issue being addressed.

Internal Scale Tests

The analysis of choice modelling data in a multinomial logit model (MNL) (McFadden, 1974) provided a statistical framework for modelling how the attributes of a particular amenity among a set of alternatives explain consumer choice responses. The standard MNL model that is typically applied to analyse CM data requires assumptions that attributes are independent and linear-in-parameters, implying that survey respondents treat different quantities of a single attribute in a uniform way. The results of many CM experiments appear to be consistent with this approach. However, there are a number of CM studies where the results suggest a more complex relationship between the levels of the attributes on offer and choice behaviour (Louviere et al., 2000). There are several reasons why a simple parameterization of internal scale differences may not be sufficient.

Respondent heterogeneity drives many of the differences. For example, proximity (and loyalty) effects have been identified in distance-decay functions where people may have higher values for local areas compared to ones further away (Concu, 2007; Hanley et al., 2003; Pate and Loomis, 1997; Sutherland and Walsh, 1985). Decision processes are another potential explanation of why responses to internal scale differences (changes in attribute levels) are not independent. In some cases respondents may prioritize between attributes in ways that treat some attributes as priors (Blamey et al., 2000) or preliminary decision points, effectively leading to nested decision structures.

Another area of potential variation from a standard treatment of respondent choices occurs when marginal effects are observed. The use of a linear additive model assumes the concept of constant marginal utility. While the use of constant marginal values may be locally correct, it may overstate the total benefits of an increase in the resource for large changes. It is entirely feasible that people have diminishing marginal utility or disutility for an attribute as the scope of the good under valuation expands. Rolfe and Windle (2003) demonstrate significant non-linearities for protection of aboriginal cultural heritage sites, with little or no increase in part-worths past the first level of a 10 per cent increase in protection for two general community samples. Windle et al. (2005) identified diminishing marginal values for estuary health in Queensland, Whitten and Bennett (2006) report evidence of diminishing marginal values for the protection of two wetlands in southern areas of Australia, and Mazur and Bennett (2009) identify diminishing marginal values for environmental protection in a river catchment in New South Wales.

Layton (2001) has demonstrated refinements in empirical estimation of discrete choice models to allow for diminishing marginal value per unit of attribute when both large and small improvements are valued. Loomis (2006) noted that most studies have not been focused on the detection of differences between marginal benefit estimates at different levels of overall supply. This implies that when supplies are at differing levels, the estimates from source studies cannot be transferred to other policy sites. He used meta-analysis regression approach to combine the findings of four studies and allow the marginal value per salmon to vary with the absolute increase in the number of salmon under various management alternatives.

Other evidence that marginal benefits vary with the scale within an attribute is provided by Morrison and Bennett (2004), who explored the effect of framing and scale of the good under valuation on value estimates in their benefit transfer study. They selected five 'representative rivers' within different geographical regions of the New South Wales and conducted CM applications on each of those rivers using samples of people living within the river catchments and outside. Scope was held constant by using the same attributes across the surveys but the attribute levels were catchment specific. Differences in value estimates for the benefits of environmental flows were found across different river types and population categories. The results suggest that local and distant populations frame trade-offs differently and that marginal benefits vary according to the scale of trade-offs.

There is other evidence that the ranges over which attributes vary have has an impact on value estimates. Dellaert et al. (1999) examined the effect of variations in attribute level differences on consumer choice consistency, and found that the choice consistency decreases as price level differences increase and absolute price levels increase.

5   SCOPE DIFFERENCES IN CHOICE MODELLING

In a CM experiment, the scope of the trade-offs that are presented to respondents are set by the geographic and policy context selected, and the selection of the attributes used in the choice sets. Trade-offs in a choice experiment can be changed by varying geographic, policy or attribute scope so that the extent of the contingent market varies. In some cases the changes can be very explicit, such as when different attributes are included in choice sets or a particular geographic region is identified. In other cases the variations are more subtle, such as when different geographic and policy contexts vary the ways in which respondents view the trade-offs of interest. Here, the impacts of different scope contexts are reviewed in more detail.

Geographic Scope Tests

A number of CM studies have been performed to identify whether value estimates are consistent when the trade-offs are framed at different levels of geographic quantity. The focus of these tests has been to identify if values can be transferred from one geographic quantity frame to another (Rolfe and Bennett, 2006). The issues can be illustrated with three similar studies performed in Australia to explicitly address geographic scope issues (Rolfe and Windle, 2008; Rolfe et al., 2006; van Bueren and Bennett, 2004).

Van Bueren and Bennett (2004) performed a number of benefit transfer tests to examine how values change across different population and frames of reference, focusing on tests for geographic scope differences. Separate surveys were undertaken to estimate community values for land and water protection in Australia at national and regional contexts. The same set of attributes was used in each survey, holding attribute scope constant, but the level of attributes differed by the geographical scope involved. Results showed that all of the implicit prices generated at a regional context exceeded those generated at a national context, indicating that framing the surveys at different levels of geographic scope generated differences.

Rolfe et al. (2006) report valuation experiments relating to floodplain development and water allocation in Central Queensland. Three split-sample CM experiments were conducted, involving the Fitzroy basin as a whole as well as two separate sub-catchments. The surveys were identical apart from the case study information and the levels for the relevant attributes. The results indicated that the implicit prices were similar between the catchment and sub-catchment studies but that the models were not equivalent. Some framing effects were identified, as the combined values for the two sub-catchments used were often larger than values for the whole catchment.

Rolfe and Windle (2008) explored the values held for environmental protection (vegetation, soils and waterways) at both state and regional catchment levels. They found that value differences between state and regional contexts were not significant. The conclusions drawn were that no adjustments are needed for benefit transfer when the scope only varies between state and regional contexts. In contrast, Mazur and Bennett (2009) found scope effects for environmental protection of a river catchment in New South Wales, where the scope of protection was defined at 10 per cent, 50 per cent and 100 per cent of the catchment.

Policy Scope: Mapping the Extent of the Contingent Market

In some situations the scope of the trade-offs to be considered are not just defined by the attributes of the good involved, but also by wider institutional and policy contexts. In many CM experiments the wider policy context is uniform across choice sets, and hence can be considered part of the way that choices are framed to respondents. For these CM experiments, scope effects do not extend to policy issues. Where a policy or institutional mechanism becomes part of the choice sets that vary between profiles, then these become part of the way in which the contingent market is scoped to respondents. There are two key ways in which policy scope can become an important part of CM experiments.

The traditional way of including policy scope has been through the use of labelled choice sets. In some cases labels for choice alternatives are used in CM experiments to convey information about institutional, governance or other aspects of a choice option. Labels are often used to categorise key choice alternatives, helping to streamline the choice process. Rolfe and Bennett (2002) report the conduct of labelled choice experiments on rainforest conservation, where the labels identified the location of the rainforests to be protected. Brisbane residents had higher values for protection options in Queensland compared to sites in New South Wales, followed by sites overseas. The use of nested models identified a structure of choice patterns that were more consistent with perceptions of responsibility driving choices rather than proximity or other factors.

An alternative way of including policy scope is to include information about the process used to achieve outcomes as part of the attribute set. There are some examples emerging of this approach, where the options presented to respondents includes not only information about the environmental outcomes but also of the policy options to achieve them. Johnston and Duke (2007) report one case study where the willingness-to-pay for agricultural land preservation varied with the policy mechanism employed. The choice experiment involved six attributes, one of which identified the policy technique and implementing agency. Roberts et al. (2008) compared two CM split samples where in one sample, probabilities were attached to the environmental outcomes described in the attribute levels (for example, 10 per cent chance of algae bloom).

Attribute Scope: Inclusion and Exclusion of Attributes

A key challenge in CM experiments is to summarize policy situations into a representative set of attributes. A researcher typically has some discretion over the number of choice alternatives and choice sets in a CM experiment

(Hensher, 2006b; Louviere et al., 2000). Options to make choice sets more realistic by including more alternatives, attributes, levels and labels have to be balanced against the desire to minimise choice complexity by reducing the number of alternatives, attributes, levels and labels.

In order to reduce task complexity and cognitive burden imposed on respondents, issues are often 'compressed' into a discrete number of attributes (Breffle and Rowe, 2002; Caussade et al., 2005; Rolfe and Bennett, 2009). However, there are also cases where attributes are 'unpacked', helping to provide more emphasis or information in a key area. Focusing on particular issues in this way appears to come with some risk. 'Unpacking' positive attributes of a good into multiple sub-attributes can make a good or service seem more desirable, while 'unpacking' attribute levels that are less desirable can make a good or service less desirable (Starmer and Sugden, 1993; Weber et al., 1988).

There may be mechanical issues associated with the selection of attributes, where the number of attributes presented can impact on the complexity of the choice task (Caussade et al., 2005; Hensher, 2006a; Rolfe and Bennett, 2009). Louviere (2001) argued that there is no empirical evidence to suggest that increasing numbers of attributes, number of choice options or numbers of choice sets (scenarios) impact mean preference parameters, but there is evidence that increases in these factors impact random component variability. In contrast, DeShazo and Fermo (2002), Hensher (2006a), Causssade et al. (2005) and Rolfe and Bennett (2009) found that changes in the design of a choice set may systematically affect both the parameter estimates as well as the variances of the error terms, other factors being held constant.

Caussade et al. (2005, p.631) indicate that the order of impact of design dimensions of model variance was *first, number of attributes; second, number of alternatives; third, range of attribute levels; fourth, number of attribute levels, and last number of choice scenarios* (sets). They found that designs with four alternatives had the highest scale parameters, followed by those with five and then three alternatives. It is likely that increasing the number of choice set dimensions has benefits in terms of increased information and choice, but beyond some point there are offsetting costs in terms of increased complexity (Rolfe and Bennett, 2009).

Attribute Scope: Definition and Presentation of Attributes

The complexity of choice set tasks can also be influenced by how attributes are defined. In this case the design dimensions of a choice experiment can be held constant while the complexity is varied by describing and scoping attributes in different ways. Little empirical work has been performed to explore the effect of changing attribute scope in this way. Rolfe et al. (2002) and Rolfe and Bennett (2002) reported the analysis of two labelled CM experiments focused on rainforest conservation where the only difference between experiments were the labels used for the choice alternatives. The labels were the locations of potential conservation activities, and hence scoped the conservation issues in different ways. By analysing the results with nested logit models, Rolfe and Bennett (2002) showed that respondents prioritized the choice alternatives differently. In this experiment, the changes in attribute scope directly influenced the choice patterns of respondents.

The use of iconic attributes raises other issues of attribute scope. In the use of iconic attributes, a 'representative attribute' can be used to signal to respondents that particular categories of environmental assets are important. The presence of causally prior attributes within a CM experiment may also influence attribute scope. The use of causally prior attributes occurs when respondents adopt decision heuristics to make choices, and identify an attribute that needs to be satisfied first before other improvements can be generated (Blamey et al., 2000). For example, improved water quality may be viewed by respondents as an 'upstream' condition that has to be satisfied before increases in fish species or recreation opportunities can occur. Defining an attribute in a way that encourages causally prior decision heuristics has implications for the way that both 'upstream' and 'downstream' attributes are scoped.

6   CONCLUSIONS

The design of a CM experiment is a challenging process requiring a combination of logic, experience and empirical detective work as described by Carson et al. (1994) and Louviere et al. (2000). The analyst designing a CM experiment has substantial control over the framing of the contingent market to survey respondents. Care has to be taken in that design stage because there is substantial evidence that the scale and scope of the trade-offs that are presented can have impacts on the choice, and ultimately valuation, process.

The material presented in this chapter can be summarized in three broad themes. First, it is misleading to bundle all variations in the amount of an amenity being offered into a general 'scope' label. It is much more useful to distinguish between scale, representing the quantity of the amenity involved, and scope, representing the types of trade-offs involved. Each of these concepts can be further distinguished in terms of whether they are internal to the choice trade-offs, or form part of the external framing of the choice task. Attribute scale and scope relate to the internal frame, while geographic scale and policy scope are key elements of the external frame.

The second broad theme is that there are sound theoretical reasons why scale and scope effects can be expected. The most important of these include diminishing marginal utility associated with increasing amounts of an amenity, sequencing effects, sub-additivity effects, and the framing of substitutes and complements. There are also sound reasons why other framing and design factors such as varying institutional settings and choice contexts may also impact on choices and values.

The third broad theme is that scale and scope effects are dependent to some extent on the way that analysts design CM experiments and frame the trade-offs. The challenge for analysts is threefold: to design contingent markets in ways that replicate the case study of interest, to ensure that framing does not exacerbate scale and scope variations, and to identify any scale or scope impacts accurately to avoid any inappropriate extrapolation of subsequent value estimates.

NOTES

1. The helpful comments of Jill Windle and Jeff Bennett are appreciated. This research has been supported through the Environmental Economics Research Hub, funded by the Australian Department of Environment and Water Heritage and the Arts under the Commonwealth Environment Research Facility.
2. Definitions from *Collins Dictionary*.

REFERENCES

Arrow, K., R. Solow, P. Portney, E. Learner, R. Radner and H. Schuman (1993), 'Report of the NOAA Panel on Contingent Valuation', *Federal Register*, **58**, 4601–14.
Bateman, I., A. Munro, B. Rhodes, C. Starmer and R. Sugden (1997), 'Does part-whole bias exist? An experimental investigation', *The Economic Journal*, **107**, 322–32.
Bennett, J.W. (1996), 'The contingent valuation method: a post-Kakadu assessment', *Agenda*, **3** (2), 185–94.
Bennett, J.W. and Blamey, R.K (2001), *The Choice Modelling Approach to Environmental Valuation*, Cheltenham, UK and Northampton, MA: Edward Elgar.
Bergland, O., K. Magnussen and S. Navrud (2002), 'Benefit transfer: testing for accuracy and reliability', in R. Florax, P. Nijkamp and K. Willis (eds), *Comparative Environmental Economic Assessment*, Cheltenham, UK and Northampton, MA, USA: Edward Elgar, pp. 117–32.
Bergstrom, J.C. and L.O. Taylor (2006), 'Using meta-analysis for benefits transfer: theory and practice', *Ecological Economics*, **60**, 351–60.
Blamey, R.K., J.W. Bennett, J.J. Louviere, M.D. Morrison and J.C. Rolfe (2000), 'The use of policy labels in environmental choice modelling studies', *Ecological Economics*, **32**, 269–86.
Blamey, R.K, J.W. Bennett, J.J. Louviere, M.D. Morrison and J.C. Rolfe (2002), 'Attribute causality in choice modelling', *Environmental and Resource Economics*, **23** (2), 167–86.

Breffle, W.S. and R.D. Rowe (2002), 'Choice question formats and natural resource trade-offs', *Land Economics*, **78** (2), 298–314.

Brouwer, R. (2000), 'Environmental value transfer: state of the art and future prospects', *Ecological Economics*, **32**, 137–52.

Brouwer, R. and F.A. Spaninks (1999), 'The validity of environmental benefits transfer: Further empirical testing', *Environmental and Resource Economics*, **14**, 95–117.

Carson, R.T. and R.C. Mitchell (1995), 'Sequencing and nesting in contingent valuation surveys', *Journal of Environmental Economics and Management*, **28**, 155–73.

Carson, R.T., J. Louviere, D. Anderson, P. Arabie, D. Bunch, D. Hensher, R. Johson, S. Kuhfeld, D. Steinberg, J. Swait, H. Timmermans and J. Wiley (1994), 'Experimental analysis of choice', *Marketing Letters*, **5** (4), 351–68.

Caussade, S., J. Ortuzar, L. Rizzi and D. Hensher (2005), 'Assessing the influence of design dimensions on stated choice experiment estimates', *Transportation Research*, **39** (7), 621–40.

Concu, G. (2007), 'Investigating distance effects on environmental values: a choice modelling approach', *Australian Journal of Agricultural and Resource Economics*, **51** (2), 175–94.

Dellaert, B.G., J.D. Brazell and J.J. Louviere (1999), 'The effect of attribute variation on consumer choice consistency', *Marketing Letters*, **10** (2), 139–47.

DeShazo, J.R. and G. Fermo (2002), 'Designing choice sets for stated preference methods: the effects of complexity on choice consistency', *Journal of Environmental Economics and Management*, **44**, 123–43.

Desvousges, W.H., F.R. Johnson, R.W. Dunford, K.J. Boyle, S.P. Hudson and K.N. Wilson (1993), 'Measuring natural resource damages with contingent valuation: tests of validity and reliability', in J.A. Hausman (ed.), *Contingent Valuation: A Critical Assessment*, Amsterdam: North-Holland, pp. 91–164.

Diamond, P.A and J.A. Hausman (1994), 'Contingent valuation: is some number better than no number?', *The Journal of Economic Perspectives*, **8** (4), 45–64.

Goldberg, I. and J. Roosen (2007), 'Scope insensitivity in health risk reduction studies: A comparison of choice experiments and the contingent valuation method for valuing safer food', *Journal of Risk and Uncertainty*, **34**, 123–44.

Hanemann, W.M. (1994), 'Valuing the environment through contingent valuation', *Journal of Economic Perspectives*, **8**, 19–43.

Hanley, N., F. Schlapfer and J. Spurgeon (2003), 'Aggregating benefits of environmental improvements: distance-decay functions for use and non-use values', *Journal of Environmental Management*, **68**, 297–304.

Hanley, N., R. Wright and W. Adamowicz (1998), 'Using choice experiments to value the environment: Design issues, current experience and future prospects', *Environmental and Resource Economics*, **11** (3–4), 413–28.

Harrison, G.W. (1992), 'Valuing public goods with the contingent valuation method: a critique of Kahneman and Knetsch', *Journal of Environmental Economics and Management*, **23**, 248–57.

Heberlein, T.A., M.A. Wilson, R.C. Bishop and N.C. Schaeffer (2005), 'Rethinking the scope test as a criterion for validity in contingent valuation', *Journal of Environmental Economics and Management*, **50**, 1–22.

Hensher, D.A. (2006a), 'Revealing differences in willingness to pay due to the dimensionalities of stated choice designs, an initial assessment', *Environmental and Resource Economics*, **34**, 7–44.

Hensher, D.A. (2006b), 'How do respondents process stated choice experiments' attribute consideration under varying information load', *Journal of Applied Econometrics*, **21**, 861–78.

Johnston, R.J. and J.M. Duke (2007), 'Willingness to pay and policy process attributes', *American Journal of Agricultural Economics*, **89** (4), 1098–115.

Kahneman, D. and J.L. Knetsch (1992), 'Valuing public goods: the purchase of moral satisfaction', *Journal of Environmental Economics and Management*, **22**, 57–70.

Layton, D.F. (2001), 'Alternative approaches for modelling concave willingness to pay functions in conjoint valuation', *American Journal of Agricultural Economics*, **83** (5), 1314–20.

Loomis, J. (2006), 'Stated preference benefit transfer approaches for estimating passive use value of wild salmon', in J. Rolfe and J. Bennett (eds), *Choice Modelling and the Transfer of Environmental Values*, Cheltenham, UK and Northampton, MA, USA: Edward Elgar, pp. 54–70.

Loomis, J.B. and E. Ekstrand (1997), 'Economic benefits of critical habitat for the Mexican spotted owl: a scope test using a multiple-bounded contingent valuation survey', *Journal of Agricultural and Resource Economics*, **22** (2), 356–66.

Louviere, J.J. (2001), 'Choice experiments: an overview of concepts and issues', in J. Bennett and R. Blamey (eds), *The Choice Modelling Approach to Environmental Valuation*, Cheltenham, UK and Northampton, MA, USA: Edward Elgar, pp. 13–36.

Louviere, J., D. Hensher and J. Swait (2000), *Stated Choice Models – Analysis and Application*, Cambridge: Cambridge University Press.

Mazur, K. and J. Bennett (2009), 'Scale and scope effects on communities' values for environmental improvements in the Namoi catchment: a choice modelling approach', Environmental Economics Research Hub Research Report No 42, Australian National University, Canberra.

McFadden, D. (1974), 'Conditional logit analysis of qualitative choice behaviour', in P. Zarembka (ed.), *Frontiers in Econometrics*, New York: Academic Press, pp. 105–42.

Mitchell, R.C. and R.T. Carson (1989), *Using Surveys to Value Public Goods: The Contingent Valuation Method*, Washington, DC: Resources for the Future.

Morrison, M. and J. Bennett (2004), 'Valuing New South Wales rivers for use in benefit transfer', *The Australian Journal of Agricultural and Resource Economics*, **48** (4), 591–611.

Pate, J. and J. Loomis (1997), 'The effect of distance on willingness to pay values: a case study of wetlands and salmon in California', *Ecological Economics*, **20**, 199–207.

Portney, P.R. (1994), 'The contingent valuation debate: why economists should care', *Journal of Economic Perspectives*, **8** (4), 3–17.

Randall, A. (1997), 'The NOAA Panel report: a new beginning or the end of an era?', *American Journal of Agricultural Economics*, **79**, 1489–94.

Randall, A. and J.P. Hoehn (1996), 'Embedding in market demand systems', *Journal of Environmental Economics and Management*, **30**, 369–80.

Roberts, D.C., T.A. Boyer and J.L. Lusk (2008), 'Preferences for environmental quality under uncertainty', *Ecological Economics*, **66** (2–3), 584–93.

Rolfe, J. and J. Bennett (eds) (2006), *Choice Modelling and the Transfer of Environmental Values*, Cheltenham, UK and Northampton, MA, USA: Edward Elgar.

Rolfe, J. and J. Bennett (2009), 'The impact of offering two versus three alternatives in Choice Modelling experiments', *Ecological Economics*, **68**, 1140–48.

Rolfe, J. and J. Windle (2003), 'Valuing the protection of aboriginal cultural heritage sites', *The Economic Record*, **79** (special issue) s85–s95.

Rolfe, J. and J. Windle (2008), 'Testing for differences in benefit transfer values between state and regional frameworks', *Australian Journal of Agricultural and Resource Economics*, **52** (2), 149–68.

Rolfe, J., J. Bennett and J. Louviere (2000), 'Choice modelling and its potential application to tropical rainforest preservation', *Ecological Economics*, **35**, 289–302.

Rolfe, J., J. Bennett and J. Louviere (2002), 'Stated values and reminders of substitute goods: testing for framing effects with choice modelling', *The Australian Journal of Agricultural and Resource Economics*, **46** (1), 1–20.

Rolfe, J., A. Loch and J. Bennett (2006), 'Testing benefit transfer with water resources in Central Queensland, Australia', in J. Rolfe and J. Bennett (eds), *Choice Modelling and the Transfer of Environmental Values*, Cheltenham, UK and Northampton, MA, USA: Edward Elgar, pp. 28–53.

Rolfe, J.C. and J.W. Bennett (2002), 'Assessing rainforest conservation demands', *Economic Analysis and Policy*, **32** (2), 51–67.

Scarpa, R., T. Gilbride, D. Campbell and D. Hensher (2009), 'Modelling attribute non-attendance in choice experiments for rural landscape valuation', *European Review of Agricultural Economics*, **36**, 151–74.

Schulze, W.D., G.H. McClelland, R.K. Lazo and R.D. Rowe (1998), 'Embedding and calibration in measuring non-use values', *Resource and Energy Economics*, **20**, 163–76.

Smith, V.K. and L.L. Osbourne (1996), 'Do contingent valuation estimates pass a "scope" test? A meta-analysis', *Journal of Environmental Economics and Management*, **31**, 287–301.

Starmer, C. and R. Sugden (1993), 'Testing for juxtaposition and event-splitting effects', *Journal of Risk and Uncertainty*, **6**, 235–54.

Sutherland, R.J. and R. Walsh (1985), 'Effect of distance on the preservation value of water quality', *Land Economics*, **61**, 281–91.

Van Bueren, M. and J. Bennett (2004), 'Towards the development of a transferable set of value estimates for environmental attributes', *Australian Journal of Agricultural and Resource Economics*, **48** (1), 1–32.

Weber, M., F. Eisenfuhr and D. von Winterfeldt (1988), 'The effects of splitting attributes on weights in multiattribute utility measurement', *Management Science*, **34**, 431–45.

Whitten, S. and J. Bennett (2006), 'Transferring the environmental values of wetlands', in J. Rolfe and J. Bennett (eds), *Choice Modelling and the Transfer of Environmental Values*, Cheltenham, UK and Northampton, MA, USA: Edward Elgar, pp. 164–90.

Windle, J., J. Rolfe and J. Grimes (2005), 'Assessing non-use values for environmental protection of an estuary in a Great Barrier Reef catchment', *Australasian Journal of Environmental Management*, **12** (3), 147–56.

14 Experimental design strategies for stated preference studies dealing with non-market goods
John M. Rose, Stuart Bain and
Michiel C.J. Bliemer

INTRODUCTION

Given that the vast majority of environmental goods are public goods not traded in real markets, the collection of high-quality data capable of eliciting reliable preference functions or estimating coherent welfare measures from surveyed respondents represents an extremely difficult task to accomplish in practice. Unlike other areas of economic study that deal primarily with private goods typically traded in real markets, the specific area of valuation related to the study of environmental and resource economics has, more than any other discipline, had to rely on stated intentions type techniques such as contingent valuation (CV) and stated choice (SC) methods in order to accomplish its goals. In this chapter, we are interested solely in SC surveys. In particular, this chapter deals specifically with the generation of experimental designs for environmental SC surveys.

In reality, an experimental design is nothing more than a matrix of numbers that researchers use to assign values to the attributes of the alternatives present within the hypothetical choice tasks of SC surveys. By using experimental design theory, the assignment of these values occurs in some systematic (that is, non-random) manner. This is done so that analysts can control as many factors as possible influencing observed choices. In creating the experimental design in a very specific and precise manner, the analyst seeks to ensure, as much as is possible, the ability to capture reliable estimates that correspond to the attributes of interest and which are not confounded (again, as far as is possible) with estimates related to other attributes or other potential sources of influence upon choice.

The process of arriving at an SC survey is a long and arduous one. Prior to the generation of the experimental design, extensive qualitative and secondary research should be undertaken to determine the relevant set of alternatives, attributes and attribute levels that will be used to make up the hypothetical choice tasks that respondents will be asked to complete as part of the final SC survey. In attempting to construct the list of finite and mutually exclusive alternatives, relevant questions that need to be asked and answered by the analyst include but are not limited to; will the experiment be labelled (the names of the alternatives have substantive meaning beyond their ordering) or unlabelled (the names of the alternatives have no substantive meaning other than their order of presentation) and will the experiment offer a no choice or status quo alternative. In arriving at the set of attributes to be used, the analyst is required to predetermine what factors are likely to be the relevant set affecting choice between the previously identified set of alternatives. With regards to the attribute levels, the analyst needs to decide what values each of the attributes should take over the course of the experiment (that is, what specific quantitative or qualitative values will be shown to respondents). Once all this has been decided, further pre-tests and piloting are also recommended. Only when the alternatives, attributes and attribute levels have been finally decided, should the researcher contemplate moving on to construct the experimental design.

This chapter first seeks to provide a brief summary of the most current experimental design methods used for constructing SC survey tasks before introducing an extension that allows for a generalisation of the most state of the art experimental design generation method. We begin with a brief illustration of some of the basic principles of experimental design which we expand upon as the chapter progresses. In doing so, we utilize the same example showing how *keeping everything else constant*, the underlying experimental design that can have a dramatic impact upon the final results obtained from SC experiments.

EXAMPLE STUDY

Let us begin with a simple example of a hypothetical environmental economic evaluation study. Consider an SC study in which respondents are asked to choose between different hypothetical policies dealing with the preservation of a forest area currently being logged for timber. Depending on the final policy adopted, a number of those employed in the logging industry will lose their jobs; however, a number of endangered animal species in the defined area may potentially be saved. Further, the policy may or may not include an option for park rangers and selected others to hunt *non-native* (that is, introduced) feral animals. Finally, to assist those who potentially become unemployed as part of implementing any policy, a fee may be introduced for those wishing to enter the area. Assume that secondary and qualitative research confirmed the above as the relevant set

Table 14.1   Relevant attributes and attribute levels

Job losses	50, 100, 150, 200
Number of endangered species saved	0, 1, 2, 3
Cost to enter park	$0, $10, $20, $30
Non-native feral animal eradication program	0 = yes, 1 = no

Outcome	Current situation	Option A	Option B
Job losses	0	50	100
Number of endangered species saved	0	1	2
Cost to enter park	$0	$10	$20
Non-native feral animal eradication program	0	No	Yes
I would choose	○	○	○

Figure 14.1   Example stated choice task

of attributes influencing choice while the same research further identified the following attribute levels as being relevant to the study (Table 14.1).

An example choice task, including a third 'status quo' alternative, is shown as Figure 14.1.

Assuming we are only interested in a linear utility specification involving solely main effects (that is, we are not interested in interaction effects, although our discussion would remain largely unaltered if we were), we postulate the following set of utility functions for the problem as described above:

$$V_1 = 0, \tag{14.1}$$

$$V_2 = \beta_{10} + \beta_1 x_{11} + \beta_2 x_{12} + \beta_3 x_{13} + \beta_4 x_{14}, \tag{14.2}$$

and

$$V_3 = \beta_{20} + \beta_1 x_{21} + \beta_2 x_{22} + \beta_3 x_{23} + \beta_4 x_{24}, \tag{14.3}$$

where x_{1k} can take the values $\{50, 100, 150, 200\}$, $x_{2k} \in \{0, 1, 2, 3\}$, $x_{3k} \in \{0, 10, 20, 30\}$, and $x_{4k} \in \{0, 1\}$. Note that in setting up the utility functions above, we have allowed for alternative specific parameters for the two hypothetical policy alternatives. While it is typical in environmental economic studies to allow for a single constant in the status quo alternative, allowing for two different constants as above allows us to account for possible biases such as left to right biases that have been found to exist in non-environmental economics SC studies in the past (see, for example, Hess and Rose, 2008, 2009).

EXPERIMENTAL DESIGN CONSIDERATIONS

For any SC study, there exist many possible experimental designs that could be constructed. The aim for the analyst is to choose a particular method and construct the design. How best to do this depends upon many different considerations. Although most environmental studies will typically involve the use of unlabelled choice tasks, the analyst must still decide whether the experiment should be treated as *labelled* or *unlabelled*. This decision is important as it impacts upon the number of parameters that will typically be estimated as part of the study. Generally, unlabelled experiments only require the estimation of generic parameters, whereas labelled experiments may require the estimation of either alternative specific or generic parameter estimates or both. Advanced knowledge of the number of likely (design-related) parameter estimates is critical as each parameter represents an additional degree of freedom required from the design. The minimum number of rows of the design (where each row corresponds to a choice task) should be equal to or greater than the number of (design-related) parameters, not including constants, plus one (for example, for our case example, we have four generic parameters, not including constants, plus one, meaning that the minimum number of choice tasks is five). Note that the inclusion of a no choice alternative does not impact upon the size of the design as it does not require the estimation of any attribute related parameter estimates. Likewise, the typical status quo method employed in many environmental economic studies where the status quo alternative is given levels which do not vary over choice tasks will also generally not add to the size of the design. This is because the typical estimation procedure dealing with such SC data is to estimate generic parameters for both the status quo and non-status quo alternatives, and hence no additional parameter estimates are required.

Another consideration typically associated with almost all experimental designs is whether to impose the *attribute level balance* property. This property exists in a design where each attribute level appears an equal number of times for each attribute over the design. Although imposing attribute level balance may restrict the design to be suboptimal, it is generally considered a desirable property. Having attribute level balance ensures that the parameters can be estimated well on the whole range of levels, instead of having data points at only some of the attribute levels. Nevertheless, the property may result in larger designs than dictated by the degrees of freedom requirement. For example, consider our case study where the final number of choice tasks decided upon must be divisible by both 2 and 4 (three of our attributes have 4 levels with one having 2 levels). Thus, while the minimum number of choice tasks required is 5, for attribute level balance we require 8, 12, or 16, and so on choice tasks to maintain attribute level balance.

The *number of attribute levels* required depends on the utility specification that is likely to be estimated in the study. If non-linear effects are expected for a certain attribute estimated using dummy or effects coding, then more than two levels need to be used for this attribute in order to be able to estimate these nonlinearities. Where dummy and/or effects coded attributes are included, then the number of levels to use for these attributes is predetermined. However, the more levels used, the higher the potential number of choice tasks required will be. Also, mixing the number of attribute levels for different attributes may yield a higher number of choice tasks (due to attribute level balance). For example, if x_{2k} had five instead of four levels (say $\{0, 1, 2, 3, 4\}$ instead of $\{0, 1, 2, 3\}$ then the minimum number of choice tasks will be 20 (since this is divisible by two, four, and five). On the other hand, if the same attribute had six levels (say $\{0, 1, 2, 3, 4, 5\}$ then a minimum of 12 choice tasks would be enough. Therefore, some researchers argue that it is not wise to mix too many different numbers of attribute levels, or at least to have all even or all odd numbers of attribute levels when generating the design.

Regarding the *attribute level range*, research suggests that using a wide range (for example, \$0–\$30) is statistically preferable to using a narrow range (for example, \$0–\$10) as this will theoretically lead to better parameter estimates (that is, parameter estimates with a smaller standard error), although using too wide a range may also be problematic (see Bliemer and Rose, 2008). The reason for this is that the attribute level range will impact upon the likely choice probabilities obtained from the design, which we show later to impact upon the expected standard errors from that design. Having too wide a range will likely result in choice tasks with dominated alternatives (at least for some attributes), whereas too narrow a range will result in alternatives which are largely indistinguishable. We have to emphasize that this is a pure statistical property and that one should take into account the practical limitations of the attribute levels. The attribute levels shown to the respondents have to make sense. Therefore, there is a trade-off between the statistical preference for a wide range and practical considerations that may limit the range.

The inclusion of *interaction effects* will also potentially impact upon the number of choice tasks required of a design. This is because each interaction effect requires a corresponding parameter estimate with each additional parameter estimate requiring an additional degree of freedom to estimate and hence an additional choice task in the design. It is for this reason that a good starting point of the design generation process is to write out the worst-case utility specification (worst case in terms of main effects and interaction effects, along with any non-linear parameterization that may be estimated once data has been collected), as generating a design with too few choice tasks will likely disqualify the analyst from estimating potentially valid utility specifications at a later stage, while generating a design with more than the minimum number of choice tasks does not preclude the estimation of simpler model forms.

Given the above, several different experimental *design generation procedures* can be considered. A *full factorial* design consists of all possible different choice tasks and with this design all possible effects (main and interaction effects) can be estimated. However, for a practical study the number of choice tasks in a full factorial design is typically too large. Therefore, most researchers rely on so-called *fractional factorial* designs, and within this class there exist many different types of designs. One could randomly select choice tasks from the full factorial, but clearly this is not the best way of doing it. Rather, one selects choice tasks in a structured manner, such that the best data from the SC experiment will be produced for estimating the model. A fractional factorial design consists of a subset of choice tasks from the full factorial. The best known fractional factorial design type is the *orthogonal design*, which aims to minimize the correlation between the attribute levels in the choice tasks. Although there exist several types of orthogonal designs, in this chapter, we consider only the most widely used orthogonal fractional factorial design method, consisting of constructing a simple orthogonal array.

More recently, several researchers have suggested other types of fractional factorial designs, so-called *D-optimal* or *D-efficient* designs. D-optimality or D-efficiency is defined in terms of variances (the roots of which are the standard errors) and covariances of the parameter estimates. The lower these (co)variances, or more precisely, the smaller the determinant of the asymptotic variance-covariance (AVC) matrix, the more efficient the experimental design. More about efficiency measures is discussed later. There exists two competing schools of thought, both applying the same optimality criterion, but making different assumptions. The first school of thought creates designs under the assumption of the null hypothesis, namely, zero valued parameter priors, while the other school assumes non-zero valued parameter priors. Clearly, in the latter case, one has to decide what these non-zero valued parameter priors are, typically leading to more efficient designs but coming at the expense of the effort to obtain some parameter priors.

The first school of thought has shown that under the null hypothesis, a design in which the attributes within each alternative are orthogonal and such that the differences in attribute levels across alternatives are maximized, is optimal (see, for example, Burgess and Street, 2003, 2005; Street and Burgess, 2004, 2007; Street et al., 2005). Assuming zero valued priors, the discrete choice model becomes a linear model and therefore an orthogonal design is optimal. The appeal of this approach is twofold. First, in taking this approach, respondents are forced to make trade-offs on each and every attribute of the design, as no two attributes in any given choice situation will, where possible, take the same value. Secondly, this approach acknowledges that discrete choice models are really difference in the utilities models (see Train 2003).

The second school of thought considers non-zero valued parameter priors, assuming that all attributes matter and that one has some prior knowledge about the parameter value (for example, even knowing simply the sign of the parameter). In this approach, researchers let go of the principle of orthogonality and construct designs in a manner that directly minimises the expected elements of the AVC matrix that will be obtained from the (non-linear) discrete choice model (see, for example, Bliemer and Rose, 2006; Bliemer et al., 2009; Carlsson and Martinsson, 2002; Ferrini and Scarpa, 2007; Fowkes, 2000; Huber and Zwerina, 1996; Kanninen, 2002; Kessels et al., 2006; Rose and Bliemer, 2008; Sándor and Wedel, 2001, 2002, 2005; Scarpa and Rose, 2008; Toner et al., 1999; Watson et al., 2000). The primary advantage of using this method is that the constructed design is related to the expected outcome of the modelling process. While the first school can prove optimality of their design (under the null hypothesis), the second school cannot (under the non-null hypothesis) and therefore these designs are typically called D-efficient designs and not D-optimal designs.

We discuss both D-optimal/efficient designs later in the chapter. In addition to examining these existing methods, we propose an approach that extends the work of Kanninen (2002). We discuss the specifics of the Kanninen approach and our extension in due course.

MAINSTREAM DESIGN CONSTRUCTION METHODS

In practice, there exist a number of different approaches that one might employ to generate a workable experimental design. The actual approach decided upon should reflect the underlying beliefs of the analyst as to what is important in generating the design. In this section, we discuss the three most widely used methods (in practice) for constructing experimental designs for SC studies.

Traditional Orthogonal Designs Methods

Historically, by far the most commonly used experimental design type used in SC studies has been *orthogonal designs*. The concept of orthogonality is related to the correlation structure between the attributes of the experimental design, with designs that display no correlation being called *orthogonal* designs. By forcing the columns of an array to display zero correlations, each column of the design will act independently of all other columns. There exist several methods for constructing an orthogonal design in practice, including but not limited to balanced incomplete blocked designs (BIBD), Latin Squares designs, L^{KJ} orthogonal fractional factorial designs (where L is the number of levels, K the number of attributes and J the number of alternatives), fractional factorial orthogonal in the differences designs, and fractional factorial designs with fold-over. We do not discuss the details of how to construct these designs here given that this has been discussed extensively elsewhere (see, for example, Bunch et al., 1996; Fowkes and Wardman, 1988; Louviere et al., 2000, or Rose and Bliemer, 2008). In this chapter we consider the most mainstream orthogonal design type only, that being the L^{KJ} orthogonal fractional factorial design.

In generating L^{KJ} orthogonal fractional factorial designs, two methods have been explored in the past. The first is to generate a design whereby the attributes of the alternatives are uncorrelated both within and between alternatives, using what is termed a simultaneous generation process (the design approach is said to be simultaneous in that all alternatives are constructed at the same time). The second approach, termed sequential generation, results in orthogonal designs that have orthogonal attribute columns only within alternatives, but not between. To construct such designs, the analyst first creates an orthogonal design for the first alternative, and creates subsequent alternatives by using the same design as for first alternative but re-arranging the rows of the design (see, for example, Louviere et al., 2000). By using the sequential approach, the analyst need only generate an orthogonal design related to the attributes of a single alternative, whereas for the simultaneous approach requires the generation of an orthogonal design that considers all attributes, irrespective of which alternative they belong to. For this reason, the sequential design approach may allow the analyst to locate designs with a smaller number of choice tasks than orthogonal designs generated using the simultaneous approach. This is because the theoretical minimum number of rows required for a design does not necessarily guarantee that an orthogonal design may be located, particularly if there is a large number of attributes or combinations of attributes with odd and even attribute levels. For the current case study, the smallest (simultaneous) fractional factorial orthogonal design that could be located has 16 choice tasks, whereas it is possible to generate using the sequential design process a design with only eight choice tasks. One limitation of the sequential design generation strategy is that such designs are appropriate only for unlabeled SC experiments where the between alternative correlation structure is not of concern.

D-optimal Design Method under the Null Hypothesis

Using the sequential design approach to generating orthogonal designs, a number of researchers have recently explored how to construct optimally the second and subsequent alternatives based on an orthogonal design constructed for the first alternative. Traditionally, researchers would simply randomly assign rows of the first alternative to make up the second and subsequent alternatives; however, this new line of research has identified a particular optimality criteria that may be used to construct efficient or optimal orthogonal SC designs specifically generated for discrete choice models. As well as maintaining (within alternative) orthogonality, these researchers suggest that SC experiments should be constructed so as to minimise the AVC matrix of the design based on the attribute level contrasts. In practice, the impact of this approach is that common attributes across alternatives are forced, as much as possible, to differ in terms of the levels shown to respondents. In this way, the trade-offs that respondents are forced to make when choosing among the set of available alternatives are maximized hence yielding maximum information as to the importance each attribute plays in choice (see, for example, Burgess and Street, 2005; Street and Burgess, 2004; Street et al., 2001, 2005). The mathematics behind calculating the AVC matrix of the attribute level contrasts as well as the optimality criterion is quite complex and beyond the scope of this chapter. Street and Burgess (2007), Street et al. (2005) and Rose and Bliemer (2008) provide detailed discussions of the exact procedures for the interested reader. Further, software exists capable of generating these types of designs such as Ngene 1.0[1] as well as an Internet website[2] (Burgess, 2007).

D-efficient Design Methods under the Non-null Hypothesis

An alternative approach to designing SC experiments is involved not with attribute level contrasts and indirectly maximizing attribute level differences, but upon directly selecting a design that is likely to provide an AVC matrix containing values which are as small as possible for a given econometric model form. As the asymptotic standard errors obtained from discrete choice models are simply the square roots of the leading diagonal of the AVC matrix of a discrete choice model, the smaller the elements of the AVC matrix (or at least the diagonal elements), the smaller the asymptotic standard errors of the model will be. Given that dividing the parameter estimates by the asymptotic standard errors results in the asymptotic *t*-ratios for the model, the smaller the asymptotic standard errors, the larger the asymptotic *t*-ratios will be for the model. Designs which attempt to minimize the elements contained within the AVC matrix are referred to as efficient designs. Note that such designs are unlikely to be orthogonal in the attributes (as we are dealing with a non-linear discrete choice model).

The AVC matrices derived when constructing D-efficient designs under the non-null hypothesis differ to those of the AVC matrices generated for optimal orthogonal designs in that efficient designs are generated in such a way as to attempt to mimic the performance of the likely model to be estimated post-data collection, whereas D-optimal designs under the null hypothesis seek to maximize the attribute level contrasts of the design, irrespective of the final model form. In this way, the objective function defining optimality in generating an efficient design may be considered a practical one in the sense that such designs seek to minimise the standard errors one is likely to obtain in practice. This is opposed to the objective function used for optimization when generating D-optimal (orthogonal) designs which says nothing about the likely final outcome of models estimated on data collected using the method, but rather only that attribute levels for similar attributes should be as different as possible across alternatives.

Unlike D-optimal designs, D-efficient designs require several strong assumptions in order to construct the design. First, the AVC matrix of discrete choice models will differ from one model type to the next. The AVC matrix of a multinomial logit (MNL) model is different to that of a nested logit or mixed multinomial logit (MMNL) model (see, for example, Bliemer and Rose, 2008, 2009). As such, the analyst must first decide what model type is likely to be estimated once data has been collected in order to decide what AVC matrix will specifically be used in generating the design. Secondly, the AVC matrix of any logit model is analytically equal to the negative inverse of the model's log-likelihood function. Independent of the specific model type, the formulas for the analytical second derivatives of logit type models retain within them the model probabilities. Given that the probabilities are a function of the utilities of the alternatives which in turn are a function of both the design attributes and the parameter estimates, to predict in advance the likely AVC matrix of a design requires advanced knowledge not just of the design (which is what is being constructed), but also of the parameter estimates themselves (which is what the design is being constructed to uncover).

In order to overcome this problem, the analyst is required to assume prior parameter estimates in a Bayesian-like approach in order to generate a design. While the assumption of priors is somewhat restrictive, it need not be as restrictive as it initially sounds. Researchers need not assume precise prior parameter values (though some researchers do resulting in what are called locally efficient designs; see for example, Carlsson and Martinsson, 2002). Rather, many researchers rely on prior parameter distributions that (hopefully) contain within their range the true population parameter. In taking this approach, the resulting Bayesian efficient design is then optimised over a range of possible parameter values, without the analyst having to know the precise population value in advance (see, for example, Sándor and Wedel, 2001, and Kessels et al., 2006). This approach however requires substantial computing time, as simulation is required in order to optimize the design over the range of possible parameter priors. Rose and Bliemer (2008) outline the precise steps used to generate this type of design. Bliemer and Rose (2008) and Bliemer et al. (2009) provide details of the analytical second derivatives for a range of logit models.

Measuring Statistical Efficiency

A number of measures have been proposed within the literature related to the statistical efficiency of experimental designs generated specifically for SC studies. As mentioned before, *D-optimal* or *D-efficient* design theory typically use what is known as the *D-efficiency* (for optimal orthogonal designs) or *D-error* (for efficient designs) as a measure of the design's efficiency. The *D-efficiency/error* relates to the determinant of either the AVC or the AVC matrix generated for a design. For both design types, the *D-* is used to indicate that the measure used is the determinant of AVC matrix being constructed. In the case of D-optimal (orthogonal) designs, the D-efficiency is typically converted to a percentage value, with values of around 90 per cent or higher said to represent desirable designs. While the D-efficiency measure is maximized, the *D-error* of efficient designs is minimized (it is also normalized to account for the number of parameters). Similar to the *D-error*, some researchers prefer to use what is known as the *A-error*, which is calculated off of the trace of the AVC matrix (also normalized to account for the number of parameter estimates).

Another measure of statistical efficiency has been proposed by Bliemer and Rose (2009). McFadden (1974) demonstrated a relationship between the AVC matrix of logit models and sample size which Bliemer and Rose (2009) exploited to calculate a measure of the sample size requirements for SC experiments. The *S-error* of a design provides the theoretical minimum sample size required in order to obtain asymptotically significant parameter estimates. As with the *D-error*, the objective is to find a design that minimises the *S-error* value. In order to calculate the S-error of a design, the analyst must also construct the AVC matrix for the design. For further details of *S-error*, see Bliemer and Rose (2009).

For the current chapter, given that we are interested in how the design will likely perform in practice, we use as our basis of comparison *D-error* and *S-error*. While we do not discount the D-efficiency measure in generating a design, we note that it is less useful as a measure of comparison in terms of how the design will perform once data has been collected.

In the next section, we develop our case example further, after which we generate three different designs corresponding to the three design types discussed above.

CASE STUDY: FURTHER ASSUMPTIONS

In order to generate an efficient design it is first necessary to assume both prior parameter estimates as well as econometric model type. In specifying the utility structure of the model, we treat the prior parameters, β_3 and β_4 as fixed parameters, whilst β_1 and β_2 are specified as random parameters drawn from normal distributions, i.e., $\beta_1 \sim N(\mu_1, \sigma_1)$ and $\beta_2 \sim N(\mu_2, \sigma_2)$ That is, we assume that the model is a MMNL model. We further assume that the model accounts for the repeated (panel) nature of SC data (see Bliemer and Rose, 2008).

In order to generate the designs, we consider a mixture of both local parameter priors (where the parameter priors are known with certainty) and Bayesian parameter priors (where there exists uncertainty about the precise parameter values). Specifically, we assume both population moments of the β_1 random parameter are not precisely known a priori, being drawn from the following (normal and uniform) distributions: $\mu_1 \sim N(-0.008, 0.001)$ and $\sigma_1 \sim U(0.002, 0.004)$. The remainder of the parameter priors are assumed to be precisely known a priori, taking the following values: $\beta_{01} = \beta_{02} = 1.7$, $\mu_2 = 1.2$, $\sigma_2 = 0.4$, $\beta_3 = -0.12$, and $\beta = -0.7$.[3]

MAINSTREAM DESIGN TYPE EXAMPLES

The three designs generated are shown in Table 14.2. The first design represents a traditional (simultaneously generated) orthogonal design generated in such a way that the correlation structure of the design columns are all zero. The second design generated is a D-optimal (sequentially orthogonal) design with a D-efficiency measure of 100 per cent. The final

Table 14.2 *Initial start designs*

		Traditional orthogonal					D-optimal orthogonal					D-efficient				
S	Alt.	X1	X2	X3	X4	Prob.	X1	X2	X3	X4	Prob.	X1	X2	X3	X4	Prob.
1	1	50	0	0	1	0.342	50	0	0	1	0.287	150	2	0	1	0.445
1	2	50	0	0	1	0.342	100	1	10	0	0.444	50	3	30	0	0.079
2	1	150	1	30	1	0.060	150	2	0	0	0.659	100	2	30	1	0.541
2	2	200	0	20	1	0.048	200	3	10	1	0.265	50	0	20	0	0.390
3	1	100	1	20	0	0.234	50	2	20	0	0.505	150	3	20	1	0.233
3	2	50	1	20	0	0.302	100	3	30	1	0.216	100	2	10	0	0.366
4	1	200	0	10	0	0.064	150	0	20	1	0.053	50	3	30	0	0.349
4	2	200	1	0	0	0.681	200	1	30	0	0.095	200	1	0	1	0.072
5	1	100	3	10	1	0.846	200	3	0	0	0.925	100	1	20	1	0.403
5	2	150	0	30	0	0.005	50	0	10	1	0.017	200	1	0	0	0.303
6	1	200	2	20	1	0.273	100	1	0	1	0.332	200	1	20	1	0.529
6	2	100	0	10	0	0.237	150	2	10	0	0.518	200	0	1	0	0.250
7	1	50	2	30	0	0.295	200	1	20	1	0.087	50	1	1	0	0.437
7	2	150	1	10	1	0.268	50	2	30	0	0.373	200	3	1	1	0.226
8	1	150	3	0	0	0.954	100	3	20	0	0.787	100	0	0	1	0.569
8	2	100	1	30	1	0.002	150	0	30	1	0.004	100	2	30	0	0.162
9	1	150	2	20	0	0.341	50	3	30	1	0.331	50	2	20	0	0.474
9	2	150	2	20	0	0.341	100	0	0	0	0.415	150	3	30	1	0.322
10	1	200	1	30	0	0.021	150	1	30	0	0.017	200	3	10	0	0.091
10	2	50	2	10	1	0.740	200	2	0	1	0.778	50	1	0	1	0.665
11	1	150	3	10	1	0.081	50	1	10	0	0.524	50	3	30	1	0.717
11	2	50	3	0	0	0.897	100	2	20	1	0.216	150	0	0	0	0.106

Table 14.2 (continued)

		Traditional orthogonal					D-optimal orthogonal					D-efficient				
S	Alt.	X1	X2	X3	X4	Prob.	X1	X2	X3	X4	Prob.	X1	X2	X3	X4	Prob.
12	1	200	0	0	1	0.218	150	3	10	1	0.801	150	0	10	1	0.320
12	2	150	3	30	1	0.330	200	0	2	0	0.015	150	1	20	0	0.319
13	1	100	2	10	0	0.724	200	0	30	0	0.007	100	0	10	0	0.435
13	2	100	2	20	1	0.108	50	1	0	1	0.769	100	2	10	1	0.056
14	1	50	1	0	0	0.610	100	2	30	1	0.006	200	1	0	0	0.134
14	2	200	2	10	0	0.293	150	3	0	0	0.951	50	2	20	0	0.815
15	1	100	3	20	1	0.129	200	2	10	1	0.164	200	2	30	1	0.047
15	2	200	3	0	1	0.781	50	3	20	0	0.693	150	0	20	0	0.628
16	1	50	0	30	1	0.012	100	0	10	0	0.293	150	0	0	0	0.070
16	2	100	3	30	0	0.589	150	1	20	1	0.122	100	3	30	1	0.062

D_b-error: 0.1274 D_b-error: 0.1238 D_b-error: 0.0807

A_b-error: 0.4109 A_b-error: 0.3315 A_b-error: 0.2887

S_b-error: 9.6046 S_b-error: 7.3828 S_b-error: 5.0920

design is a D-efficient design generated constructed using the prior parameters as outlined above.

At the bottom of Table 14.2, the D_b-*error*, A_b-*error* and S_b-*error* are shown. The subscript b is used to represent the fact that the measures shown were calculated assuming a Bayesian prior parameter distribution. As can be seen from the table, the two orthogonal designs produce very similar D_b-*error* values although the D-optimal orthogonal design produces a lower A_b-*error* value. The lower A_b-*error* value suggests that this design will likely produce smaller standard errors than the traditional orthogonal design, which is confirmed by the smaller S_b-*error*. Assuming that the prior parameters are correct and that the panel version of the MMNL is correct, then the efficient design is likely to outperform the other two design types on all three measures. This finding is not surprising given that the design was optimized specifically on the D_b-error criteria we are using to compare the three designs on.

AN ISSUE WITH EFFICIENT DESIGNS AND A POSSIBLE SOLUTION?

Any constraint one places on an experimental design generated specifically for the purposes of modelling discrete choices will likely impact upon the overall efficiency of that design, with orthogonality representing just one such normally imposed constraint. A second constraint often imposed on designs is attribute level balance. Attribute level balance occurs when each level of an attribute is forced to occur an equal number of times within the design. This constraint is typically imposed so that each point in preference space (represented by the attribute levels) is covered an equal number of times of the course of the design. The attribute level balance constraint is often imposed on efficient designs, although this need not be the case. Typically, when this constraint is relaxed, it is necessary to impose a minimum number of times each level must appear, otherwise the attribute levels of the design will tend to go to the extremes of the attribute level range, thus not allowing for tests of non-linearity in preference. This is because designs with attributes only at the end points will generally place less constraints on the values the choice probabilities can take, although designs with too wide an attribute level range may tend to produce strictly dominated alternatives if only the end points of the attribute levels are used. Yu et al. (2008) and Kessels et al. (2008) overcome this problem by effects coding all attributes, such that there is no need to impose any attribute level balance constraints. However, this will yield many more parameters, hence larger designs. Nevertheless, attribute level balance remains a dominant assumption in constructing experimental designs for SC studies.

Where such a constraint is maintained (as with the three previous designs), the overall efficiency of a design may be impacted upon as changing one attribute level in one choice situation may result in an overall improvement in the design, but such a change would require that another attribute level be changed somewhere else in the design, possibly resulting in an overall worsening of overall efficiency of the design.

Toner et al. (1999), Fowkes (2000) and Kanninen (2002) offer a number of different design methods which we collectively call optimal choice probability designs that are designed to overcome this problem. Both Toner et al. and Kanninen show analytically that utility or probability balance in choice tasks represent an undesirable property, and in doing so suggest rules that minimize the variance of estimates in an optimal manner, based on desirable or what Toner et al. refer to as magic *p*s. Although using a different set of arguments, Fowkes (2000) arrived at a similar conclusion deriving a set of designs he termed boundary value designs. In each case, $K - 1$ attribute levels are first generated for each J alternative, typically using an orthogonal or optimal orthogonal approach. The last Kth attribute for each alternative is then generated as a continuous variable (usually a price attribute). The values of these continuous variables are chosen such that the choice probabilities take certain values that minimize the elements of the AVC matrix under the assumption of non-zero prior parameters, and as such are consistent with D-optimality. Toner et al. (1999) achieves a similar result to those reported by Kanninen and Fowkes. The boundary value method of Fowkes is somewhat different in derivation although the implications remain the same. Toner et al. (1999), Kanninen (2002) and Johnson et al. (2006) have determined the desirable probabilities for a limited number of designs (that is, those involving two alternatives), although non-linear programming may be used to determine these for a wider number of designs. We now go on to discuss these types of designs in detail.

OPTIMAL CHOICE PROBABILITY DESIGNS

In order to generate an *optimal choice probability* design, the first step is to generate a design with all non-continuous attribute levels. This initial design should have the same number of design dimensions (that is, alternatives, attributes, attribute levels and choice situations) with the exception of the kth attribute which is to be treated as continuous. This design should typically also, where possible, display the attribute level balance property. For the kth attribute, any attribute levels can be provided as long as they do not violate attribute level balance and hence require a different number of rows be generated. For example, assuming the price attribute as the attribute to be later treated as continuous, assigning it two attribute levels for a design to be with nine rows will require a change in the number of rows required. Also, while not necessary, the specific levels chosen are best selected if they are within the range that will be allowed when the attribute is later treated as continuous. For example, if in the final design, the analyst will allow the price attribute to take any value between $0 and $20, then the attribute levels for price in the initial design should be within this range also. In generating the initial design, any type of design can be constructed. Note that, in generating the design with continuous attribute levels, only the attributes that are allowed to take on continuous levels will be changed. That is, all other attributes will be fixed based on the initial design. Kanninen (2002) and Johnson et al. (2006) suggest using optimal orthogonal designs as the initial start design; however, other design types might provide more efficient results, particularly if they are closer to the 'optimal' level of statistical efficiency.

The next step is to select attribute levels for the kth attribute such that the choice probabilities for each choice situation in the design assume certain values. In selecting which attribute to treat as continuous, it is necessary that the attribute conceptually also be continuous (such as price). Thus, the attribute selected should not be qualitative but rather quantitative in nature. Note that as with efficient designs, the generation of choice probability designs requires the use of prior parameter estimates in order to determine the choice probabilities over the design. If zero-valued priors are assumed, as with optimal orthogonal designs, then the choice probabilities will simply be fixed and equal to $1/J$ and it will not be possible to generate the design. In allocating the attribute levels, the desirable choice probabilities that the analyst should attempt to aim for are shown in Table 14.3 for a small number of designs. In generating values for the kth attribute, the analyst may have to let go of the attribute level balance assumption common in generating designs, and further, may have to let go of the assumption that the attribute can only take on integer values.

The probabilities shown in Table 14.3 were derived analytically for the MNL model only, and unfortunately are known for designs of the dimensions reported within the table. Additional restrictive assumptions exist for this design generation method. For example, the method is limited not only the model assumed, but also the number of alternatives and attributes that can be examined. Further, the method also assumes generic parameters, and hence is not designed to handle labelled alternatives. The choice probabilities also assume prior parameter values, and hence are subject to

Table 14.3   Optimal choice probability values for specific designs

Number of attributes (K)	Number of unique choice situations in the design	Optimal choice-percentage split for two-alternative model
2	2	0.82/0.18
3	4	0.77/0.23
4	4	0.74/0.26
5	8	0.72/0.28
6	8	0.70/0.30
7	8	0.68/0.32
8	8	0.67/0.33

Source: Adapted from Johnson et al. (2006).

the same assumptions as per efficient designs. Finally, the procedures outlined in Kanninen (2002) and Johnson et al. (2006) are limited to locally optimal designs (that is, where the prior parameter values are known with 100 per cent certainty).

Given the above limitations, rather than rely on these probabilities which are known only for designs generated for MNL models, we explore here the use of an algorithm that does not require the analytical derivation of the most desirable choice probabilities (it is not certain that these can be derived outside of the assumptions listed above). In particular, we operationalise the Nelder–Mead algorithm (Nelder and Mead, 1965) to search for an optimal design. A detailed description of the algorithm is given in the Appendix to this chapter.

OPTIMAL CHOICE PROBABILITY DESIGN EXAMPLES

While Kanninen (2002) and Johnson et al. (2006) suggest using optimal orthogonal designs as the initial start design, we generate three different optimal choice probability designs based on the designs given in Table 14.2. In generating the designs, we make the same assumptions as before, however we now allow the third attribute to take non-integer values anywhere within the range of 0 and 30. Table 14.4 shows the three generated designs. As before, we provide D_b-error, A_b-error and S_b-error values for each of the designs at the base of the table.

All three errors for the first two design types improve over the equivalent designs shown in Table 14.2. Note however that the A_b- and S_b-errors of the optimal choice probability design constructed from the initial efficient

Table 14.4 Final designs

		Traditional orthogonal					Optimal orthogonal					Efficient				
S	Alt.	X1	X2	X3	X4	Prob.	X1	X2	X3	X4	Prob.	X1	X2	X3	X4	Prob.
1	1	150	0	5.8670	1	0.243	50	0	1.2440	1	0.445	150	2	1.7317	1	0.565
1	2	50	0	29.8362	1	0.022	100	1	29.9082	0	0.079	50	3	28.3324	0	0.293
2	1	150	1	23.8771	1	0.079	150	2	0.3744	0	0.541	100	2	28.4095	1	0.225
2	2	200	0	0.5401	1	0.296	200	3	5.2793	1	0.390	50	0	18.3837	0	0.151
3	1	100	3	26.2232	0	0.644	50	2	29.7444	0	0.233	150	3	6.1730	1	0.782
3	2	50	1	29.8062	0	0.050	100	3	28.9317	1	0.366	100	2	21.9078	0	0.096
4	1	200	0	0.2674	0	0.422	150	0	0.3641	1	0.349	50	3	29.5369	0	0.467
4	2	200	1	22.1967	0	0.107	200	1	28.1403	0	0.072	200	1	0.2256	1	0.305
5	1	100	3	27.8657	1	0.353	200	3	27.8376	0	0.403	100	1	15.2318	1	0.094
5	2	150	0	0.1165	0	0.353	50	0	0.1651	1	0.303	200	1	0.2236	0	0.656
6	1	200	2	0.7844	1	0.642	100	1	0.0161	1	0.529	200	1	21.2217	1	0.069
6	2	100	0	2.0805	0	0.191	150	2	20.4986	0	0.250	200	0	1.6002	0	0.409
7	1	50	2	17.3122	0	0.487	200	1	1.0554	1	0.437	50	1	4.7989	0	0.367
7	2	150	1	0.0619	1	0.331	50	2	29.7694	0	0.226	200	3	9.1622	1	0.520
8	1	150	3	26.9874	0	0.382	100	3	26.9020	0	0.569	100	0	0.2064	1	0.329
8	2	100	1	2.1603	1	0.392	150	0	0.1655	1	0.162	100	2	29.2543	0	0.257
9	1	50	2	29.9779	0	0.061	50	3	23.7711	1	0.474	50	2	10.9847	0	0.689
9	2	150	2	3.2300	0	0.818	100	0	0.3314	0	0.322	150	3	23.2498	1	0.170
10	1	200	1	0.0887	0	0.478	150	1	17.9196	0	0.091	200	3	17.5291	0	0.503
10	2	50	2	14.2951	1	0.344	200	2	3.3461	1	0.665	50	1	1.3632	1	0.353
11	1	150	3	2.6309	1	0.605	50	1	4.2528	0	0.717	50	3	28.6298	1	0.391
11	2	50	3	18.4067	0	0.327	100	2	22.9206	1	0.106	150	0	0.3519	0	0.333

Table 14.4 (continued)

S	Alt.	Traditional orthogonal					Optimal orthogonal					Efficient				
		X1	X2	X3	X4	Prob.	X1	X2	X3	X4	Prob.	X1	X2	X3	X4	Prob.
12	1	200	0	23.0717	1	0.019	150	3	28.1713	1	0.320	150	0	1.3394	1	0.318
12	2	150	3	29.7592	1	0.410	200	0	0.2873	0	0.319	150	1	27.7212	0	0.095
13	1	100	2	20.0506	0	0.147	200	0	0.9889	0	0.435	100	0	3.7186	0	0.119
13	2	100	2	0.8217	1	0.735	50	1	29.3072	1	0.056	100	2	1.1642	1	0.762
14	1	50	1	2.3948	0	0.441	100	2	5.3281	1	0.134	200	1	0.0164	0	0.528
14	2	200	2	5.2640	0	0.462	150	3	3.4252	0	0.815	50	2	17.0721	1	0.277
15	1	100	1	28.4825	1	0.042	200	2	29.0994	1	0.047	200	2	29.8620	0	0.263
15	2	200	3	26.6597	1	0.417	50	3	29.3998	0	0.628	150	0	27.7814	1	0.017
16	1	50	0	0.4434	1	0.254	100	0	25.6054	0	0.070	150	0	0.5945	0	0.356
16	2	100	3	28.4824	0	0.494	150	1	29.5542	1	0.062	100	3	29.2082	1	0.330

D_b-error: 0.0870
A_b-error: 0.3038
S_b-error: 5.7861

D_b-error: 0.0891
A_b-error: 0.2927
S_b-error: 5.4774

D_b-error: 0.07804
A_b-error: 0.2923
S_b-error: 5.2303

design actually get worse. This situation occurs as the optimality criterion that was applied was based on the D_b-*error* and not the A_b- or S_b-*errors*. There could be two reasons for the resulting larger A_b-*error*: (1) since the A_b-*error* is simply an average of the diagonal values, larger values of the standard errors are weighted more, hence the increase in a single standard error can outweight the decrease in many other standard errors, and (2) the covariances will be different across the two designs (and not necessarily smaller), which may have a positive influence in the D_b-*error*. Similar logic applies to the S_b-*error* which also works only with the standard error values.

A comparison of the three designs reveals that the efficiency measures of the first two designs are now more comparable to that of the third. Note, however, that this is possible only by letting go of orthogonality (at least in terms of the continuous attribute). Indeed, all designs now require a minimum of six respondents (rounding up) in order for all parameters (means and standard deviation parameters) to be statistically significant at the 95 per cent level. Further, note that this number represents a theoretical minimum required to obtain statistically significant parameter estimates only and that a larger sample size would possibly be required in order to achieve parameter stability and/or population generalizability.

CONCLUDING REMARKS

In this chapter, we have provided an overview of the current state of art in terms of generating experimental designs specifically for SC type studies. In addition, we introduce for the first time the most general approach to date for generating efficient or optimal SC designs. Previous attempts to generate such designs have been limited to studies with very specific design dimensions. Here, with the use of the Nelder–Mead algorithm, we have been able to extend designs allowing for continuous attribute levels to designs of any dimension, while at the same time, extending the theory to allow for Bayesian D-optimal designs (rather than just for locally D-optimal designs) as well as to other model types beyond the MNL model.

While this represents a significant advancement, there is still work to be done. The experimental design world remains fractured, stuck in dogmatic and what appears to many to be diagrammatically perpendicular world views. What is now required more than anything, is for these different schools of thought to come together and create a unified theory of experimental design for SC studies. Such a unified theory is not that far off, and indeed, we provide a glimpse of it here. These different theories of experimental design are not mutually exclusive, and indeed, can be accommodated within a single theory.

Finally, what we have presented here is an examination of the literature dealing with the statistical efficiency of SC experimental designs. Statistical efficiency represents but one side of the coin. While there exists a vast literature dealing with behavioural impacts of various design dimensions upon choice, what is lacking is research combining both statistical efficiency and what can be thought of as behavioural efficiency. Such a combination, represents to our way of thinking, the next frontier.

NOTES

1. www.choice-metrics.com.
2. http://crsu.science.uts.edu.au/choice/choice.html (accessed 14 July 2008).
3. Note that any parameter values could have been chosen. These were selected purely for demonstrative purposes only. Had different prior parameters been chosen instead, the results reported may have varied considerably. We discuss this in the discussion section of the chapter.

REFERENCES

Bliemer, M.C. and J.M. Rose (2006), 'Designing stated choice experiments: the state of the art', accepted for presentation at 11th International Conference on Travel Behaviour Research, Kyoto, Japan.

Bliemer, M.C.J. and J.M Rose (2008), 'Construction of experimental designs for mixed Logit models allowing for correlation across choice observations', Transportation Research Board Annual Meeting, Washington, DC.

Bliemer, M.C. and J.M. Rose (2009), 'Efficiency and sample size requirements for stated choice experiments', Transportation Research Board Annual Meeting, Washington, DC.

Bliemer, M.C.J., J.M. Rose and D.A. Hensher (2009), 'Constructing efficient stated choice experiments allowing for differences in error variances across subsets of alternatives', *Transportation Research Part B*, **43** (1), 19–35.

Bunch, D.S., J.J. Louviere and D.A. Anderson (1996), 'A comparison of experimental design strategies for Multinomial Logit Models: the case of generic attributes', working paper, Graduate School of Management, University of California at Davis.

Burgess, L. (2007), Discrete Choice Experiments (computer software), Department of Mathematical Sciences, University of Technology, Sydney, available at: http://crsu.science.uts.edu.au/choice/ (accessed 14 July 2008).

Burgess, L. and S. Street (2003), 'Optimal designs for 2k choice experiments', *Communications in Statistics: Theory and Methods*, **32**, 2185–206.

Burgess, L. and D.J. Street (2005), 'Optimal designs for choice experiments with asymmetric attributes', *Journal of Statistical Planning and Inference*, **134**, 288–301.

Carlsson, F. and P. Martinsson (2002), 'Design techniques for stated preference methods in health economics', *Health Economics*, **12**, 281–94.

Ferrini, S. and R. Scarpa (2007), 'Designs with a-priori information for nonmarket valuation with choice-experiments: a Monte Carlo study', *Journal of Environmental Economics and Management*, **53**, 342–63.

Fowkes, A.S. (2000), 'Recent developments in stated preference techniques in transport research', in J. de D. Ortuzar (ed.), *Stated Preference Modelling Techniques*, London: PTRC Education and Research Services Ltd, pp. 91–101.

Fowkes, A.S. and M.R. Wardman (1988), 'The design of stated preference travel choice experiments with particular regard to inter-personal taste variations', *Journal of Transport Economics and Policy*, **22**, 27–44.

Fowkes, A.S., M. Wardman and D. Holden (1993), 'Non-orthogonal stated preference design', *Proceedings of the PTRC Summer Annual Meeting*, Manchester, pp. 91–7.

Hess, S. and J.M. Rose (2008), 'Intra-respondent taste heterogeneity in instantaneous panel surveys', Transportation Research Board Annual Meeting, Washington, DC.

Hess, S. and J.M. Rose (2009), 'Should reference alternatives in pivot design SC surveys be treated differently?', *Environment and Planning A*, **42** (3), 297–317.

Huber, J. and K. Zwerina (1996), 'The importance of utility balance and efficient choice designs', *Journal of Marketing Research*, **33**, 307–17.

Johnson, F.R., B.J. Kanninen and M. Bingham (2006), 'Experimental design for stated choice studies', in B.J. Kanninen (ed.), *Valuing Environmental Amenities Using Stated Choice Studies: A Common Sense Approach to Theory and Practice*, Dordrecht: Springer, pp. 159–202.

Kanninen, B.J. (2002), 'Optimal design for multinomial choice experiments', *Journal of Marketing Research*, **39**, 214–17.

Kessels, R., P. Goos and M. Vandebroek (2006), 'A comparison of criteria to design efficient choice experiments', *Journal of Marketing Research*, **43** (3), 409–19.

Kessels, R., J. Bradley, P. Goos and M. Vandebroek (2008), 'Recommendations on the use of Bayesian optimal designs for choice experiments', *Quality and Reliability Engineering International*, **24** (6), 737–44.

Louviere, J.J., D.A. Hensher and J.D. Swait (2000), *Stated Choice Methods: Analysis and Application*, Cambridge: Cambridge University Press.

McFadden, D. (1974), 'Conditional logit analysis of qualitative choice behaviour', in P. Zarembka (ed.), *Frontiers in Econometrics*, New York: Academic Press, pp. 105–42.

Nelder, J.A. and R. Mead (1965), 'A simplex method for function minimization', *The Computer Journal*, **7** (4), 308–13.

Rose, J.M. and M.C.J. Bliemer (2008), 'Stated preference experimental design strategies', in D.A. Hensher and K.J. Button (eds), *Handbook of Transport Modelling*, Oxford: Elsevier, pp. 151–80.

Sándor, Z. and M. Wedel (2001), 'Designing conjoint choice experiments using managers' prior beliefs', *Journal of Marketing Research*, **38**, 430–44.

Sándor, Z. and M. Wedel (2002), 'Profile construction in experimental choice designs for mixed logit models', *Marketing Science*, **21** (4), 455–75.

Sándor, Z. and M. Wedel (2005), 'Heterogeneous conjoint choice designs', *Journal of Marketing Research*, **42**, 210–18.

Scarpa, R. and J.M. Rose (2008), 'Designs efficiency for non-market valuation with choice modelling: how to measure it, what to report and why', *Australian Journal of Agricultural and Resource Economics*, **52** (3), 253–82.

Street, D.J. and L. Burgess (2004), 'Optimal and near-optimal pairs for the estimation of effects in 2-level choice experiments', *Journal of Statistical Planning and Inference*, **118**, 185–99.

Street, D.J. and L. Burgess (2007), *The Construction of Optimal Stated Choice Experiments: Theory and Methods*, Hoboken, NJ: Wiley.

Street, D.J., D.S. Bunce and B.J. Moore (2001), 'Optimal designs for 2^k paired comparison experiments', *Communications in Statistics, Theory, and Methods*, **30** (10), 2149–71.

Street, D.J., L. Burgess and J.J. Louviere (2005), 'Quick and easy choice sets: Constructing optimal and nearly optimal stated choice experiments', *International Journal of Research in Marketing*, **22**, 459–70.

Toner, J.P., S.D. Clark, S.M. Grant-Muller and A.S. Fowkes (1999), 'Anything you can do, we can do better: a provocative introduction to a new approach to stated preference design', *WCTR Proceedings*, **3**, 107–20.

Train, K. (2003), *Discrete Choice Methods with Simulation*, Cambridge: Cambridge University Press.

Watson, S.M., J.P. Toner, A.S. Fowkes and M.R. Wardman (2000), 'Efficiency properties of orthogonal stated preference designs', in J. de D. Ortuzar (ed.), *Stated Preference Modelling Techniques*, London: PTRC Education and Research Services Ltd, pp. 91–101.

Yu, J., P. Goos and M. Vanderbroek (2008), 'Model-robust design of conjoint choice experiments', *Communications in Statistics: Simulation and Computation*, **37** (8), 1603–21.

APPENDIX: NELDER–MEAD ALGORITHM

The Nelder–Mead method Nelder and Mead (1965) is a computational technique for solving non-linear optimisation problems. The method is what is known as a *local search* technique (also referred to as an *incomplete* method). This means that although the method will locate a solution to a problem, that solution may only be *locally* optimal rather than *globally* optimal (so there may exist a better solution that the method fails to find). The motivation for the use of local methods is that guaranteeing the optimality of a solution is for many problems too computationally intensive to be feasible and is often of little practical benefit. Although in theory there are situations where the Nelder--Mead method will not terminate, in practice the finite precision and bounds of the floating point numbers used in digital computers guarantee that the method will (eventually) converge and terminate.

Operation

The method maintains a set of tentative solutions. The size of this set is determined by the number of unknowns in the problem. For a problem with N unknowns, a set of $N + 1$ tentative solutions will be maintained. With respect to optimising SP experimental designs with continuous attributes, the number of unknowns is the number of continuous attributes multiplied by the number of rows in the design. For the initial set of solutions, the levels for the continuous attributes are allocated randomly. Following the initial random allocation of attribute levels, the algorithm iteratively either improves upon the current worst tentative solution or shrinks all tentative solutions towards the best solution. The specific process is as follows.

Reflection/extension: the centroid of the set of tentative solutions (excluding the worst) is first calculated. A new tentative solution is obtained by reflecting the worst solution through this centroid, the rationale being that moving away from the worst solution towards the others should result in an improved solution. If the reflected solution does not improve upon the objective value of the worst solution the procedure skips to contraction. Otherwise, if the new solution is an improvement, a further extension away from the worst solution is considered. When the worst solution is a distance d from the centroid then the reflected and extended solutions are a distance of $2d$ and $3d$ respectively[1] from the worst solution. The better of these two solutions replaces the worst tentative solution and the iteration is complete.

Contraction: if reflection does not result in an improved solution, alternate solutions involving smaller changes are considered. Two solutions are considered: one halfway between the current worst and the centroid, the second halfway between the centroid and the reflected solution. Continuing the previous discussion, these solutions will be distances of 0.5*d* and 1.5*d* from the worst solution respectively. If neither of these solutions improves upon the worst the method instead applies shrinking. Otherwise, the contracted solution with the better objective function valuation is adopted in place of the current worst and the iteration is complete.

Shrinking: if neither of the above steps has produced an improved solution, then all tentative solutions (including the worst) are moved towards the best solution by a factor of 0.5, irrespective of whether this leads to improvements in their respective objective function valuations. This concludes the iteration.

Unless the procedure exhausts its computational resources (that is, a specified time or number of iterations has elapsed) it will continue to iterate until all tentative solutions are within a distance δ of the best solution. For a design with N rows and K continuous attributes, δ is defined to be:

$$\delta = \alpha N \sum_{k=1}^{K} (\max_k - \min_k)^2$$

where α is a user-definable value within the range $0 < \alpha < 1$. Smaller values of α lead to tighter convergence criteria and hence more iterations prior to convergence.

Multiple Runs and Tries

As with most local search algorithms, the solution obtained will depend on the starting conditions (the initial set of random tentative solutions). Running the procedure multiple times from different starting locations ensures that a single bad starting location does not unduly prejudice the final outcome. The version of the Nelder–Mead procedure implemented in NGene, the software used in generating designs in this chapter, allows multiple repeated *runs* and *tries* for this reason.

Each run is entirely independent and may involve multiple tries. Tries are not independent. Within a run, the best solution from each try is conveyed to the subsequent try (as one of the initial tentative solutions) so only the first try of a run uses an entirely random set of initial solutions. This ensures that each try within a run produces an improved (or at least not worsened) solution. A try ends when computational resources are exhausted or the tentative solutions converge. If computational resources remain, a new try begins.

As runs are independent, additional runs do not necessarily lead to improved solutions. It must also be noted that on the first run, a single copy of the design that is initially passed to the procedure is preserved as a tentative solution, meaning that on this run only, the solution set for the first try is not entirely random.

Note

1. The coefficients of distance used in the Nelder–Mead method are arbitrary. The values reported here are those commonly used.

15 Incentive and information properties of preference questions: commentary and extensions
Richard T. Carson and Theodore Groves

INTRODUCTION

This chapter is both a commentary on and extension of Carson and Groves (2007) (hereafter CG) The substantial attention the paper has received has been enormously gratifying. Reception of CG has largely been positive with little if any substantive criticism directed toward it; and, there are many papers now being presented at conferences that are testing or relying on various aspects of it.

Our remarks are organized into a series of short sections. The first points out that the main purpose of CG was to extend the revealed preference paradigm to cover some types of survey responses. The second notes that CG provides the theoretical foundation that some critics of contingent valuation (CV) had argued was missing. The third takes the concepts of 'hypothetical' and 'hypothetical bias' head on and argues that these concepts are, for the most part, ill-defined or simply wrong and have done enormous damage to clear and careful thinking about the nature of the response to stated preference questions. The fourth examines the properties of cheap talk which is often proposed as a way to reduce hypothetical bias. The fifth provides some elaboration on CG and the issue of how to interpret information extracted from preferences questions. The sixth poses an answer to the often asked question: is a single binary discrete choice (SBC) question always the best elicitation format for a researcher to use? The seventh provides some elaboration on the payment card elicitation format, which in recent years has seen a resurgence. The eighth turns to an examination of some of the properties of the now widely used discrete choice experiment. The ninth considers the usefulness of economic experiments to help determine the performance of preference elicitation formats. The last section addresses the relationship between CG and the behaviouralist critique of neoclassical economics with a focus on the different-answers-to-the-same-underlying-question issue.

EXTENDING THE REVEALED PREFERENCE PARADIGM

The CG paper has not, of course, quelled objections by some economists to the use of preference information obtained from surveys to place monetary values on goods. Nor should it have. The paper's purpose was to suggest economists should think about surveys as a source of 'revealed' preference information. As long as the preference information collected in surveys is used by governments and private firms to help make decisions, then people *should* use the opportunity provided by their survey response to help influence those decisions. In this sense, responses to survey questions meeting the set of conditions CG term 'consequential' are no different than any other type of behaviour that economists use to infer information about preferences. One way to view CG is as just another evolutionary step along the path pioneered by Bowen (1943) who early on recognized that voting represented economic behaviour with respect to public goods and Becker (1978) who saw that the allocation of time between activities and even behaviour as intimate as marriage were reflective of underlying utility in the standard sense of neoclassical economics.

PROVIDING A THEORETICAL FRAMEWORK

Carson and Groves (2007) provide the underlying theoretical framework that Cummings and Harrison (1994, pp. 115–17) correctly pointed out was missing with respect to the use of the contingent valuation method (CVM):

> There exists no theory that relates to individual valuation behavior in markets or referendums under conditions in which the good being purchased or the issue on which people are to vote is hypothetical and implied economic commitments are hypothetical. Therefore, as a theoretical basis for applications of the CVM, one must presume that the received economic theory of individual behavior in markets where real economic commitments are made, or the majority rule principle derived in social choice theory, is relevant for the hypothetical context of the CVM. The consistency of people's valuation behavior in the CVM with that assumed in value theory or the majority rule principle is, of course, an empirical question. Unfortunately, there does not currently exist a body of empirical evidence that might establish this consistency in any compelling way. Thus there exists no basis for drawing unequivocal conclusions as to the theoretical substance of values derived with the CVM.

Carson and Groves (2007) provide this theoretical foundation by first dividing questions into two types, consequential and inconsequential. For a question to be consequential, survey respondents need to believe, at least probabilistically, that their responses to the survey may influence some decision they care about. For consequential survey questions, neo-classical economic theory is relevant in terms of the incentives respondents face in answering the question. Fortunately, most CV surveys fall into this category, as they usually ask about something the respondent cares about (even if it is only the possibility of increased taxes) and are clearly intended to be used as an input to some decision making process. We contend that it is implausible to believe that someone would go to the expense of conducting a survey if it were clearly a priori that the agency was going to ignore the information it supplies. Inconsequential questions are those for which there is either no chance of influencing a government or firm decision and/or when utility is not changed by the decision to be made. For inconsequential decisions, any response is as good as any other response in terms of its influence on the respondent's utility level. Inconsequential questions can easily be created in a laboratory situation but are harder to do so convincingly in an actual field survey. Thus, as emphasized by CG, it is inappropriate to lump all survey questions together and label them as 'hypothetical'. As CG note, the difficulty with the word hypothetical is that it is ill-defined, an issue to which we now turn.

HYPOTHETICAL SURVEY QUESTIONS AND HYPOTHETICAL BIAS

Critics of the use of stated preference surveys are quick with the word 'hypothetical' as a pejorative adjective in front of 'survey', 'question' or 'bias'. But what does the term hypothetical mean? Dictionary definitions include: (1) related to a hypothesis, (2) assumed or thought to exist, and (3) as a synonym for the logical term conditional, sometimes in the context of a conjecture in a legal situation. While this last definition is consistent with the use of the term 'contingent' as in a CV survey, the critical aspect to note is that *none* of these definitions explicitly embody the definition of having 'no influence' on a decision to be made. This, however, is the way the term is often used by economists when referring to surveys, and forms the basis of how most tests of hypothetical bias are operationalized in the experimental economics literature.[1]

In CG's framework these tests of hypothetical bias are tests of consequential versus inconsequential questions. Such tests, to be blunt, are *completely useless* in terms of determining the properties of consequential questions. As such, much of the discussion in the existing literature (for example, Murphy, et al., 2005) about hypothetical bias is misguided because much of the evidence from experimental tests is simply irrelevant.[2] What then is left? A very large meta-analysis (Carson et al., 1996) suggests that estimates based on contingent valuation are highly correlated with (and if anything, slightly smaller on average) than estimates based on household production functions and hedonic pricing. A substantial body of evidence re-examined every couple of years suggests that political polling on two candidate races and referendums taken close to elections by the standards of economic forecasting are excellent predictors on average of actual voting. A much smaller number of comparisons between referendum votes and directly comparable CV questions also find close correspondence between the two. There are repeated demonstrations that survey-based estimates of how much people would be willing to contribute voluntarily are substantially higher than actual contributions and indications that surveys tend to over-predict the purchases of newly introduced consumer goods.[3] This pattern of results is predicted by the CG framework. It is, however, not predicted if respondents always truthfully respond to preference questions in surveys or if there is always a substantial 'hypothetical bias' effect in these surveys.

The usual claim of widespread hypothetical bias in stated preference surveys comes from irrelevant experimental tests using an inconsequential treatment as the incorrect stand-in for a survey question or from field comparisons involving voluntary contributions or purchases of new private goods. That no predictions follow from neoclassical economic theory for inconsequential questions has already been noted.[4] The other two situations where claims of hypothetical bias tend to originate are both similar in nature in that positive survey responses may be reasonably expected to increase the likelihood that the good will be made available in the future and the agent would then have the option to get to contribute towards/purchase it at a later date. This provides an incentive for the respondents to overstate, which is what tends to be observed in practice, consistent with CG's prediction. There is also an incentive to free ride in terms of the actual contribution with respect to the public good while payment for the private good is necessary in the sense that it cannot be obtained without payment. The use of voluntary contributions to provide a public good provides the classic illustration of why the concept of hypothetical bias is ill-defined if not just simply wrong. Neoclassical theory suggests the survey should overestimate true willingness-to-pay (WTP) while actual contributions should underestimate true WTP. Why would anyone define the (hypothetical) bias of using the survey estimate as the difference between the estimated and the actual voluntary contribution?

CHEAP TALK

There is almost a complete disconnect between how the term cheap talk is used in the game theory literature and its use in the non-market valuation literature. From a theoretical perspective, cheap talk is an interesting communications concept first examined by Crawford and Sobel (1982) for games without a dominant strategy as a way of altering the nature of equilibrium strategies.[5] Ironically, this literature shows that talk is not 'cheap' when it can influence the actions of others. What was thought of initially as a costless way of signalling, in contrast to the original work on costly signalling by Spence (1974), turned out to be quite consequential in the right circumstances. Two parties with objectives that were not perfectly aligned or diametrically opposed might be able to use a 'cheap talk' signal to reach a mutually more advantageous outcome. While the cheap talk signal is costless to send, the economic value of the signal need not be zero and can be calculated for each party as the difference in economic value of the outcomes achieved with and without its use. As long as the signal has non-zero economic value, agents are not indifferent to its use. Cheap talk in the usual game theory context is not intended to alter the strategic incentives of a game nor does it supply any information about a particular agent's payoff options but rather yields information about the preferences of other agent(s) that is potentially useful for coordination on one or more equilibrium solutions.

The 'cheap talk' language in stated preference surveys tells respondents that some other respondents lie when they answer survey questions and, as such, the fraction of people who would actually vote in favour is smaller than the fraction that says yes in the survey (for example, Cummings and Taylor, 1999). This cheap talk script is an explicit attempt to introduce the notion of hypothetical bias. While this language was clearly inspired by the game theory theoretic literature on cheap talk, no one has ever laid out a formal economic model of how or why cheap talk should have an influence on survey responses.[6] Indeed, the use of the term cheap talk in the game theoretical literature, which is focused on the use of costless signals to helping the parties coordinate on more desirable outcomes, is sufficiently different from the use of the term cheap talk in the non-market valuation literature so as to be a source of confusion.

Cheap talks' standard implementation in the non-market valuation literature has been with an SBC question for a public good, although not necessarily in a context that meets the CG conditions for incentive compatibility. We ignore that issue here and assume that the SBC question is incentive compatible, but that raises another question. An incentive-compatible SBC question has a dominant strategy response so it is unclear what role cheap talk is supposed to be playing. The stated purpose of cheap talk as explained by those implementing it in stated preference surveys is to reduce hypothetical bias. The problem is that anything that reduces WTP estimates tends to be seen as accomplishing this objective, but as we have pointed out earlier, the notion of hypothetical bias is ill-defined. Looking, for instance, at the main cheap talk script used in Cummings and Taylor (1999), the question that a rational respondent should ask is why is there a divergence between the survey response and the actual vote? There are many possible speculations, a lower quality good and the failure of some agents to follow through with actually paying. Unfortunately, these interpretations of the cheap talk script should have the effect of lowering the probability of a yes answer for some respondents. Because cheap talk should not have an impact unless it induces a change in the characteristics of the good or the payment obligation in situations where the agent has a dominant strategy, it should not be surprising that empirical tests of cheap talk produce erratic and inconsistent results (for example, Aadland and Caplan, 2006).

Parsing the language of different cheap talk scripts reveals 'hard' and 'soft' cheap talk versions.[7] The hard cheap talk version tells a respondent that some respondents lie when they say 'yes' in surveys. It is not clear how a respondent should interpret such a statement and it clashes with the usual social norm of truth telling that survey researchers try to advance in surveys. It is not hard to imagine interpretations that violate the standard notion of cheap talk which should alter the answer that some respondents give. For instance, it is possible that some respondents see the statement as saying that other respondents had had buyer's remorse which might increase uncertainty over the characteristics of the good in a negative manner. Another interpretation is that some respondents might see this as a statement that other respondents were going to shirk their obligation to pay. This could, in turn, either decrease the likelihood of a particular respondent saying yes, either due to a reduced probability that the good would be provided if there were shirkers or through fairness considerations. It might also increase the likelihood of a yes answer if the respondent thought the cheap talk language indicated a possibility that people can shirk. No doubt one could argue over the plausibility or relevance of any of these interpretations or advance others, some of which may result in the appearance of a higher WTP. The point that CG make is that a researcher needs to consider seriously the informational content of survey statements and the influence they might have on respondents. The strong version of cheap talk simply has too many interpretations as to why it might have an effect and some of these interpretations lead to undesirable changes in the responses given to a survey question.

The soft version of cheap talk invokes the notion of a divergence between a casual survey response and what respondents would like to do if they carefully considered their budget situation. It differs from the strong version of cheap talk in that it does not invoke other respondents explicitly lying when answering survey questions. By focusing on individual failure to consider payment obligations as the source of the problem, it does not raise the issue of potential problems with the good. The soft version of cheap talk stresses the need for the person answering the survey to make sure that they could actually pay and recognize what the commitment they are making is. It has some similarities both with respect to content and intent to language used in some earlier contingent valuation studies that explicitly invoked the respondent's budget constraint and provided an opportunity to reconsider their response.

This soft version of cheap talk may reduce WTP estimates if there is a random component to respondent answers and it reduces that random component in an asymmetric manner.[8] Reducing the random component by inducing respondents to take more care in their answers is desirable from a policy perspective, although it is important to note that doing so can sometimes produce divergences with behaviour in actual markets where much less time and effort is often put into making decisions than in a survey context. The asymmetric nature of the cheap talk script by concentrating on the payment aspects rather than on the desirable quality of the good to be provided will tend to make WTP estimates more conservative.

When one moves away from an elicitation format in which a respondent has a dominant strategy to one that does not, then cheap talk can have an impact on a respondent's optimal answer. Finding a difference in estimates with and without using a cheap talk script should not be taken as an indication that hypothetical bias is present. A simple example extending an incentive-compatible SBC to a multinomial choice question with three alternatives illustrates the issue. Suppose a respondent is offered three choices A (the status quo option), B and C, where the agent's preferences are $C > A > B$. If the cheap talk script alters the respondent's perception of the fraction in favour of A in a downward direction, the respondent's optimal choice may now well be A, to avoid the worst option of B. This action clearly lowers the estimate of WTP for C, yielding the effect attributed to hypothetical bias. While the nature of the problem with cheap talk in this case is particularly easy to see, the ability of cheap talk to influence respondent beliefs about priors concerning particular goods and/or their attributes in more general settings where respondents do not have dominant strategies is conceptually straightforward to show. Hence, cheap talk can have an influence (potentially undesirable) on consumer choices in these situations both in surveys and actual markets. The issue of how information provided in a survey influences respondent beliefs concerning the preferences of other agents is one that naturally follows from the CG framework but it remains largely unexplored from an empirical perspective.

EXTRACTING PREFERENCE INFORMATION

Carson and Groves (2007) suggest that the interpretation of data from stated preference surveys is much more complicated than previously thought. Most researchers using such data had implicitly or explicitly assumed that people truthfully answered the questions they asked. Carson and Groves (2007) argue that in general, this assumption is likely to be false if the survey question is consequential and the respondent is acting like a rational economic agent. The conditions under which truthful preference revelation is always in the respondent's best interest are often hard and sometimes impossible to meet. However, one of the most important but often overlooked implications of CG is that even in the absence of incentive for truthful preference revelation, much useful information can be obtained from stated preference data. The key question that CG addressed was how to interpret such information and the nature of the deviations from truthful preference revelation that were likely to be observed in particular instances.

IS A SINGLE BINARY DISCRETE CHOICE ALWAYS THE BEST FORMAT?

Under specific conditions noted by CG, an SBC question for a pure public good is incentive compatible in the sense that truthful preference revelation is a respondent's dominant strategy. This, however, does not imply that stated preference surveys should always use this elicitation format. First, the incentive compatibility result requires auxiliary conditions to be met, and this is often difficult and sometimes impossible to do. This qualification is true of markets, voting and surveys. Second, when the SBC question being asked is incentive compatible, the preference information that it provides to the researcher is very limited. All a respondent's choice can do is increase or decrease the likelihood that the specified good is provided at the specified cost. This means that surveys using an SBC question require large samples and substantial pre-testing to help determine the range and placement of the cost amounts used. As such, a researcher may want to use an elicitation format that provides more preference information.

The main implication from CG on this point is that preference information from these alternative formats may be distorted. For instance, CG argue that a zero spike in the estimated WTP distribution is a natural consequence of the incentive structure induced by an open-ended matching question since a respondent should report a zero WTP if their true WTP is lower than the expected cost if the good is provided. There can, of course, in particular instances be alternative explanations for the observed phenomena that have a different interpretation. Many people could actually be indifferent to having the good supplied rather than simply having WTP values below expected cost.

There are two other aspects of an SBC question that are worth noting. The first is a corollary to the sparse nature of the information obtained from this elicitation format. Statistical precision of estimates either requires very large sample sizes and/or making strong assumptions about the nature of the underlying latent WTP distribution. Many of the claims about the SBC format overestimating WTP seem traceable to one of two problems: (1) making an inappropriate distributional assumption, and (2) inappropriate treatment of the right tail of the distribution. An example of the first problem is estimating a logit or probit model with the log of price as the stimulus variable. The second problem has cursed almost all welfare estimation irrespective of the source of the data obtained and has many variants. For travel cost models, functional form assumptions rather than actual data are relied upon to choke-off demand beyond some point. While stated preference questions can often push the prices for which reliable information can be obtained, both higher and lower than what is available in a market context, extremely high and extremely low prices should not be seen as plausible by respondents. As such, CG argue that rational respondents will answer the question with the cost information they think is relevant. The need for posing only realistic/credible questions cannot be emphasized enough. A more subtle variant of the right tail problem is the failure to recognize that data issues unrelated to the properties of the elicitation format may contaminate the data generating process. These include respondent confusion and the interviewer incorrectly recording the answer or the data entry incorrectly transferring the response. Note that these problems also occur with respect to data received from market transactions. In that context, they are often less obvious and less problematic as long as the highest price observed in the market is far from choking off demand or if the researcher is only interested in estimating marginal changes in WTP with respect to changes in an attribute rather than total WTP. The implications of consumer confusion with respect to both survey responses and market purchases is an issue that deserves more attention.

Second, a binary discrete choice question is most appropriate where there are two alternatives. A natural example is the status quo versus an alternative involving a public good (for example, status quo level of air quality in a city versus an alternative level). The critical feature is that only one level of air quality can be supplied so that any question that puts more than one alternative to the status quo into play unravels the SBC incentive properties. The issue is quite different when multiple additions to the status quo can be made available such as new fishing locations or new products. In this switch from public to quasi-public/private goods, the SBC question loses much of its attractiveness. The relationship between the nature of the good and the properties of the elicitation format developed by CG still appears to be under-appreciated.

A RESURGENCE OF THE PAYMENT CARD FORMAT

One of the more interesting developments in recent years has been the emergence of the payment card format first proposed in Mitchell and Carson's (1989) early work as the most popular matching elicitation format. The purest version of a matching elicitation format, the open-ended direct question, finds many respondents at a loss as to how to answer. At first this was thought to be related to asking about an unfamiliar public good but familiarity is not the main factor. In most western societies, making decisions in response to posted prices is the norm. In such a context, choice is the economic primitive which reveals preferences.

Interestingly, original criticism of the payment card was based on the anchoring behaviour with respect to the starting cost amount used, as seen in the bidding game format. Carson and Groves (2007) argue that this anchoring behaviour should be expected if the initially asked about cost is thought by the respondent to be correlated with the good's actual cost, which seems like a natural inference for respondents to make. Rather than encouraging a vague type of anchoring, the array of amounts on a payment card we conjecture may do two things. The first follows from the usual language of a payment card to pick any amount on the card.[9] This subtly converts the question into a choice question but one with a sufficiently large number of options that it ends up approximating a continuous matching response. The second is that the sequence of amounts on the payment card appears to increase uncertainty over the actual cost of the programme relative to the expectation that is formed in the open-ended direct question. Carson and Groves (2007) shows that increasing uncertainty with respect to cost in the matching format tends to increase the optimal stated WTP response towards its true value from below under most plausible belief structures. This may result in the payment card producing conservative WTP estimates, but not grossly conservative estimates. The theoretical drawback is that the payment card cannot be guaranteed to always provide incentives for revealing WTP amounts equal to or less than true WTP. In practice, there are usually only a small number of suspect very high WTP responses. Whether these responses are inconsistent with income levels and other covariates may be checked using regression procedures designed to identify outliers.

CHOICE EXPERIMENTS

The increasingly popular discrete choice experiment (DCE) format received limited treatment in CG beyond a few key results. Carson and Groves (2007)'s starting point was to note that the SBC question, to which they devoted considerable attention, is the simplest case of a DCE. Moving from an SBC with two alternatives to a multinomial question with $k > 2$ alternatives generally causes a loss of incentive compatibility even if (1) the payment mechanism is coercive, (2) no other decision is potentially influenced by the response to the question, and (3) a take-it-or-leave it offer is made. The fundamental reason for this is that, if only one good is to be supplied, then a particular respondent's optimal choice should depend upon beliefs about the choices that are likely to be made by other respondents. As such, truthful preference revelation can no longer be a dominant strategy for all consumers and belief structures as it is in the case of SBC. When a survey's influence on the agency's decision comes through a plurality aggregation rule, for example, it is easy to show that, if all respondents have completely flat (that is, uninformative) prior assumptions about the choices likely to be made by other respondents, then truthful preference revelation is the optimal strategy.[10] The question for empirical researchers then is how likely is it for the flat prior assumption to hold? What is not known though without imposing a lot of structure on the problem is how a consumer should trade-off a weak but non-flat prior assumption against the strength of preference for a particular alternative. This is the situation that is likely to hold in most situations.

Carson and Groves (2007) also note that the truthful preference revelation problem in a multinomial choice question can go away in the special case where all but one of the $k-1$ of the goods rather than just one of good is provided.[11] It is easy to show in this situation that the multinomial choice question is effectively a SBC of the respondent's most preferred alternative paired against a single stochastically chosen less preferred alternative. This context is most likely to be applicable to quasi-public and private goods. Again, however, the situation facing empirical researchers is likely to be the intermediate case where there is uncertainty over the number of alternatives that might be provided.

Many DCE's utilize more than one choice set. This introduces a new issue. How does the agency aggregate responses across choice sets? Randomly picking one choice (under the assumption that respondents are expected utility maximizers) provides them with an incentive to treat each choice set as independent. While it is possible to provide assurances to participants in a laboratory experiment that this is what is being done, such a statement may not be credible in the context of a survey, as it suffers the same problem that CG point out occurs with any survey implementation of the Becker et al. (1964) mechanism. It may not be plausible to respondents that information collected in a survey would be discarded and not used. Most plausible aggregation rules result in a situation where the optimal response by some respondents to one choice set is contingent on the response they gave in another choice set.

A key insight of CG was that the nature of deviations from truthful preference revelation in non-incentive compatible DCEs should not manifest themselves as random behaviour. Most of the tests comparing consumer preferences estimated from DCEs to similar estimates using behaviour revealed in a market context are now based on whether the preference parameters from the two approaches are consistent, up to a constant scale (variance) factor.[12] Such tests, however, do not have much power against many forms of strategic behaviour as they are partially or completely confounded with changes in the scale factor. The objective of non-truthful revelation is to drive down price (for an existing good), to help induce provision (for a new good in the case where later purchase is an option) and/or to take account of the perceived preferences of other agents under some type of plurality decision rule. In none of these cases is random deviation from truthful preference revelation optimal.

The usual deviation from truthful preference revelation will be for respondents to sometimes indicate that their second most preferred option is the choice that they would make from the set available. A violation of the independence of irrelevant alternative (IIA) assumption results from this action.[13] A slightly different way to see the nature of the IIA violation is to note that the choice between any two alternatives now depends on the presence or absence of other alternatives. Independence of irrelevant alternative violations are typically seen in data from DCEs. It is straightforward to see how this type of IIA violation inflates the variance since the implicit variance has to increase to explain why the second favourite option was indicated as the choice out of the set of options. It is sometimes argued that strategic behaviour in a DCE is a difficult task for respondents to undertake, but all respondents have to do is to act as if they are more (or less) price sensitive than they actually are when the bundle of attributes they most prefer in a choice set is priced higher than they expected it be, given the other alternatives in the current or previous choice sets.[14] There are, of course, many other reasons posited for the ubiquitous IIA violations observed. The point we wish to make is that deviations from the standard conditional logit model now typically modelled as preference heterogeneity in a random parameters sense can also be generated by the sort of non-truthful preference revelation that one might expect to see in a DCE.

The broader message from CG is that a researcher needs to step back and ask the question: what should a respondent answering a DCE be trying to accomplish? The most troubling answer is 'nothing', as this implies that the questions being asked are not consequential. By asking this question, CG provide an insight into a long-standing but little recognized puzzle. For private goods, choice questions tend to overestimate the propensity to buy a new product potentially being introduced into the market, while at the same time choice questions for existing products produce estimates that suggest survey respondents are more price sensitive than actual customers in stores. Neither result is surprising once one realizes that a respondent who potentially wants a new product to be available should act less price sensitive than they truly are to increase the likelihood of it being offered for sale in the market, while for an existing good, the same respondent should act more price sensitive in hopes of reducing the price the good is sold for.

Seeing different prices for the same or a closely related good can also influence a respondent's optimal answers to a sequential DCE. For instance, with a coercive payment mechanism for a pure public good, some respondents may rationally say 'no' if they have seen the same good or a closely related good earlier for a lower price.[15] There are other interpretations of what impact having the respondent seeing multiple prices for the same or closely related good can have. Take for instance the case of being offered the good at a higher price. The respondent may be more likely say 'no' even though their WTP exceeds the higher priced asked because they presume the good can be supplied at the first priced asked. This can lead to the appearance of starting point bias because answers to subsequent questions are 'anchored' on the first price seen, as it is deemed the most credible. A wide variety of different behaviours such as price averaging and completely ignoring very high or very low prices are plausible depending on how divergent information concerning prices is translated by the respondent into beliefs about what price will actually be paid if the good is supplied.

The general difficulty with a survey that presents the respondent with a sequence of choice sets is that the researcher would like the respondent to treat each choice set as independent of the other, but there may be no reason for a rational respondent to do so. Failure to treat the choice sets as independent could be manifest in any number of ways but one way (Day et al., 2009) appears to be for the respondent to accept the attribute levels other than cost and then to adjust the perceptions of the actual cost to be paid (including uncertainty about cost in the case of a coercive payment mechanism). This can be seen in respondents who either become much more or much less price sensitive than they would be in an incentive compatible SBC or the actual marketplace. The particular effect that should be expected depends on the nature of the payment obligation and how respondents believe the agency will use the information with respect to price (or other attributes).[16]

THE USEFULNESS OF ECONOMIC EXPERIMENTS

Economic experiments, both laboratory and field, have the potential to shed considerable light on the incentive and informational properties of survey elicitation formats. Their track record to date, however, has been quite mixed. Much of the problem stems from an obsession to show whether hypothetical bias exists, which is an understandable research endeavour given the scepticism many economists have concerning the use of surveys.

The most common experiment has been a blunt instrument testing the hypothesis that respondents always tell the truth, irrespective of the incentives they face for preference revelation, rather than a test of any theoretical prediction from economic theory. A well-known and widely cited example is Cummings et al. (1995). This paper compares the percentage who say 'yes' that they would pay a specified amount for various private goods when payment is required to the percentage who say 'yes' in a treatment where it is made clear that the question being asked is purely hypothetical in the sense that they will neither pay for nor receive the good. They find that more subjects in the 'real' treatment say 'yes' than in the 'hypothetical' treatment. This result has led some researchers to believe that contingent valuation overestimates and is frequently invoked by critics as a reason why contingent valuation methods should not be used. But consider this experiment through the lens of CG. If respondents considered the second treatment to be inconsequential, then economic theory makes no prediction with respect to comparing the two treatments.[17] It may be useful to ask the question: what results would the researcher have expected to see if statements made in the second treatment that the response was inconsequential were ignored? In that case, anyone who thought that they might want to accept a future offer to obtain the good should say 'yes' because saying 'yes' might increase the likelihood that such an offer would be made and the respondent could decide at that point whether to accept it.[18] Thus, if the second treatment was taken by respondents to be inconsequential, then it is not clear why the comparison is of any interest to economists. If the treatment was taken as consequential, then the theoretically predicted result for a private good was observed.

Carson and Groves (2007) has inspired a substantial amount of experimental work and it is beyond the scope of our effort here to comprehensively review it, although we believe that in a few years from now this would be a worthwhile endeavour. Carson et al. (2004) provide experimental results supporting a key implication of the CG framework: the probability of a vote on a public good being binding does not influence the fraction responding 'yes' as long as it is positive. There are two other findings from this study. First, a purely hypothetical case (probability of the vote being binding is zero) does behave differently from treatments where the probability of the vote being binding is positive. The empirical estimates are overestimates which is consistent with past experimental work, suggesting that results from the purely hypothetical case should not be relied upon as an indication of how consequential questions work.[19] Second, creating an explicit linkage between two decisions influences the response to a question asked about only one of those decisions. While the nature of the linkage was made obvious to subjects, the response to it was clearly inconsistent with the belief that respondents always truthfully reveal their preferences and provides a note of caution with respect to making the assumption that respondents are not capable of linking multiple issues.

Some of the most interesting papers we have seen have taken a step away from the generic (and, as CG argue, ill-defined) question of whether contingent valuation overestimates, to look at the nuts and bolts of how specific elicitation formats work under much more controlled circumstances using induced rather than home-grown preferences.[20] Doing so allows clearer identification of deviations from theoretical predictions and the ability to better sort out what type of belief structures subjects are using in particular contexts. One of the key findings that emerges in this work is that subjects make optimization errors, an issue that CG do not consider. Taylor et al. (2001) show that optimization errors using a referendum format requiring payment are relatively common, even though the aggregate results were consistent with what one would have expected under truthful preference revelation. Using induced values, Palomé (2003) shows that about half of the subjects responded truthfully and that those who did not respond truthfully were much more likely to under-declare (41 per cent) versus over-declare (12 per cent). Vossler and McKee (2006) look at several different elicitation mechanisms and show that they differ in terms of the fraction of subjects making optimization errors. An intriguing result in this paper is that asking subjects about how certain they are about their answers induced the appearance of uncertainty even where there was none. Collins and Vossler (2009) used induced preferences and looked at the difference in choices made by respondents when faced with three options. They create a context in which a subject should view all three of the options as having an equal probability of being chosen by other agents. In situations involving equal prior assumptions with respect to the choice of other agents, CG argue that the multinomial choice question with three options is incentive compatible. Collins and Vossler's overall results are consistent with truthful preference revelation, albeit with optimization errors. Interestingly, treatments that move away from easy to understand plurality rules for determining outcomes toward more complicated schemes generally appear to induce a higher fraction of optimization errors. The lesson from all these studies is that errors of optimization are likely to be more common than often thought and can vary with the nature of the task. Theoretical work on the nature and implications of such optimization errors is clearly needed, as most random utility models ascribe the error component to specification error and factors observable to the agent but not the analyst.

The induced value framework can also be used to examine other key issues related to the properties of elicitation. For instance, Carson et al. (2009) show that one can achieve incentive compatibility in a double-bounded discrete choice question if the link between the two questions can be broken. This is easy to do in a laboratory experiment but hard to do in an actual field survey. By tracing out the steps involved, they are able to isolate the source of the problem which is the ability to guarantee the independence of the two questions. This, in turn, may provide some insight into situations where the independence of the two questions is more likely to approximately hold.

BEHAVIOURALIST CRITIQUE

The CG paper presents a set of neoclassical predictions that stand in stark contrast with several of the key predictions associated with the behavioral critique of neoclassical economics. Chief among these is the assertion that the core problem with the assumption of neoclassical economic behaviour (that is, Tversky et al., 1990) is that it should produce estimates that are 'procedurally invariant', where the classic examples are the divergences in the implicit preferences suggested by answers to choice and matching questions. Carson and Groves (2007) suggests that observing such procedural invariance under neoclassical economic behaviour is highly unlikely, as most approaches to obtaining preference information differ either in terms of their incentive structure with respect to truthful preference revelation and/or with respect to the nature of the information that a procedure conveyed. Carson and Groves (2007) predict procedural invariance will be violated and often provides guidance on the direction of the divergence that should be observed. A broad array of empirical evidence supports these predictions.[21]

Carson and Groves do not claim that neoclassical economic theory is not vulnerable to the behavioural critique. We do believe, though, that to the extent the behavioral critique is valid, it is unlikely to have different implications for consequential surveys than other types of economic behaviour. In this sense, it is inconsistent to act as if there are behavioral economics related problems with surveys used for valuation purposes that do not permeate data used to infer preference information obtained from other sources. The main distinction would appear to be that in a survey context it is easier to run experiments to examine the role of different types of effects. Given the ability of surveys to frame questions for respondents that avoid some decision-making problems and facilitate transparency, one might even argue that preference information elicited from well constructed surveys should play a larger role in helping to formulate policies that increase social welfare.

One of the most interesting directions for future research we believe is how the CG neoclassical framework and various predictions from behavioral economics interact. At the heart of CG's reading of the empirical evidence is that neoclassical marginal conditions appear to hold while much of the behavioural critique concerns stepping back to a much more primitive level regarding behaviour. Bernheim and Rangel (2009) provide an examination of what welfare economics might look like if it is based on consumer choice which is influenced by factors identified by the behavioural critique.

NOTES

1. This definition is surprising given Samuelson's (1954) early recognition that if the government relied on questionnaires of the public for preference information, it would be in the interest of respondents to exploit that opportunity for their own selfish gain.

2. Murphy et al. (2005) presciently state that their 'results are quite sensitive to model specification, which will remain a problem until a comprehensive theory of hypothetical bias is developed.'

3. It is worth noting here that the cleanest recent comparison in the literature to the ideal situation put forth by CG is Johnson (2006) and in Chapter 9 of this volume. This study looks at a case where a survey with a binary discrete choice question on a water supply issue in Rhode Island was first administered as an input to the policy-making process and then a subsequent binding referendum vote was held at one of the price points. At the $250 price used in the binding referendum, the percentage in favour was 46 per cent while in the survey the percentage in favour was 48 per cent, with the difference not statistically significant (p = .69).

4. Inconsequential questions in many contexts are odd in that they invite speculation as to their potentially hidden purpose. In many experimental contexts participants may believe that if they indicate responses consistent with higher (or in some contexts lower) WTP amounts that they will be more likely to be given the opportunity to participate in subsequent rounds where real money can be earned. This possibility makes the interpretation of the result of inconsequential treatments in economics experiments even more difficult to interpret.

5. See Farrell and Gibbons (1989) for further theoretical development and Farrell and Rabin (1996) for a very readable review.

6. Cummings and Taylor at the end of their paper suggest potential psychological explanations related to priming.

7. The environmental valuation literature (for example, Aadland and Caplan, 2006) sometimes refers to long and short versions of cheap talk that have some overlap with but do not directly correspond to the hard and soft labels we use here.

8. Interestingly, Bulte et al. (2005) comparing treatments using a cheap talk script to those emphasizing the consequential nature of the survey find no difference in the aggregate estimates. In contrast, treatments that appear very hypothetical tend to result in higher WTP estimates.

9. Most work on payment cards has focused on whether restricting the range of the amounts shown on a payment card can influence estimated WTP (Covey et al., 2007; Dubourg et al., 1997; Rowe et al., 1996) to which there are mixed results. Under CG, the range of amounts displayed on a payment card can have an influence on both expected cost and the level of uncertainty surrounding that amount. Earlier researchers (for example, Mitchell and Carson, 1989) looked at placing the cost of other goods (public and private) on the payment card. These, too, can have an influence on formation of cost expectations. Dubourg et al. (1997) demonstrate a pure psychological anchoring effect by giving half of the sample a payment card starting with low numbers (and increasing) and the other half the sample a payment card starting with high numbers (and decreasing). This may be an indication that one of the approaches has violated standard conversation conventions (Grice, 1975).

10. Note that this is a sufficient condition rather than a necessary condition, so an empirical researcher is not able to conclude that a choice question is not incentive compatible if respondents do not hold a flat prior assumption.

11. This holds under the maintained assumption that the respondent gets utility from at most one of the goods in the choice set. Otherwise, one has to take account of the relationship between goods in the set and their joint consumption.

12. Choice models inherently produce estimates of (β/σ) rather than β, where β is the preference parameter of interest and σ is the scale factor. Some earlier tests comparing stated and revealed preference data made the mistake of comparing parameter estimates implicitly assuming that the scale factor in the two types of data was the same. Swait and Louviere (1993) and Haab et al. (1999) show that one needs to take account of the difference in scale factors in between survey and market/experimental data in comparing estimates since discrete choice models inherently generate parameter estimates confounded with a scale factor. In a particular context, survey data may be associated with a smaller

or larger random component than data from other sources. Further, the particular elicitation format and specific features of it, such as the number of attributes and/or attribute levels, may influence the magnitude of the random component. In spite of calls (for example, Louviere et al., 2002) for more research on factors influencing the magnitude and nature of the random component, there is still too little work on this topic relative to work concentrating on factors that might influence location shifts in parameters.

13. To see this, consider the case where there are three options (A, B and C), rank ordered for convenience in terms of a respondent's preferences. A is thought to have little chance of being implemented given beliefs about other agent's preferences but is close to B in attribute space with B being strongly preferred to C. At the heart of IIA violations is a dependence on the choice between two alternatives in the presence of one or more alternatives in the choice set.

14. If respondents adopt this simple strategy, then as CG argue, it is possible to correctly recover marginal WTP estimates with respect to changes in attribute levels. This is because the biased price/scale effect cancels out in the standard approach to obtaining marginal WTP estimates. Most comparisons in the literature (for example, Carlsson and Martinsson, 2001) look at marginal rather than total WTP. One of the few papers to look at both is Lusk and Schroeder (2004). They found in the context of a private good that marginal WTP estimates are similar between stated preference and experimental treatments while the total WTP estimates differed.

15. For an example documenting such behaviour, see Day et al. (2009). For private goods, this type of effect could go either way depending upon whether the respondent was more interested in influencing the price of the good or the probability that it was offered for sale.

16. An under-appreciated issue in surveys briefly raised by CG and explored in depth (Corrigan et al., 2008; Zhao and Kling, 2001, 2004) is the issue of *when* a consumer is making an irrevocable commitment to pay for a good if supplied. We suspect that some of the observed differences in WTP (and WTA) are really the result of subtle divergences between treatments on this dimension of 'commitment dynamic' that is inferred by respondents/experiment participants but not recognized by the researchers involved.

17. The general difficulty we see with the 'pure hypothetical' implementation in many experiments is its lack of plausibility. With money being spent to gather data from them, subjects should speculate as to the use that data will be put and respond accordingly. As long as some subjects believe that saying 'yes' or giving high WTP amounts will make it more likely that they will advance, in the sense of being made future offers, then there may be an intrinsic tendency of purely hypothetical treatments to overestimate.

18. The issue with the experiment from this perspective is the assumption that public and private goods had the same theoretical properties. This assumption appears to have stemmed from the belief that if an elicitation procedure is not 'well-behaved' with private goods then it will not be well-behaved with public goods. This belief is pervasive in the literature even though it has no basis in neoclassical economic theory.

19. While this overestimate result may be an empirical regularity, without any theoretical basis it is unclear why such an empirical regularity exists.

20. This comment should not be taken as suggesting that home-grown values (that is, preferences that are not induced by the experimenter) should never be used, but rather, more caution should be taken when they are. The researcher should first ask whether the question can be best addressed using induced values. Herriges et al. (2007) and Vossler and Evans (2009) provide interesting experiments that explore the implications of CG's consequentiality using home-grown values. Both papers find similar results in quite different contexts. The concluding sentence of the Herriges et al. (2007) paper's abstract provides a nice summary: 'We find evidence consistent with the knife-edge theoretical results, namely that the willingness to pay distributions are equal among those believing the survey to be at least minimally consequential, and divergent for those believing that the survey is irrelevant for policy purposes.' We believe that more work on how to best induce consequentiality in preference surveys is clearly needed.

21. We have given short treatment to the information aspects of the CG framework. Most experiments and surveys comparing different treatments have implicitly assumed that all information provided is taken at face value and clearly understood. A good example is the Powe and Bateman (2004) study which looks at the well-known external scope test (Carson and Mitchell, 1993, 1995) using flood protection schemes involving different parts of the Broadlands area in the UK. Their results suggest respondents are not sensitive to enacting the scheme for specific areas and for the entire Broadlands, a troubling finding. However, 41 per cent of respondents do not consider a scheme involving the whole area realistic. This fraction is much higher than the fraction finding the scheme unrealistic for specific areas. Not seeing a scheme as realistic is closely tied to not being willing to pay anything for it, a behaviour one might expect of rational agents. After controlling for whether the respondent sees particular schemes as realistic, the theoretically expected result that WTP for the more inclusive area is larger is now obtained. Their simple take home message is that performing like-for-like scope tests is harder than it seems.

REFERENCES

Aadland, D. and A.J. Caplan (2006), 'Cheap talk revisited: new evidence from CVM', *Journal of Economic Behavior and Organization*, **60**, 562–78.

Becker, G.M., M.H. DeGroot and J. Marschak (1964), 'Measuring utility by a single response sequential method', *Behavioral Science*, **9**, 226–32.

Becker, G.S. (1978), *The Economic Approach to Human Behavior*, Chicago, IL: University of Chicago Press.

Bernheim, B.D. and A. Rangel (2009), 'Beyond revealed preference: choice theoretic foundations for behavioral welfare economics', *Quarterly Journal of Economics*, **124**, 51–104.

Bowen, H.R. (1943), 'The Interpretation of Voting in the Allocation of Economic Resources', *Quarterly Journal of Economics*, **58**, 27–48.

Bulte, E., S. Gerking, J.A. List and A. de Zeeuw (2005), 'The effect of varying the causes of environmental problems on stated WTP: evidence from a field study', *Journal of Environmental Economics and Management*, **49**, 330–42.

Carlsson, F. and P. Martinsson (2001), 'Do hypothetical and actual marginal willingness to pay differ in choice experiments?', *Journal of Environmental Economics and Management*, **27**, 179–92.

Carson, K.S., S.M. Chilton and W.G. Hutchinson (2009), 'Necessary conditions for incentive compatibility in double referenda', *Journal of Environmental Economics and Management*, **57**, 219–25.

Carson, R.T. and T. Groves (2007), 'Incentive and information properties of preference questions', *Environmental and Resource Economics*, **37**, 181–210.

Carson, R.T., T. Groves and J. List (2004), 'Probabilistic influence and supplemental benefits: a field test of the two key assumptions underlying stated preferences', paper presented at NBER Public Economics Workshop, Palo Alto, March.

Carson, R.T., N.E. Flores, K.M. Martin and J.L. Wright (1996), 'Contingent valuation and revealed preference methodologies: comparing the estimates for quasi-public goods', *Land Economics*, **72**, 80–99.

Carson, R.T. and R.C. Mitchell (1993), 'The issue of scope in contingent valuation studies', *American Journal of Agricultural Economics*, **75**, 1263–7.

Carson, R.T. and R.C. Mitchell (1995), 'Sequencing and nesting in contingent valuation studies', *Journal of Environmental Economics and Management*, **28**, 155–73.

Collins, J.P. and C.A. Vossler (2009), 'Incentive compatibility tests of choice experiment value elicitation methods', *Journal of Environmental Economics and Management*, **58**, 226–35.

Corrigan, J.R., C.L. Kling and J. Zhao (2008), 'Willingness to pay and the cost of commitment: an empirical specification test', *Environmental and Resource Economics*, **40**, 285–98.

Covey, J., G. Loomes, and I.J. Bateman (2007), 'Valuing risk reductions: testing for range biases in payment card and random card sorting procedures', *Journal of Environmental Planning and Management*, **50**, 467–82.

Crawford, V.P. and J. Sobel (1982), 'Strategic information transmission', *Econometrica*, **50**, 1431–51.

Cummings, R.G. and G.W Harrison (1994), 'Contingent valuation', in R.A. Eblen and W.R. Eblen (eds), *Encyclopedia of the Environment*, Boston, MA: Houghton Mifflin, pp. 115–17.

Cummings, R.G., G.W. Harrison and E.E. Rutström (1995), 'Homegrown values and hypothetical surveys: is the dichotomous choice approach incentive compatible?', *American Economic Review*, **85**, 260–66.

Cummings, R.G. and L.O. Taylor (1999), 'Unbiased value estimates for environmental goods: a cheap talk design for the contingent valuation method', *American Economic Review*, **89**, 649–65.

Day, B., I.J. Bateman, R.T. Carson, D. Dupont, J.J. Louviere, S. Morimoto, R. Scarpa and P. Wang (2009), 'Task independence in stated preference studies: a test of order effect explanations', CSERGE working paper EDM 09-14, Centre for Social and Economic Research on the Global Environment, University of East Anglia.

Dubourg, W. B., M.W. Jones-Lee, G. Loomes (1997), 'Imprecise preferences and survey design in contingent valuation', *Economica*, **64**, 681–702.

Farrell, J. and R. Gibbons (1989), 'Cheap talk can matter in bargaining', *Journal of Economic Theory*, **48**, 221–3.

Farrell, J. and M. Rabin (1996), 'Cheap talk', *Journal of Economic Perspectives*, **10**, 103–18.

Grice, H. (1975), 'Logic and conversation', in P. Cole and T. Morgan (eds), *Syntax and Semantics: Vol. 3, Speech Acts*, New York: Seminar Press.

Haab, T.C., J.C. Huang and J.C. Whitehead (1999), 'Are hypothetical referenda incentive compatible? A comment', *Journal of Political Economy*, **107**, 186–96.

Herriges, J., C.L. Kling, C.C. Liu and J. Tobias (2007), 'What are the consequences of consequentially', paper presented at Allied Social Sciences Meeting, Chicago, January.

Johnson, R.J. (2006), 'Is hypothetical bias universal: validating contingent valuation responses by a binding referendum', *Journal of Environmental Economics and Management*, **52**, 469–81.

Louviere, J.J., D. Street, A. Ainslie, T.A. Cameron, R.T. Carson, J.R. DeShazo, D. Hensher, R. Kohn and T. Marley (2002), 'Dissecting the random component', *Marketing Letters*, **13**, 177–93.

Lusk, J.L. and T.C. Schroeder (2004), 'Are choice experiments incentive compatible? A test with quality differentiated beefsteaks', *American Journal of Agricultural Economics*, **86**, 467–82.

Mitchell, R.C. and R.T. Carson (1989), *Using Surveys to Value Public Goods: The Contingent Valuation Method*, Washington, DC: Resources for the Future.

Murphy, J.J., P.G. Allen, T.H. Stevens and D. Weatherhead (2005), 'A meta analysis of hypothetical bias in stated preference surveys', *Environmental and Resource Economics*, **30**, 313–25.

Palomé, P. (2003), 'Experimental evidence on deliberate missrepresentation in referendum contingent valuation', *Journal of Economic Behavior and Organization*, **52**, 387–401.

Powe, N.A. and I.J. Bateman (2004), 'Investigating insensitivity to scope: a split sample test of perceived scheme realism', *Land Economics*, **80**, 258–71.

Rowe, R., W.D. Schuzle and W.S. Breffle (1996), 'A test for payment card bias', *Journal of Environmental Economics and Management*, **31**, 178–85.

Samuelson, P.A. (1954), 'The pure theory of public expenditure', *Review of Economics and Statistics*, **36**, 387–89.

Spence, M. (1974), *Market Signaling: Informational Transfer in Hiring and Related Screening Processes*, Cambridge, MA: Harvard University Press.

Swait, J and J.J. Louviere (1993), 'The role of the scale parameter in estimation and comparison of multinomial logit models', *Journal of Marketing Research*, **30**, 305–14.

Taylor, L.O., M. McKee, S.K. Laury and R.G. Cummings (2001), 'Induced value tests of the referendum voting mechanism', *Economic Letters*, **71**, 61–5.

Tversky, A., P. Slovic and D. Kahneman (1990), 'The causes of preference reversals', *American Economic Review*, **80**, 204–17.

Vossler, C.A. and M.F. Evans (2009), 'Bridging the gap between the field and the lab: environmental goods, policy maker input, consequentiality', *Journal of Environmental Economics and Management*, **58**, 338–45.

Vossler, C.A. and M. McKee (2006), 'Induced value tests of contingent valuation elicitation mechanisms', *Environmental and Resource Economics*, **35**, 137–68.

Zhao, J. and C.L. Kling (2001), 'A new explanation for the WTP/WTA disparity', *Economic Letters*, **73**, 293–300.

Zhao, J. and C.L. Kling (2004), 'Willingness to pay, compensating variation and the cost of commitment', *Economic Inquiry*, **42**, 503–17.

16 Valid value estimates and value estimate validation: better methods and better testing for stated preference research[1]
Ian J. Bateman

INTRODUCTION

This chapter provides personal reflections on some of the recent stated preference valuation studies I have been fortunate enough to be involved in and attempts to draw out some common themes and findings with the hope that these might form the basis for future research in the area. In so doing I draw upon the work of a large number of colleagues to whom I am deeply indebted.[2]

The background to this work is the rise in applied cost–benefit analysis which has progressively spread out from the confines of a few government departments in a small number of countries to now represent one of the major approaches to decision-making across the world. This expansion is most marked in countries such as the USA and the UK where economic approaches in general and cost–benefit analysis in particular now underpins the work of a vast array of decision-making by government and its agencies, being applied to fields as diverse as water quality management, road building, health planning, climate change mitigation, and so on.

Because cost–benefit analysis seeks to place values (conventionally measured in monetary units) on all the benefits and costs (including opportunity costs) of a given project, its growing application has necessarily entailed an increased institutional acceptance of techniques for valuing preferences for non-market goods. This, in turn, has resulted in a massive expansion in valuation studies, developing from just a few early applications in the post-war decades to a discernable increase in the 1980s and a veritable explosion in the 1990s and on with increasing momentum to the present day.

While early applications mainly featured revealed preference methods using travel cost and hedonic pricing approaches, the explosion of the last two decades has been dominated by stated preference (SP) techniques and in particular the contingent valuation (CV) and discrete choice experiment (DCE) methods. There have now been literally thousands of CV valuation studies (Carson, 2010) and the number of DCE studies is rapidly catching up. Therefore this chapter addresses a burgeoning field of research. It is motivated by a concern that, while the analytical techniques being applied to SP research have greatly improved over this period of development, less attention has been given to some of the simple requirements for ensuring that valuation survey respondents actually understand the task set for them. We tackle this issue through two themes: examining techniques for enhancing understanding valuation tasks, and testing the validity of resulting responses. In essence then, this chapter concerns how to elicit valid value estimates and then conduct value estimate validation.

VALID VALUE ESTIMATES

One of the key assumptions of any SP study is that, at the point when a respondent answers a valuation question they know their personal preferences for the good in question and hence their personal willingness-to-pay (WTP) for that good. Note that this does not imply that the respondent will necessarily reply in a way which reveals that true value. The more that an individual can lower the price they have to pay for a good below their WTP then the greater will be their consumer surplus. Therefore respondents have a strategic incentive to misrepresent their WTP and there is a substantial literature on this matter, much of it focused upon the link between study design and the potential for strategic behaviour (Carson and Groves, 2007, and Chapter 15 of this volume). Of course this does not mean that all respondents will indeed misrepresent their true WTP all or indeed any of the time. Some, perhaps most, will always strive to tell the truth. However, even with a strategy-proof design and truthful respondents, individuals cannot report what they do not know. This starts to be a problem where SP studies present survey respondents with goods they have little prior knowledge of or have never considered in WTP terms. In such cases the study questionnaire needs to provide sufficient information to respondents regarding the good under investigation that they can determine their robust preferences and WTP for that good prior to them answering the valuation question. This is a tall order. Surveys are often around 20 minutes long and during that period they not only have to describe the good in question, its provision change, the contingent market mechanism through which payments are made and goods provided (the 'institution', which we consider in more detail below), but a scenario and its context which justifies all of this attention, as well as a considerable degree of additional questions intended to characterize the respondent to allow for validity analysis and aggregation of responses to some wider population.

Some commentators have argued that the information provided and time allowed for deliberation compares favourably to that typically involved in many similar value decisions such as ordering a meal in a restaurant. However, a key difference here is experience. Most respondents have considerable experience of making the latter decisions. They are familiar with the units in which such goods are presented, have often undertaken the task of trading them off against money and have frequently consumed the latter. Respondents are therefore starting from a very well-informed basis of understanding. While such conditions can apply to some non-market goods (for example, outdoor recreation and similar use values), it is not obvious that they hold for all such cases, especially those less familiar examples (for example, biodiversity conservation and similar non-use goods). Here it is unlikely that respondents will hold prior notions of their WTP (indeed they may never have considered their preferences for such goods) and therefore have to formulate this during the course of the interview which, as discussed, may not allow much time for reflection. These problems are likely to be exaggerated when those goods are presented in unfamiliar units and using novel institutions. Individuals are born with instincts but not well-formed economic preferences. Preferences then must be the product of some degree of interaction with the world.

All SP surveys assume that, by the time a valuation choice response is made, the respondent has understood the nature of the institution being presented to them. To re-clarify, by institution we mean the contingent (hypothetical) market in which they have to operate in order to express their preferences. This might seem a trivial matter; the questionnaire has to specify the nature of the exercise in order that individuals can respond to it. However, in practice respondents are often presented with a situation with which they have little or no prior experience. For example (to criticize my own work from the outset), Bateman et al. (1995) use what is generally considered the gold standard format for eliciting WTP responses in CV studies; the single discrete choice question. However, even here respondents face a novel situation of a government backed referendum regarding the cost of a proposed scheme to prevent saline inundation in a wetland national park. A problem here is that, unlike most of the real-world trade-off decisions people make every day, these respondents had no prior experience of such an institution. This is very different to, say, the institution in which many people make the numerical bulk of their valuation decisions; the supermarket. The average individual has experienced literally thousands of supermarket purchases and has overwhelming experience to draw upon. They know exactly how such markets work and in effect understand completely how their WTP decisions (placing a good in a basket) relate to the final outcome. This is not the case in stated preference surveys. For the majority of individuals this will be the first survey they have ever participated in and for all but a very few (unfortunate) individuals this will be their only experience of a hypothetical WTP survey.

So what is likely to happen when respondents are presented with an SP survey concerning an unfamiliar good, presented in novel units via an institution they have no experience of and are asked to undertake a trade-off against money; a comparison they have not previously considered? One likely reaction is greater uncertainty and indeed many SP studies report low degrees of explanation. Again criticizing our own work, Bateman et al. (1995) report R^2 values ranging from about 20 per cent down as low as 5 per cent. Now to some extent this is likely to reflect the obvious difficulty of capturing the complex array of preference drivers held by individuals within a standard length valuation survey. That said, it also reflects that underlying uncertainty experienced by individuals placed into such novel situations. Nevertheless, to some degree uncertainty is of lesser importance provided that the obtained general picture of preferences and values is unbiased. However, critics of SP valuation techniques argue that this may not be the case in such situations (see, for example, Green et al., 1998). Instead some claim that, faced with such uncertainty, respondents face high cognitive load and respond by using rules of thumb, heuristic shortcuts in the form of perceived cues interpreted from the framing of questions (Tversky and Kahneman, 1974). In effect they use these cues to construct preferences (Slovic, 1995) from which they can then provide valuation responses.

While both sides of the argument may recoil at the thought, the constructed preferences argument can be seen as the flip side to the discovered preference hypothesis (DPH) proposed by Plott (1996). The DPH argues that stable and theoretically consistent preferences are typically the product of experience gained through practice and repetition. Plott notes that markets provide an ideal environment for such repetition and learning through which individuals can discover both how best to achieve goals within the operating rules of that market (a process which Braga and Starmer, 2005, refer to as 'institutional learning'). In effect SP proponents contend that the survey interview process can provide sufficient information for respondents to discover their own, theoretically consistent preferences and correspondent WTP values.

This chapter attempts to find a midway between the critics and proponents of SP methods (probably incurring the wrath of both on the way!). I argue that, in cases where individuals have well formed prior preferences for non-market goods then carefully designed SP studies can pass robust tests of validity. Furthermore, in certain cases where conventionally estimated values fail such validity tests, I argue that there are a number of techniques which can be employed to enhance respondents' understanding and even experience of the task in front of them so as to allow them to discover theoretically consistent preferences. However, I also note that, in the absence of such techniques there is clear evidence that many respondents do resort to the heuristic cues made available by the framing of a valuation question in order to formulate their response. In the latter cases a change in question framing which economic theory would see as irrelevant can substantially alter responses and resulting values.[3]

VALUE ESTIMATE VALIDATION

All of the above assertions about SP elicited values being either valid or invalid ultimately rely upon some form of testing. Validity testing is therefore central to any attempt to improve methodology and thus forms the second major theme of this chapter.

The most generally adopted 'gold standard' for valuation validation is the 'scope sensitivity' test, endorsed by the National Oceanic Atmospheric Administration (NOAA) 'Blue Ribbon' CV panel and described by them as 'a willingness to pay somewhat more for more of a good' (Arrow et al., 1993). The notion that one would expect WTP to rise as the provision of a good increased seems immediately appealing. However, in practice such a test has a major flaw in that we have no clear prior expectation about what a 'correct' answer should be. More specifically we have no way of knowing what degree of scope sensitivity is reasonable. So, for example, if a respondent is faced with a valuation scenario in which the provision of some non-market good is doubled, should we expect total WTP for that good to also double, or to increase by more than double or less? All outcomes are eminently feasible.[4] Indeed even a zero increase in total WTP is perfectly defensible in cases of satiation. In fact the only outcome that seems a priori to be problematic is if total value fell as the provision of a good increased. This is clearly an unsatisfactory basis for any validity test; if almost any outcome is defensible then this fails to be a reliable way to assess the usefulness of a study.

Given the weakness of the scope sensitivity test we need to find alternative validation analyses which have clear a priori expectations regarding results which signal validity or not. Fortunately there is a large literature from the field of experimental economics which provides a suite of such tests. These tests draw upon the very fundamentals of economic principles to provide clearly falsifiable Popperian hypotheses. Here tests have unambiguous results which either conform to economic theory or not. The latter anomalous findings provide clear evidence that the originating studies are not yielding preferences which conform to the requirements of cost–benefit analyses and so cannot be used for economic decision making. This chapter provides a series of empirical analyses which rely upon such tests drawn from a variety of empirical contexts. Their findings suggest patterns for which SP methods and contexts provide reliable values; and by elimination, which do not.

OVERVIEW OF EMPIRICAL ILLUSTRATIONS

The case studies presented in this chapter are chosen to illustrate our argument that greater attention needs to be focused upon some of the basic elements of SP applications. We start by considering whether or not prior experience of a given good and the contingent institution actually influences the theoretical consistency of SP responses. Not surprisingly this study shows that the absence of such experience is strongly correlated with significant anomalies in elicited preferences. We further illustrate this point by showing how such inconsistent preferences are likely to be malleable and responsive to the framing of SP questions in ways which significantly affect resulting WTP values. We further illustrate this problem by considering how, even with a more familiar good and a recently developed SP technique, prominent features of an unfamiliar contingent institution can still affect WTP. The somewhat pessimistic tone of these initial applications then lightens when we consider explicit strategies to tackle the problem of low prior experience. First, I show that by repeatedly exposing respondents to a contingent institution we can significantly reduce and eventually eliminate anomalous responses to be left with theoretically consistent preferences. Then I show how altering the way in which contingent changes in provision are presented to respondents can again radically reduce the incidence of anomalous responses in SP surveys. I conclude by arguing that a combination of these approaches can substantially improve the validity of such studies even when assessed via unambiguous testing protocols.

DOES PRIOR PREFERENCE MATTER?

This first case study illustrates both the impacts that can occur when we consider low experience goods for which survey respondents do not have prior preferences and the principle of using tests with clear a priori expectations regarding anomalous or theoretically consistent results.

Figure 16.1 illustrates potential bundles of two goods, A and B. Initially

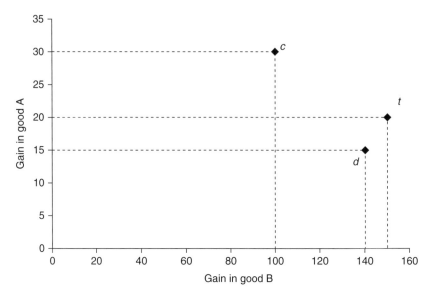

Figure 16.1   An asymmetrically dominated choice set

ignore bundle *d* and consider bundles *c* and *t*. Relative to *c*, bundle *t* offers more of good B but less good A. One can readily imagine specifications in which some individuals prefer bundle *c* while others prefer *t*. Now consider bundle *d*. This offers less of both goods A and B than good *t*; in effect it is 'dominated' by *t* which is better on both dimensions (note however, that *d* is not completely dominated by *c* and because of this *d* is referred to as being 'asymmetrically dominated').[5]

Examining Figure 16.1 we can see that, for an individual who holds preferences consistent with economic theory, it is irrelevant whether bundle *d* is included in the choice set or not; as it is completely dominated by bundle *t* the choice remains between *t* and *c*. Bundle *d* is therefore an 'irrelevant alternative' for anyone with economic preferences. Now this observation provides us with a clear and unambiguous test of preference consistency; the addition of bundle *d* should have no impact on respondents' choices. If it does have an effect then we are clearly not dealing with well-formed, standard economic preferences.

To demonstrate the potential usefulness of such a test and examine the effects of prior preference on the theoretical consistency of values, Alistair Munro, Greg Poe and I, together with students from the University of East Anglia, designed an SP study of visitors to a lake in Norfolk, UK. Two groups of visitors used this lake, one for boating and the other for bankside walking, both of which were surveyed.[6] This lake was chosen for

Table 16.1   Choices made by visitors to a lake choosing between bundles of gains in both lake surface flowers and boating facilities

Bundle *c* has larger gains of lake surface flowers.
Bundle *t* has larger gains in boating facilities.
Bundle *d* is asymmetrically dominated by *t*.

Sample (sample size)	Bundles presented to sample	Number (and % of sample) choosing bundle *c*	Number (and % of sample) choosing bundle *t*	Number (and % of sample) choosing bundle *d*
Sample I (144)	*c* and *t*	102 (71%)	42 (29%)	Not shown
Sample II (150)	*c*, *t* and *d*	102 (68%)	44 (29%)	4 (3%)

Note: The relative positions of bundles *c*, *t* and *d* are as shown in Figure 16.1.

study because, not long before the survey, it had been the centre of a local debate, featured in regional media reports, regarding whether the lake should be managed mainly to enhance boating or walking. A specific issue concerned whether the lake should be managed to increase substantially the number of flowering water plants on the surface of the lake with just a modest increase in facilities for boaters, or whether the latter should increase substantially and the former only marginally. These trade-offs naturally lend themselves to the specification of an asymmetric dominance experiment and three options were specified along the lines of bundles *c* (favouring water flowers), *t* (favouring boating) and *d* (dominated by *t*) as in Figure 16.1. We had prior expectations that walkers would favour bundle *c* and that boaters would prefer bundle *t*.

Unbeknown to them, the survey respondents were randomly assigned to two treatments. Sample I were presented with a choice between options *c* and *t* whereas Sample II were asked to choose between bundles *c*, *t* and *d*. Table 16.1 presents details of the choices made by these two groups.

Examining Table 16.1 notice that in both samples almost identical proportions choose bundle *t* (the same applies to bundle *c* and as expected very few people choose the dominated bundle *d*). Statistical testing confirms that there is no significant difference between Samples I and II (p = 0.451). Therefore there is no evidence of anomalies here and respondents appear to have preferences for the goods on offer which conform to the expectations of economic theory.

The same respondents were also asked to make choices regarding a second set of bundles. Here the bundles were made up of increases in the number of species of bankside plants and the number of species of

Table 16.2   Choices made by visitors to a lake choosing between bundles of gains in both bankside flowers or birds

Bundle *c* has larger gains of bankside flowers.
Bundle *t* has larger gains in bankside birds.
Bundle *d* is asymmetrically dominated by *t*.

Sample (sample size)	Bundles presented to sample	Number (and % of sample) choosing bundle *c*	Number (and % of sample) choosing bundle *t*	Number (and % of sample) choosing bundle *d*
Sample I (144)	*c* and *t*	72 (50%)	72 (50%)	Not shown
Sample II (150)	*c, t* and *d*	46 (31%)	103 (69%)	1 (<1%)

Note: The relative positions of bundles *c, t* and *d* are as shown in Figure 16.1. Note that *d* is asymmetrically dominated by *t*.

Source: Adapted from Bateman et al. (2008a).

bankside nesting birds. Again analogues of bundles *c, t* and (asymmetrically dominated) *d* were defined with one sample choosing between *c* and *t* and the other choosing between *c, t* and *d*. Table 16.2 details results from the SP responses to these treatments.

In marked contrast to the findings of Table 16.1, the results shown in Table 16.2 show that the irrelevant alternative *d* has a very substantial impact on choices. Specifically, while only one (seemingly irrational) chose bundle *d*, its introduction significantly increases the probability that a respondent will choose bundle *t* ($p < 0.01$) raising this from 0.50 to 0.69, an increase of nearly 40 per cent. This phenomena, of the introduction of an apparently irrelevant dominated bundle increasing the probability of individuals choosing the dominant bundle is known as the 'asymmetric dominance effect' and is a clear violation of the requirements for well formed, theoretically consistent, economic preferences. Such anomalies provide clear and unambiguous grounds for rejecting the validity of such preferences.

Why should the experiments reported in Tables 16.1 and 16.2 yield such diverse results? Following Ockham's Razor, the most obvious and likely explanation seems to be that, while the former concerns a choice between goods which the respondents clearly have prior preferences for, the latter does not. In the first experiment each respondent is either a walker or a boater and therefore has clear preferences regarding which bundle they prefer; boaters prefer *t* as it delivers greater gains in boat access, walkers prefer *c* as it provides greater scenic beauty for their walks.

The introduction of bundle *d* does not help either group make up their mind regarding which option they prefer. It is therefore truly an irrelevant alternative and has no impact on choices. However, the second experiment concerns a case in which respondents do not have any clear prior preference. Both goods within a bundle are likely to be seen as equally good things and indeed it is interesting to note that the sample presented only with bundles *c* and *t* divided exactly equally over which they chose. However, the introduction of dominated bundle *d* very substantially shifted stated preferences in favour of dominant bundle *t*. The psychology here seems to be that respondents faced with the two bundles *c* and *t* cannot easily decide which they prefer, but the introduction of *d* provides a simple decision heuristic, while they may not have clear preferences regarding bankside flowers and birds, clearly bundle *t* is better than bundle *d* and therefore the former provides a low risk alternative; while all the bundles may be difficult to evaluate one (*t*) is clearly better than another (*d*) and so is chosen.

The possibility of such clear effects arising from poorly formed prior preferences is a challenge to SP research, particularly if such anomalies are seen to transfer onto elicited WTP values. To examine this all of the respondents in the second experiment were asked to state their WTP for their chosen option. Respondents in sample I who chose bundle *t* stated a mean WTP for that option of £18.49 whereas those who chose the same bundle in sample II stated an average WTP of £24.35; a highly statistically significant ($p < 0.01$) increase of one-third in stated values[7] (for further details see Bateman et al., 2008a).

MANIPULATING MALLEABLE PREFERENCES

Our asymmetric dominance results suggest that, in the absence of clear understanding of a good, stated preferences are malleable and hence can be manipulated by changes to the questionnaire design. This is not a new finding; indeed the advertising industry is predicated on such knowledge and manufacturers spend millions of dollars every day attempting to exploit such effects. By understanding the heuristics which consumers use to make many purchases, advertisers can present goods in an advantageous light and induce purchases or increase WTP. Of course, the unscrupulous economist could also play at this game in an effort to increase WTP for a poorly understood good.

While not meaning to impugn the scruples of my co-authors, Bateman et al., (2010) investigate the potential for such effects by applying advertising techniques to what seemed likely to be poorly formed preferences;

those concerning the conservation of a relatively little known yet potentially charismatic species; the Sumatran tiger.

A split-sample survey of 600 respondents was undertaken at locations across the UK. Survey respondents were given a simple choice between two tubs of margarine identical in all respects except price and that one was designated as being produced using palm oil from 'tiger friendly' plantations which undertook measures to maintain prey species, while the other was made using conventionally produced techniques. The price of the two goods was varied across treatments and the difference between the two was adjusted up or down in response to individuals' choices until respondents' maximum willingness-to-pay (WTP) for the 'tiger friendly' margarine was established.

One of the objectives of the study was to examine the impact of both information and presentation upon stated WTP. That information should change WTP is entirely in accordance with economic theory (Munro and Hanley, 1999). A split sample approach tested the effect of two levels of information, the first simply describing the nature of the 'tiger friendly' approach to production while the second informed respondents of the decline in numbers of Sumatran tigers from roughly 1000 in 1978 to around 500 now. While the first treatment yielded a WTP equivalent to a 15 per cent price premium above conventionally produced margarine, not surprisingly the additional information leads to a further, statistically significant increase, this time to 21 per cent higher than WTP for the conventional product. As noted, such an effect is in line with conventional expectations and would not of itself lead us to doubt the validity of responses. However, a further increase in the price premium to some 36 per cent is achieved by the simple addition, on top of previous information, of a picture of tiger cubs. Figure 16.2 provides an illustration of this photograph and its effect. Statistical tests showed that this value is significantly greater than either of the preceding sums and illustrates the extent to which such malleable preferences can be influenced.

FRAMING EFFECTS IN CONTINGENT VALUATIONS OF FAMILIAR GOODS

The previous case study concerned a relatively unfamiliar good; conserving the Sumatran tiger. However, problems can arise even when stated preference methods are used to value more commonplace goods if the contingent market institutions are unfamiliar. In such cases survey respondents can again embark on a hunt for heuristic shortcuts to answer such questions, again resulting in the question frame having an impact on

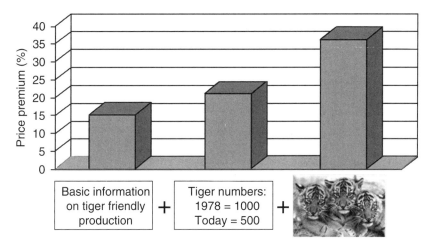

Figure 16.2   Price premium for 'tiger-friendly' palm oil products under three treatments

elicited values. Such effects are likely to be exacerbated by frames which appear to readily offer such cues.

As an examples of this we can consider an application of the 'one-and-one-half bid' (OOHB) contingent valuation method proposed by Cooper et al. (2002). Here the survey respondent is initially told that the cost of a scheme lies between some specified lower ($L) and higher ($H) amount. In an 'ascending sequence' (LH) the respondent is asked if they would pay the $L amount. Here a 'No' response terminates the procedure while a 'Yes' results in the $H amount being asked. The reverse order is followed in a 'descending sequence' (HL).

Cooper et al. prove that the OOHB approach delivers gains in statistical efficiency over the standard single dichotomous choice approach advocated by Carson and Groves (2007). However, this says nothing about whether the estimates produced by the OOHB method are unbiased. In Bateman et al. (2009c) we examine the procedural invariance properties of the method, testing whether apparently irrelevant alternations in question framing impact upon elicited values. For example, given that the OOHB approach informs respondents about both the $L and $H amounts in advance, one might not expect a switch in the ordering in which those amounts are then presented to respondents to impact on responses.[8]

Bateman et al. (2009c) consider a good which has frequently featured in previous SP studies; the reduction of eutrophication problems affecting rivers and lakes near to where respondents live. This change was to be effected via the installation of technology at sewage works to address household contribution to this problem with payments being collected via increases to water bills. The study design comprised a number of pairs of amounts arranged in either ascending (LH) or descending (HL) sequences. A split sample design was employed with bid pairs and sequences being randomly allocated across respondents. Valuation data were collected via a face-to-face, at-home survey of 1,254 UK households.

Table 16.3 presents findings from this study, disaggregating these first into the ascending and descending sequence and within those further dividing results into the individual value pairs seen by a single subsample of respondents.

Examining the first row of the ascending sequence (LH) we can see that the results pass a money dimension scope sensitivity test in that, while 90 per cent of respondents were willing to pay £10 for the reduction of eutrophication, less than half of those individuals were willing to pay £50 for the same good. However, as discussed previously, such tests are a relatively weak guide to the validity of values. Indeed, as Ariely et al. (2003) show, there is a strong impetus toward internal consistency within a given respondent's answers, irrespective of whether the initial response is affected by objectively irrelevant information (an effect they term 'coherent arbitrariness').

Given this, we need to undertake external validity tests across respondents facing different framing treatments. Here the results are less encouraging. For simplicity consider the acceptance rates for the £100 bid amount, which is presented within a range of frames, sometimes being the lower amount of a pair of values, while in other treatments it is the higher amount. In all, the £100 bid amount appears in ten different combinations. However, acceptance rates vary from 22.1 per cent to 61.5 per cent across these treatments. Furthermore, closer inspection shows a clear pattern in these results. When the £100 amount is the lower of a pair, acceptance rates vary from 42.1 per cent to 61.5 per cent. However, when £100 is the higher of a pair, acceptance rates decline to between 22.1 per cent and 36.6 per cent. This highly significant difference in response rates is further exacerbated by the relative difference between amounts in a pair. When the £100 amount is very much larger than a preceding sum then acceptance rates are particularly depressed. The opposite effect arises in sequences where £100 is the smaller of the pair; as the higher amount is increased so acceptance rates for the £100 amount rise.

Why is this happening? Given that we are confident that the notion of cleaning up local rivers is more familiar to UK residents than schemes to conserve tigers in Sumatra, the most likely cause is the unfamiliarity of the contingent institution itself. It is, after all, an unusual experience to be asked about one's preferences regarding environmental public goods; and

Table 16.3   Comparison of bid acceptance rates across treatments[†]

Ascending sequence (LH)

Label	LOW 1 Initial bid amount	Acceptance rate	HIGH 2 Follow-up bid amount	Acceptance rate[††]
LH1	10	90.1%	50	46.5%
LH2	50	55.7%	100	23.7%
LH3	100	42.1%	150	26.3%
LH4	100	46.9%	200	9.2%
LH5	25	82.1%	100	22.1%
LH6	75	41.6%	100	32.7%
LH7	48.50	52.6%	98.50	18.6%

Descending sequence (HL)

Label	HIGH 1 Initial bid amount	Acceptance rate	LOW 2 Follow-up bid amount	Acceptance rate[††]
HL1	50	59.4%	10	90.1%
HL2	100	36.6%	50	65.6%
HL3	150	38.9%	100	48.4%
HL4	200	28.1%	100	61.5%
HL5	100	30.5%	25	85.3%
HL6	100	31.1%	75	42.2%

Notes:
[†]   Total sample size = 1254 households. Sample sizes within each treatment vary from a minimum of 90 to a maximum of 106 households. Bid amounts are in GB pounds.
[††] Acceptance (rejection) rates for follow-up questions include as 'Yes' ('No') responses those respondents who were not asked the second question because they had implicitly accepted (rejected) this amount in their initial response.

Source: Bateman et al. (2009c).

stranger still to have to convert those preferences into the money dimension. If, as is almost certainly the case for the vast majority of individuals, there is no prior experience of such a task then it seems perfectly reasonable that respondents will search for heuristic cues with which to formulate responses. The OOHB question framework provides ample cues in that there is an obvious strategic response to the pair of values presented. It is a strange respondent indeed who would rather pay more than less for a given good. Therefore the lower amount of a pair of values is always to be preferred irrespective of its absolute level. Hence we can readily predict the outcome that acceptance rates for a given amount will be greater when paired with a higher amount than a lower one; a result which our findings confirm.

Now, importantly, this need not mean that the responses to SP surveys are meaningless. Far from it; indeed when we model the data obtained from this study and take account of whether respondents were presented with either ascending or descending value pairs we find mean WTP values of £79.37 for the former treatment and £99.35 for the latter.[9] While these differences are statistically significant ($p < 0.001$) nevertheless, given the wide variation of treatments presented in the experiment it seems likely that underlying WTP would fall within the range described by these estimates. Indeed we find such an approach to investigating the robustness of values to framing effects an appealing strategy for informing decision-makers about the variability in values. Often such a range will be perfectly acceptable for decision purposes. If scheme costs lie either side of this range then the economic appraisal is complete and the scheme either passes or fails a cost–benefit test. This is very likely to be the case and, even if costs actually do fall within this range, then the study remains informative as it tells the decision-makers that costs and benefits are somewhat similar. Again this is often sufficient for a decision to be made, especially when a decision-maker is considering a number of alternative options others of which may, if similarly assessed, provide clear net benefits. Nevertheless any study design approach which reduces such uncertainty is clearly worth investigating. We now turn to consider such an approach.

LEARNING DESIGN CONTINGENT VALUATION (LDCV)

The findings of the previous experiment show that, even if an SP study concerns a local good which is relatively easy to convey to respondents, bias can still arise due to unfamiliarity with the contingent institution leading to individuals seeking heuristic cues from the question framing.

One strategy for addressing this problem is to help respondents learn about that institution through repeated exposure. This approach draws upon Braga and Starmer (2005), who in turn build upon the discovered preference hypothesis (DPH) proposed by Plott (1996). This argues that stable and theoretically consistent preferences are learnt through repetition rather than being inherent. Braga and Starmer extend this to define two types of learning: 'institutional learning' through which an individual finds out how a given market works, and 'value learning' where the individual finds out about their value for a good. In the 'learning design contingent valuation' (LDCV) method Bateman et al. (2008b) encourage and test for both types of learning through a design which exposes respondents to repeated CV exercises using the same contingent institution to value a set of similar goods.

That set of similar goods is provided by defining a number of farm animal welfare schemes, each one concerning an increase in living space for different species, these being laying hens, chicks, cows and pigs. The particular contingent institution adopted for the study was the 'double bound contingent valuation' (DBCV) format first proposed by Hanemann et al. (1991). This has similarities with the OOHB method in that each respondent faces two CV bid amounts, however now these are presented sequentially with the respondent unaware that the initial amount will be followed by a second (the latter amount being higher if the response to the first question was positive and lower otherwise). While this is an appealing method in principle, and generates substantial gains in statistical efficiency over a single question format, in practice applications of the DBCV method have consistently reported an anomalous result that mean WTP obtained from responses to the initial 'first bound' question is significantly higher than that obtained from responses to the follow-up 'second bound' question. This finding is such a general regularity that it is widely considered as a 'stylized fact' concerning the DBCV method (Carson and Groves, 2007).

A number of possible explanations of the DBCV anomaly have been proposed. Carson and Groves (2007) focus upon possible strategic reactions to the presentation of a second amount while Bateman et al. (2001), Cooper et al. (2002) and DeShazo (2002) note the adverse psychological responses which may arise from the presentation of an unanticipated second amount, particularly where that is higher than the first. The lack of prior experience underpinning these 'surprise' arguments can be directly addressed by repeatedly exposing respondents to DBCV formats and examining whether associated first bound versus second bound anomalies decay with that repetition.

To test whether repeated exposure to contingent institutions reduced

Table 16.4   Institutional learning tests: differences between mean WTP for SB and DB estimates for each good

Scheme	Estimate	Value	Std. err.	t-ratio	H_0: $\mu_{SB} = \mu_{DB}$ (Prob.)
Sample I					
$HENS_1^1$	μ_{SB}	£4.72			
	μ_{DB}	£2.74			
	Δ_1^1	£1.98	£1.21	1.64	0.10
$CHICK_2^1$	μ_{SB}	£2.68			
	μ_{DB}	£2.51			
	Δ_2^1	£0.17	£0.17	1.00	0.32
$COWS_3^1$	μ_{SB}	£3.10			
	μ_{DB}	£2.87			
	Δ_3^1	£0.23	£0.26	0.88	0.38
$PIGS_4^1$	μ_{SB}	£2.07			
	μ_{DB}	£2.06			
	Δ_4^1	£0.01	£0.15	0.07	0.95
Sample II					
$PIGS_1^2$	μ_{SB}	£2.98			
	μ_{DB}	£2.38			
	Δ_1^2	£0.60	£0.25	2.40	0.02

Note: $\Delta_j^i = \mu_{SB} - \mu_{DB}$ for good X_j^i.

Source: Bateman et al. (2008b).

the rate of anomaly among valuation responses, a random sample of respondents was initially presented with a DBCV question concerning the hen welfare good, followed by similar questions for the chick welfare good, then for cows, then pigs. The test throughout was to examine the significance of any difference between the first and second bound DBCV response with the learning expectation being that this difference will reduce across repetitions. Just in case there was some confounding due to the order in which goods were presented a second sample was only presented with a DBCV exercise concerning the pig welfare good; the last task presented to the learning treatment sample. Comparison of responses to the pig welfare good across treatments should provide a further test of consistency.

The first column of Table 16.4 indicates the various goods and treatments in our experiment with the superscript denoting sample (where 1 = the learning treatment) and the subscript denoting the order of presentation to that sample. The second column denotes three measures, where μ_{SB} is the mean WTP from the first bound (referred to as the 'single bound', hence SB) response, μ_{DB} is the mean from the double bound (DB) model[10] and $\Delta_j^i = \mu_{SB} - \mu_{DB}$ for good X_j^i. The next column provides estimates for these measures followed by the standard error of the difference in WTP from the single and double bound models. The final two columns report the t ratio and p-value statistics testing whether that difference is statistically significant.

Considering the sample I (learning treatment) responses from Table 16.1, we can see that the first good presented to respondents (when institutional familiarity will be at its lowest) results in very marked differences between the SB and DB results with the latter being not much more than half the former. However, the resulting difference in values declines from 42 per cent of the SB response in the first question to between 6 and 7 per cent in the next two goods falling to below 1 per cent for the final good. This shows a marked decline in divergence between SB and DB values within sample I. Furthermore when we conduct an across individual test by comparing the final good valued by sample I with the same good valued as the first and only valuation task faced by sample II we see the difference dramatically increase from completely insignificant to highly significant levels.

It seems that the repetition of valuation tasks promotes institutional learning to the extent that associated response anomalies completely disappear.[11] Indeed, given that the SB versus DB difference is an accepted stylized fact of the DBCV approach, such results are both remarkable and encouraging. However, the findings of Table 16.4 reflect an increase in the internal consistency of respondents within the learning treatment sample. Such a result is a necessary but insufficient test for robust preferences. Ariely et al. (2003) argue that individuals are very good at keeping their answers internally consistent but that they can 'anchor' those answers to some initial cue, even when it is blatantly arbitrary. In a fascinating test of this hypothesis Ariely et al. (2003) ask individuals to give separate values for two bottles of wine, one being described as being of 'average' quality while the other is labelled as a 'fine' wine. Ariely et al. note that respondents maintained strong internal consistency of values with the fine wine always valued above the average wine, but that WTP for both wines were strongly anchored to an obviously random starting point, in this case the final two digits of the respondents' self-reported social security number.

Ariely et al. (2003) use a test of association or 'anchoring' between the randomly assigned starting point and the final valuation as a method for distinguishing theoretically consistent, learned values from those based upon anomalous, coherently arbitrary preferences. This is a strong test to

Table 16.5   *Value learning test: estimates of DB model with anchoring coefficient γ, testing whether second response is anchored on the first bid level*

Good	Variable	Coeff.	Std. err.	t-ratio	P
Sample I					
HENS$_1^1$	α_{DB}	0.786	(0.22)	3.57	
	β_{DB}	−0.224	(0.11)	−2.04	
	γ_1^1	0.670	(0.17)	4.03	<0.001
CHICK$_2^1$	α_{DB}	1.392	(0.28)	4.94	
	β_{DB}	−0.551	(0.12)	−4.65	
	γ_2^1	0.146	(0.15)	0.98	0.329
COWS$_3^1$	α_{DB}	1.198	(0.37)	3.26	
	β_{DB}	−0.391	(0.13)	−2.92	
	γ_3^1	0.334	(0.17)	2.00	0.047
PIGS$_4^1$	α_{DB}	1.427	(0.30)	4.76	
	β_{DB}	−0.691	(0.14)	−4.94	
	γ_4^1	−0.026	(0.18)	−0.14	0.886
Sample II					
PIGS$_1^2$	α_{DB}	1.194	(0.26)	4.59	
	β_{DB}	−0.497	(0.13)	−3.82	
	γ_1^2	0.315	(0.15)	2.07	0.040

Source: Bateman et al. (2008b).

pass which has frequently failed in previous valuation experiments (Green et al., 1998), and so we adopt this approach in our LDCV study by examining whether DBCV responses are anchored to the first amount presented to respondents within each good. Previous tests of such effects within the DBCV format have found clear evidence of anchoring and hence had to reject the hypothesis that such responses are unbiased (Herriges and Shogren, 1996).

Table 16.5 reports the findings of our anchoring test. For each good a double bound model is estimated as a function of an intercept (α_{DB}) a slope on the bid amount (β_{DB}) and an anchoring coefficient (γ) testing any association with the initial bid amount randomly assigned to each respondent. The table reports estimated coefficients for each of these terms with tests showing that, as expected, in all cases α_{DB} and β_{DB} are statistically significant. Despite this, results for the first good presented to the learning treatment sample show that the estimated anchoring coefficient is positive and highly significant. This shows the classic anchoring result that, the higher the initial bid presented to a respondent, the higher their stated WTP.

However, this anchoring term becomes insignificant for the second good suggesting that, once respondents discover their preferences for a good they no longer need to rely upon the anchoring heuristic to formulate their value responses. Note that the first and second goods are chosen to be very similar (welfare improvements for hens then chicks). However, this is not the case when we move to consider the third good which concerns a much bigger animal; cows. Interestingly anchoring reasserts itself in this novel good situation. It is tempting to conclude that the substantial change in good means that respondents again have to discover their preferences and once more resort to the anchoring heuristic. Further support for this argument is obtained from the final good (pig welfare), which concerns a good more similar to the preceding one. Again anchoring effects decline to become insignificant. Out of sample support for this argument is obtained by comparing the latter result with that for the same good presented as the first (and only) good seen by sample 2. Here respondents have no previous experience upon which to discover robust preferences and the anchoring term is now clearly significant.

The findings from this study suggest that providing respondents with hands-on experience of contingent institutions can reduce framing anomalies to insignificant levels. To some extent this is likely to be provided by discrete choice experiment (DCE) methods as these present respondents with repeated choices between respecifications of the goods in question (achieved by decomposing the good into its utility bearing attributes and varying the levels of those attributes within each choice option). Note, however, that our previous findings suggest that the preferences elicited in such experiments are likely to change and develop through the course of the exercise; a hypothesis supported by recent empirical testing (Day et al., unpub.). These findings show that preferences are liable to shift substantially early on in a DCE experiment before settling down to a stable level. This echoes the preference discovery process suggested in our CV results and indicates that some allowance for this process may be required in assessing stable WTP sums.

READILY COMPREHENDED DESCRIPTIONS OF GOODS: VIRTUAL REALITY CHOICE EXPERIMENTS (VRCE)

Our final study builds on those presented above, using a DCE framework to encourage repetition induced experience of the contingent institution. However, it addresses a further fundamental aspect of SP study design which analysts have to tackle in order to reduce respondent reliance upon

342 The international handbook on non-market environmental valuation

framing heuristics; conveying clearly understood descriptions of goods. This issue is so basic that it has, I believe, become somewhat overlooked in valuation guideline documents. Yet if the respondent does not readily comprehend the good on offer then at best we will induce unwanted uncertainty into valuation responses and at worst positively encourage reliance upon framing heuristics.

To some extent common approaches to applying the DCE method may exacerbate the difficulty of comprehending the goods under evaluation. While applications may well introduce the general issue using accessible, often visual, stimuli (for example, by showing survey respondents pictures of a land area which is going to be affected by some policy), the actual choice questions from which valuations are derived are almost always presented as a series of numeric levels for each of the attributes which define the good.

There is a substantial literature highlighting problems which many individuals experience in correctly understanding numeric information (Hsee, 1996; Mathews et al., 2006). This is likely to be greatly compounded when those numbers apply to unfamiliar units. Yet a substantial number of SP studies appear to employ such undesirable combinations. For example a recent study conducted in the UK presented respondents with one attribute detailing the number of metres per kilometre of dry stone wall field boundary which would be restored under an option, three attributes concerning the number of hectares of different land use types that would change and two further attributes, one descriptive and the other monetary. Even if we ignore the fact that most UK residents use Imperial rather than metric units, it seems unlikely that the bulk of respondents in this study felt that say the area measurements were as readily comprehended as the monetary cost attribute.

This is a serious problem for DCE studies; if some attributes are readily comprehended while others are not, it seems reasonable that the former will play a larger role in determining respondents' choices. However, this may not reflect preferences. Those low comprehension attributes may indeed be the main drivers of preference, yet if they are not presented in ways which are readily understood then respondents will struggle to accurately represent their preferences within the choices they make.

There is a growing consensus among best-practice guides that the most effective route for promoting such comprehension is via the use of visual stimuli (Krupnick and Adamowicz, 2006; Mathews et al., 2006). This conclusion draws in part upon a substantial, long-standing and ongoing literature showing that the presentation of information in visual form can, in many situations, greatly enhance its evaluability. Early findings include the work of MacGregor and Slovic (1986) who show that visual displays outperform conventional information in terms of respondents being able to correctly assess factual outcomes. More recently Lipkus and Hollands (1999) show that visual information outperforms numeric data as a basis for the accurate comprehension of risk. Indeed the evaluation of health care risks has provided a number of examples where visual information has consistently outperformed equivalent numeric information as a route for minimizing perception and judgement errors. For example, Hibbard et al., (2002) found that individuals asked to pick the best health insurance plan from an array of satisfaction ratings chose an inferior plan 45 per cent of the time. However, the simple addition of visual information reduced error rates to only 16 per cent.

The use of visual stimuli seems particularly appropriate for goods which are most readily 'consumed' visually; landscape goods being an obvious example. Few members of the public really understand how big 1 hectare or 1 acre actually is. Therefore complex trade-offs across multiples of these units attached to differing land use types seem likely to impose a high cognitive burden on respondents. The challenge is to find naturalistic methods of conveying information using techniques which utilize the way in which people conventionally understand the attributes of goods. For landscape goods this would appear to be in terms of what people can see.

In order to examine the possibility that cognitively challenging numeric information may induce reliance upon framing heuristics in choice experiments, as well as to investigate the potential for visual information to overcome this problem we undertook a DCE study of a landscape change issue (Bateman et al., 2009d). As part of this experiment we investigated the role which virtual reality (VR) imaging techniques may play in providing realistic representations of both present and potential future landscapes. The validity of the resulting virtual reality choice experiment (VRCE) approach was, as before, tested via a split sample design using clear-cut anomaly testing as the criterion for whether resultant stated preferences conformed to economic expectations or not.

In selecting an appropriate anomaly test we considered the likely heuristic response of an individual faced with a DCE question containing attribute levels which were not readily comprehended. Suppose, as is typical, the DCE question format consisted of attributes defined by numeric values. Taking a recent landscape valuation study as an example, a given option might include an increase of 5500 ha of one land use type and a reduction of 17 700 ha in another while a second option offers an increase of 2700 ha of the former and a reduction of 1560 ha in the latter; with both options containing several other attributes. Suppose also that a respondent found this combination of numbers and units difficult to comprehend. What response heuristics might this respondent latch on to in order to answer these challenging questions? One reasonable approach might be to try and convert these attribute levels into simpler gains and losses, the size of which were at best only computed in relative terms. So, an option which offers two gains might end up being seen as better than one which offers a mix of gains and losses, irrespective of their absolute size. A characteristic pattern associated with such patterns of heuristic thinking is the gains–loss anomaly in which a unit loss is accorded a value which is disproportionally large relative to that given to a unit gain.

While the gains–loss phenomena has been the subject of ongoing debate and interpretation in the valuation literature (Hanemann, 1999; Sugden, 1999) experimental tests using real payment scenarios reveal levels of disparity which are not commensurate with conventional theory (Bateman et al., 1997). Within the context of a given valuation study the presence of some level of gains-loss anomaly is not that surprising and a review of the literature confirms it is commonplace across non-market and even market contexts (Horowitz and McConnell, 2002). However, our study set out to examine whether the use of numeric attribute levels and unfamiliar units might exacerbate the gains-loss disparity and if so whether VR generated visual alternatives might significantly reduce this problem.

The VRCE design was implemented through a case study of coastal land use change at Holme, UK. Here a DCE format design was used to examine preferences and associated values for changes from agricultural land into two alternative land uses: nature reserve and flooded. These, along with a cost level (a local tax increases collected through a universally inclusive mechanism) formed the attributes of the experiment. All respondents were initially presented with the type of information which any typical land use valuation study would include such as maps of the area detailing current land use and photographs of each of the alternative land use types. An unseen random process was then used to allocate participants into three treatments as follows:

1. NUMERIC_ONLY treatment. Here the DCE choice tasks were presented in the standard manner with numeric levels for each of the alternative land use attributes.
2. VR_ONLY treatment: Here the choice tasks presented solely as VR 'flythroughs' (images which move the respondent through the landscape of each option showing them what the land would look like under that scenario).
3. VR&NUMERIC treatment: Here respondents were presented with choices described both as VR flythroughs and in standard numeric form.

	Status quo	Scheme A
Area of the site that is nature reserve (hectares)	93	123
Area of the site that is flooded (hectares)	30	50
Area of the site that is farmland (hectares)	151	101
Addition to your annual water bill	£0	£5
Your choice	☐	☐

Figure 16.3   Standard (numeric only) approach to conveying land use options

In all treatments the level of the cost attribute was always presented numerically. Choices were defined by comparing a given option with the attribute levels describing the status quo. This simplest of choice formats was adopted and used throughout the study to reduce any extraneous sources of complexity and allow for a cleaner comparison between the values generated by the three treatments outlined above.

Figure 16.3 illustrates an example question posed to respondents facing the NUMERIC_ONLY treatment. Here, as per most DCE studies, attribute levels are given in numeric form. To attempt to give the standard approach as good a chance as possible of being comprehended, the case study area was chosen so as to avoid large and potentially complex numbers being used in each column. This is contrasted with the VR provided visual representation of options presented to the VR_ONLY and VR&NUMERIC treatments, examples of which are given in Figure 16.4.

Results from the experiment are summarised in Figure 16.5 which details derived values for changes in nature reserve. This shows that responses from the standard NUMERIC_ONLY treatment yield very strong gain-loss asymmetry; a unit loss is valued at well over four times the WTP for a unit gain producing the kinked value curve symptomatic of this anomaly. Results from the VR_ONLY and VR&NUMERIC treatments are insignificantly different from each other but very strongly significantly different from the NUMERIC_ONLY treatment. In contrast the degree

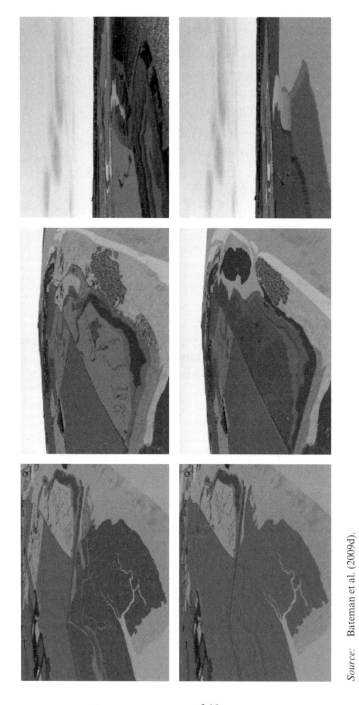

Source: Bateman et al. (2009d).

Figure 16.4   VR visualizations of the status quo (upper row) and various alternative land use scenarios (of which one example given in the lower row) from different viewing points

346

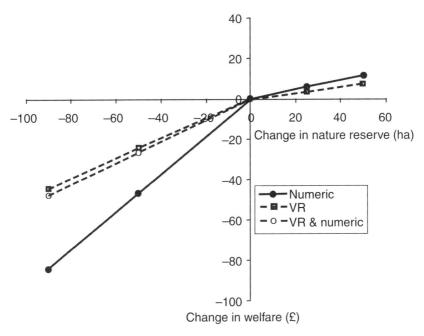

Source: Bateman et al. (2009d).

Figure 16.5 *Value functions for changes in area of nature reserve by treatment group*

of gains-loss asymmetry is now much reduced (if not insignificant) and the resulting valuation function is much smoother. It is clear that the use of visual imagery has very markedly reduced what is often seen as the most robust of all anomalies.

CONCLUSIONS

The case studies presented in this chapter can be seen as providing some hopefully common-sense guidance for future SP studies which we can summarize as 'Ask reasonable questions, in reasonable ways, with reasonable tests'.

Valuation questions need to address goods for which individuals either have well formed prior preferences, or for which those preferences can readily and consistently be discovered within the confines of an SP survey. Put simply, analysts should attempt to avoid asking questions to which people do not know the answer or can not easily work it. The biggest problem is that respondents *will* give answers even if they do not understand the question. In cases where respondents do not know their preferences by the time a valuation question is asked, the majority will infer that the good in question must be important and hence valuable – otherwise the survey would not be going on. Hence they will hunt for clues as to the 'correct' response, taking the question frame as a good source of heuristic short cuts to provide those answers. Such situations will lead to framing effects which bias valuations and make them unsuitable for decision purposes. In such circumstances analysts need to assist respondents to understand the goods being presented to them. Adopting naturalistic representations of those goods is a vital part of that undertaking and the findings of the previous study suggest that very significant reductions in anomalies can be provided when goods are presented in readily comprehended ways.

Just as individuals can struggle when faced with unfamiliar goods that they are being asked to value, so they can find the contingent institutions hypothesized in many non-market valuation studies challenging and difficult to comprehend. Here, a number of studies have been presented that provide reasons to be hopeful that, through repeated exposure to such institutions, respondents can learn and understand how they work so that associated anomalies become insignificant. Indeed, cases such as our LDCV example suggest that institutional learning can be a swift process providing rapid reductions in rates of anomaly from even one repetition of a contingent market.

Throughout the chapter we have stressed the need for better testing as the way to guide the development of methodology. The conventional scope sensitivity test lacks clear prior expectations and therefore is not a sufficient validation of valuation findings. However, experimental economics has provided a rich source of unambiguous tests focusing upon the presence or absence of anomalies. It is to be hoped that future testing will adopt these definitive approaches to validation rather than continuing to rely upon an approach which is inherently open to interpretation and subjectivity.

While we feel that this general approach to design, valuation and validation might provide a useful avenue to progress future SP research we fully recognize that there are important further issues which require addressing and will end by considering one of these. Most of the studies described in this chapter concern methods in which respondents are presented with multiple valuation questions. A concern with this is that any departure from the single question CV format is liable to present respondents with the opportunity to strategically misrepresent their preferences (Carson and Groves, 2007). The most obvious form of such strategic behaviour is when respondents pretend to have lower WTP than they really do in an attempt to secure provision of a good at the lowest possible cost. This problem directly conflicts with the repeated questioning approach which underpins most of the reductions in anomalies reported in this chapter. We therefore have a dilemma in that the strategic behaviour argument supports the use of a single question while the experience and learning approach emphasizes that repetition of valuation exercises improves experience and lowers the rate of anomalies. One possible solution to this quandary is to make the repetition process overtly a training exercises in which respondents are clearly informed that early questions are merely practice rounds. This should enhance familiarity with the contingent institution. It may even enhance the discovery of preferences if the goods used in the practice rounds are of a similar type.[12] The experienced respondent can then be presented with a single, incentive compatible 'for-real' valuation question, being clearly informed that responses to this final exercise will be used for decision purposes. It is to be hoped that this mix of repetition, learning, experience and incentive compatibility, complemented by robust validity testing, will provide a superior methodology for future non-market valuation studies.

NOTES

1. The research reported in this chapter was supported by: the ChREAM project which is funded by the UK Research Councils' Rural Economy and Land Use (RELU) Programme, funder reference: RES-227-25-0024; the SEER project which is funded by the UK Economic and Social Research Council (ESRC), funder ref: RES-060-25-0063; and the Economics for the Environment Consultancy (EFTEC), London. We are grateful to all funders for their support.
2. The names of these co-authors are given in the references listed at the end of this paper. However, I would not want to infer that they would necessarily agree with the arguments put forward in this chapter (especially as I am confident that the views expressed here include elements that both SP supporters and critics will disagree with). I am also grateful to a wider group who have generously shared their time and diverse thoughts with me over the years; they know who they are – thank you.
3. Furthermore, in ongoing work not reviewed here but with related early papers given in Bateman et al. (2009a, 2009b), we argue that there may be classes of goods for which the prospects of robust SP based valuation are not favourable (for example, non-use values for conservation of specific species). In such situations coat-effective provision of safe minimum standards may be a viable alternative to valuation (Bateman, 2009). See, for example, Crowards (1998), Turner et al. (1998) and Fisher et al. (2008).
4. The one exception is likely to be studies concerning valuations of increased life expectancy where one can construct theoretically based arguments supporting the expectation of approximate linearity (after income effects) in scope sensitivity.
5. These labels are taken from the literature on asymmetric dominance effects (see, for example, Huber et al., 1982) which refers to c as the 'competitor' to t, the 'target', while d refers to the 'decoy' bundle.
6. This survey was organized and in the main conducted by Alex Arnell, then of UEA.

7. Interestingly, the addition of bundle *d* lowers WTP among those who choose bundle *c* from £15.45 to £13.81; a reduction of more than 10 per cent although this difference is not statistically significant.
8. One could only defend such an expectation by inferring that the order of presentation in itself was deemed to have information content.
9. These figures are obtained using non-parametric modelling. Parametric models yield values of £75.86 and £101.43 respectively; again these differences are statistically significant at the 0.001 level (see Bateman et al., 2009c, for details).
10. Note that, as the amount presented to respondents in the second bound question is determined by the first bound amount and the respondent's answer to that it would be incorrect to only model second bound responses here (doing so would artificially exacerbate the difference between the first and second bound response). For further discussion see Bateman et al. (2008b)
11. Note that there is a counter explanation of these findings which posits that all but the initial response should be ignored due to the potential for strategic behaviour once multiple questions are asked of respondents (see Carson and Groves, 2007). We consider the implications of this argument in the conclusions to this chapter.
12. This may also improve the awareness of substitutes. However, ultimately the best form of experience has to be repeated consumption. While this obviously complicates valuation studies nevertheless it does seem an extremely fruitful avenue for future research.

REFERENCES

Ariely, D., G. Loewenstein and D. Prelec (2003), '"Coherent arbitrariness": stable demand curves without stable preferences', *Quarterly Journal of Economics*, **118** (1), 73–105.

Arrow, K., R. Solow, P.R. Portney, E.E. Leamer, R. Radner and H. Schuman, H. (1993), 'Report of the NOAA panel on contingent valuation', *Federal Register*, **58**, 4601–14.

Bateman, I.J. (2009), 'Economic analysis for ecosystem assessments: application to the UK National Ecosystem Assessment (NEA)', CSERGE Working Paper EDM 09-12, Centre for Social and Economic Research on the Global Environment, University of East Anglia.

Bateman, I.J., K. Bolt, B.H. Day, S. Ferrini, G. Loomes, M. Scasny, M.B. Kohlová and H. Skopková (2009a), 'Can stated preferences yield robust estimates of the value of statistical life? Lab and field applications of conventional and novel techniques for estimating adult and child VSL within an environmental context', presented at the 17th Annual Conference of the European Association of Environmental and Resource Economists (EAERE 2009), Department of Spatial Economics of the Faculty of Economics and Business Administration and the Institute for Environmental Studies, Vrije Universiteit, Amsterdam, 24–27 June.

Bateman, I.J., D. Burgess, W.G. Hutchinson and D.I. Matthews (2008b), 'Contrasting NOAA guidelines with learning design contingent valuation (LDCV): preference learning versus coherent arbitrariness', *Journal of Environmental Economics and Management*, **55**, 127–41.

Bateman, I.J., E. Coombes, B. Fisher, E. Fitzherbert, D.W. Glew and R. Naidoo (2009b), 'Saving Sumatra's species: combining economics and ecology to define an efficient and self-sustaining program for inducing conservation within oil palm plantations', CSERGE Working Paper EDM-2009-03, Centre for Social and Economic Research on the Global Environment, University of East Anglia.

Bateman, I.J., B.H. Day, D. Dupont and S. Georgiou (2009c), 'Procedural invariance testing of the one-and-one-half-bound dichotomous choice elicitation method', *Review of Economics and Statistics*, **91** (4), 806–20, doi:10.1162/rest.91.4.806.

Bateman, I.J., B.H. Day, A.P. Jones and S. Jude (2009d), 'Reducing gains/loss asymmetry: a virtual reality choice experiment (VRCE) valuing land use change', *Journal of Environmental Economics and Management*, **58**, 106–18, doi:10.1016/j.jeem.2008.05.003.

Bateman, I.J., B. Fisher, E. Fitzherbert, D. Glew and R. Naidoo (2010), 'Tigers, markets and palm oil: market potential for conservation', *Oryx*, in press.

Bateman, I.J., I.H. Langford, A.P. Jones and G.N. Kerr (2001), 'Bound and path effects in multiple-bound dichotomous choice contingent valuation', *Resource and Energy Economics*, **23** (3), 191–213.

Bateman, I.J., I.H. Langford, R.K. Turner, K.G. Willis and G.D. Garrod (1995), 'Elicitation and truncation effects in contingent valuation studies', *Ecological Economics*, **12** (2), 161–79, DOI: 10.1016/0921-8009(94)00044-V.

Bateman, I.J., A. Munro and G.L. Poe (2008a), 'Asymmetric dominance effects in choice experiments and contingent valuation', *Land Economics*, **84**, 115–27.

Bateman, I.J., A. Munro, B. Rhodes, C. Starmer and R. Sugden (1997), 'A test of the theory of reference-dependent preferences', *Quarterly Journal of Economics*, **112** (2), 479–505.

Braga, Jacinto and Chris Starmer (2005), 'Preference anomalies, preference elicitation and the discovered preference hypothesis', *Environmental and Resource Economics*, **32** (1), 55–89.

Carson, R.T. (2010), *Contingent Valuation: A Comprehensive Bibliography and History*, Cheltenham, UK and Northampton, MA, USA: Edward Elgar.

Carson, R.T. and Groves, T. (2007), 'Incentive and informational properties of preference questions', *Environmental and Resource Economics*, **37**, 181–210, DOI 10.1007/s10640-007-9124-5.

Cooper, Joseph, W. Michael Hanemann and Giovanni Signorello (2002), 'One-and-one-half-bound dichotomous choice contingent valuation', *Review of Economics and Statistics*, **84** (4), 742–50.

Crowards, T.M. (1998), 'Safe minimum standards: costs and opportunities', *Ecological Economics*, **25**, 303–14.

Day, B.H., I.J. Bateman, R.T. Carson, D. Dupont, J.J. Louviere, S. Morimoto, R. Scarpa and P. Wang (unpublished), 'Task independence in stated preference studies: a test of order effect explanations', available from author.

DeShazo, J.R. (2002), 'Designing transactions without framing effects in iterative question formats', *Journal of Environmental Economics and Management*, **43** (3), 360–85.

Fisher, B., K. Turner, M. Zylstra, R. Brouwer, R. de Groot, S. Farber, P. Ferraro, R. Green, D. Hadley, J. Harlow, P. Jefferiss, C. Kirkby, P. Morling, S. Mowatt, R. Naidoo, J. Paavola, B. Strassburg, D. Yu and A. Balmford, (2008), 'Ecosystem services and economic theory: integration for policy-relevant research', *Ecological Applications*, **18** (8), 2050–67.

Green, D., K.E. Jacowitz, D. Kahneman and D. McFadden (1998), 'Referendum contingent valuation, anchoring, and willingness to pay for public goods', *Resource and Energy Economics*, **20**, 85–116.

Hanemann, W.M. (1999), 'Neo-classical economic theory and contingent valuation', in I.J. Bateman and K.G. Willis (eds), *Valuing Environmental Preferences: Theory and Practice of the Contingent Valuation Method in the US, EU, and Developing Countries*, Oxford: Oxford University Press, pp. 42–96.

Hanemann, M., J. Loomis and B. Kanninen (1991), 'Statistical efficiency of double-bounded dichotomous choice contingent valuation', *American Journal of Agricultural Economics*, **73**, 1255–63.

Herriges, J.A. and J.F. Shogren (1996), 'Starting point bias in dichotomous choice valuation with follow-up questioning', *Journal of Environmental Economics and Management*, **30** (1), 112–31.

Hibbard J.H, P. Slovic, E.M. Peters and M. Finucane (2002), 'Strategies for reporting health plan performance information to consumers: evidence from controlled studies', *Health Services Research*, **37** (2), 291–313.

Horowitz, J. K. and K.E. McConnell (2002), 'A review of WTA/WTP studies', *Journal of Environmental Economics and Management*, **44**, 426–47.

Hsee, C.K. (1996), 'The evaluability hypothesis: an explanation for preference reversals between joint and separate evaluations of alternatives', *Organizational Behavior and Human Decision Processes*, **67**, 242–57.

Huber, J., J.W. Payne and C. Puto (1982), 'Adding asymmetrically dominated alternatives: Violations of regularity and the similarity hypothesis', *Journal of Consumer Research*, **9**, 90–98.

Krupnick, A. and W.L Adamowicz (2006), 'Supporting questions in stated choice studies', in B. Kanninen (ed.), *Valuing Environmental Amenities Using Stated Choice Studies: A Common Sense Approach to Theory and Practice*, vol. 8, Dordrecht: Springer, pp. 43–65.

Lipkus, I.M. and J.G. Hollands (1999), 'The visual communication of risk', *Journal of the National Cancer Institute Monographs*, **25**, 149–63

MacGregor, D. and P. Slovic (1986), 'Graphic representation of judgmental information', *Human–Computer Interaction*, **2**, 179–200.

Mathews, K.E., M.L. Freeman and W.H. Desvousges (2006), 'How and how much? The role of information in stated choice questionnaires', in B. Kanninen (ed.), *Valuing Environmental Amenities Using Stated Choice Studies: A Common Sense Approach to Theory and Practice*, vol. 8, Dordrecht: Springer, pp. 111–33.

Munro, A. and N. Hanley (1999), 'Information, uncertainty and contingent valuation', in I.J. Bateman and K.G. Willis (eds), *Valuing Environmental Preferences: Theory and Practice of the Contingent Valuation Method in the US, EC and Developing Countries*, OUP.

Plott, Charles R. (1996), 'Rational individual behavior in markets and social choice processes: the discovered preference hypothesis', in K. Arrow, E. Colombatto, M. Perleman and C. Schmidt (eds), *Rational Foundations of Economic Behavior*, London: Macmillan and NY: St. Martin's, pp. 225–50.

Slovic, P. (1995), 'The construction of preferences', *American Psychologist*, **50**, 364–71.

Sugden, R. (1999), 'Alternatives to the neo-classical theory of choice', in Ian Bateman and Kenneth G. Willis (eds), *Valuing Environmental Preferences: Theory and Practice of the Contingent Valuation Method in the US, EU, and Developing Countries*, Oxford: Oxford University Press.

Turner, R.K., W.N. Adger and R. Brouwer (1998), 'Ecosystem services value, research needs, and policy relevance: a commentary', *Ecological Economics*, **25** (1), 61–5, doi:10.1016/S0921-8009(98)00018-4.

Tversky, Amos and Daniel Kahneman (1974), 'Judgment under uncertainty: heuristics and biases', *Science*, **185** (4157), 1124–31.

17 Evaluating benefit transfer for Canadian water quality improvements using US/Canada metadata: an application of international meta-analysis

Paul J. Thomassin and Robert J. Johnston

Benefit transfer is often unavoidable in contemporary policy analysis. Even in the absence of comprehensive cost–benefit analysis, policy analysts are increasingly asked to incorporate estimates of non-market value into policy evaluations. Benefit transfer becomes particularly relevant, however, when government policies mandate that benefits and costs be considered in management plans; for example river basin management in the UK (Hanley et al., 2006a, 2006b) or as required by Executive Orders 12866, 13258 and 13422 for major US Government rules (Griffiths and Wheeler, 2005). In many cases, policy analysts do not have the time or resources necessary to undertake primary valuation studies of policy impacts, and in some cases are prevented from doing so by requirements imposed by statutes such as the Paperwork Reduction Act in the USA (Griffiths and Wheeler, 2005; Iovanna and Griffiths, 2006; Johnston and Rosenberger, 2010). As a result, policy analysts must rely on other means – namely, benefit transfer – to provide estimates.

Early benefit transfers almost exclusively applied unit value transfers, in which unadjusted welfare estimates from non-market research at a 'study site' were used to approximate benefits at a 'policy site.' Loomis (1992) is widely credited with initiating a movement away from these simple unit value transfers and towards benefit function transfer (BFTs), with benefit functions drawn from individual primary studies in the literature. The consensus of the contemporary literature is that benefit function transfers usually outperform unit value transfers (Johnston and Rosenberger, 2010; Rosenberger and Stanley, 2006), although contrary or non-conclusive findings have been reported (e.g., Brouwer, 2000; Brouwer and Bateman, 2005; Ready et al., 2004), and unit value transfers are still commonly used within agency policy analysis (Johnston and Rosenberger, 2010). The availability of applicable site-specific benefit functions, however, is limited, particularly those drawn from study sites of sufficient similarity to the policy sites in question. In cases for which a closely matching study site function is not available, a parameterized meta-analytic benefit function, estimated using a meta-regression model (MRM) of many primary study results, can provide the analyst with a viable alternative (Bergstrom and Taylor, 2006; Rosenberger and Loomis, 2000).

Benefit function transfer applications of meta-analysis (MA) typically involve the use of MRMs in which the dependent variable in a Bayesian or classical regression model is a summary welfare statistic (for example, willingness-to-pay estimate) drawn from comparable primary studies. Independent variables in the MRM characterize attributes of the resource, policy, site and affected population that are hypothesized to explain observed variation in the dependent variable across primary study observations (Nelson and Kennedy, 2009). The estimated regression equation characterizes a value surface that reflects multidimensional patterns in estimated willingness-to-pay (WTP) across the empirical observations that comprise the metadata. The use of the estimated regression equation for BFT requires that the analyst then assign values (that is, choose variable levels) for independent variables reflecting conditions or attributes at an unstudied policy site, so that a transferable WTP prediction can be obtained (Stapler and Johnston, 2009). The advantages of using a BFT derived from meta-analysis can include: (1) improved estimates of central tendency and the distribution of value in the metadata when a large number of studies are used in the regression analysis, (2) the ability to control for the effects of methodological variables, and (3) an ability to account for differences between the study and policy sites across site, policy and population attributes not present in benefit functions derived from single studies (Shrestha and Loomis, 2001). As a result, MRM BFT can offer the analyst a greater capacity to adjust for attributes of the policy or site for which welfare estimates are desired. Although the use of meta-analysis for BFT has been given increased attention during the past ten years, the literature provides mixed conclusions and arguments regarding its suitability and empirical performance (see Johnston and Rosenberger, 2010, for a summary).

The use of meta-analysis to estimate BFTs requires a large number of primary studies that measure WTP for the non-market commodity in question. Some countries, such as the USA and the UK, have an extensive published valuation literature from which such studies may be drawn. Many other countries, however, have less extensive collections of non-market valuation studies. In such cases, options for within-country benefit transfer are limited – using meta-analysis or otherwise – causing some to explore options for international meta-analysis and/or benefit transfer (Johnston and Thomassin, 2010; Ready and Navrud, 2006; Ready et al., 2004). The methods used in international benefit transfer parallel those applicable within a single country. Options include standard site-to-site unit transfers or BFTs adjusted for exchange rates and other cross-border differences (Brouwer and Bateman, 2005; Kristófersson and Navrud, 2007; Ready and Navrud, 2006; Ready et al., 2004), as well MRMs estimated with multiple country data (Brander et al., 2007; Brouwer et al., 1999; Lindhjem and Navrud, 2008; Santos, 1998). In the latter case, the metadata include observations from both foreign and domestic studies, providing sufficient information for statistical estimation of an MRM. As noted by Johnston and Thomassin (2010), 'multinational MRMs may be particularly tempting in countries for which a relatively small number of primary studies are available, both reducing the likelihood of a good site match for site-to-site BFT and the number of in-country studies suitable for MA'. An additional benefit of meta-analysis in such cases is the ability to identify systematic value surface differences between nations, thereby promoting more informed WTP adjustments.

The reliability of any MRM BFT – international or otherwise – depends on the characteristics of the metadata, among other factors (Johnston and Rosenberger, 2010; Nelson and Kennedy, 2009; Rosenberger and Stanley, 2006). The first step in developing international metadata is to identify the primary studies to be included. This is usually done through a systematic search of both the published and grey literatures of the countries to be included in the metadata. In recent years, this process has been facilitated by the availability of valuation databases such as the Environmental Valuation Reference Inventory (EVRI, n.d.). EVRI was founded in 2002 and is now the largest international searchable database of valuation studies. It includes over 2500 valuation studies from a variety of countries, with a majority of the studies coming from countries that sponsor the database (Canada, the USA, the UK, France, Australia and New Zealand; these countries are together known as the EVRI Club). EVRI provides the analyst with the ability to search for studies based on a number of categories including study area and population characteristics, study method, environmental good or service, and estimated value. The searchable database allows researchers and policy analysts to identify primary studies that are potentially comparable to the policy site whether the metadata is being constructed for in-country or international benefit transfer.

Although databases such as EVRI enhance the ease with which multinational metadata may be compiled, the ability of resulting MRMs to ameliorate the challenges of international benefit transfer remains unclear. The environmental economics literature includes a number of multinational MRMs, but provides only limited evidence regarding differences in WTP value surfaces across countries (Johnston and Rosenberger, 2010).

Such differences can be crucial to the validity and reliability of benefit transfers. Only a small number of works provide detailed guidance regarding difficulties involved in the estimation and use of multinational MRMs for benefit transfer (for example, Lindhjem and Navrud, 2008; Ready and Navrud, 2006). Despite increasing use of MRMs in environmental economics, reliable transfers are not assured (Bergstrom and Taylor, 2006; Johnston and Rosenberger, 2010; Johnston and Thomassin, 2010; Moeltner et al., 2007; Nelson and Kennedy, 2009; Smith and Pattanayak, 2002); such challenges are often magnified when metadata pool observations across different countries.

This chapter considers the empirical possibilities and challenges for international benefit transfer in which multinational metadata combine valuation estimates from a data-rich and data-poor country, in order to conduct BFT in the latter. Results are drawn from an MRM conducted to identify systematic components of WTP for surface water quality improvements across US and Canadian observations and isolate differences in value surfaces between the two countries, developed to support benefit transfer for Canadian policy development. The metadata include stated preference valuation studies that estimate total (use and nonuse) WTP for water quality changes that affect aquatic life habitats or recreational uses – a type of primary study with few Canadian examples. The goals of the paper are to (1) assess the properties of a multinational (US and Canadian) MRM compared to a single-country (US) analogue, (2) illustrate the potential information which may be derived as well as the analytical challenges, (3) assess the relative performance of related BFTs using out-of-sample convergent validity tests, and (4) comment on the reliability of the various methods that could be used for benefit transfer within our case-study context.

INTERNATIONAL META-ANALYSIS

Developing metadata for a domestic MRM requires the analyst to reconcile individual observations from primary studies to ensure that there is consistency in variable definition and measurement, particularly for the dependent variable. This task becomes more complicated when dealing with multinational metadata. Here we distinguish between *international* benefit transfer (transfer from a study site in one country to a policy site in another) and *multinational* meta-analysis used for benefit transfer in one or more countries (meta-analysis in which metadata include observations from multiple countries). Similar challenges, however, confront both types of benefit transfer.

Several authors (Ready and Navrud, 2006; Ready et al., 2004) have identified issues that must be addressed when developing multinational metadata or conducting international benefit transfer. These can include: (1) currency conversion between countries, (2) adjustments to account for differences between the characteristics of the commodity, the context in which it is provided, and the characteristics of users or affected populations, (3) potential adjustments for differences in wealth versus income across countries, (4) cultural differences between countries that influence value, (5) differences in the size of the market in different countries; that is, the size of the population that values the environmental good, and (6) whether values should be adjusted when they are transferred into another country's context. Although some of these issues are similar to those made within domestic benefit transfers, the international dimension can magnify the complications involved and the potential importance of appropriate adjustments. In some cases, however, meta-analysis can provide a means to ameliorate or reveal potential complications that affect other transfer methods (Rosenberger and Johnston, 2009). For example, an appropriately specified multinational MRM might reveal systematic differences in value surfaces across different countries and thereby promote more appropriate BFTs.

Analysts considering the development of metadata from multiple countries can also face non-trivial challenges related to study heterogeneity and sample selection considerations across nations (Lindhjem and Navrud, 2008; Rosenberger and Johnston, 2009), because the heterogeneity of study attributes across countries may be greater than that of the same attributes within countries (Lindhjem and Navrud, 2008; Ready and Navrud, 2006). This can lead to questions regarding the appropriateness of data pooling (Lindhjem and Navrud, 2008). In addition, sample selection patterns may vary across countries. For example, some countries such as the US have accumulated a wide and varied literature of non-market valuation. Many other countries, however, do not have such a rich non-market valuation literature. This can lead to concerns regarding research priority selection bias, methodological selection bias, publication selection bias and metadata sample selection bias (Hoehn 2006; Johnston et al., 2006; Rosenberger and Johnston, 2009; Rosenberger and Stanley, 2006; Stanley 2005), as well as the broader interpretability of metadata dominated by observations from a single country.

The valuation literature includes a number of multinational MRMs (for example, Brander et al., 2006, 2007; Brouwer et al., 1999; Lindhjem and Navrud, 2008; Santos, 1998, 2007), but the authors are aware of few articles that offer in-depth discussion of the complexities involved with multinational MA and related benefit transfers (for example, Lindhjem and Navrud, 2008). Multinational meta-analyses often give scant attention to the empirical challenges associated with multinational data. As a result, there is little evidence to indicate whether or not MRMs estimated from multinational metadata are a valid alternative to other, simpler approaches for benefit transfer (Johnston and Thomassin, 2010). The few studies that have undertaken BFT based on MRMs estimated from multinational metadata suggest that there is the potential for large transfer errors, particularly when metadata include observations from three or more countries (Brander et al., 2007; Lindhjem and Navrud, 2008).

The present chapter explores issues related to the estimation and use of multinational MRMs for benefit transfer, focusing on a more restricted and perhaps viable class of multinational MRM based on metadata from two similar and neighbouring countries, the USA and Canada. We give particular emphasis to a case in which a large number of valuation studies from a data-rich country (here, the USA) are combined a smaller number of studies from a relatively data-poorer country (here, Canada) to estimate an MRM for purposes of BFT in the country with a less extensive valuation literature. The policy context involves BFT for Agriculture and Agri-Food Canada (AAFC) proposals to reduce agriculture-related movement of sediments, nutrients, pathogens, pesticides and salts into Canadian surface waters. Although policymakers originally expressed a desire for a meta-analysis from Canadian data alone, such a model was infeasible because of the lack of sufficient Canadian studies. For this reason, the present metadata combine US and Canadian observations, providing at least a potential means to estimate a benefit meta-function that incorporates greater information than one based solely on Canadian data.

The analysis is designed to allow direct comparisons to a parallel US MRM, as well as a prior US-only MRM drawn from similar metadata (Johnston et al., 2005). The contrast of parallel single and multiple country MRMs provides insight into the robustness of results to multinational data pooling. The contrast also illustrates challenges involved in the estimation and interpretation of a multinational MRM across even similar countries, and allows a comparison of results between countries without the additional complexity involved in meta-analysis involving data from three or more countries. Particular emphasis is given to reliability of resulting BFTs for use in Canadian policy contexts compared to alternative transfer methods, as revealed by a battery of convergent validity assessments.

DATA AND EMPIRICAL MODEL

The assessment draws from the original metadata of Johnston and Thomassin (2010), including stated preference studies that estimate US and Canadian total (use and non-use) WTP for water quality changes that affect aquatic life habitats or recreational uses. This dataset extends the metadata of Johnston et al. (2005) with a set of comparable Canadian observations to estimate a joint Canadian–US value surface. The metadata were limited to stated preference studies to ensure that a consistent Hicksian welfare measure was pooled across all observations, following guidance from the meta-analysis literature (Bergstrom and Taylor, 2006; Nelson and Kennedy, 2009; Smith et al., 2002). Specific criteria for study selection are found in Johnston and Thomassin (2010).

The metadata include 90 observations from 36 unique studies published between 1981 and 2003. Sixteen of the observations were from Canadian studies; these represent 17 per cent of the metadata. Many of the studies in the metadata include multiple estimates of WTP based on in-study variations in such factors as the extent of the amenity (that is, water quality) change, elicitation methods, water body type, recreational activities affected and species affected. Canadian observations are drawn from two studies (Brox et al., 1996; Dupont, 2003). Despite an extensive review of the literature no other Canadian studies could be found that met all inclusion criteria. Brox et al. (1996) provide various estimates of WTP for water quality improvements in the Grand River Watershed in Ontario, only one of which met all inclusion criteria. Dupont (2003) estimates WTP for water quality improvements that support different types of aquatic life and recreational activities in nearby Hamilton Harbor, also in Ontario; this study provides the majority of Canadian observations in the metadata. Both studies are associated with western Lake Ontario waters or watersheds in relatively urbanized areas, and both address waters with significant recreational use. Hence, as emphasized by Johnston and Thomassin (2010), MRM results must be interpreted not only with respect to the number of Canadian observations in the metadata, but also with regard to the geographic range and characteristics of the Canadian waters that are represented.

The remaining 74 observations in the metadata are from US studies and are described in Johnston et al. (2005). The US studies cover a broad range of systemic components, that is, population attributes and methodological approaches. For example, the US studies cover a number of geographical locations (Pacific, Southeast, Northeast, plains and multiple regions), water body types (lakes, single rivers, multiple rivers, ponds, and so on), and resource attributes (fish species, multiple species, shellfish species, unspecified species). This provides variation and degrees of freedom in the metadata unavailable from Canadian studies alone, but also assumes that data from the USA and Canada are suitable for pooling.

Table 17.1 summarizes characteristics for included studies, a large

Table 17.1   Characteristics of studies included in meta-analysis

Citation for study	Number of obs. in metadata	State or region	Species affected	Methodology	Adjusted WTP values[a]
Aiken (1985)	1	CO	Game fish	Contingent valuation (CV) – multiple methods[b]	$167.98
Anderson and Edwards (1986)	1	RI	Unspecified	Contingent valuation (CV) – open ended	$157.14
Azevedo et al. (2001)	5	IA	Game fish	CV – discrete choice	$17.76–$118.68
Bockstael et al. (1989)	2	MD	Unspecified	CV – discrete choice	$65.80–$209.51
Brox et al. (1996)	1	Ontario (Canada)	Unspecified	CV – payment card	$15.07
Cameron and Huppert (1989)	1	CA	Game fish	CV – discrete choice	$43.07
Carson et al. (1994)	2	CA	Game fish; multiple categories	CV – discrete choice	$35.83–$67.47
Clonts and Malone (1990)	3	AL	Unspecified	CV – iterative bidding	$68.10–$110.85
Croke et al. (1987)	9	IL	All recreational fish; none	CV – iterative bidding	$53.31–$81.46
Cronin (1982)	4	DC	All recreational fish	CV – open ended	$61.85–$212.73
Desvousges et al. (1983)	2	PA	Unspecified	CV – discrete choice	$111.41–$220.24
De Zoysa (1995)	2	OH	Multiple categories	CV – discrete choice	$35.88–$61.02
Dupont (2003)	15	Ontario (Canada)	Unspecified; fish	CV – discrete choice	$6.60–$61.24[c]
Farber and Griner (2000)	3	PA	All recreational fish	CV – discrete choice	$44.22–$105.58
Hayes et al. (1992)	2	RI	Shellfish; none	CV – discrete choice	$339.72–$351.47

Table 17.1 (continued)

Citation for study	Number of obs. in metadata	State or region	Species affected	Methodology	Adjusted WTP values[a]
Herriges and Shogren (1996)	2	IA	All recreational fish	CV – discrete choice	$53.66–$180.35
Huang et al. (1997)	2	NC	Multiple categories	CV – discrete choice; revealed and stated preference	$221.75–$228.07
Kaoru (1993)	1	MA	Shellfish	CV – open ended	$190.10
Lant and Roberts (1990)	3	IA/IL	Game fish; all recreational fish	CV – discrete choice	$107.86–$134.18
Loomis (1996)	1	WA	Game fish	CV – discrete choice	$80.93
Lyke (1993)	2	WI	Game fish	CV – discrete choice	$51.96–$84.99
Magat et al. (2000)	2	CO/NC	All aquatic species	CV – iterative bidding	$114.49–$376.61
Matthews et al. (1999)	2	MN	All aquatic species	CV – discrete choice	$15.77–$22.01
Mitchell and Carson (1981)	1	National	All aquatic species	CV – discrete choice	$242.34
Olsen et al. (1991)	3	Pacific NW	Game fish	CV – open ended	$34.48–$107.59
Roberts and Leitch (1997)	1	MN/SD	Multiple categories	CV – discrete choice	$7.26
Rowe et al. (1985)	1	CO	Game fish	CV – open ended	$117.04
Sanders et al. (1990)	4	CO	Unspecified	CV – open ended	$70.44–$171.59
Schulze et al. (1995)	2	MT	Multiple categories	CV – discrete choice	$15.08–$21.16
Stumborg et al. (2001)	2	WI	Multiple categories	CV – discrete choice	$57.90–$88.38
Sutherland and Walsh (1985)	1	MT	Unspecified	CV – open ended	$126.98

Table 17.1   (continued)

Citation for study	Number of obs. in metadata	State or region	Species affected	Methodology	Adjusted WTP values[a]
Welle (1986)	6	MN	Multiple categories; game fish	multiple methods	$95.30–$207.32
Wey (1990)	2	RI	Shellfish	multiple methods	$55.61–$200.50
Whitehead and Groothuis (1992)	3	NC	All recreational fish	CV – open ended	$27.74–$46.23
Whitehead et al. (1995)	2	NC	Multiple categories	CV – iterative bidding	$68.08–$97.91
Whittington et al. (1994)	1	TX	All aquatic species	CV – discrete choice	$169.32

Notes:
a   As noted in the text, reported WTP values apply to different levels of water quality change. All WTP estimates are converted to 2002 US dollars and rounded to the nearest cent, and hence may not match exactly the raw WTP estimates reported in source studies. Where multiple WTP estimates are available from a given study, the range of values is presented.
b   The author averaged WTP estimates derived from both open-ended and iterative bidding methods to obtain a single reported WTP estimate.
c   WTP estimates for nested policy options were summed in some cases to obtain total WTP estimates for combined policies.

number of which were identified through their inclusion in EVRI (Johnston and Thomassin, 2010; Johnston et al., 2005). This highlights the important role of valuation databases for metadata construction (Johnston and Thomassin, 2009). The extensive filtering of studies (each original study had to be carefully read in detail) and data transformations required to complete the metadata (see Johnston and Thomassin, 2010; Johnston et al., 2005), however, also suggest the extensive work required to transform or extend data in EVRI into a form useful for meta-analysis and benefit transfer. That is, EVRI should be viewed as an excellent 'starting point' for research and policy analysis, but comprehensive analysis requires data beyond that included in the database (Johnston and Thomassin, 2009).

Table 17.2 provides a description and summary statistics of the variables included in the model, including WTP values (the dependent variable in the MRM). Monetary values for WTP values were converted to 2002 US dollar equivalents. For US observations, this required transformation

Table 17.2 Meta-analysis variables and descriptive statistics

Variable	Description	Units and measurement	Mean (std. dev.)
ln_WTP	Natural log of willingness-to-pay for specified resource improvements. WTP for all studies was converted to 2002 US dollars as detailed in main text.	Natural log of dollars (Range: 1.98 to 5.93)	4.21 (0.91)
year_indx	Year in which the study was conducted, converted to an index by subtracting 1970.	Year Index (Range: 3 to 31)	19.80 (6.42)
discrete_ch	Binary variable indicating that WTP was estimated using a discrete choice survey instrument.	Binary (Range: 0 or 1)	0.44 (0.50)
voluntary	Binary variable indicating that WTP was estimated using a payment vehicle described as voluntary.	Binary (Range: 0 or 1)	0.06 (0.24)
interview	Binary variable indicating that the survey was conducted using in-person interviews.	Binary (Range: 0 or 1)	0.15 (0.36)
mail	Binary variable indicating that the survey was conducted through the mail.	Binary (Range: 0 or 1)	0.63 (0.49)
lump_sum	Binary variable indicating that payments were to occur on something other than a long-term annual basis (for example, a single lump sum payment).	Binary (Range: 0 or 1)	0.33 (0.47)
wq_change	Change in mean water quality, specified on the Resources for the Future (RFF) water quality ladder. Defined as the difference between baseline and post-improvement quality. Where the original study (survey) did not use the RFF water quality ladder, we mapped water quality descriptions to analogous levels on the RFF ladder to derive water quality change (see text). Note that this variable was only included in the model as part of an interaction term (*WQ_fish*, *WQ_shell*, *WQ_many*, *WQ_non*).	Water quality ladder units (Range: 0.5 to 5.75)	See individual WQ variables below
wq_ladder	Binary variable indicating that the original survey reported resource changes using a standard RFF water quality ladder.	Binary (Range: 0 or 1)	0.27 (0.45)

Table 17.2   (continued)

Variable	Description	Units and measurement	Mean (std. dev.)
protest_ bids	Binary variable indicating that protest bids were excluded when estimating WTP.	Binary (Range: 0 or 1)	0.38 (0.49)
outlier_ bids	Binary variable indicating that outlier bids were excluded when estimating WTP.	Binary (Range: 0 or 1)	0.19 (0.39)
hi_ response	Binary variable indicating that the survey response rate exceeds 74% (that is, 75% or above).	Binary (Range: 0 or 1)	0.26 (0.44)
income	Mean income of survey respondents, either as reported by the original survey or calculated based on Census averages for the original surveyed region.	Dollars (Range: 30396 to 137693)	44956.14 (12590.26)
nonusers	Binary variable indicating that the survey is implemented over a population of nonusers (default category for this dummy is a survey of any population that includes users).	Binary (Range: 0 or 1)	0.21 (0.41)
estuary_ bay	Binary variable indicating that resource change explicitly takes place in an estuary or large bay (default is a change in a river).	Binary (Range: 0 or 1)	0.12 (0.33)
lake	Binary variable indicating that resource change explicitly takes place over a single lake.	Binary (Range: 0 or 1)	0.26 (0.44)
Salt_pond	Binary variable indicating that resource change explicitly takes place over multiple salt ponds.	Binary (Range: 0 or 1)	0.04 (0.20)
regional_ fresh	Binary variable indicating that resource change explicitly takes place in multiple fresh water bodies in an identified geographical region.	Binary (Range: 0 or 1)	0.31 (0.46)
southeast	Binary variable indicating that survey was conducted in the USDA Southeast region (default is Northeast region).	Binary (Range: 0 or 1)	0.10 (0.31)
pacif_ mount	Binary variable indicating that survey was conducted in the USDA Pacific / Mountain region.	Binary (Range: 0 or 1)	0.17 (0.37)

Table 17.2 (continued)

Variable	Description	Units and measurement	Mean (std. dev.)
plains	Binary variable indicating that survey was conducted in the USDA Northern or Southern Plains region.	Binary (Range: 0 or 1)	0.02 (0.14)
mult_reg	Binary variable indicating that survey included respondents from more than one of the regions.	Binary (Range: 0 or 1)	0.03 (0.17)
Canada	Binary variable indicating that survey was conducted in Canada.	Binary (Range: 0 or 1)	0.17 (0.37)
WQ_fish	Interaction variable: *wq_change* multiplied by a binary variable identifying studies in which water quality improvements are stated to benefit only fin fish. Default is zero (that is, change did not affect fish).	Water quality ladder units (Range: 0.5 to 5.75)	1.13 (1.47)
WQ_shell	Interaction variable: *wq_change* multiplied by a binary variable identifying studies in which water quality improvements are stated to benefit only shellfish. Default is zero (that is, change did not affect shellfish).	Water quality ladder units (Range: 0.5 to 4.00)	0.10 (0.58)
WQ_many	Interaction variable: *wq_change* multiplied by a binary variable identifying studies in which water quality improvements are stated to benefit multiple species types. Default is zero (that is, change did not affect multiple species).	Water quality ladder units (Range: 0.5 to 4.00)	0.53 (1.12)
WQ_non	Interaction variable: *wq_change* multiplied by a binary variable identifying studies in which species benefiting from water quality improvements remain unspecified. Default is zero (that is, change did not affect unspecified species).	Water quality ladder units (Range: 0.5 to 2.5)	0.53 (0.93)
fishplus	Binary variable identifying studies in which a substantial fish population or harvest change is reported in the survey.	Binary (Range: 0 or 1)	0.20 (0.40)

Table 17.2   (continued)

Variable	Description	Units and measurement	Mean (std. dev.)
baseline	Baseline water quality, specified on the RFF water quality ladder.	Water quality ladder units (Range: 0 to 7)	4.61 (2.27)
baseline_ Canada	Interaction variable: *baseline* multiplied by *Canada*.	Water quality ladder units (Range: 0 to 7)	(1.76) 0.76

using the US Bureau of Labor Statistics non-seasonally adjusted average Consumer Price Index (CPI) for all urban consumers. For Canadian observations, parallel adjustments were made using the Statistics Canada Consumer Price Index (2007). Canadian observations were then adjusted to US Dollar equivalents using the average annual G5 exchange rates published by the Board of Governors of the Federal Reserve System (USA). These adjustments ensure that monetary amounts are comparable across observations. Even after these adjustments there was a large variation in WTP estimates in the metadata; these values ranged from $6.60 to $376.61 with an average value of $95.42.

Two MRMs were developed for convergent validity tests of benefit transfer reliability. The first MRM incorporates all metadata observations into the analysis (including all US and Canadian observations) and is designated the US/Canada model. A second MRM was developed using only the US observations and is designated the US model. A separate model including only Canadian observations could not be estimated because of degrees of freedom limitations that resulted from the small number of Canadian observations.

Both MRMs apply a maximum likelihood, multi-level (random effects) model to take into account the potential correlations between multiple observations from individual studies, as well as the potential for heteroskedastic errors that could otherwise lead to inefficient, inconsistent parameter estimates (Rosenberger and Loomis, 2000). In all cases MRMs are specified as unweighted semi-log regression models following Johnston and Thomassin (2010), with the natural log of the estimated household WTP for water quality improvements in aquatic habitat as the dependent variable. This was regressed over 29 variables, including 22 variables that characterized the resource attributes, socioeconomic characteristics, and policy context (X_j; $j = 22$) and seven variables characterizing the methodological approaches of the primary studies in the metadata (Y_k; k = 7). The functional form is given by:

$$\ln WTP_{Np} = \alpha + \sum_{j=1}^{J}\beta_j X_j + \sum_{k=1}^{K}\theta_k Y_{jk} + e_{Np} + u_p \qquad (17.1)$$

where the subscripts N and p index each observation included in the meta-data (N) and an index of each unique study (p), and parameters to be estimated are given by α, β_j and θ_k. The two error terms in the model; u_p and e_{Np}, include the study level error that is shared by all observations from the same study and the standard *iid* estimation level error with a mean of zero and constant variance, respectively (Shretha and Loomis, 2003).

Among the most critical aspects of metadata construction reflected in Table 17.2 are the methods used to reconcile variable definitions across observations (Bergstrom and Taylor, 2006; Johnston et al., 2005; Smith and Pattanayak, 2002; Smith et al., 2002). Among the reconciled variables most central to the model are those characterizing water quality. Many (26) observations in the metadata characterize quality changes using variants of the Resources for the Future (RFF) water quality ladder (McClelland, 1974; Mitchell and Carson, 1989, p. 342; Vaughan, 1986). The ladder allows the use of objective water quality parameters such as dissolved oxygen to characterize suitability for particular human uses (Johnston and Besedin, 2009; Vaughan, 1986). For studies that did not include the water quality ladder as an original study element, the descriptions of water quality that were included – either using descriptive (for example, suitable for swimming) or objective criteria – are used to map water quality measures to the RFF ladder following Johnston et al. (2005). To account for the possibility of systematic biases involved in mapping descriptive water quality measures to the RFF ladder, the binary variable *wq_ladder* is defined. This variable identifies studies in which the water quality ladder measurements were an original component of the survey instrument. For comparison, an alternative means of coordinating water quality measurements across studies is illustrated by Van Houtven et al. (2007).

The metadata and associated MRMs also allow the estimated partial slope associated with water quality changes to vary as a function of the primary affected species group. Following Johnston et al. (2005), water quality variables (see above) were included in the model as a set of interactions with dummy variables characterizing the primary species affected by water quality change, as noted in the original studies. These interaction variables distinguish the effects of water quality change for fish (*WQ_fish*), shellfish (*WQ_shell*), multiple species (*WQ_many*), and non-specified species (*WQ_non*).

Three BFTs are drawn from the two sets of MRM results, from which convergent validity tests are used to characterize transfer reliability. In all cases, we follow the original motivation for our MRM estimation (that is, benefit transfer for Canadian policy development) and forecast WTP for all Canadian observations in the sample ($N = 16$). These transferred values are then compared to the original WTP estimates generated by the primary study observation in question following standard mechanisms for convergent validity testing in benefit transfer (Rosenberger and Stanley, 2006).

The three tested BFTs are distinguished first by the MRM used to generate welfare estimates and second by assumptions that determine the treatment of methodological variables within each BFT (Johnston et al., 2006; Stapler and Johnston, 2009). The latter issue is a concern for MRM BFT because methodological variables are often shown to influence WTP within meta-analysis, but values for these variables cannot be observed from the policy site (because no study has been conducted in the actual BFT settings) (Johnston et al., 2006). The first BFT draws from the US/Canada MRM and assumes that the methodological attributes of the Canadian studies are known. This follows the 'best-case' scenario of Stapler and Johnston (2009) that is available within a convergent validity framework but not within real world BFTs where no policy site study is available.

The second BFT also draws from the US/Canada MRM to predict WTP values for Canadian observations, but assumes that the methodological attributes of the Canadian observations are not known. This BFT reflects a more realistic situation – universal within real-world applications of benefit transfer – in which no policy site study exists from which to observe methodological variable values. Here, we follow standard practice and use the mean of the methodological variable levels to forecast WTP within the BFT, again following Stapler and Johnston (2009). This model is designated as the US/Canada model with the mean methodological attribute assumption.

The third BFT uses results from the *US-only* MRM to forecast out-of-sample values for each *Canadian* observation in the full Canada/US meta-data. Other than this difference, methods and variable assignments for the assessment mirror those in the second BFT above, using mean Canadian values for methodological variable value assignments. Within this third BFT, estimates of WTP of the Canadian observations were predicted using the US MRM without any adjustments for systematic differences between US and Canadian WTP. This would mirror a situation in which a policy analyst sought to predict WTP for Canadian policy development using information from a published US-only MRM such as that of Johnston et al. (2005).

For comparison, performance of the three MRM BFTs described above is contrasted to that from a simple unit value benefit transfer. For this transfer, the mean value of WTP (2002 $US) over Canadian observations was used as an alternative transfer value for each observation. The unit transfer value estimated is a modification of the approach used by Lindhjem and Navrud (2008). In our test, $n - 1$ of the Canadian observations (where n in this case is the number of Canadian observations in the sample) are used to estimate the average unit value; this unadjusted unit value is then used to predict WTP for the single omitted observation. This provides an out-of-sample comparison for each observation, based on an average unit value for all other observations. Such mean value unit transfers might be applied in countries where a closely-matching study site function is not available, and in the absence of a good site match analysts transfer a mean WTP over all available in-country studies (Johnston and Thomassin, 2010). Transfer error in this case is calculated as the difference between predicted and observed WTP, presented as an absolute value percentage following standard convention (Rosenberger and Stanley, 2006).

RESULTS AND DISCUSSION

The MRM results are given in Table 17.3; these mirror original results provided by Johnston and Thomassin (2010). Model variables are jointly significant at $p < 0.0001$ for both the US/Canada and US models as determined by likelihood ratio tests (-2 log likelihood $\chi^2 = 121.2$ and 92.9, respectively). Twenty-five of the 29 variables in the US/Canada model are statistically significant at $p < 0.10$; most are significant at $p < 0.01$. Most variables in the US model (24 of 27) are also statistically significant. The statistical properties of the models compare well to prior meta-analyses in the literature (Nelson and Kennedy, 2009). Statistically significant variables in the model have expected signs and general magnitudes as suggested by theory, intuition and previous literature (Table 17.3). Results are relatively robust between the US/Canada and US models. Among variables shared across both models, both statistical significance and magnitudes are similar in nearly all instances. Although these results should be interpreted in light of the relatively small number of observations from Canadian studies, such findings appear promising for commensurability of value surfaces across Canadian and US metadata. That is, most results are robust to the addition of Canadian observations to the metadata. These results aside, results also point to statistically significant and large magnitude divergences between Canadian and US WTP estimates and some value surfaces.

Table 17.3   Meta-regression results

Moderator	Canada/US model		US model	
	Coefficient	Pr > |t|	Coefficient	Pr > |t|
intercept	5.6916	0.0001	5.5760	0.0001
year_indx	−0.1199	0.0001	−0.1259	0.0001
discrete_ch	0.914	0.0001	0.9793	0.0001
voluntary	−0.8621	0.0024	−1.1338	0.0001
income	0.0000012	0.8008	0.0000022	0.6071
wq_ladder	−0.2557	0.2499	−0.2340	0.2534
protest_bids	0.9282	0.0001	0.9701	0.0001
outlier_bids	−0.6459	0.0001	−0.7129	0.0001
hi_response	−0.9348	0.0001	−0.9565	0.0001
lake	0.7220	0.0069	0.8279	0.0005
estuary_bay	0.2248	0.1903	0.2377	0.1582
salt_pond	0.9361	0.0007	1.0027	0.0007
regional_fresh	0.3034	0.0203	0.3735	0.0010
southeast	1.0504	0.0004	1.2393	0.0001
plains	−0.8693	0.0022	−0.9809	0.0001
pacif_mount	−0.3415	0.0133	−0.3570	0.0089
mult_reg	0.5502	0.0105	0.4967	0.0224
Canada	−5.6777	0.0001	−	−
nonusers	−0.6084	0.0001	−0.5256	0.0001
WQ_fish	0.1989	0.0001	0.1598	0.0016
WQ_shell	0.2924	0.0001	0.2501	0.0006
WQ_many	0.2259	0.0013	0.1814	0.0111
WQ_non	0.3439	0.0001	0.3093	0.0010
fishplus	0.6477	0.0003	0.8745	0.0001
baseline	−0.1085	0.0189	−0.1219	0.0072
baseline_Canada	0.7759	0.0001	−	−
interview	1.1594	0.0001	1.3079	0.0001
mail	0.3019	0.1759	0.4733	0.0240
lump_sum	0.5716	0.0021	0.5440	0.0011
−2 log likelihood χ^2	121.2	0.0001	92.9	0.0001
Covariance factors				
Study level (σ_u^2)	0.0000		0.0000	
Residual (σ_e^2)	0.1480		0.1472	
Observations (N)	97		81	

Two additional variables are included in the US/Canada model to account for differences in WTP between estimates from Canadian observations and those from US observations. The first variable, *Canada*, is a binary variable that indicates the country of origin for the study (Table

17.2). The parameter estimate for this variable is large and is statistically significant at $p < 0.0001$. This result was robust in the preliminary models that were estimated as well as in the final model. The results suggest that Canadian WTP is significantly lower than US WTP for changes in water quality, holding all else constant, even after adjustments are made for exchange rates and other differences between the countries. The second variable distinguishing US and Canadian observations in the model is the interactive variable *baseline_Canada*, calculated as *(Canada × baseline)*. The coefficient for this variable is statistically significant but is counter-intuitive in sign. The impact of the combination of the *baseline* and the *baseline_Canada* parameter estimates suggests that Canadians are willing to pay greater amounts for quality improvements in water bodies that begin with higher baseline quality levels (Johnston and Thomassin, 2010).

The differences between the two countries reflected in these two variables could be the result of several factors such as variations in the number of substitutes and compliments across the country observations, differences in preferences between the respondents in Canada and the US, unobserved variables related to the geography or socio-economic factors of where the studies were undertaken, and the potential that Canadians might view improvements in higher-quality water bodies as being relatively more cost-effective. The lack of Canadian studies and observations in the metadata make it difficult to provide explanations for these differences and thus these suggestions can only be seen as speculative. A further discussion of the details of the models and value surfaces can be found in Johnston and Thomassin (2010).

Benefit Transfer Reliability

The lack of Canadian studies quantifying WTP for water quality changes provides at least some justification for the use of international benefit transfer, but concerns exists about the transfer errors that may result. To quantify the types of errors that might result here, out-of-sample benefit transfer errors were measured for the four above-noted methods used to estimate WTP for improved water quality across the 16 Canadian observations. These include: (1) the use of the US/Canada MRM assuming known methodological variable values, that is, the best case, (2) the use of the US/Canada MRM with mean values for the methodological variables, (3) a unit value comparison based on the average WTP for Canadian observations, and (4) the use of the US MRM with mean values for methodological variables.

For BFTs (1) and (2) the convergent validity test is implemented following methods of Stapler and Johnston (2009). Similar methods are used by Brander et al. (2007) and Lindhjem and Navrud (2008), among others. The approach may be summarized as follows. Assume that one has meta-data with $n = 1 \ldots N$ unique observations. The first step is the omission of the nth observation from the metadata, which is the same as a hold-out sample comprised of a single observation. The MRM is then fitted (that is, parameters are estimated) using the remaining $N - 1$ observations. This is iterated for each $n = 1 \ldots N$ observation, resulting in a vector of N unique parameter estimates, each corresponding to the omission of the nth obser-vation. For each $n = 1 \ldots N$ observation, the nth observation is not part of the metadata during estimation of the nth model iteration, and is hence an out-of-sample observation corresponding to the vector of parameter estimates resulting from that iteration (Stapler and Johnston, 2009).

Parameter estimates for the nth model iteration are combined with independent variable values for the nth observation (omitted in that model iteration) to generate a WTP forecast for the omitted, and hence out of sample, nth observation. As MRM results are only used to forecast WTP for the nth observation omitted from each estimated model, the result is N out-of-sample WTP forecasts, each drawn from a unique MRM estima-tion. Transfer error is assessed through comparisons of the predicted and actual WTP value for each of the N observations (Brander et al., 2007; Lindhjem and Navrud, 2008; Stapler and Johnston, 2009). This approach is repeated for each of the 16 Canadian observations in the sample, with errors in WTP prediction (that is, transfer errors) represented as an abso-lute value percentage of the original primary study WTP estimate.

For BFT approach (4), the Canadian observations are already 'out of sample,' as the MRM used to predict WTP includes only US observations. Hence, in this case, the parameter estimates in Table 17.3 are combined with independent variable values for each Canadian observation to gener-ate a WTP forecast for that observation. Transfer error is again assessed through comparison of the predicted and actual WTP value for each observation, with errors reported as average absolute value percentages.

Table 17.4 provides detailed results of the convergent validity test using MRM method (1), the BFT conducted using the US/Canada model with actual methodological variable values from Canadian observations. In this case, the mean absolute transfer error over the 16 Canadian observa-tions was 41.34 per cent with a range of 0.94 per cent to 174.77 per cent. This transfer error falls within the range of the transfer errors found in the review by Rosenberger and Stanley (2006), and is relatively modest com-pared to errors reported in other studies in the benefit transfer literature. Results suggest reasonable performance of meta-function transfer, with estimates that can at least provide broad approximations of 'true' WTP as estimated by site-specific primary studies.

Table 17.4 *Transfer accuracy for Canadian observations: out-of-sample US/Canada meta-function*

Canadian obs.	Predicted WTP: meta-function transfer (2002 $US)	Primary study WTP (2002 $US)	Absolute value % error (meta-function transfer)	Scenario
1	$28.22	$41.86	32.57%	*WQ_non* = 2.5, *baseline* = 4.5, *lake* = 1
2	$32.05	$23.30	37.55%	*WQ_non* = 2.5, *baseline* = 4.5, *lake* = 1
3	$17.21	$13.88	24.00%	*WQ_non* = 2.5, *baseline* = 4.5, *lake* = 1, *nonusers* = 1
4	$30.77	$11.20	174.77%	*WQ_fish* = 0.5, *baseline* = 4.5, *lake* = 1, *fishplus* = 1
5	$27.99	$21.98	27.37%	*WQ_non* = 0.5, *baseline* = 4.5, *lake* = 1, *fishplus* = 1
6	$16.93	$6.60	156.44%	*WQ_non* = 0.5, *baseline* = 4.5, *lake* = 1, *fishplus* = 1, *nonusers* = 1
7	$38.44	$61.24	37.23%	*WQ_fish* = 2.5, *baseline* = 4.5, *lake* = 1, *fishplus* = 1
8	$40.56	$40.18	0.94%	*WQ_non* = 2.5, *baseline* = 4.5, *lake* = 1, *fishplus* = 1
9	$22.33	$19.96	11.89%	*WQ_non* = 2.5, *baseline* = 4.5, *lake* = 1, *fishplus* = 1, *nonusers* = 1
10	$40.37	$41.91	3.66%	*WQ_fish* = 2.5, *baseline* = 4.5, *lake* = 1, *fishplus* = 1
11	$39.78	$46.90	15.17%	*WQ_non* = 2.5, *baseline* = 4.5, *lake* = 1, *fishplus* = 1
12	$22.08	$21.56	2.40%	*WQ_non* = 2.5, *baseline* = 4.5, *lake* = 1, *fishplus* = 1, *nonusers* = 1
13	$12.39	$24.09	48.56%	*WQ_non* = 0.25, *baseline* = 4.5, *lake* = 1
14	$13.90	$14.29	2.69%	*WQ_non* = 0.25, *baseline* = 4.5, *lake* = 1
15	$7.56	$7.69	1.71%	*WQ_non* = 0.25, *baseline* = 4.5, *lake* = 1, *nonusers* = 1
16	$2.33	$15.07	84.53%	*WQ_non* = 1, *baseline* = 7, *regional_fresh* = 1
Mean % error (absolute value)			41.34%	

Table 17.5   Mean absolute percentage transfer error: benefit function transfer for Canadian observations

Benefit transfer approaches	Mean	Median	Std. dev.	Min.	Max.
US/Canada MRM (best-case methodological variable values)	41.34	25.69	53.39	0.94	174.77
US/Canada MRM (mean methodological variable values)	37.01	19.53	44.44	2.73	152.19
Average unit value – Canadian studies	74.32	41.87	80.61	6.82	289.76
US MRM (mean methodological variable values)	1059.41	923.88	661.97	401.34	2632.80

A comparison of summarized performance from the MRM BFT method (1) to results from alternative transfer methods (2) through (4) is given in Table 17.5. Interestingly, the mean absolute percentage transfer error decreases from 41.34 per cent to 37.01 per cent when BFTs use the mean value for methodological attributes to predict WTP estimates. That is, the particular pattern of results found for the MRM and the Canadian observations results in a situation in which improved transfer accuracy occurs when one uses the mean value for methodological variables across all Canadian observations within the BFT, rather than using the unique methodological variable values from each observation. Standard deviations are also smaller when using the mean methodological assumption (Table 17.5). The relatively accurate performance of BFT method (2) corresponds to the general conclusions of Stapler and Johnston (2009) that support the use of mean methodological variable values for MRM BFTs.

By comparison, the average unit value transfer BFT results in a 74.32 per cent average absolute value error (Table 17.5). This is approximately twice the size of similar errors from both US/Canada BFTs. Similar patterns are seen in median absolute value percentage errors. Although these errors still fall within the general range of transfer errors found in the review of Rosenberger and Stanley (2006), results strongly support the use of the US/Canada MRMs for BFT over the use of a simple average unit value transfer from Canadian observations alone. This mirrors the general support for MRM BFT approaches in the literature more broadly (Johnston and Rosenberger, 2010).

The final BFT method uses the US-only MRM with mean methodological variable values to predict WTP for Canadian observations (method 3 described above). In contrast to the moderate generalization errors found in the US/Canada MRM BFTs (methods 1 and 2), errors from

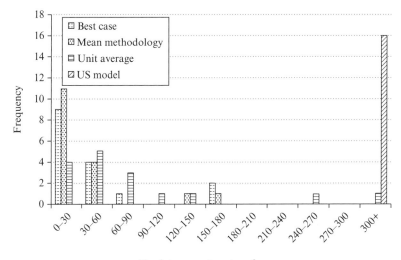

Figure 17.1   Distribution of the absolute percentage transfer error using four approaches

the US-only MRM results would likely render transfers unsuitable for applied use, with an average absolute value error exceeding 1059 per cent. All statistical properties of this approach demonstrate poor performance compared to alternative transfer methods (Table 17.5), including poorer performance than a simple transfer of average unit values from Canadian studies. Combined results in Table 17.5 illustrate the potential benefits of pooling US and Canadian data to generate a multinational MRM as a means to approximate Canadian WTP values, compared to the use of an MRM estimated solely from US observations. They also suggest the hazards of using a single-country MRM (here, the US model) to conduct BFT for another country (here, Canada). In this case, differences in preferences and context have a major influence on the benefit transfer results.

Summary statistics of transfer performance, however, provide only a partial perspective. To provide an alternative and perhaps more revealing perspective, Figures 17.1–17.3 illustrate the distribution of benefit transfer errors and changes across different transfer methods. The distribution of WTP absolute percentage transfer errors over all four methods is shown by Figure 17.1. As shown by the figure, similar distribution patterns result from both the BFTs based on the US/Canada MRM, regardless of the treatment of methodological variable values when calculating WTP. Both BFTs are characterized by a large number of transfer errors falling within

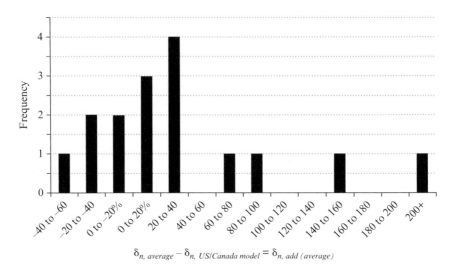

$$\delta_{n,\,average} - \delta_{n,\,US/Canada\ model} = \delta_{n,\,add\ (average)}$$

Figure 17.2   Change in the transfer accuracy for Canadian observations comparing unit value transfer with US/Canada model benefit function transfer

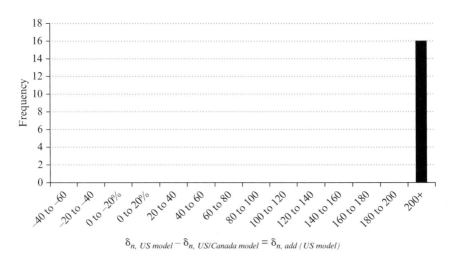

$$\delta_{n,\,US\ model} - \delta_{n,\,US/Canada\ model} = \delta_{n,\,add\ (US\ model)}$$

Figure 17.3   Change in the transfer accuracy for Canadian observations comparing US/Canada and US-only models

the 0 to 30 per cent range; 9 out of 16 estimates for the 'best case' treatment of methodological variable values (BFT method 1) and 11 out of 16 estimates for the mean value treatment (BFT method 2). The tail of the transfer error distribution under method 1 has a slightly thicker tail than that under method 2, but both methods have a maximum error between 150 and 180 per cent. In contrast to the similar performance of both BFTs based on the US/Canada MRM, the average unit value transfer shows a distribution skewed towards larger errors. Only four out of 16 predictions fall in the 0 to 30 per cent error range, and the largest number of estimates fall in the 30 to 60 per cent error range (five out of 16 estimates). The largest absolute value error from unit value transfer (309 per cent) also far exceeds those under either of the US/Canada MRM transfers.

The use of US-only MRM results to conduct meta-function benefit transfers for Canadian observations provides even less satisfactory results. All estimates of transfer error fall in the greater than 300 per cent range. The best estimate from this BFT has an absolute percentage transfer error of 311 per cent, while the worst estimate has an absolute percentage transfer error of 3717 per cent. Nine of the estimates have absolute percentage transfer errors of greater than 1000 per cent. Combined results from Table 17.5 and Figure 17.1 illustrate the potential benefits of pooling US and Canadian data to generate a multinational MA as a means to approximate Canadian WTP values, compared with the use of a MA estimated solely from US observations. They also suggest the hazards of using a single-country MRM (here, the US model) to conduct BFT to another country. Put another way, results suggest that information from valuation research within country in which a policy site is located may be crucial for reliable MRM BFTs. We emphasize that the poor performance of the US-only MRM is applicable only when used to predict WTP for out-of-sample Canadian observations; the model is much more reliable when used to predict WTP for US observations (these results are omitted for conciseness).

Note that transfer errors for specific observations may diverge from the average absolute value percentage transfer error for each method. Hence, one may also characterize differences in transfer performance based on a summary of the difference in absolute value transfer errors across each individual observation. Figures 17.2 and 17.3 provide the distribution of change in transfer accuracy for individual Canadian observations when comparing transfers from the most accurate US/Canada MRM BFT (method 2) and the two worst-performing approaches, average unit value transfer (Figure 17.2) and US-only MRM BFT (Figure 17.3). In both cases, the difference in transfer accuracy is given by the variable $\delta_{n, add}$, where $\delta_{n, add} > 0$ for an individual observation indicates that transfer error under the best performing US/Canada MRM BFT is smaller than the alternative approach. In contrast, $\delta_{n,\ add} < 0$ for an individual observation indicates that transfer error under the best performing US/Canada MRM BFT is larger than the alternative approach. Note that because the original percentage transfer errors are measured as absolute values, $\delta_{n,\ add}$ measures the difference in absolute value percentage error magnitude irrespective of sign (that is, whether the original error was of positive or negative sign).

As shown by Figure 17.2, transfer errors for individual observations can improve or worsen when comparing the best performing MRM BFT to an average unit value transfer. However, the majority of observations (11 out of 16) show improved performance for MRM BFT. Most changes in transfer error are smaller than 60 per cent irrespective of direction, although in four cases difference between errors under MRM BFT and unit value transfer differ by more than 60 per cent, with MRM BFT outperforming unit value transfer in all of these 'large difference' cases. In contrast, $\delta_{n,\ add}$ is greater than 200 per cent for all observations when comparing accuracy between the US-only MRM BFT and the best performing US/Canada MRM BFT (Figure 17.3), with a range between 357 per cent and 2497 per cent. Taken together, results from Figures 17.1–17.3 mirror the general conclusions above; improved accuracy is found when using the US/Canada MRM for benefit transfer, compared with alternative approaches.

Overall, results of the present analysis are promising for at least the prospect of obtaining inferences regarding value surfaces and benefit transfer possibilities from multiple country metadata that supplements observations from a relatively data-poor country with those from a data-rich country. Results here show robust statistical properties of the US/Canada MRM compared with the US-only model. Results also suggest systematic differences between Canadian and US WTP for surface water quality improvements. Out-of-sample convergent validity assessments provide evidence that multinational MRMs can support low-to-moderate error BFTs. Such findings may be particularly relevant when the sample of studies available within a particular country precludes a good site-to-site match for standard benefit function or even unit value transfer. In such cases, multinational MRMs might offer an alternative means to generate transferable benefit functions. However, even in this case caution is advised, as a country with insufficient studies for domestic benefit transfers will likely provide a relatively small quantity of data for meta-analysis, thereby necessitating the type of small sample caveats emphasized here.

Results also highlight the substantial risks involved in international site-to-site BFTs that do not capitalize on potential insights available through meta-analysis. Findings here suggest that site-to-site transfer between US and Canadian sites would risk substantial generalization errors related to the systematic divergences in value surfaces between the two countries. Canadian WTP appears to be systematically lower than US WTP for otherwise identical water quality improvement policies and contexts, at least considering the available sample of studies. Canadian studies also appear to have different WTP patterns related to baseline quality. Results such as these point to the risk of significant error in multinational MRMs that do not specify models to allow for at least some systematic variation in WTP across countries. These findings also suggest that researchers should exercise extreme caution when conducting unadjusted BFT between the two countries – as results here show systematic differences in WTP that, if not corrected using meta-analysis, could result in large generalization errors.

Of course, whether or not any given transfer error is acceptable depends on the purpose of the benefit transfer and the requirement for accuracy (Bergstrom and DeCivita, 1999; Johnston and Rosenberger, 2010). There are situations where relatively large percentage errors can be taken into account, at least partially, either through the analytical process or the decision-making framework. Such situations might include benefit–cost analysis in which the analyst can undertake additional sensitivity analysis or adjust decision rules to allow for the possibility of large transfer errors. In other situations, such as compensation for damages in a legal situation, the size of the transfer errors can preclude the use of benefit transfer because of the requirement for accuracy in determining compensation or mitigation. In these situations, the cost of undertaking primary research must be weighed against the increase in accuracy that would likely result.

CONCLUSIONS

Results of the present analysis are promising for at least the prospect of obtaining inferences regarding value surfaces from metadata that supplements observations from a relatively data-poor country with those from a data-rich country. The US/Canada MRM estimated here has robust statistical properties when compared to the US-only MRM. Statistical results also, however, suggest that there are systematic differences in WTP for improved water quality between Canada and the USA. This latter finding supports the hypotheses that individuals in different countries may have different values for otherwise similar environmental resources, and that meta-analysis or alternative mechanisms may be required to adjust for systemic value differences between countries when implementing benefit transfers. Results also highlight the risks involved in international site-to-site BFTs or unit value transfers that do not capitalize on potential insights available through meta-analysis.

Out-of-sample convergent validity assessments drawn from the US/ Canada MRMs provide evidence that multinational meta-analysis can provide a source of low-to-moderate error benefit transfers. Here, the most accurate transfers were from BFTs that used the US/Canada MRM. Benefit function transfers were able to account for systematic differences between Canadian and US WTP, resulting in transfer errors in a broadly acceptable range for at least some policy applications. Such findings may be particularly relevant when the sample of studies available within a particular country precludes a good site-to-site match for standard within-country BFT. In such cases, multinational MRMs might offer an alternative means to generate transferable benefit functions. Findings here also suggest that unadjusted site-to-site transfer between US and Canadian sites, or the use of an MRM derived from US-only data to predict WTP for Canadian sites, risks substantial generalization errors related to the systematic divergences in value surfaces between countries.

Although the multinational MRM shows promise in the present application, caution is advised in generalizing these findings. Countries with insufficient studies for domestic benefit transfers will likely provide a relatively small quantity of metadata, thereby necessitating the type of small sample caveats emphasized here. In this case the meta-function transfer allows adjustments for systematic WTP differences between the two countries, but limitations in the Canadian sample size preclude a more comprehensive analysis of systematically varying slopes for all moderator variables. As a result, there might be significant value surface differences between the two countries that remain unidentified.

Future research will be required to provide a more comprehensive analysis of such issues and to assess the most appropriate ways to leverage data from multiple countries to improve benefit transfer. For example, as more primary studies in Canada become available they should be added to the metadata and the MRM models should be re-estimated in order to investigate whether model properties are robust as more primary studies are added. Metadata expansion could be facilitated by further development of searchable valuation databases such as EVRI (Thomassin et al., 2009). More broadly, current results suggest that practitioners should exercise extreme caution in potential applications of site-to-site BFT between even similar and neighbouring countries. While meta-analysis may assist practitioners in ameliorating some of the potential problems with international benefit transfer, additional work will be required to assess the broader capacity of multinational MRMs to promote reliable benefit transfers. In the absence of this and other empirical evidence, the broader viability of international benefit transfer will remain uncertain.

REFERENCES

Aiken, R.A. (1985), 'Public benefits of environmental protection in Colorado', Master's thesis, Department of Economics, Colorado State University.

Anderson, G.D. and S.F. Edwards (1986), 'Protecting Rhode Island's coastal salt ponds: an economic assessment of downzoning', *Coastal Zone Management*, **14** (1–2), 67–91.

Azevedo, C., J.A. Herriges and C.L. Kling (2001), 'Valuing preservation and improvements of water quality in Clear Lake', Staff Report 01-SR 94, Center for Agricultural and Rural Development (CARD), Iowa State University.

Bergstrom, J.C. and P. De Civita (1999), 'Status of benefits transfer in the United States and Canada: a review', *Canadian Journal of Agricultural Economics*, **47** (1), 79–87.

Bergstrom, J.C. and L.O. Taylor (2006), 'Using meta-analysis for benefits transfer: theory and practice', *Ecological Economics*, **60** (2), 351–60.

Bockstael, N.E., K.E. McConnell and I.E. Strand (1989), 'Measuring the benefits of improvements in water quality: the Chesapeake Bay', *Marine Resource Economics*, **6** (1), 1–18.

Brander, L. M., R. J. G. M. Florax and J. E. Verrmaat (2006), 'The empirics of wetland valuation: a comprehensive summary and a meta-analysis of the literature', *Environmental and Resource Economics*, **33** (2), 223–50.

Brander, L.M., P. van Beukering and H. Cesar (2007), 'The recreational value of coral reefs: a meta-analysis', *Ecological Economics*, **63** (1), 209–18.

Brouwer, R. (2000), 'Environmental value transfer: state of the art and future prospects', *Ecological Economics*, **32**, 137–52.

Brouwer, R. and I.J. Bateman (2005), 'Benefit transfer of willingness to pay estimates and functions for health-risk reductions: a cross-country analysis', *Journal of Health Economics*, **24**, 591–611.

Brouwer, R., I.H. Langford, I.J. Bateman and R.K. Turner (1999), 'A meta-analysis of wetland contingent valuation studies', *Regional Environmental Change*, **1** (1), 47–57.

Brox, J.A., R.C. Kumar and K.R. Stollery (1996), 'Willingness to pay for water quality and supply enhancements in the grand river watershed', *Canadian Water Resources Journal*, **21** (3), 275–86.

Cameron, T.A. and D.D. Huppert (1989), 'OLS versus ML estimation of non-market resource values with payment card interval data', *Journal of Environmental Economics and Management*, **17** (3), 230–46.

Carson, R.T., W.M. Hanemann, R.J. Kopp, J.A. Krosnick, R.C. Mitchell, S. Presser, P.A. Ruud and V.K. Smith (1994), 'Prospective interim lost use value due to DDT and PCB contamination in the Southern California Bight', vol. 2, unpublished report to the National Oceanic and Atmospheric Administration, Natural Resources Damage Assessment Inc., La Jolla, CA.

Clonts, H.A. and J.W. Malone (1990), 'Preservation attitudes and consumer surplus in free flowing rivers', in J. Vining (ed.), *Social Science and Natural Resource Recreation Management*, Boulder, CO: Westview Press, pp. 301–17.

Croke, K., R.G. Fabian and G. Brenniman (1987), 'Estimating the value of improved water quality in an urban river system', *Journal of Environmental Systems*, **16** (1), 13–24.

Cronin, F.J. (1982), 'Valuing nonmarket goods through contingent markets', Report PNL-4255, Pacific Northwest Laboratory, Richland, WA.

De Zoysa, A.D.N. (1995), 'A benefit evaluation of programs to enhance groundwater quality, surface water quality and wetland habitat in Northwest Ohio', PhD dissertation, Department of Agricultural Economics and Rural Sociology, Ohio State University.

Desvousges, W.H., V.K. Smith and M.P. McGivney (1983), *A Comparison of Alternative*

Approaches for Estimating Recreation and Related Benefits of Water Quality Improvements, Washington, DC: US Environmental Protection Agency, Economic Analysis Division.

Dupont, D.P. (2003), 'CVM embedding effects when there are active, potentially active and passive users of environmental goods', *Environmental and Resource Economics*, **25** (3), 319–41.

EVRI (n.d.), *Environmental Valuation Resource Inventory*, available at http://www.evri.ca/ (accessed 15 January 2010).

Farber, S. and B. Griner (2000), 'Valuing watershed quality improvements using conjoint analysis', *Ecological Economics*, **34** (1), 63–76.

Griffiths, C. and W. Wheeler (2005), 'Benefit–cost analysis of regulations affecting surface water quality in the United States', in R. Brouwer and D. Pearce (eds), *Cost–Benefit Analysis and Water Resource Management*, Cheltenham, UK and Northampton, MA, USA: Edward Elgar, pp. 223–50.

Hanley, N., S. Colombo, D. Tinch, A. Black and A. Aftab (2006a), 'Estimating the benefits of water quality improvements under the Water Framework Directive: are benefits transferable?', *European Review of Agricultural Economics*, **33**, 391–413.

Hanley, N., R.E. Wright and B. Alvarez-Farizo (2006b), 'Estimating the economic value of improvements in river ecology using choice experiments: an application to the Water Framework Directive', *Journal of Environmental Management*, **78**, 183–93.

Hayes, K.M., T.J. Tyrrell and G. Anderson (1992), 'Estimating the benefits of water quality improvements in the Upper Narragansett Bay', *Marine Resource Economics*, **7** (1), 75–85.

Herriges, J.A. and J.F. Shogren (1996), 'Starting point bias in dichotomous choice valuation with follow-up questioning', *Journal of Environmental Economics and Management*, **30** (1), 112–31.

Hoehn, J.P. (2006), 'Methods to address selection effects in the meta regression and transfer of ecosystem values', *Ecological Economics*, **60**, 389–98.

Huang, J.C., T.C. Haab and J.C. Whitehead (1997), 'Willingness to pay for quality improvements: should revealed and stated preference data be combined?', *Journal of Environmental Economics and Management*, **34** (3), 240–55.

Iovanna, R. and C. Griffiths (2006), 'Clean water, ecological benefits, and benefits transfer: a work in progress at the USA EPA', *Ecological Economics*, **60**, 473–82.

Johnston, R.J. and E.Y. Besedin (2009), 'Benefits transfer and meta-analysis: estimating willingness to pay for aquatic resource improvements', in H.W. Thurston, M.T. Heberling and A. Schrecongost (eds), *Environmental Economics for Watershed Restoration*, Boca Raton, FL: CRC Press, Taylor and Francis Group, pp. 95–120.

Johnston, R.J. and R.S. Rosenberger (2010), 'Methods, trends and controversies in contemporary benefit transfer', *Journal of Economic Surveys*, **24** (3), 479–510.

Johnston, R.J. and P.J. Thomassin (2009), 'Evaluating the Environmental Valuation Reference Inventory (EVRI): results from a survey of actual and potential users', *AERE (Association of Environmental and Resource Economists) Newsletter*, **29** (1), 33–38.

Johnston, R.J. and P.J. Thomassin (2010), 'Willingness to pay for water quality improvements in the United States and Canada: considering possibilities for international meta-analysis and benefit transfer', *Agricultural and Resource Economic Review*, **39** (1), 114–31.

Johnston, R.J., E.Y. Besedin and M.H. Ranson (2006), 'Characterizing the effects of valuation methodology in function-based benefit transfer', *Ecological Economics*, **60**, 407–19.

Johnston, R.J., E.Y. Besedin, R. Iovanna, C. Miller, R. Wardwell and M. Ranson (2005), 'Systematic variation in willingness to pay for aquatic resource improvements and implications for benefit transfer: a meta-analysis', *Canadian Journal of Agricultural Economics*, **53** (2–3), 221–48.

Kaoru, Y. (1993), 'Differentiating use and nonuse values for coastal pond water quality improvements', *Environmental and Resource Economics*, **3** (5), 487–94.

Kristófersson, D. and S. Navrud (2007), 'Can use and non-use values be transferred across countries?', in S. Navrud and R. Ready (eds), *Environmental Value Transfer: Issues and Methods*, Dordrecht: Springer, pp. 207–26.

Lant, C.L. and R.S. Roberts (1990), 'Greenbelts in the cornbelt: riparian wetlands, intrinsic values, and market failure', *Environment and Planning A*, **22** (10), 1375–88.

Lindhjem, H. and S. Navrud (2008), 'How reliable are meta-analyses for international benefit transfers?', *Ecological Economics*, **66** (2–3), 425–35.

Loomis, J.B. (1992), 'The evolution of a more rigorous approach to benefit transfer: benefit function transfer', *Water Resources Research*, **38**, 701–05.

Loomis, J.B. (1996), 'How large is the extent of the market for public goods: evidence from a nationwide contingent valuation survey', *Applied Economics*, **28** (7), 779–82.

Lyke, A.J. (1993), 'Discrete choice models to value changes in environmental quality: a great lakes case study', PhD dissertation, Department of Agricultural Economics, University of Wisconsin-Madison.

Magat, W.A., J. Huber, K.W. Viscusi and J. Bell (2000), 'An iterative choice approach to valuing clean lakes, rivers, and streams', *Journal of Risk and Uncertainty*, **21** (1), 7–43.

Matthews, L.G., F.R. Homans and K.W. Easter (1999), 'Reducing phosphorous pollution in the Minnesota River: how much is it worth?', unpublished report, Department of Applied Economics, University of Minnesota.

McClelland, N.I. (1974), 'Water Quality Index application in the Kansas River Basin', report to US EPA Region VII, Kansas City, MO.

Mitchell, R.C. and R.T. Carson (1981), 'An experiment in determining willingness to pay for national water quality improvements', unpublished preliminary draft report to the US Environmental Protection Agency, Washington, DC: Resources for the Future.

Mitchell, R.C. and R.T. Carson (1989), *Using Surveys to Value Public Goods: The Contingent Valuation Method*, Washington, DC: Resources for the Future.

Moeltner, K., K.J. Boyle and R.W. Patterson (2007), 'Meta-analysis and benefit transfer for resource valuation – addressing classical challenges with Bayesian modeling', *Journal of Environmental Economics and Management*, **53** (2), 250–69.

Nelson, J.P. and P.E. Kennedy (2009), 'The use (and abuse) of meta-analysis in environmental and resource economics: an assessment', *Environmental and Resource Economics*, **42** (3), 345–77.

Olsen, D., J. Richards and R.D. Scott (1991), 'Existence and sport values for doubling the size of Columbia River Basin salmon and steelhead runs', *Rivers*, **2** (1), 44–56.

Ready, R. and S. Navrud (2006), 'International benefit transfer: methods and validity test', *Ecological Economics*, **60** (2), 429–34.

Ready, R., S. Navrud, B. Day, R. Dubourg, F. Machado, S. Mourato, F. Spaninks and M.X.V. Rodriquez (2004), 'Benefit transfer in Europe: how reliable are transfers between countries?', *Environmental and Resource Economics*, **29**, 67–82.

Roberts, L.A. and J.A. Leitch (1997), 'Economic valuation of some wetland outputs of Mud Lake', Agricultural Economics Report No. 381, Department of Agricultural Economics, North Dakota Agricultural Experiment Station, North Dakota State University.

Rosenberger, R.S. and R.J. Johnston (2009), 'Selection effects in meta-analysis and benefit transfer: avoiding unintended consequences', *Land Economics*, **85** (3), 410–28.

Rosenberger, R.S. and J.B. Loomis (2000), 'Using meta-analysis for benefit transfer: in-sample convergent validity tests of an outdoor recreation database', *Water Resources Research*, **36** (4), 1097–107.

Rosenberger, R.S. and T.D. Stanley (2006), 'Measurement, generalization, and publication: sources of error in benefit transfers and their management', *Ecological Economics*, **60**, 372–78.

Rowe, R.D., W.D. Schulze, B. Hurd and D. Orr (1985), 'Economic assessment of damage related to the Eagle Mine Facility', unpublished report, Energy and Resource Consultants, Boulder, CO.

Sanders, L.B., R.G. Walsh and J.B. Loomis (1990), 'Toward empirical estimation of the total value of protecting rivers', *Water Resources Research*, **26** (7), 1345–57.

Santos, J.M.L. (1998), *The Economic Valuation of Landscape Change: Theory and Policies for Land Use and Conservation*, Cheltenham, UK and Northampton, MA, USA: Edward Elgar.

Santos, J.M.L. (2007), 'Transferring landscape values: how and how accurately?', in S. Navrud and R. Ready (eds), *Environmental Value Transfer: Issues and Methods*, Dordrecht: Springer, pp. 45–76.

Schulze, W.D., R.D. Rowe, W.S. Breffle, R.R. Boyce and G.H. McClelland (1995), *Contingent Valuation of Natural Resource Damages Due to Injuries to the Upper Clark Fork River Basin*, State of Montana, Natural Resource Damage Litigation Program, Boulder, CO: RCG/Hagler Bailly.

Shrestha, R.K. and J.B. Loomis (2001), 'Testing a meta-analysis model for benefit transfer in international outdoor recreation', *Ecological Economics*, **39**, 67–83.

Shrestha, R.K. and J.B. Loomis (2003), 'Meta-analytic benefit transfer of outdoor recreation economic values: testing out-of-sample convergent validity', *Environmental and Resource Economics*, **25** (1), 79–100.

Smith, V.K. and S.K. Pattanayak (2002), 'Is meta-analysis a Noah's Ark for non-market valuation?', *Environmental and Resource Economics*, **22** (1–2), 271–96.

Smith, V.K., G. Van Houtven and S.K. Pattanayak (2002), 'Benefit transfer via preference calibration: "prudential algebra" for policy', *Land Economics*, **78** (1), 132–52.

Stanley, T.D. (2005), 'Beyond publication bias', *Journal of Economic Surveys*, **19**, 309–45.

Stapler, R.W. and R.J. Johnston (2009), 'Meta-analysis, benefit transfer, and methodological covariates: implications for transfer error', *Environmental and Resource Economics*, **42** (2), 227–46.

Statistics Canada (2007), *The Consumer Price Index*, Catalogue no. 62-001-XIE, Ottawa: Supply and Services Canada.

Stumborg, B.E., K.A. Baerenklau and R.C. Bishop (2001), 'Nonpoint source pollution and present values: a contingent valuation of Lake Mendota', *Review of Agricultural Economics*, **23** (1), 120–32.

Sutherland, R.J. and R.G. Walsh (1985), 'Effect of distance on the preservation value of water quality', *Land Economics*, **61** (3), 282–91.

Thomassin, P.J., R.J. Johnston, I. Turpin and M. Lebbos (2009), *EVRI Review: Literature Review, Surveys and Website Analysis*, final report, Environment Canada, April.

Van Houtven, G., J. Powers and S.K. Pattanayak (2007), 'Valuing water quality improvements in the United States using meta-analysis: is the glass half-full or half-empty for national policy analysis?', *Resource and Energy Economics*, **29** (3), 206–28.

Vaughan, W.J. (1986), 'The RFF water quality ladder', in R.C. Mitchell and R.T. Carson, *The Use of Contingent Valuation Data for Benefit/Cost Analysis in Water Pollution Control, Final Report*, Washington, DC: Resources for the Future.

Welle, P.G. (1986), 'Potential economic impacts of acid deposition: a contingent valuation study of Minnesota', PhD dissertation, Department of Agricultural Economics, University of Wisconsin-Madison.

Wey, K.A. (1990), 'Social welfare analysis of congestion and water quality of Great Salt Pond, Block Island, Rhode Island', PhD dissertation, Department of Resource Economics, University of Rhode Island.

Whitehead, J.C. and P.A. Groothuis (1992), 'Economic benefits of improved water quality: a case study of North Carolina's Tar-Pamlico River', *Rivers*, **3** (3), 170–78.

Whitehead, J.C., G.C. Blomquist, T.J. Hoban and W.B. Clifford (1995), 'Assessing the validity and reliability of contingent values: a comparison of on-site users, off-site users, and non-users', *Journal of Environmental Economics and Management*, **29** (2), 238–51.

Whittington, D., G. Cassidy, D. Amaral, E. McClelland, H. Wang and C. Poulos (1994), 'The economic value of improving the environmental quality of Galveston Bay', GBNEP-38, Department of Environmental Sciences and Engineering, University of North Carolina at Chapel Hill.

Index